POLITICS, PARTIES, AND ELECTIONS IN AMERICA

SEVENTH EDITION

Brian F. Schaffner

University of Massachusetts, Amherst

WADSWORTH
CENGAGE Learning

Australia • Brazil • Japan • Korea • Mexico • Singapore • Spain • United Kingdom • United States

WADSWORTH
CENGAGE Learning

Politics, Parties, and Elections in America, Seventh Edition
Brian F. Schaffner

Assistant Editor: Katherine Hayes

Editorial Assistant: Angela Hodge

Marketing Manager: Amy Whitaker

Marketing Coordinator: Josh Hendrick

Marketing Communications Manager: Heather Baxley

Content Project Management: PreMediaGlobal

Art Director: Linda Helcher

Print Buyer: Fola Orekoya

Rights Acquisitions Account Manager, Text: Katie Huha

Rights Acquisitions Account Manager, Image: Mandy Groszko

Production Service: PreMediaGlobal

Cover Designer: Rokusek Design

For product information and technology assistance, contact us at **Cengage Learning Customer & Sales Support, 1-800-354-9706.**

For permission to use material from this text or product, submit all requests online at **www.cengage.com/permissions**. Further permissions questions can be e-mailed to **permissionrequest@cengage.com.**

Library of Congress Control Number: 2010929102

Student Edition:

ISBN-13: 978-0-495-89916-7

ISBN-10: 0-495-89916-X

Wadsworth
20 Channel Center Street,
Boston, MA 02210
USA

Cengage Learning is a leading provider of customized learning solutions with office locations around the globe, including Singapore, the United Kingdom, Australia, Mexico, Brazil, and Japan. Locate your local office at **www.cengage.com/global**.

Cengage Learning products are represented in Canada by Nelson Education, Ltd.

To learn more about Wadsworth, visit **www.cengage.com/wadsworth**

Purchase any of our products at your local college store or at our preferred online store **www.cengagebrain.com**.

Printed in the United States of America
1 2 3 4 5 6 7 14 13 12 11 10

CONTENTS

PREFACE

It is striking how quickly things can change in the world of politics. Just a decade ago, the dominant theme in political parties textbooks was one of party decline. Scholars and pundits questioned whether parties were relevant to citizens any longer and discussed the dire consequences of this irrelevance for the political system. But the increasing homogeneity of the party coalitions along with critical events such as the 2000 Florida recount, 9/11, the conflicts in Iraq and Afghanistan, and the health-care reform legislation, have created a very different landscape. These changes, and others, hold important implications for how political parties function in our political system. The conversation about political parties is now focused on "red states" and "blue states" and the increasing partisan polarization in American politics. Indeed, rather than worry about the consequences of party decline, many pundits and scholars now wonder if parties matter *too* much. Clearly much has changed in the study of political parties and these changes have provided much of the material for the seventh edition of this book.

Through its first five editions, John F. Bibby did a fine job of producing one of the most comprehensive texts on political parties. One of the major strengths of this book has been its attention to historical context while also remaining contemporary in its focus. In taking over this book from Professor Bibby, I have endeavored to keep intact much of what has made this book so strong. The attention to historical context remains, as does the book's central theme of parties influencing and being influenced by the electoral context within which they operate.

While the core concepts in the book carry over from previous editions, much has changed in recent years and the shifting political landscape has provided me with plenty of material with which to augment the previous work and add new insight to this seventh edition. Partisan polarization has become more than just a buzzword for politicians, pundits, and academics and the subject deserves serious attention in any contemporary parties text. This edition was written to incorporate this new reality of American politics. Nearly every chapter has been further revised to incorporate information and research about the polarized political environment. This is particularly true for Chapters 7, 8, and 9, which expand on the causes and consequences of polarization among voters, candidates, and office holders. Polarization is also one of the themes of the book's conclusion in Chapter 10.

Of course, much has changed in the American political landscape even since the last edition of this book was published in 2007. The 2008 election proved to be one of the most fascinating and historical elections in decades. Previous editions of this book noted that modern presidential nomination campaigns tended to be won by the frontrunner and generally did not last long at all. Of course, the epic battle between Hillary Clinton and Barack Obama for the Democratic Party's nomination turned that conventional wisdom on its head. This edition of the book focuses significant attention on how Obama was able to come from behind in the polls to win the nomination and why the nomination race carried on for so long without a clear winner.

Obama's 2008 campaign was also innovative in other ways as well. First, his fund-raising success was unprecedented and allowed him to become the first major party candidate to forego public funding during both the primary and general election campaigns. This edition of the text examines not only how Obama was able to raise such large sums, but also what it means for how future presidential campaigns are financed. Second, Obama was also highly entrepreneurial in how he used the Internet and other technological innovations to build support and target individuals during the campaign. A description of these innovations and what they mean for how parties approach future campaigns is an important part of this new edition. Third, Obama became the first African American ever elected to the presidency, and his campaign for that office challenged many Americans to reflect on the role of race in modern politics. This new edition describes some of the initial research that has debated whether race influenced voters' support for Obama.

Finally, Obama's first term in office has been an eventful one. He took office with large Democratic majorities in both the House and the Senate, and Democrats have used their unified control of government to pursue much of their agenda. Particularly controversial were Democratic efforts to reform the nation's health-care system. Over nearly a full year, Congress and the nation debated whether and how to reform health care and given the nature of modern politics, it is no surprise to find that politicians and the public were highly polarized on the issue. Nevertheless, with strong leadership from Nancy Pelosi and Harry Reid, Democrats were ultimately able to pass a health-care reform bill that the president signed into law. The efforts to pass this major legislation provide abundant material for a revised discussion of the role of party in government in Chapter 9.

I am grateful to many people not only for their help with this text, but also for putting me in the position in my career to have this opportunity. With regard to the latter, my professors at Indiana University, including Pat Sellers, Jerry Wright, Bob Huckfeldt, Dave Weaver, Leroy Rieselbach, Margie Hershey, and John Williams, provided me with the highest quality training to enter the academic world. As an undergraduate, my very first upper division class in political science was on political parties and I owe much of my interest in the subject to John Clark who taught that class, sparked my interest in getting a PhD, and later became my colleague and friend. At American University, Jim Thurber was a very supportive mentor and friend and my year at the National Science Foundation was enriched by my good fortune in working with so many smart and kind political scientists, including Susan Haire, Wendy Martinek, Frank Scioli, Harold Clarke, and especially Brian Humes. Since the last edition, I have moved to the University of Massachusetts, Amherst, where my new colleagues have been extremely welcoming. In particular, I want to thank the members of our American politics group, Maryann Barakso, Ray La Raja, Tatishe Nteta, Jesse Rhodes, and Dean Robinson as well as John Hird, who is as supportive a department chair as one could ever hope for.

Several people contributed a great deal to this edition. John Bibby deserves my highest appreciation not only for creating a wonderful foundation upon which to build, but also for trusting me to take his book forward. I also want to thank the Wadsworth team, including Carolyn Merrill and Angela Hodge, as well as David Tatom and Janise Fry, who originally brought me in on this project. My research assistant, Mel Tarsi, was very important for the timely completion of the book.

Most of all, I would like to thank my family. My parents, John and Karen Schaffner, sparked my interest in politics at a young age, and my sisters, Laura and Georgia, have always been there to support me. I am particularly grateful to Maryann, Sarah, and Ellie, who patiently tolerated all of the late nights (and the laptop that seemed to be permanently attached to me) as the deadline approached. Without their love and support, none of this would be possible.

Brian F. Schaffner

PARTIES AND POLITICS IN AMERICA: AN OVERVIEW

CHAPTER CONTENTS

Anyone who seriously studies American political parties is confronted with a series of seeming contradictions and confusing conditions. The framers of the Constitution feared parties—James Madison attacked them in the Federalist Papers and George Washington warned against them in his farewell address—and citizens and political commentators continue to blame parties for much that appears to be wrong with politics. At the same time, parties thrive in America, and many scholars believe that they are absolutely necessary for the functioning of democracy.

If your general outlook toward political parties and the two-party system is negative, you are hardly alone. Nearly two-thirds of American citizens believe that the United States needs a viable third party, and in 2007, only 37 percent said that "the two-party system does a pretty good job of addressing the issues that are most important." In the past, a common complaint about American parties was that they were about as different from each other as Tweedledum and Tweedledee. That is, "there's not a dime's worth of difference between them." In recent decades, voters have become concerned that the parties are too different, have too many disagreements, and are generally not willing to compromise with each other. Thus, in a recent poll, 81 percent of Americans agreed that 2009 was "a period of division where the parties held fast to their positions and showed little willingness to compromise."

Despite Americans' complaints about the parties, they are clearly relevant to the political system. In the 2008 election, fewer than 2 percent of the voters actually cast ballots for third-party candidates. Well over half of the citizenry consider themselves either Republicans or Democrats, while a majority of those who claim to be independents actually lean toward one of the major parties and demonstrate considerable party loyalty in their voting. The Republican and Democratic party organizations have developed broadly based and relatively stable followings. Only the nominees of the Republican and Democratic parties stand a reasonable chance to win the presidency, congressional seats, governorships, or positions in the state legislatures. Furthermore, these bodies are organized on a partisan basis, with key power positions allocated to members of the majority party.

It also makes an important difference which party wins elections. The vast expansion of social welfare programs that occurred under President Johnson was possible only because of the Democrats' landslide victory of 1964. Similarly, President Reagan's program of lower taxes and retrenchment of domestic programs was possible because Republicans won the presidency in 1980 and 1984 and controlled the Senate from 1981 to 1986. And when President Obama took office along with a Democratic majority in Congress, a broad-sweeping reform of the health care system was made possible. These patterns point to the unique character of American political parties. They count among their affiliates the vast majority of the voters. They nominate candidates and contest the major offices in the land. They staff formal organizational structures at the national level and in the fifty states. They organize the executive and legislative branches in Washington and the states. And they exert tremendous influence on governmental policy. Despite these signs of strength and pervasiveness, American parties have few formal ("card-carrying") members, are often understaffed and in financial straits, are sometimes disunited in terms of policy direction, and are fragmented in terms of power. These puzzling aspects of American political parties dramatize many of the major concerns of this book:

- The unique character of political parties as institutions for aggregating political influence
- The functions performed by political parties within the American political system
- The impact of institutional factors (e.g., separation of powers, direct primaries) on American parties
- The relationship of parties to voters, candidates, officeholders, and interest groups
- The ongoing processes of change in the party system
- The impact of parties on governmental policy
- The changing role of parties in the American political system

THE NATURE OF POLITICS

What is politics? In common usage, it is the unseemly machinations of the ambitious and self-serving to gain advantage over others; it is the subverting of the public welfare for group or partisan advantage; it is the never-ending struggle between the Republicans and the Democrats; and it is what happens in government—in Washington or the statehouses of Sacramento, Harrisburg, Springfield, Baton Rouge, or Cheyenne. Generally, when one is accused of acting politically, there is a suspicion that less than wholesome activities are afoot.

But when these pejorative connotations are removed, the essence of politics is *power*—the ability of one person to get another person to behave in a desired manner. Politics and the use of power inevitably involve *conflict* because what people want from life differs—they have different values—and because there is a scarcity of life's prized objectives (e.g., wealth, security, prestige, and power). In its most basic sense, then, politics is concerned with "Who Gets What, When, and How."[1]

Whether a political system works depends to a large degree upon whether society's inevitable political conflicts among competing interests can be resolved and managed via bargaining and compromise. If the processes of bargaining and compromise enable competing interests to get enough of what they want, it is possible for these interests to continue to cooperate and not disrupt the whole legal structure of government. Politics, therefore, can be viewed as a process of conflict management.

The political process, however, involves more than keeping the lid on the passions of social conflict. It is also the process through which individuals and groups organize and act collectively to achieve social goals—individual freedom, public health, quality education, national security, economic opportunity, clean air, and water.

When politics is stripped of its unsavory normative connotations and viewed in its essentials, it can be seen as a basic social process involving (1) the acquisition, retention, and exercise of power; (2) the expression and management of conflicts; and (3) collective action. In each of these aspects of politics, political parties play a central role. Parties help determine who governs, who wins or loses public policy disputes, and the extent of the win or loss.

THE NATURE OF PARTY

In spite of their acknowledged impact on American government, political parties have proved to be elusive creatures for social commentators to define. One famous characterization was that of Edmund Burke, the British philosopher and member of Parliament, who in 1770 offered a classic ideologically oriented definition: "Party is a body of men united, for promoting by their joint endeavors the national interest, upon some particular principle in which they are all agreed."[2] Whatever relevance this conception of party had for eighteenth-century England, it is clearly inappropriate for American political parties, which have never been noted for their ideological purity. Conservatives, moderates, and liberals are found in both the Republican and Democratic parties, albeit not in the same proportions. Furthermore, it is not uncommon for senators and representatives to vote in opposition to their party colleagues in excess of 40 percent of the time. Definitions stressing organizational structure (i.e., the existence of a hierarchy of organizations—county committees, state central committees, and national committees) are also inadequate because parties include masses of voters as well as dues-paying members, officials or staff, candidates, their supporters, campaign consultants, and government officials.

A definition of parties better adapted to the modern American and Western democratic contexts is that provided by political scientist Leon D. Epstein: "Any group, however loosely organized, seeking to elect government officeholders under a given label."[3] This definition allows for the lack of ideological and policy unity so apparent in American parties. It also accommodates the wide variety of party organizations in the country, which range from the disciplined urban machines of the Mayor Richard J. Daley era in Chicago to the well-financed and professionally staffed Republican and Democratic National Committees, to the underfinanced and disorganized, but loyal, bands of volunteers who run local party organizations in regions where their party has virtually no chance of winning elections. The Epstein conception of party also takes into account two special aspects of parties: (1) their preoccupation with contesting elections and (2) the fact that it is only parties that run candidates on their own labels.

As V. O. Key, Jr., pointed out, "The fundamental difficulty about the term 'political party' is that it is applied without discrimination to many groups and near groups."[4] He therefore urged students of parties to recognize them as tripartite social structures composed of the following elements (Figure 1.1):

- *The party in the electorate:* voters with a sense of loyalty to and identification with the party
- *The party organization:* party officials, committees, volunteer workers, and paid staff
- *The party in government:* party candidates for governmental office and public officeholders at the local, state, and national levels

American parties, therefore, are structures that contain a variety of components: from the weakly committed voter who usually supports the party's candidates to the dedicated activist with an ideological commitment who volunteers time and treasure; from the party boss seeking to run a disciplined patronage-dispensing organization to the public official who, while elected on a party level, seeks to project an image independent of party. As Paul Allen Beck

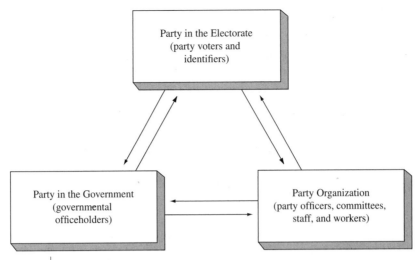

FIGURE 1.1 | THE TRIPARTITE STRUCTURE OF AMERICAN POLITICAL PARTIES

Source: "The three-part political party," p. 12, from *Party Politics in America*, 8th ed., by Paul Allen Beck. Copyright © 1997 by Addison-Wesley Educational Publishers, Inc. Reprinted by permission of Pearson Education, Inc.

has noted, the political party "embraces the widest range of involvement and commitment."[5]

THE FUNCTIONS OF PARTIES

Parties serve many functions in the United States, including:

- Serving as intermediaries between citizens and government
- Nominating candidates for office
- Contesting elections
- Organizing government
- Providing accountability
- Managing conflict

SERVING AS INTERMEDIARIES

Wherever free elections have been conducted on a continuing basis at the national or regional level, political parties exist. This basic fact is suggestive of the fundamental role of parties in a democratic society. They are intermediary or linkage mechanisms between the mass of the citizenry and their government. Parties function as institutions to bring scattered elements of the public together, to define objectives, and to work collectively to achieve those objectives through governmental policy. Parties, therefore, are involved in aggregating societal interests, recruiting leadership, compromising competing demands, contesting elections, and seeking to organize governments.

Parties developed as the old bases of governmental authority (e.g., divine right of kings) crumbled before the democratic revolutions of the eighteenth and nineteenth centuries and governments came to be seen as deriving their powers from the people. To legitimize their positions, leaders were compelled to appeal to the voters. Such appeals required the development of organizations to communicate with and mobilize the masses. V. O. Key, Jr., summarized the process of party development in the Western democracies as follows:

> As democratic theory spread, those dissatisfied with the old order rallied the masses ... against the established holders of authority. In effect the outs played demagogue, lined up the unwashed in their support, and, at the elections, by superiority of numbers and organization they bested those dominant in government. Those who suffered such indignities were compelled in self-defense to defer to the people, no matter how distasteful it was, and to form organizations to solicit electoral support.[6]

As will be discussed in the following chapter, the development of American parties generally follows the pattern Key outlined. America was the first nation to transfer executive power from one faction to another via an election (the election of 1800), and this feat was accomplished by a political party. The United States thereby became the first nation with modern political parties organized on a national basis with broad membership, in contrast to the parliamentary factions that existed in Great Britain.

Many political scientists believe that parties are the principal intermediary between the citizens and their government. E. E. Schattschneider, for example, opened his 1942 classic study with the assertion that "political parties created democracy and modern democracy is unthinkable save in terms of parties."[7] And more recently, Samuel Huntington, in a cross-national study, observed that parties were distinctive institutions of the modern state whose function "is to organize participation, to aggregate interests, to serve as the link between social forces and the government."[8] Even if such statements overstate the role of parties, parties do permeate every aspect of national and state government and politics. As Sarah McCally Morehouse has reminded us, it is Republicans and Democrats who "make the major decisions regarding who pays and who receives."[9]

In their role as intermediaries, parties must compete with other institutions. They share the linkage functions with interest groups, which exist in infinite variety—labor unions; business and trade associations; professional organizations; racial, ethnic, and religious groups; single-issue groups; ideological groups. The electronic media, including television and the Internet, also function as an intermediary between government and the people. The party's place in the political system as an intermediary institution is illustrated in Figure 1.2.

NOMINATING CANDIDATES

The determination of which names shall appear on the general election ballot—the narrowing of the voter's choice—is a critical stage in the electoral process. The nominating process controls the voter's range of choice and thus severely limits who is eligible for public office. For the candidate—both incumbent and challenger—the nomination is a hurdle that must be cleared if entry into elective politics is to be

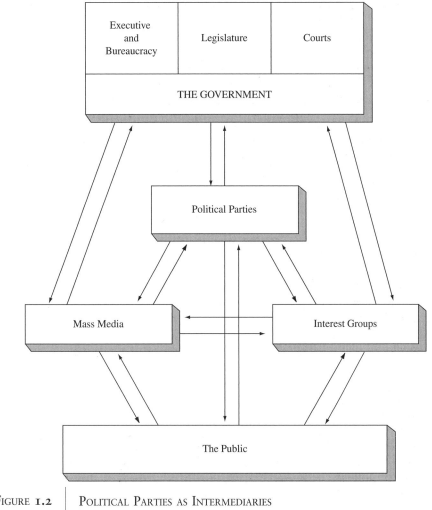

FIGURE 1.2 | POLITICAL PARTIES AS INTERMEDIARIES

---

achieved. In the United States, virtually all national and most major state elected officials are nominated by political parties. So crucial is the nomination process to the parties that Schattschneider concluded:

> Unless the party makes authoritative and effective nominations, it cannot stay in business.... The nature of the nominating procedure determines the nature of the party; he who can make nominations is the owner of the party.[10]

Although interest groups, political action committees (PACs), pollsters, campaign consultants, and candidate organizations seek to influence nominating decisions, it is ultimately the party that makes nominations. And without a party nomination, the record demonstrates that it is virtually impossible to gain major elected office. No one has been elected president since the development of modern parties in the early 1800s without a partisan nomination. Following the

2008 elections, all members of the House and Senate except two independent senators were either Democrats or Republicans. Since 1942, only five persons have been elected governor as independents or minor-party candidates; and after the 2008 elections, only 20 state legislators among a national total of 7,382 were neither Republican nor Democrat (excluding Nebraska's nonpartisan legislature).

The outcome of partisan nominations can dramatically influence a party's electoral prospects and its future course of development. For example, the Democrats' 1972 nomination of Senator George McGovern (S. Dak.), who was widely perceived to be far to the left of the average Democratic voter and American citizen, doomed the party to a landslide defeat and sowed the seeds for continuing divisiveness between liberals and moderates that contributed to ensuing losses of the presidency.

Similarly, Senator Barry Goldwater's (Ariz.) capture of the 1964 Republican nomination led to that party's disastrous defeat, as the nominee was seen by voters to be substantially more conservative than they were. His nomination, however, signaled the growing conservative movement within the party. This movement helped develop the cadre of rank-and-file workers devoted to conservative ideology that made it possible for Ronald Reagan to challenge incumbent President Gerald R. Ford for the 1976 Grand Old Party (GOP) nomination and then easily win the 1980 election. In nominating Ronald Reagan for president, the Republican Party significantly altered the course of American history because he was the first post–New Deal president to seriously attempt to limit the growth of federal domestic programs and expenditures.

The impact of the nomination process upon the House of Representatives since the 1980s has been striking. As the South became more competitive between the Republican and Democratic parties, conservatives were increasingly drawn to the GOP. At the same time, the Voting Rights Act of 1965 made it possible for black voters, who are overwhelmingly Democratic, to participate in the electoral process. The net effect of these changes was to make the Democratic Party in the South more liberal than in the past and, therefore, it nominated congressional candidates who reflected the national party's policy orientation instead of the traditional southern conservative view. The nomination and election of these moderate to liberal southern Democrats gave the Democratic Party in the House increased unity in roll call votes and enabled it to control the chamber's agenda and policy output from the mid-1980s until 1995.[11] At the same time, the infusion of white southern conservatives into the Republican nominating primaries has resulted in GOP nominees with decidedly conservative policy views. As the electoral realignment of the region progressed in the 1990s and in the 2000s, these conservatives were elected in larger and larger numbers, thereby creating a Republican party in the House characterized by an overwhelmingly conservative policy orientation.

Control of the party nominating process has gradually shifted from the hands of the party organization to the party in the electorate. Nominations for congressional and state office since the 1920s have been made via the direct primary, in which party voters select the nominee. In presidential nominations, the party leadership's voice has similarly been diminished with the rise of the presidential primary as the principal method of selecting national convention delegates.

CONTESTING ELECTIONS AND CHANNELING THE VOTE

Normally, in the general election stage, the parties mobilize the electorate and channel it either to the Democratic or Republican candidate. Given the physical size of the country, the masses of people involved, the diverse interests at stake, the number of states, the pace of social change, and the variety of political cultures, it is quite remarkable how successful the parties are in channeling the vote. The Republicans and Democrats can rely upon the partisan commitment of most voters to guide their election-day choices; but they cannot rely only on latent partisanship among the electorate. Partisans must be activated to turn out and actually vote; independents must be persuaded; and opposition party identifiers must be wooed and at least temporarily converted. In these activities, parties play a central role, but they are not exclusively party tasks. These responsibilities are shared with interest groups, candidate organizations, and campaign consultants.

ORGANIZING THE GOVERNMENT

For governmental institutions to operate with at least a modest degree of effectiveness, they require a division of labor, leadership, and rules; that is, they must be organized. The job of organizing government has fallen to the political parties. For example, Congress and most state legislatures are organized on a partisan basis. (Nebraska's nonpartisan legislature is an exception.) With their majority status following the 2000 elections, Republicans held the leadership roles of Speaker of the House, Senate Majority Leader, committee chairs, and subcommittee chairs and thereby largely determined the agenda and decisions of the chamber. However, when Senator James Jeffords (Vt.) switched from Republican to independent early in 2001, the Democrats became the chamber's majority party and claimed the leadership posts, only to relinquish those posts back to the Republicans after losing Senate seats in 2002. The executive branch is also organized on a primarily partisan basis. Presidential appointments go almost exclusively to members of the president's party. Indeed, most policy-making officers of the executive branch must gain a clearance from party officials at the national, state, and local levels prior to their appointment.

The constitutional separation of powers was intended by the Founders to encourage tension between the Congress and the president so that neither branch would become too powerful and threaten individual liberties. However sound the Founders' theory may have been, it is also clear that modern government requires legislative-executive coordination if societal needs and international obligations are to be met. An important source of such policy coordination is the tie of partisanship. Presidents tend to work primarily through their fellow partisans in Congress to achieve their policy goals. At the same time, leaders of the president's party in Congress, lacking formal power to control their party members, rely on the prestige and influence of the White House to exert leverage for party unity on roll call votes. Presidents' influence on their congressional party is normally at its zenith during the first two years of their term, when fellow party members are seeking to enhance the president's record for the next presidential election. The impact of presidential leadership can be impressive. For example, President Lyndon Johnson wielded

BOX 1.1	ELECTIONS, COLLECTIVE ACTION PROBLEMS, AND POLITICAL PARTIES

It is necessary to pool the resources and efforts of a large number of voters to win elections. However, this often leads to a collective action problem—when large numbers of people are involved, there is an incentive to free ride since any single person's contribution is unlikely to be missed. After all, it is time-consuming for citizens to inform themselves about candidates and to bother to turn out to vote at the polls, particularly given the small likelihood that their vote will decide an election. Candidates face the problem of having to inform and mobilize large numbers of citizens, a task that political parties make easier in two ways:

- Party labels as brand names—No matter where in the country you might be, you always know what to expect when you enter a McDonald's restaurant. Similarly, when a candidate runs as a Democrat or Republican, you can reasonably assume what he or she might stand for. In this way, political-party labels transmit a great deal of information to voters much more efficiently than if each candidate had to educate the public about their positions on the issues individually.
- Economies of scale—When you go out for pizza with your friends, you probably try to buy an entire pizza to share rather than each buying your own slice. After all, buying the whole pie together is more cost-efficient. Similarly, candidates could spend vast resources trying to mobilize supporters individually, but it makes far more sense to go in together and run as a party to more cost-efficiently mobilize supporters to vote for all of the party's candidates.

Source: John H. Aldrich, *Why Parties?* (Chicago: University of Chicago Press, 1995).

heavy Democratic congressional majorities to enact his Great Society social welfare program after the 1964 election, and in 1981 Ronald Reagan worked through a Republican majority in the Senate to set a conservative agenda for Congress. Even a president whose party does not control the House or Senate counts upon the loyalty of fellow partisans in Congress to achieve his policy goals. Presidents George H. W. Bush and Bill Clinton, for example, relied upon congressional partisans to sustain their vetoes in order to achieve bargaining leverage on legislation with the opposition party leaders. Of course, the president's ability to rely upon fellow partisans in Congress varies with conditions—especially the popular support enjoyed by the president. When that support diminishes, so does the president's capacity to hold the party together in support of favored programs in Congress, as the first two years of the Obama administration demonstrated.

PROVIDING PUBLIC ACCOUNTABILITY

Democratic governments derive their powers from the people. Fred I. Greenstein, therefore, has suggested a simple and workable definition of democracy as a political system in which "citizens have a relatively high degree of control over their leaders."[12] Parties provide voters with a means to hold public officials accountable for the actions of government. They therefore make a contribution to citizen control of government.

The contemporary political world is extremely complex. The array of issues and candidates upon which the model citizen should be informed in a general election is almost mind-boggling. Political power in the United States is divided among the legislative, executive, and judicial branches and among national, state, and local governments. The voter, therefore, is expected to make informed choices for officials at all levels and in several branches of government. There are choices for offices from president to county registrar of deeds, and issues from combating terrorism to the administration of county courts. Fortunately, the voter can respond to these tangled questions in terms of a few simple criteria and is not required to spend all available time studying politics.

Party labels enable voters to sort out this complexity and vote for the candidates of their preferred party—the party they perceive to be closest to their interests. Because each major elected official wears a party label—a type of political brand name—voters can also assign to the party in power either credit or, more likely, blame for the state of the union. Without party labels to sort out the candidates and issues, the average voter would be at sea with no compass for a guide.

Additionally, parties can contribute to citizen control of government because they are forced to advocate policies that will retain the support of their traditional constituencies while at the same time seeking additional votes among the unaffiliated or the disaffected members of the opposition party. The very uncertainty of electoral outcomes prevents parties from becoming excessively complacent because retention of office requires a constant reassessment of public sentiments. As a result, parties and candidates spend millions of dollars in both election and nonelection years on public-opinion surveys of voter sentiments.

The process of citizen control of government to which parties contribute is indirect, of course, and imperfect in nature. It is not a matter of voters instructing their leaders on the specific policies that they want the government to follow. Rather, periodic elections using party labels give the voters a chance to register their general reaction to a party's stewardship in office. The voters' judgment can be positive, as in the case of Ronald Reagan's (1984) and Bill Clinton's (1996) reelection victories, or be negative—witness the voter's rejection of reelection bids by Jimmy Carter (1980) and George H. W. Bush (1992). There is scant evidence, however, that in these elections voters were voting for specific governmental policies advocated by the winning candidates. They were rendering a general verdict on the incumbents' performance in office and, based upon past performance, their likely ability to deal with future problems.[13]

MANAGING CONFLICT

Because people vary in their goals and values and because what people want is often in short supply, conflict is inevitable in society. A stable governmental order, therefore, requires mechanisms for compromising competing group demands. Conflict must be managed and American parties have traditionally played a significant role in reconciling competing group demands.

Winning elections within a two-party system requires building broadly based coalitions. Inevitably, the elements of such coalitions will have somewhat divergent objectives. For example, the dominant Democratic New Deal coalition forged by

President Franklin D. Roosevelt during the 1930s contained such contentious elements as white Protestant southerners, blacks, northern urban Catholics, blue-collar workers, Jews, and farmers. The conflicts inherent in this alignment have been juggled with varying degrees of success since the 1930s. Within the Congress, for example, the Democrats have practiced the politics of "inclusive compromise," in which Democratic representatives from urban areas have supported farm price supports, while rural Democrats have voted for federally subsidized housing and urban development programs, and both groups have backed federal water projects for their party members from the arid Western states.[14] Uneasy alliances also exist within the GOP, which since the 1980s has sought to accommodate the interests of business-oriented economic conservatives as well as the social policy concerns of religious conservatives. As these examples suggest, within the American political system many group conflicts in society have been settled *within* the parties.

PARTIES AS COMPETITORS FOR POLITICAL INFLUENCE

As prominent as parties are in the American political order, they do not have the field to themselves. They must compete for political influence with candidate organizations, campaign consultants, interest groups, and the mass media. In recent years, the ability of parties to compete for a place in the campaign process has been weakened by the growing role of a professional corps of consultants and experts skilled in the latest campaign techniques and technologies. To a significant degree, these professional consultants operate outside the regular party organizations and are closely tied to the organizations of individual candidates. Even well-financed and professionally staffed party organizations at the national, state, and local levels find it impossible to provide their candidates with all the technical assistance—media experts, pollsters, direct-mail specialists, campaign managers—that they require. Recognizing the value of these specialists, the candidates, therefore, often seek to employ this type of talent using funds that have been raised independently of the parties. In the process, the candidates have become less dependent upon their party organizations at election time. This sense of independence from party is often reflected in the behavior of candidates after they have won public office.

Parties also face stiff competition from organized groups in terms of funding campaigns. Election costs are constantly and dramatically rising, and the parties cannot fund (and are often forbidden by law from funding) all or even major shares of the costs of campaigns. Increasingly, interest groups have come to play a larger role in funding candidates. The Campaign Finance Institute estimates that interest groups raised over $400 million during the 2008 election campaign. Organizations such as Planned Parenthood, the AFL-CIO, the Sierra Club, the National Rifle Association, and the Chamber of Commerce are heavily engaged in issue-advocacy campaigns that utilize media advertising on a massive, multi-million-dollar scale. Issue-advocacy campaigns, which do not explicitly call for the election or defeat of a candidate and are indistinguishable to the average voter from a candidate's own ads, enable interest groups not only to assist their favored candidates, but also to influence the issue agenda of the campaign.

The electronic news media, including television and the Internet, are also competitors with the parties for political influence. To a large degree, political reality for most Americans is what they see on the cable news programs or on their favorite blogs or Internet new sites. Americans get their news mainly from television. Television, therefore, has come to play a major role in politics and especially in presidential nomination contests. Internet news sites have become increasingly popular as well, providing more opportunities for political activists to reach citizens directly via blogs or news sites.

By the 1970s the bulk of the national convention delegates were chosen in presidential primaries—mass elections that in 2008 attracted over 55 million voters. In the sequence of presidential primaries that run from January to June of presidential election years, it is essential that a candidate establish the image of a winner, that is, momentum. Being interpreted as the winner of an early primary is necessary to gain media coverage, achieve standing in the polls, and raise funds for the next in a long series of primaries. But as Austin Ranney has pointed out, "Doing best in the early primaries is not simply a matter of getting more votes than the other candidates; it is getting substantially more votes than expected."[15] And it is the news media who decide what is expected. For example, during much of 2007, the news media portrayed Hillary Clinton as the undisputed frontrunner for the Democratic nomination. But Obama was able to win the Iowa caucuses in early January, giving him the momentum he needed to continue his campaign and eventually capture the nomination. John McCain's bid for the Republican nomination seemed all but doomed just a few months before the New Hampshire primary. But a victory in New Hampshire provided him with the momentum he needed to catapult to the front of the field and go on to win the Republican nomination.

In effect, what has been happening in presidential politics is that the traditional role of screening the candidates is being shifted away from party leaders—governors, members of Congress, state and local party chairs, and mayors—to the mass media and the participants in presidential primaries. The party role in presidential nominations has not been eliminated, but the age of party-leadership domination of presidential nominations has clearly passed. The news media has become a powerful, competing intermediary institution.

Some observers concerned with the rise of campaign consultants, PACs, interest groups' issue-advocacy campaigns, and news media have predicted a bleak future for American parties. There were even apocalyptic visions of partyless politics. But the parties have demonstrated qualities of adaptability, durability, and resilience. As succeeding chapters will demonstrate, three elements of the party retain significant influence: the party in the electorate retains the allegiance of over 60 percent of the voters who identify with one of the two major parties; the party in government dominates decision making in Congress; and the first decade of this century has witnessed a renewal of strength in both national and state party organizations.

PARTIES AND INTEREST GROUPS: THERE IS A DIFFERENCE!

Interest groups engage in many of the same activities as political parties. They seek to influence nominations, elect favored candidates, influence the appointment of officials to the executive branch, and influence governmental decisions. Although there are surface similarities, parties are unique institutions that can be distinguished from interest groups.

PARTIES RUN CANDIDATES UNDER THEIR OWN LABELS

No matter how much interest groups may concern themselves with elections through endorsements and support of candidates in primaries and general elections, it is only the parties that run candidates on their own labels. There are no candidates for major office that run under the label of the AFL-CIO, the U.S. Chamber of Commerce, the NAACP, the American Bar Association, or the Methodist Church. Only parties assume responsibility for the candidates that run under their banners, and only parties act as agents of public accountability for the actions of their affiliated officeholders.

PARTIES HAVE BROAD ISSUE CONCERNS

Interest groups reflect the concerns of persons who share a common viewpoint or set of attitudes and wish to further those interests through governmental policy. Normally these interests are quite narrow in scope, reflecting the special concerns of the membership and not the full gamut of governmental policies. The National Association of Home Builders, for example, is primarily concerned about federal housing policy and interest rates; the Tobacco Institute worries about regulation of smoking; the American Legion seeks benefits for former members of the armed forces and advocates a strong defense; the Wildlife Federation seeks sanctuary for wildlife through environmental protection; and so on. Most interest groups have clear priorities in terms of the issues to which they devote attention, and they do not strain the unity of their organizations or their treasuries by getting involved in issues of only marginal interest to the membership. Even broadly based organizations like the AFL-CIO, which seeks to influence a wide range of governmental policies, have clear priorities that reflect the bread-and-butter concerns of union members.

Political parties, by contrast, take stands on the whole spectrum of issues with which government deals—foreign, fiscal, welfare, education, transportation, health, racial, environmental, science, energy, and social policy. No other political organization has a breadth of policy concerns comparable to that of political parties.

PARTIES GIVE PRIORITY TO CONTROLLING THE PERSONNEL OF GOVERNMENT

However broad the policy concerns of parties may be, they tend to give priority in the United States to winning elections. Parties want to control the personnel of government. To achieve this end, American parties have shown great flexibility in terms of their policy positions and willingness to accommodate a wide variety of different views in their midst. Although Republican and Democratic members of Congress as a group show distinctly different voting patterns on major issues, it is also true that each party contains significant though differing proportions of conservatives, moderates, and liberals. Ideological purity takes a backseat to winning elections for American parties. By contrast, interest groups like the American Association of Retired Persons, the National Organization of Women, or the American Medical Association are concerned first and foremost with governmental policy.

Most groups are concerned about who is elected or appointed only because of the policies these officeholders will promulgate, not out of a desire to put fellow group members in public office. As a result, most interest groups support candidates in both parties whom they see as capable of advancing group aims.

PARTIES ARE QUASI-PUBLIC ORGANIZATIONS

Interest groups like the American Bankers Association, the American Farm Bureau Federation, the Teamsters, Common Cause, or the American Library Association are private associations. They operate under minimal governmental regulation and enjoy all the protections of the First Amendment. Parties are quite different organizations. In the United States, they are heavily regulated by federal and especially state statutes. These statutes provide legal definitions of parties, mandate organizational structures and procedures, define membership, and specify how certain party functions like nominating candidates will be carried out. American parties are, therefore, quasi-public institutions, whereas interest groups are private associations.[16]

PARTIES HAVE A UNIQUE RELATIONSHIP TO THEIR CLIENTELE

As Paul Allen Beck has observed, other political organizations, like interest groups, seek to attract the support of persons beyond their membership, but such persons always remain outside the group. But the persons in the electorate being wooed by parties are permitted to take part through the direct primary in the most important activities of the party—the nomination of its candidates and the selection of its leadership. "The American party is an open, inclusive, and semipublic political organization composed of its own clientele, a tangible organization, and personnel in government. As such it stands alone and unique in the American political system."[17]

THE STATE OF PARTIES IN THE TWENTY-FIRST CENTURY

While Americans have not always embraced political parties, parties have been a stable force in the nation's political history. As discussed in Chapter 2, party conflict has been institutionalized in the United States. Americans expect electoral contests between two parties, with the victorious party organizing the government and the opposition party maintaining a steady barrage of criticism. Nevertheless, the increasing failure of citizens to affiliate themselves with either party during the second half of the twentieth century led many scholars and commentators to wonder whether parties were becoming less relevant to voters and political elites. Throughout this text, I will not only discuss the many functions that parties perform in our political system, but I will also address their continued salience, particularly in light of the increasing political polarization evident during the past decade. Ultimately, I demonstrate that parties remain central to our political system and that they have become increasingly relevant to citizens, activists, and office holders in recent years.

NOTES

1. Harold Lasswell, *Politics: Who Gets What, When, and How* (New York: McGraw-Hill, 1936).

2. Edmund Burke, "Thoughts on the Cause of Present Discontents," in *The Works of Edmund Burke*, vol. 1 (Boston: Little, Brown, 1871), p. 151.

3. Leon D. Epstein, *Political Parties in Western Democracies* (New York: Praeger, 1967), p. 9.

4. V. O. Key, Jr., *Politics, Parties, and Pressure Groups*, 5th ed. (New York: Crowell, 1964), p. 163.

5. Paul Allen Beck, *Party Politics in America*, 8th ed. (New York: Longman, 1997), p. 13.

6. Key, *Politics, Parties, and Pressure Groups*, p. 201.

7. E. E. Schattschneider, *Party Government* (New York: Holt, Rinehart and Winston, 1942), p. 1.

8. Samuel Huntington, *Political Order in Changing Societies* (New Haven, Conn.: Yale University Press, 1980), p. 91.

9. Sarah McCally Morehouse, *State Politics, Parties and Policy* (New York: Holt, Rinehart and Winston, 1981), p. 29.

10. Schattschneider, *Party Government*, p. 64.

11. David W. Rohde, "Something's Happening Here; What It Is Ain't Exactly Clear: Southern Democrats in the House of Representatives," in Morris P. Fiorina and David W. Rohde, eds., *Home Style and Washington Work: Studies in Congressional Politics* (Ann Arbor: University of Michigan Press, 1989), pp. 137–163; and Nicol C. Rae, *Southern Democrats* (New York: Oxford University Press, 1994).

12. Fred I. Greenstein, *The American Party System and the American People*, 2nd ed. (Englewood Cliffs, N.J.: Prentice Hall, 1970), p. 2.

13. Paul R. Abramson, John H. Aldrich, and David W. Rohde, *Change and Continuity in the 1996 Elections* (Washington, D.C.: CQ Press, 1998), pp. 146–150.

14. David Mayhew, *Party Loyalty among Congressmen: The Differences between Democrats and Republicans, 1947–1962* (Cambridge, Mass.: Harvard University Press, 1966).

15. Austin Ranney, *Channels of Power: The Impact of Television on American Politics* (New York: Basic Books, 1983), p. 95.

16. See Leon D. Epstein's discussion of political parties as public utilities in his book *Political Parties in the American Mold* (Madison: University of Wisconsin Press, 1986), ch. 6; see also Jack W. Peltason, "Constitutional Law for Parties," in Nelson W. Polsby and Raymond E. Wolfinger, eds., *On Parties: Essays Honoring Austin Ranney* (Berkeley: Institute of Governmental Studies, University of California, Berkeley, 1999), pp. 9–41.

17. Beck, *Party Politics*, p. 13.

THE PARTY BATTLE IN AMERICA

CHAPTER CONTENTS

Organized partisanship was an unplanned development. In their plan for the Republic, the framers of the Constitution did not envision a president nominated by party conventions, partisan slates of presidential electors, or a Congress organized on the basis of partisanship. Early leaders like Washington, Hamilton, and Madison believed that parties would be divisive and would undermine the public interest. Their grand design was not to create "a system of party government under a constitution but rather a constitutional government that would check and control parties."[1] Fearing the impending rise of parties, Washington's Farewell Address in 1796 sounded a warning call:

> [The Spirit of party] serves always to distract the Public Councils and enfeeble the Public administration. It agitates the Community with ill-founded jealousies and false alarms, kindles the animosity of one party against another, foments occasional riot and insurrection. It opens the door to foreign influence and corruption, which find a facilitated access to the government itself through the channels of party passions....

Such misgivings about parties have remained a persistent element of American political culture. Early in the twentieth century, when party conflict had been institutionalized, progressive reformers succeeded in imposing upon parties severe regulations that stripped them of such functions as control of the nominating process. In the 1970s, Congress passed legislation that aided their rivals—the political action committees (PACs). A strong strain of apprehension and dissatisfaction concerning the role of political parties continues to flourish among the citizenry. Polls conducted during the 1990s revealed that a majority of Americans preferred to have the presidency and Congress controlled by different parties; 40 percent would like to have candidates run without party labels; and only 8 percent said that a candidate's party was most important to them in choosing a president.[2] Thus, from the beginning of the Republic to the present, political parties have functioned in an environment never entirely hospitable to their presence. American parties may have evolved into durable institutions that command substantial numbers of adherents, but the public remains skeptical of them.

PARTY REALIGNMENTS IN AMERICAN HISTORY

Throughout American party history, there have been periodic electoral *realignments*. During a realignment, significant changes occur within the electorate: a minority party becomes the majority party (1860, 1932); one party achieves an infusion of strength that enables it to remain dominant (1896); significant changes in the partisan loyalties of voters develop (1860, 1932). In a penetrating analysis of critical elections in American history, Walter Dean Burnham noted that realignments tend to occur when major crises intrude on the society and economy and "politics as usual" is not adequate to deal with the problems.[3] Paul Abramson, John Aldrich, and David Rohde outline five attributes of realignments:[4]

1. The regional support for the parties changes.
2. The social groups supporting the parties change.
3. New groups of citizens are mobilized and become part of the electorate.
4. Voters change not just which party they vote for, but also the party that they identify with.
5. Realignments are typically caused by new issues that divide citizens.

The last point is particularly important, as it provides insight into why realignments occur. Typically, realignments are caused when a new issue arises that fractures the current coalitions supporting each of the major parties. This causes a reorganization of support for the parties with major consequences for the party system, including highly polarized campaigns and heightened public interest, which together result in a critical realignment of voters. For example, the slavery issue arose in the mid-1800s and provided dilemmas for both parties. As noted below, the Whigs largely avoided taking a clear position on the issue of slavery, while the Democratic Party was badly fractured. This led to the dissolution of the Whigs during the 1850s and the emergence of the Republican Party. The critical election of 1860 solidified a realignment as the Republican Party emerged and ran Abraham Lincoln as its candidate and the Democratic Party showed just how divided it was by running two separate candidates for president. Ultimately, the Republican Party became the party of the North—and the dominant national party—while the Democratic Party was the party of the South. This change amounted to a significant alteration in the political landscape and provides one of the quintessential examples of the phenomenon of realignment.

According to most scholars of political parties, there have been either four or five realignments in the United States—1828, 1860, 1896, 1932, and perhaps 1968. Political scientists use these realignments to divide American political history into six party systems. Table 2.1 provides an overview of the historical development of party systems, and these party systems are described in the sections that follow.

THE FIRST PARTY SYSTEM, 1788–1824: FEDERALISTS, REPUBLICANS, AND ONE-PARTY FACTIONALISM

American parties were born in the policy conflict between Hamilton and Jefferson during the Washington administration. As their disputes intensified, each turned to his supporters within the Congress, and factional alliances between leaders of the executive and legislative branches developed. The emerging parties, therefore, developed out of national divisions, not state politics. It was, however, the Jeffersonians who first sought to broaden their operations beyond the nation's capital by endorsing candidates for Congress and the Electoral College. Later they developed slates of candidates for state offices.[5] The Federalists, led by Hamilton and Adams, were forced to follow suit and compete for support within the mass electorate. The Federalists, however, were reluctant party organizers whose initial reaction to the party organizing activities of Jefferson's Democratic-Republicans was to bemoan their rivals' appeals to the public. As Hamilton noted, the Federalists "erred in relying so much on the rectitude and utility of their measures as to have neglected the cultivation of popular favor by fair and justifiable expedients."[6] Historians are in general agreement that the dramatic extension of party organizations at the local level in the election of 1800 and the aggressive organizing of the Democratic-Republicans in support of Jefferson contributed to his election over John Adams.[7] The nomination of presidential candidates by party caucuses in Congress is further evidence of the emergence of party organizations.

The Federalists were advocates of a positive national government capable of nation building and the protection of American business interests. In foreign affairs,

TABLE 2.1 | PARTY SYSTEMS IN AMERICAN HISTORY

Party System	Dates	Competing Parties	Characteristics/Comments
First Party System	1788–1824	Federalists vs. Democratic-Republicans	Parties emerge in 1790s. One-party factionalism within Democratic-Republican Party after 1820.
Second Party System	1828–1854	Democrats vs. Whigs	Balanced two-party competition, with Democrats the dominant party.
Third Party System	1856–1896	Republicans vs. Democrats	Republican dominance from 1862 to 1874, balanced two-party competition from 1874 to 1896. Sectionalism in political conflict.
Fourth Party System	1896–1928	Republicans vs. Democrats	Republican dominance except for period of intraparty schism in 1912. Continued sectionalism.
Fifth Party System	1932–1968	Republicans vs. Democrats	Democratic dominance and formation of the New Deal Democratic coalition; in the 1950s, the coalition starts to fray and the era of divided party control of the government begins.
Sixth Party System	1968–present	Republicans vs. Democrats	Weakened partisanship among the voters; candidate-centered politics; blacks becoming overwhelmingly Democratic; southern whites shift to the Republicans; split-ticket voting; divided government; after the 1994 elections, the Republicans regain control of Congress for the first time since 1954; alternating party control of the presidency; frequent third-party eruptions (1968, 1980, 1992, 1996, 2000).

they sided with the British against the revolutionary regime of France. In terms of electoral bases of support, the Federalists tended to be the established leadership strata in most of the states, while their challengers were Jeffersonians. Federalists were distinguished by being persons of old wealth, respectable occupations, and higher levels of formal education. By contrast, the Democratic-Republicans tended to draw support from less elite elements of society. They were fearful of the strong national government emerging under the Federalists and were protectors of agricultural interests. They were aligned with the French in foreign affairs.

Federalist electoral support suffered a precipitous decline after the Federalists' defeat in 1800. This decline is related to the Federalists' failure, as the party of the

American elite, to respond in as timely a manner as the Democratic-Republicans to the popular and democratic style of politics that was developing.[8] After 1816, the Federalists disappeared as a national political party capable of contesting for the presidency and competed only in a few states, such as Massachusetts and Delaware. The Jeffersonians were triumphant, and the first era of partisan competition was over. The "Era of Good Feeling" that followed was a period of partyless politics characterized by factionalism among leaders, all of whom claimed to be Republicans. Since all elected officials belonged to one party, it was impossible for President James Monroe to exercise any party discipline over Congress and coherent action by Congress became impossible to achieve.

Factionalism within the dominant Democratic-Republican Party led to the collapse of the congressional caucus system of presidential nominations. Because there was no opposition party, the winner of the caucus nomination was assured of election. The congressional caucus, however, had never been popular. It was seen more and more as an undemocratic device as states dropped the property-ownership restrictions on voting, thereby extending the franchise to all white males. In 1824, when the congressional caucus nominated William Crawford for president, it was inevitable that other ambitious politicians would challenge Crawford in the general election. The 1824 election became a four-way contest among Crawford, John Quincy Adams, Andrew Jackson, and Henry Clay. As a result, no candidate received a majority in the electoral college. The House of Representatives, after much bickering and maneuvering, finally chose Adams. His administration was characterized by intense intraparty conflict between his followers and those of Jackson. The "Era of Good Feeling" was at an end, and the expanded electorate stood ready for political mobilization by political parties.

What set this First Party System apart from those that have followed was the fact that neither Federalists nor Democratic-Republicans were born into families with these affiliations. There were no traditional party loyalties upon which to build electoral support and sustain parties. Political activists had not had their party identification passed on to them by parents and friends through reinforcing patterns of interaction. As Everett Carll Ladd has noted,

> The absence of inherited loyalties in the new party system of the first period, together with the rudimentary character of party organization and the prevailing tendency to see party as, at best, a necessary evil, made the new party growth relatively superficial. The roots of party simply did not run deep.[9]

THE SECOND PARTY SYSTEM, 1828–1854: DEMOCRATS VERSUS WHIGS IN TWO-PARTY COMPETITIVE POLITICS

Andrew Jackson, the popular hero of the Battle of New Orleans, defeated Adams in 1828 and gained reelection over Clay in 1832. These elections were fought in a transitional era of bifactional politics within the dominant Democratic-Republican Party. Both Jackson and Adams used variations on the Republican name as their party labels in 1828, as did Clay in 1832, when Jackson switched to the Democratic label. By 1834, the amalgam of forces and groups opposed to Jackson's policies had coalesced sufficiently to form an opposition party, the Whigs. An era of unusually close two-party competition followed.

This Second Party System came into being during a period when American political life was being democratized: slates of presidential electors were popularly elected; property qualifications for voting were dropped; and electoral participation increased dramatically. For example, voter turnout increased from 26.9 percent of eligible voters in 1824 to 78.9 percent in 1848.[10] Party nominating procedures were also opened to wider participation as the congressional caucus was replaced by the national convention.

In the two decades that followed Jackson's reelection in 1832, the Whigs and Democrats were engaged in an intense struggle for the newly expanded electorate. They engaged in popularized campaigning—torchlight parades, rallies, picnics, campaign songs, and slogans like "Tippecanoe and Tyler too." Both parties organized state and local parties and ran full slates of candidates under a party label. In this atmosphere of partisan mobilization, voters began to see themselves as either Whigs or Democrats.[11] Unlike the Federalists, who had been reluctant to court popular support, the Whigs did so with zeal. As the national minority party, one of their favorite techniques was to run military heroes with an appeal above party for president. They did this in four of six elections and were successful twice—in 1840 with William Henry Harrison and in 1848 with Zachary Taylor. In nine of eleven elections, however, the majority Democrats won control of the Congress.

Both the Democrats and the Whigs were truly national parties that engaged in relatively close competition not only at the national level but also in each region and in most states. For example, old bastions of Jefferson's such as Georgia, North Carolina, Louisiana, and Tennessee divided their support quite evenly between the Whigs and Democrats, as did the Middle Atlantic states. Ladd has observed that during the 1836–1852 period, the "United States had less regional variation in voting than at any other time in history."[12] This lack of sectionalism in American politics was a tribute to the skills of Democratic and Whig leaders in balancing the interests of farmers, manufacturing and mercantile factions, nativists, immigrants, Catholics, and Protestants. Both parties were broad coalitions that sought backing throughout the country, with the Whigs attracting proportionately more support from manufacturing and trading interests, planters, and established Protestants, whereas the Democrats did well among newly enfranchised voters, western farmers, Catholics, and new immigrants.

The absence of highly salient issues that might have divided the nation along sectional lines also contributed to the ability of the two parties to compete in all regions. However, when racial and slavery issues reached crisis proportions in the 1850s, the Whigs and Democrats were confronted with a nation divided along sectional lines. This national schism was reflected in the parties that split into Northern and Southern factions because neither was able to satisfy both regions. America then entered its Third Party System.

THE THIRD PARTY SYSTEM, 1856–1896: ASCENDANT REPUBLICANS VERSUS DEMOCRATS

Culturally and economically, the South became increasingly distinct from the rest of the nation during the 1840s and 1850s. Abolitionist sentiment gained support in the North, demonstrating the force of a compelling moral issue, whereas the South

continued to harbor the institution of slavery. In addition, the two regions' economies were developing quite differently. The South concentrated almost exclusively
on agriculture, especially cotton, whereas the North was becoming more industrial,
urban, and mixed in its ethnic composition. In addition, the population and wealth
of the North were growing at a much more rapid rate than those of the South.
These economic and cultural differences inevitably led to political conflicts over
the direction of national policy. The sectional rivalries created by those differences
came into their sharpest conflict because of the ceaseless westward expansion of the
nation. Western settlement required the Congress and the parties to confront
the issues of whether slavery would be permitted in the territories and whether the
new states would be admitted as slave or free states. Any change in the number of
free and slave states threatened to upset the delicate balance of power in the
national government. Both the Whigs and Democrats were unable to reconcile the
sectional conflicts within their ranks, and as a result the electorate went through a
major realignment in the 1850s and 1860s.

The Democrats' situation was made difficult by the powerful position occupied
by its southern wing. In Congress, the Democrats were dominated by southerners
determined to maintain the institution of slavery and protect the political position
of the South by insisting that the balance of free and slave states not be upset
when new states were admitted to the Union. The South was also strengthened by
the two-thirds rule used by the Democratic national nominating conventions. This
procedure guaranteed the South a veto over the selection of presidential nominees.
As a result, the party could only agree to nominate weak "neutralist" or "dough-
face" candidates like Franklin Pierce (1852) and James Buchanan (1856). With
weak presidents and a southern-led Congress, it was not possible for the government to resolve the slavery issue.

In the midst of this sectional turmoil over the extension of slavery, the Whig
Party dissolved. The Whigs had traditionally been the party of national integration
and accommodation between the North and South. But with the intensification of
northern hostility toward slavery and heightened sectional sentiments in the South,
the Whigs' position was undermined in both regions. Faced with declining electoral
support, a schism between its northern and southern wings, and the emergence of
the antislavery Republican Party in the North, the Whig Party ceased to be a major
electoral force after the elections of 1854.[13] There was a transition period toward
two-party competition between the Republicans and Democrats between 1854 and
1860. In the presidential election of 1856, the new Republican Party—composed of
abolitionists, Free Soilers, and dissident northern Whigs and Democrats—came in
second to Democrats, as James Buchanan defeated General John C. Fremont. The
remaining Whigs nominated former President Millard Fillmore under the American
party banner and came in a dismal third. No candidate received a majority of the
popular vote. The deterioration of the old party system continued in 1860. In the
North, the election was a contest between Stephen A. Douglas, the nominee of
northern Democrats, and former Whig Abraham Lincoln, the Republican nominee.
In the South, southern Democrat John C. Breckenridge contested former southern
Whig John Bell. Again, no candidate received a popular vote majority, though
Lincoln was able to gain 59.4 percent of the electoral vote and 39.8 percent of the
popular vote.

The Republican Party dominated in the 1864–1874 period. The successful prosecution of the Civil War identified the Grand Old Party (GOP) with the Union, patriotism, and humanitarianism. But Republican strength did not rest on emotionalism alone. The party forged an alliance among several important interest groups: farmers through the Homestead Act and free land in the West, business and labor through support for a high protective tariff, entrepreneurs through federal land grants to build transcontinental railroads linking the West and North (and bypassing the South), and veterans through pensions. By imposing Reconstruction upon the South, the post–Civil War Radical Republicans in Congress sought to control the South through black votes and the support of carpetbaggers. Both parties were sectional. The GOP was dominant in the North and West, but it had little popular support in the South. The Democrats, by contrast, were a southern-based party. The party's addiction to free trade did, however, give it some northern business allies.[14] In addition, the Democrats gained substantial support among Roman Catholic immigrants in cities of the North. After 1874 and the end of Reconstruction, the Republicans and Democrats started to compete on a more even basis up until 1896. They alternated control of the presidency and Congress, but the post–Civil War period was primarily an era of Republican dominance in national political life.

In addition to the disappearance of the Whigs and the emergence of the Republicans as the dominant political party, two other significant developments occurred during the era of the Third Party System. One was the growth, particularly in the Middle Atlantic and some midwestern states and cities, of patronage-based party organizations or machines. Organized to address the growing needs of communities for services in the wake of massive waves of immigration and economic growth, there were also extremely effective in controlling nominations and mobilizing party votes on Election Day.[15] Ironically, the Third Party System was also the era that ushered in the Australian ballot (ballots printed at government expense instead of party-printed ballots, and provision for casting one's vote in secret), which had the effect of weakening the party machines. The Australian ballot movement gave the voter new independence from parties in making electoral choices. It was no longer public knowledge how people voted, and using government-provided ballots made it easier for citizens to split their ballots.

THE FOURTH PARTY SYSTEM, 1896–1928: REPUBLICAN DOMINANCE RENEWED

The period following the Civil War was a time of immense social and economic change with far-reaching consequences for electoral politics. The United States ceased to be a primarily agrarian society and became an industrialized and urban nation. By 1890, more people were employed in manufacturing than in agriculture, and by the end of the 1920s, only one family in four was involved in agriculture. On the eve of the Civil War, no American city had contained a million people, but by the close of the 1920s, cities with a population in excess of a million inhabitants were becoming commonplace—New York, Chicago, Philadelphia, and Los Angeles. Transportation advances, like the completion of the great transcontinental railroads, linked the East and West and made the nation more interdependent. Rail mileage grew from 8,500 in 1850 to 193,000 in 1900. This was also the era of the rise of the corporation—mammoth enterprises like Standard Oil and U.S. Steel. The ethnic makeup of the population also changed as waves of immigrants entered the country largely from non–English-speaking nations of Europe.

The economic and social revolution that was transforming America posed new problems for the political system. Radical agrarian movements swept the nation (e.g., the Grangers Farmers' Alliance and the Greenbackers).

Third-party movements also formed. The most significant was the People's Party (Populist), which in 1892 garnered over 1 million votes and twenty-two electoral votes on a radical platform that demanded the inflation of the currency through unlimited coinage of silver, nationalization of railroads and telephone/telegraph companies, and institution of an income tax. These movements reflected the major economic dislocations that were occurring. There was agrarian discontent with the growing power of corporations and the frequently depressed state of the farm economy. The late 1800s also witnessed the rise of labor organizations, reflecting the discontent of urban workers with their status in the new industrial order.

Neither the dominant Republicans nor the "me too" Democrats were responsive initially to these popular protest movements. In 1896, however, the forces of agrarian radicalism captured the Democratic presidential nomination for William Jennings Bryan, whose platform was a challenge to the existing industrial order. A key plank in the Democrats' platform was a call for free and unlimited coinage of silver and gold at a ratio of sixteen to one. In adopting this position, the Democrats appropriated the principal program of the Populists and made a dramatic appeal to farmers, debtors, and western mining interests. The Democrats were also the party of a low tariff.

Seeking to bolster their post–Civil War coalition, the Republicans countered by advocating the gold standard and opposing the inflationary free coinage of silver; and they maintained their position as the party of the high protective tariff. Their stand on the silver issue cost them the support of western states, but the high protective tariff position brought them renewed support among urban workers, who blamed the depression of the 1890s on the low tariff policies of the Democratic Cleveland administration. William McKinley, the Republican candidate, was able to run on the themes of "Prosperity—Sound Money—Good Markets and Employment for Labor—A Full Dinner Bucket." Mark Hanna, the Ohio industrialist and skilled Republican campaign manager, also mobilized business interests, terrified by Bryan and his policies, to give generous and overwhelming support to the GOP.

The election of 1896 transformed the political landscape and realigned the electorate. The Republican coalition forged during and after the Civil War received an infusion of support, especially among urban dwellers of the Northeast. McKinley carried the nation's ten largest cities and increased the GOP vote in working-, middle-, and upper-class wards. Bryan was the sectional candidate of the agrarian South, the Plains, and the silver mining states of the West. He had little appeal to the industrializing East and Middle West, where the bulk of the population and electoral votes were located. V. O. Key has observed that the Democratic loss of 1896 "was so demoralizing and so thorough that the party made little headway in regrouping its forces until 1916."[16] Indeed, the Democrats elected only one president in the period between 1896 and 1928, and Woodrow Wilson's 1912 election was possible only because of a major schism within the dominant Republican coalition.

In that year, the festering internal Republican conflict between the traditional conservatives of the industrial-financial centers of the Northeast and the Progressive reformers of the Middle West and West broke wide open. Theodore Roosevelt, after failing to capture the GOP nomination from President William Howard Taft, ran as a candidate of the Progressive Party. Roosevelt split the Republican vote and actually outpolled Taft in popular votes (27.4 percent to 23.2 percent). This division permitted a brief Democratic interlude under Wilson. After World War I, the fire was out of the Progressive movement and Americans yearned for normalcy. In this postwar atmosphere, the Republicans asserted their dominance with impressive victories in 1920, 1924, and 1928. Although the Republicans won the election of 1928, the election returns gave evidence of expanding Democratic strength. The Democratic percentage of the popular vote jumped from 28.8 in 1924 to 40.8 in 1928, and the party's presidential ticket carried Massachusetts and Rhode Island, an indication of its appeal to voters in Catholic, urban, and industrial centers. Democratic support was thus developing in the growing metropolitan and manufacturing centers, whereas the GOP tended to be dominant in northern and eastern rural precincts.[17]

The Fourth Party System was an era of diminished interparty competition. In the seven presidential elections after 1896, the average Republican share of the national two-party vote was 57.7 percent, while the Democrats received 42.3 percent. In four of these elections, the gap between the Republican and Democratic vote exceeded ten percentage points—the usual definition of a landslide. This was in sharp contrast to the evenness of competition between 1876 and 1896, when in 1880, 1884, and 1892 less than one percentage point separated the two parties' share of the popular vote for president. The post-1896 lack of competitiveness was also reflected in state elections. Regional voting patterns were sharply differentiated. The South, especially after the disenfranchisement of blacks via devices like the poll tax and white primary, became even more overwhelmingly Democratic (see Figure 2.1). In the rest of the nation, however, the Republicans were dominant. In twenty-two states of the North and West, the Republicans received more than 60 percent of the vote on average in the presidential elections from 1896 to 1928.[18]

The Progressive reform movement of this period had a profound impact on American parties, even though the Progressives never succeeded in forming a major party. It was during the Fourth Party System era that the direct primary was instituted as the principal method of nominating candidates. The primary weakened the capacity of parties to control the nominating process and enabled candidates to make direct appeals to the voters. In addition, as Kristi Anderson has noted, women's achievement of suffrage in 1920 further "helped solidify the movement from the partisan-structured politics of the nineteenth century to the politics of advertising, interest groups, and candidates that characterize the twentieth century."[19] The presidential primary was also born in this period. Another major change in the legal environment of parties was the imposition of governmental regulation, primarily by the states. Primary laws frequently regulated party organizational structure, and campaign finance was also brought within the purview of the law. Parties became quasi-public agencies subject to legislative control.[20]

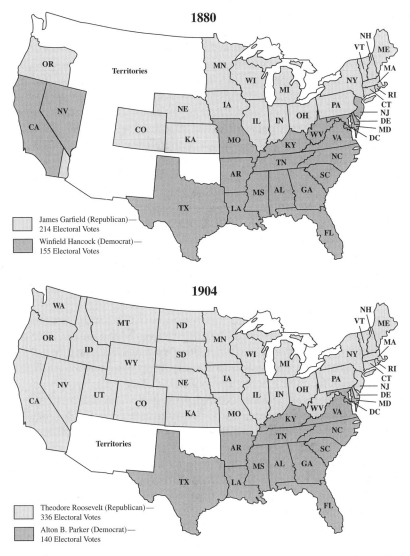

1880

James Garfield (Republican)—
214 Electoral Votes

Winfield Hancock (Democrat)—
155 Electoral Votes

1904

Theodore Roosevelt (Republican)—
336 Electoral Votes

Alton B. Parker (Democrat)—
140 Electoral Votes

FIGURE 2.1   SECTIONALISM IN AMERICAN POLITICS DURING THE POST–CIVIL WAR
ERA AND EARLY TWENTIETH CENTURY

THE FIFTH PARTY SYSTEM, 1932–1968: THE DEMOCRATIC NEW DEAL ERA

President Herbert Hoover had been in office less than a year when the stock market crash signaled the beginning of the Great Depression of the 1930s. The election of 1932 was a major benchmark in American political history. It marked a realignment of the electorate from a Republican to a Democratic majority. The New Deal coalition that supported Franklin D. Roosevelt was formed. Like the old

Republican coalition, the new Democratic majority was an amalgam of disparate and sometimes conflicting elements. White southerners, still wedded to the cause of white supremacy, were a core group, as were Catholic urban workers, mostly recent immigrants from eastern and southern Europe who had been socialized to political life by the urban political machines. These Catholic voters had also been drawn to the Democratic banner by the antiprohibitionist candidacy of a coreligionist, Governor Al Smith of New York, in 1928. Blue-collar workers, especially organized labor, rallied to support Roosevelt in the face of rising unemployment. Blacks forsook the party of Lincoln to back the Democrats; the already economically depressed black society was severely rocked by the Depression. Jews, who heretofore had been predominantly Republican, also became identified with the Democratic Party because of the Depression and Roosevelt's leadership against Nazi Germany. In addition, young people entering the ranks of the electorate in the 1930s and 1940s tended to become Democrats. The Democrats were riding a wave of demographic change. Urban ethnics, Catholics, blue-collar workers, and blacks were becoming a more and more significant proportion of the electorate, while the traditional Republican base of white Protestants, small-town residents, farmers, and middle-class businesspersons constituted a shrinking share of the population.

Franklin Roosevelt's election and his New Deal social welfare policies, which instituted an American version of the welfare state, had long-run weakening consequences for the traditional, patronage-based urban party organizations. New social insurance programs (like Social Security and unemployment compensation) were effectively insulated from patronage-type politics and served as models for later federal grant-in-aid programs that emphasized professionalism in state and local government.[21] The New Deal social welfare programs not only further weakened the patronage base of the machines, but they also took from the machines their traditional function of providing welfare services to the deprived urban populations.

The New Deal Democratic electoral coalition forged by Roosevelt proved to be an enduring alliance. Between 1932 and 1948, the Democrats won the White House all five times and lost control of the Congress only once, in 1946. Divisions within the dominant coalition, however, appeared as early as the late 1930s, when conservative southern Democratic representatives and senators began to dissent from Roosevelt's social welfare policies. The North/South split within the party became even more pronounced after 1948 and into the 1960s, when northern Democratic leaders like Senator Hubert Humphrey (Minn.) led the party into taking a strong stand on civil rights issues.

Since the 1930s, the Republican Party has remained the minority party. At least twice, after electoral disasters in 1936 and 1964, it was written off by political commentators as terminally ill. Its obituaries were prepared prematurely, however, because each time the party staged a timely comeback, demonstrating the resiliency of two-party competition in the United States. In 1952, Republicans used a strategy long favored by minority parties to help them win the presidency and Congress. Like the Whigs of 1840 and 1848, the GOP nominated a national hero, General Dwight D. Eisenhower, the charismatic commander of Allied forces in Europe during World War II. Running on the slogan "I like Ike," the Republicans made major inroads into all elements of the New Deal coalition while holding the traditional

Republican vote. Particularly noteworthy was Eisenhower's support in the heretofore solidly Democratic South, where he carried states of the old Confederacy such as Virginia, Texas, Florida, and Tennessee. The Eisenhower years proved to be a period of consolidation in American politics. The new Republican administration and Congress did not move to repeal the policies of the New Deal. Rather, they accepted the New Deal programs and made only minor modifications. With this Republican acceptance, the Roosevelt New Deal legacy ceased to be the divisive force in American politics that it had been. One of Eisenhower's Republican successors, Ronald Reagan, could even be heard praising and quoting Roosevelt in the 1980s.

Running on a theme of "Peace and Prosperity," Eisenhower swept to an even more overwhelming victory in 1956. The election, however, confirmed the continuing minority status of the GOP, which lost seats in the House and Senate despite the landslide election of the president. The normal Democratic majority reasserted itself in 1960 and 1964 with the elections of John F. Kennedy and Lyndon B. Johnson. The huge congressional majorities that Johnson carried into office with him in 1964 enabled the party to enact his Great Society programs—a massive expansion of social welfare assistance that was carried out largely through extensive grant-in-aid programs to state and local governments. After the Democrats' landslide win of 1964, however, the divisions within the Democratic Party intensified as the party split over such issues as race relations, the Vietnam War, defense policy, crime and civil disorder, and social policy.

THE SIXTH PARTY SYSTEM, 1968–2000: THE POST–NEW DEAL ERA—DEALIGNMENT AND DIVIDED GOVERNMENT

The period from 1964 through 1968 was a transition period into a post–New Deal party system. Between 1952 and 1964, there was little change in the aggregate distribution of partisanship among the electorate. This steady state of electoral partisanship, however, underwent significant changes during the mid- to late 1960s. Among the significant changes were the following: (1) black voters increased their political participation levels and increased their affiliation with the Democratic Party, resulting in the virtual disappearance of black Republican identification as Democratic presidents endorsed civil rights legislation and the 1964 GOP presidential nominee, Barry Goldwater, opposed it; (2) partisanship declined as more voters identified themselves as independents and tended not to see the relevance of parties; (3) white southerners, once a mainstay of the Democratic electoral coalition, moved into the Republican fold; and (4) support for the Democrats declined among their other traditional support groups such as Catholics and blue-collar workers.[22] In addition, television, an information source that tends to discourage rather than encourage stable party loyalties, became the dominant campaign medium.[23]

The coming together of these forces in the 1960s helped to create and institutionalize, in the 1980s and 1990s, a *candidate-centered party system,* in which neither the Republicans nor the Democrats constituted a true majority party and voters were heavily guided by candidate appeals. The Democrats lost the majority status they had from the New Deal to President Lyndon Johnson's Great Society era in the early 1960s; and the Republicans, while having staged a comeback, were not able to pick up the majority party mantle from the Democrats.

This absence of a party commanding the loyalties of a majority of voters differentiates the current party system from previous party systems, which did have dominant majority parties among the voters. The declining impact of partisanship within the electorate can be seen in a comparison of the pre- and post-1960s eras. Thus, an analysis of presidential elections from 1840 to 1960 shows that changes in the vote from one election to the next were due primarily to differences in the ability of the parties to mobilize their partisan identifiers rather than the conversion of voters from supporting one party to supporting the other.[24] Beginning in the 1960s, however, such conversions became the principal force causing interelection vote shifts. This change has been attributed primarily to the ability of candidates to appeal directly to the public and to woo voters away from the opposition. The candidate-centered nature of elections is also clearly in evidence at the congressional level. Students of congressional elections have found that up until 1960 there was no systematic personal advantage attached to being an incumbent. After 1960, however, there has been sustained advantage attached to incumbency.[25] Indeed, at least 90 percent of the incumbents normally win reelection in House elections, and Senate incumbents' reelection statistics are not far below those of their House colleagues.

An additional indicator of the weakening of party ties among voters was the emergence of unusually strong third-party and independent candidates in four presidential elections during the post–New Deal era. Even before Ross Perot became a household name in 1992 (capturing the largest vote percentage of any non–major-party candidate since Theodore Roosevelt in 1912) and 1996, there was Governor George Wallace's (Ala.) 1968 run for the presidency, which garnered 13.5 percent of the vote and carried five Deep South states with forty-six electoral votes, as well as Representative John B. Anderson's (Ill.) 1980 independent candidacy, which netted 6.6 percent of the popular vote but no electoral votes. More recently, Ralph Nader's third-party candidacy garnered more than 2.5 percent of the vote in 2000 and likely kept Al Gore from winning Florida and the election.

With voters guided less than in the past by partisanship, split-ticket voting became commonplace during this period and divided party control of the presidency and Congress a regular occurrence. Thus, in twenty-six of the thirty-two years between Richard Nixon's first election in 1968 and the return of one-party control by the Republicans after the 2000 election (briefly interrupted when Senator James Jeffords of Vermont defected from the GOP in early 2001), different parties controlled the White House and at least one chamber of the Congress. A similar pattern has emerged at the state level, where divided government also occurs on a regular basis.

In this era of candidate-centered politics, party organizations neither control the nomination process nor run their nominees' campaigns. Rather, the parties play the role of providing services, particularly money, to their candidates. As a result, the Sixth Party System has been characterized by political scientist John H. Aldrich as one in which the parties operate in service to their candidates.[26]

Most political scientists agree that the Sixth Party System was born more out of dealignment than realignment. And while dealignment—the weakening of party loyalties among the electorate—has occurred, this does not fully account for changes witnessed during this period. In fact, the most significant change during this period may have taken place in the South, which did undergo substantial realignment. Until the middle of the twentieth century, there was almost a complete absence of a Republican presence in the South. White southerners, even conservative white southerners, continued to have disdain for Abraham Lincoln's Republican Party, choosing instead to ally themselves with Democrats. However, the passage of civil rights legislation during the 1960s and the candidacy of conservative Republican Barry Goldwater set in motion a dramatic realignment that would fundamentally alter the landscape of party politics in the South. The issue of race divided the Democratic Party in the South and provided an opportunity for Republicans to win the support of conservative white southerners who no longer supported the policies espoused by Democrats.

Figure 2.2 presents the percentage of southerners and nonsoutherners who reported affiliating with the Republican Party from 1956 to 2008. In 1956, approximately 20 percent of southerners affiliated with the Republican Party, compared with over 40 percent of those residing elsewhere. However, while the percentage of people affiliating with the Republican Party remained relatively stable in the rest of the United States, it climbed steadily in the South during this period, and by 2008 the Republican presence in the southern electorate was significantly greater than outside the South. Voters' changed party identification meant that Republicans began winning elections in the South. In 1960, Republicans did not hold any southern Senate seats and won fewer than 10 percent of the House contests; by 2009, Republicans held 15 of the 22 southern seats in the Senate and 72 of the 124 House seats. While realignment occurred only in the South, the phenomenon had important consequences for the national political landscape. Gains by southern Republicans provided the foundation for taking control of Congress in 1994 and provided the basis for the increasing polarization of the national parties in the 1990s and 2000s.[27]

FIGURE **2.2** | PERCENT AFFILIATING WITH THE REPUBLICAN PARTY IN THE SOUTH AND NON-SOUTH, 1956–2008

Source: National Election Studies.

| BOX 2.1 | PARTISAN POLARIZATION IN CONTEMPORARY POLITICS? |

Reporters, pundits, and many academics have noted the increasing polarization among the electorate in recent years. The polarization manifests itself as a seemingly deep divide between Republicans and Democrats (or red states and blue states). There are many reasons cited for this increased polarization:

- *Partisan parity*. The electorate is very evenly divided between the two major parties, with nearly equal shares of citizens affiliating with each party. This close division has raised the electoral stakes, resulting in close and bitter contests such as the 2000 and 2004 presidential campaigns. The 2000 presidential election, in which Al Gore won the popular vote but lost the electoral college vote by the narrowest of margins, angered many Democrats and increased the partisan divide in subsequent years.
- *News media*. While the politics may have become more polarized, the news media only serve to reinforce this polarization by focusing on the most bitter and divisive aspects of politics.
- *Congressional redistricting*. After the 2000 census, most congressional districts were drawn to be very safe for either Republicans or Democrats. Representatives hailing from these uncompetitive districts can afford to be more extreme in their politics because it is unnecessary to reach out to moderates to win reelection.
- *Issues*. Many of the issues at stake in recent campaigns have also been particularly polarizing. The Iraq War drove a wedge between those supporting and opposing the continued deployment of U.S. forces in Iraq. In addition, divisive morality issues such as gay marriage and abortion have taken on particular prominence in recent years, as well as debates about the preservation of civil liberties while fighting terrorism.

Ultimately, these factors, and many others, combine to create an electorate for whom partisan divisions are more salient than in previous decades. Consider that during the 2004 campaign, 90 percent of registered voters said that the stakes were higher than they had been in previous elections and 76 percent were "afraid" of what might happen if their preferred candidate did not win.

Source: Geoffrey C. Layman Thomas M. Carsey, and Juliana Menasce Horowitz, "Party Polarization in American Politics: Characteristics, Causes, and Consequences," *Annual Review of Political Science* (Vol. 9, 2006) pp. 83–110.

TWENTY-FIRST CENTURY PARTY POLITICS: A RENEWED ERA OF PARTISAN POLARIZATION?

By the early 1990s, scholars were suggesting that parties had lost much of their influence, particularly among the American public. However, during the first decade of the twenty-first century, there are signs of a significant renewal of partisanship among the American public. This pattern has not been reflected by changes in the share of the American public who identifies with a party; those figures have not changed much at all during the past two decades. However, Americans who do identify with a party are now more ideologically homogenous. For example, in the early 1980s, one-third of American conservatives identified as Democrats. By 2004, that figure had dropped to just 14 percent. During the first decade of the twenty-first century, over 80 percent of conservatives identify with the Republican Party and four of every five liberals are Democrats. Thus, partisanship and ideology have become fundamentally linked in recent decades. In fact, by 2004, just 2 percent of Americans classified themselves as both liberal and Republican, while less than 5 percent said they were conservative Democrats.

As Americans have polarized along partisan lines, parties have become increasingly important to their political decisions. In the past decade, it has become less common for voters to support candidates from the opposite party, or to split their tickets by voting for a presidential candidate from one party and a congressional candidate from another party. According to the exit polls in 2008, 71 percent of voters classified themselves as either a Democrat or Republican, and only one in ten of these voters reported casting a ballot for the candidate from the other party. And Americans are not just divided when it comes to their vote choices. By the end of Obama's first year in office, over 80 percent of Republicans disapproved of the job he was doing as president while over 80 percent of Democrats approved, a partisan divide similar to that experienced by George W. Bush during the earlier part of the decade.

Overall, it appears as though the patterns of dealignment that persisted during the latter half of the twentieth century may be on the wane. While Americans have not become significantly more likely to claim party allegiances during the past decade, those allegiances appear to mean more than they did several decades ago. They are more powerful determinants of how Americans vote and evaluate politicians and issues than they once were, which has led to the conventional wisdom that America has become a more polarized nation.

MINOR PARTIES IN AMERICAN POLITICS

The presidential candidacies of Ross Perot in 1992 and 1996 and the formation of his Reform Party, the election of non–major-party governors in four states during the 1990s, and Ralph Nader becoming the nominee of the Green Party in 2000 sparked renewed interest in minor parties. These events are a reminder that the United States does not have a pure two-party system, since in every election year minor parties run candidates for president (more than fifteen candidates in 2004). Some of these parties have long histories; for example, the Socialist and Prohibition parties. However, such doctrinal parties are not operating elements of the party system. They are, instead, like "rivulets alongside the main stream of party life," maintaining an "isolated existence."[28] Similarly, the so-called new parties, such as the Green, Libertarian, and Right-to-Life parties, which have distinctive cultural orientations, also operate largely outside the mainstream of American politics. However, a steady current of "recurring short-lived, minor party eruptions" have been closely tied to the party system.[29] Only the Republican Party, which replaced the Whigs between 1854 and 1856, when the nation was in the throes of a sectional split over slavery, has ever achieved major party status. Most have been short-lived, and none has had a realistic chance of electing a president. The most successful third-party or independent presidential candidacies were those of Theodore Roosevelt (Progressive Party, 27 percent of vote) in 1912, Ross Perot (independent, 18.9 percent of the vote) in 1992, and George Wallace (American Independent Party, 13.5 percent of the vote) in 1968.

THE IMPACT AND ROLE OF MINOR PARTIES

Third-party protests have been closely associated with the early stages of every major electoral realignment since the 1830s and hence have been called a "protorealignment phenomenon."[30] On these occasions, the rise of third parties has reflected the inability of the major parties to meet the expectations of large segments of the public. Thus, the Free Soil Party (1848) arose prior to the collapse of the Whigs and the emergence of the Republicans; the Populist eruption in 1892 occurred before the landmark realigning election of 1896 between McKinley and Bryan; the La Follette Progressive movement of 1924 was a precursor to the creation of the New Deal Democratic coalition in the 1930s. The Dixiecrat (States' Rights Party) revolt of southern Democrats in 1948 and George Wallace's run for the presidency as the American Independent Party candidate in 1968 foreshadowed the weakening of the New Deal–Democratic coalition and the beginning of the Sixth Party System.

Third-party and independent candidates have also helped to give prominence to certain issues and forced these issues onto the public agenda when the major parties were unwilling to confront them: for example, the Free Soilers on the slavery issue; the Populists on the plight of farmers of the Great Plains and West; the Progressives of 1912 and 1924 on the economic dislocations created by industrialization and urbanization; and Perot (1992) on huge federal budget deficits. However, it is possible to overstate the extent to which third parties advocate and build public support for causes that the major parties are then forced to adopt as their own. Thus, it is commonly asserted that the Socialist Party's advocacy of such policies as a minimum wage law for over twenty years led to its becoming a part of Franklin Roosevelt's New Deal program. Yet, as Paul Allen Beck has observed, "Unfortunately, there is no way of testing what might have happened had there been no Socialist Party," and one of the lessons of party history is that "major parties grasp new programs and proposals in their 'time of ripeness' when large numbers of Americans have done so and when such a course is therefore useful to the parties."[31]

BOX 2.2	SIGNIFICANT THIRD-PARTY ERUPTIONS AND INDEPENDENT CANDIDATES

Since the early days of the Republic, periodic third-party eruptions have raised important issues and affected future electoral alignments, election outcomes, and the nature of the party system. Although frequent, these third-party movements have been short-lived, and only one, the Republican Party, which emerged between 1854 and 1856, achieved major party status. Few had success winning more than a small number of electoral votes. In the post–World War II years, there has been an increase in the number of independent presidential candidates, and even candidates who have formed third parties have run highly personalized campaigns without a real party organization supporting them or a full slate of candidates for other offices.

Anti-Masonic Party
The Anti-Masons were America's first third party and an early manifestation of fundamentalist Christian distrust of the establishment and secularism. The party is best

continued

SIGNIFICANT THIRD-PARTY ERUPTIONS AND INDEPENDENT CANDIDATES *continued*

remembered for instituting the national convention in 1831 as the method for nominating presidential candidates. In 1833, it merged with the National Republicans to form the Whig Party.

Free Soil Party
Formed in 1848, the Free Soilers opposed the extension of slavery in newly acquired territories and advocated a homestead act to provide free land to settlers. By 1854, the party had been absorbed into the newly formed Republican Party.

American (Know Nothing) Party
This anti-immigrant and anti-Catholic party achieved electoral successes at the state level in 1854 as the old Democratic/Whig party system was collapsing. Amid the sectional turmoil of the pre–Civil War period, it quickly faded out of existence.

Constitutional Union Party
An offshoot of the Whig Party composed of conservatives opposed to the candidacy of Abraham Lincoln in 1860, the Constitutional Union Party carried three southern states and then dissolved amid secession of the South and the Civil War.

Southern Democratic Party
This was a splinter party reflecting the schism between the northern and southern wings of the Democratic Party in 1860. Its presidential nominee carried most of the southern states and garnered seventy-two electoral votes. The party dissolved after the secession of the South.

Liberal Republican Party
As a party of dissident Republican reformers opposed to Reconstruction and the corruption of the Grant administration, the Liberal Republicans nominated *New York Tribune* editor Andrew Greeley as their presidential nominee. Greeley was also endorsed and nominated by the Democrats, but the alliance's weak showing in 1872 led to its breakup and the disbanding of the Liberal Republicans.

People's (Populist) Party
As an agrarian radical movement that swept across the West and South during the farm depression of the 1890s, the Populists called for government ownership of railroads, free coinage of silver, an income tax, and an eight-hour work day. Its presidential candidate carried five states in 1892. Four years later, Populists captured control of the Democratic national convention and nominated William Jennings Bryan.

Progressive (Bull Moose) Party of 1912
The Bull Moose Progressive Party was Theodore Roosevelt's vehicle to regain the presidency after he was denied the GOP nomination by President William Howard Taft. Roosevelt's candidacy reflected the split between the Progressive and Stalwart wings of the Republican Party. By coming in second in the popular voting, Roosevelt split the Republican vote and enabled the Democratic candidate, Woodrow Wilson, to be elected with 42 percent of the vote. Roosevelt returned to the GOP four years later.

continued

SIGNIFICANT THIRD-PARTY ERUPTIONS AND INDEPENDENT
CANDIDATES *continued*

Progressive Party of 1924

Led by Senator Robert La Follette of Wisconsin, the Progressives sought to build a base of farmer and labor supporters with a program calling for government ownership of railroads, protection for organized labor, direct primaries, and approval of wars by referendums. La Follette carried only his home state and died shortly after the election. His party died with him.

States' Rights Party of 1948

The so-called Dixiecrats were a splinter group of southern Democrats opposed to their party's strong civil rights plank. They made no attempt to organize a separate party but instead used the existing southern state Democratic Party machinery. The Dixiecrats returned to the Democratic fold after the election, in which they carried four states.

American Independent Party of 1968

With the Democratic Party wracked by internal dissension over civil rights, law and order, and the Vietnam War, Alabama Governor George Wallace emerged as the candidate of segregationist, traditionalist, and anti-Washington elements of the electorate. He won five southern states and made inroads among blue-collar workers, but in 1972 he returned to the Democratic Party.

Independent John B. Anderson of 1980

After failing to win the Republican nomination, the moderate GOP congressman from Illinois ran as an independent seeking to be a centrist candidate between Republican Ronald Reagan on the right and Democrat Jimmy Carter on the left. Even though he lacked an organization, adequate financing, and a compelling issue, he won 6.6 percent of the vote. He retired from politics after the election.

H. Ross Perot, Independent in 1992 and Reform Party Candidate in 1996

Taking advantage of public disenchantment with the major party nominees in 1992, the Texas billionaire mounted a personally financed campaign for the presidency that emphasized the dangers of a huge federal budget deficit. He collected the largest percentage of popular vote (18.9) for an independent candidate since Teddy Roosevelt in 1912, but he did not win a single electoral vote. For the 1996 campaign, Perot created and funded his own party, the Reform Party, but saw his popular vote fall to 8.4 percent. Racked by internal dissension, the party's nomination was captured in 2000 by a renegade right-wing Republican, Pat Buchanan, who received only 0.43 percent of the vote in spite of having received $12.6 million in public funding.

Ralph Nader, Green Party in 2000 and 2004

Running as a dedicated environmentalist, liberal advocate of expanded social welfare programs, and an ardent opponent of free trade and corporate interests, to which he claimed the major parties were beholden, Nader won only 2.7 percent of the vote. However, by taking votes away from Al Gore in critical states such as Florida, he may have enabled George W. Bush to win in the electoral college. In 2004, his support dwindled significantly, capturing less than 0.5 percent of the national vote.

Source: John F. Bibby and L. Sandy Maisel, *Two Parties—Or More? The American Party System* (Boulder, Colo.: Westview, 1998). Copyright © 1998 John F. Bibby and L. Sandy Maisel. Reprinted by permission of the Perseus Books Group.

BOX 2.3	WAS RALPH NADER RESPONSIBLE FOR THE BUSH PRESIDENCY?

Ever wondered how the world might have been different if Al Gore had won Florida in 2000 instead of George W. Bush? Gore appeared on *Saturday Night Live* in 2006 pretending that he had in fact won and that he was addressing the nation as its president. Among his fictional presidential achievements that he humorously trumpeted were an end to global warming, gas prices of 19 cents per gallon, and a budget surplus of $11 trillion. The spoof was a vivid reminder of how close the 2000 election had been. And while Gore may still agonize over the myriad of factors that cost him the 2000 election, none may be as clearly to blame as the candidacy of third-party candidate Ralph Nader.

Though Nader only captured 2 percent of the vote in Florida, the nearly 100,000 people who voted for him in the Sunshine State was more than enough to overcome a Bush margin of victory that was smaller than 1,000 votes. Political scientists have found that while many Nader voters would not have voted at all if he had failed to run, between 32 and 40 percent of them would have cast ballots for Gore and only as many as 17 percent would have voted for Bush. Based on those estimates, Gore would have won Florida by more than 20,000 votes if Nader had not run. This would have secured the presidency for Gore and altered the course of American history. Thus, even though third-party candidates are rarely successful in winning office in their own right, they can influence electoral outcomes in important ways.

Source: Christopher S. P. Magee, "Third-Party Candidates and the 2000 Presidential Election," *Social Science Quarterly* (Vol. 84, No. 3, 2003), pp. 574–595.

Furthermore, new issues in their incubation period do not depend exclusively upon minor parties to bring them to the fore. Interest groups, the mass media, prominent citizens, and factions *within* the parties can also be more effective than minor parties in issue advocacy. It is widely accepted, for example, that an interest group, the Anti-Saloon League, was a far more powerful force in the enactment of Prohibition than was the Prohibition Party.[32]

MINOR PARTIES AT THE STATE LEVEL

The partisan alignment of voters at the state level has tended to follow the national pattern. During the long domination of electoral politics by the Republicans and Democrats since the 1850s, state politics has been a struggle mainly between the Democrats and the GOP, just as it has been for the presidency and Congress. State party organizations, though primarily concerned about winning state-level offices, have made effective use of their parties' national followings in state races. However, there have been several minor parties of consequence existing on their own local bases of support rather than as extensions or offshoots of minor parties at the national level. In several instances, these parties achieved electoral success before withering or being absorbed into the major parties.

- *Minnesota's Farmer-Labor Party.* This party was created in the 1920s by Populists who mobilized hard-pressed farmers and laborers to challenge the state's dominant Republican Party. It was so successful that it temporarily replaced the Democrats as the Republicans' principal opposition, thereby creating a three-party system in the state. In 1930, the Farmer-Labor alliance even won the governorship. However, in the 1940s, the pull of national political alignments overcame the party, and after suffering successive defeats, it merged with the Democrats to form the Democratic Farmer-Labor (DFL) Party.

- *Wisconsin's Progressive Party.* Like Minnesota, Wisconsin also had a brief interlude when a third party, led by the sons of Robert La Follette, the 1924 Progressive presidential candidate, emerged to challenge the Republicans and Democrats. Between 1934 and 1946, the state had a three-party system in which the most meaningful competition took place between the Republicans and the liberal Progressives, who succeeded in winning gubernatorial, senatorial, and congressional elections along with control of the state legislature. Just as the tides of national politics swept over Minnesota in the 1940s, as liberal and labor elements of the electorate were attracted to the national Democratic Party, the Progressives found themselves steadily losing supporters. Facing likely defeat for reelection as a third-party candidate and in the face of a projected Republican electoral sweep, Senator Robert M. La Follette, Jr., decided in 1946 that pragmatism dictated that the Progressives should disband and move back into the Republican Party.
- *New York's Multiparty System.* A distinctive party system has developed in the Empire State due to a type of election law that enhances the status of minor parties and institutionalizes their existence. New York permits candidates to receive the nomination of more than one party. Candidates' names can appear on the ballot under the label of multiple parties. This "cross-filing" or "fusion ticket" arrangement has encouraged various interests to seek leverage over the major parties by creating minor parties. Among the options available to minor parties under cross-filing are nominating the candidate of an allied major party and thereby gaining influence within the major party by providing votes crucial for victory. With the potential to affect election outcomes, the minor parties can pressure an allied party to nominate a favored candidate or face the prospect of the minor party either running a candidate of its own, thereby taking votes away from their normally allied party's nominee. Minor parties in New York also have the option of nominating the candidate of the party with which they are not normally allied. Through the use of these tactics, the Liberal Party has exerted substantial influence over its customary ally, the Democrats. The Conservative Party and, to a lesser degree, the Right-to-Life Party have become forces to be reckoned with in state Republican politics.

THIRD-PARTY AND INDEPENDENT GOVERNORS

In 1990, two well-known former Republican officeholders, Walter Hickel (Alaska) and Lowell Weicker (Conn.), were elected governor in their states on minor-party tickets. In spite of these breakthroughs, both men found the problem of sustaining a third-party challenge to the major parties a feat bordering on the impossible. Parties such as Hickel's Alaska Independence Party and Weicker's A Connecticut Party lacked an organizational infrastructure and were overly dependent upon a single, prominent, maverick politician. When these two former Republicans were not on the ballot in 1994, their parties floundered and sank.

In Maine, Angus King, a former Democrat and high-tech millionaire running as an independent, won the governorship in 1994 and a landslide reelection victory in 1998. His popularity has stemmed from his emphasis on economic development, while also taking into account environmental concerns. Unlike Hickel and Weicker, King has not tried to form a third party.

In 1998, minor-party candidate Jesse "The Body" Ventura, a former professional wrestler, actor, and suburban mayor, emerged to capture the Minnesota governorship by upsetting the major-party nominees, an incumbent Democratic attorney general and a Republican mayor of St. Paul. Ventura's populist, straight-talking rhetoric, tough-guy image, and showmanship enabled Ross Perot's Reform Party to gain its first major electoral victory. However, Ventura quit the Reform Party as it became engulfed in internecine warfare during 2000 and he formed the Independence Party of Minnesota. Although he has retained his personal popularity, Ventura has not given priority to party building and the party has had difficulty recruiting candidates.

SOME LESSONS FROM PARTY HISTORY

This brief overview of party history in the United States provides the main contours of party development and permits us to make several observations about the nature of the American party system. Throughout the party history of the United States, the following traits can be observed:

- Normally, just two major parties compete for power.
- Parties rely on broad-based coalitions of citizens.
- The Democratic and Republican parties are quite durable features in American political life.

WHY TWO PARTIES? SOME EXPLANATIONS

Although there have been transitional periods characterized by factionalism within the dominant party (1824–1832) and interludes when third parties or independent candidates posed a major threat to the major parties (1892, 1912, 1924, 1992), party competition in the United States has been predominantly of the two-party variety. Even when one of the major parties disintegrated, the two-party division reestablished itself. And although one party frequently has been overwhelmingly dominant in the national government, the opposition party has been able to retain the loyalty of a sizable segment of the electorate. Despite the prevalence of this pattern of two-party competition, scholars have had difficulty explaining the persistence of dualism. Certainly, there is no one cause of the phenomenon.

THE INSTITUTIONAL EXPLANATION

A French political scientist by the name of Maurice Duverger proposed that the basis for a two-party system is the standard American arrangement for electing national and state legislators, the single-member district system—whoever receives a plurality of the vote is elected. In contrast to proportional representation, which uses multimember districts and rewards all serious parties with their proportionate share of the legislative seats, the single-member system permits only one party to win in any given district. It is a system that affords only two parties a reasonable chance of victory. Third or minor parties are normally condemned to perpetual electoral defeat—not a prescription for longevity—unless they can combine forces with a larger party. The single-member system certainly creates incentives for two broadly based parties capable of winning legislative district pluralities. The role of this electoral system in creating a two-party system became known as Duverger's Law; however, this is a misnomer. Scientific laws are generally meant to be universally true, but the experience of other nations—the Third Republic of France, Canada, and the United Kingdom—suggests that single-member districts by themselves are not a sufficient answer to the question of why America has two parties. The single-member district can only encourage this type of competition.[33]

Two-party competition is also encouraged by the Electoral College system for choosing presidents. Election as president requires an absolute majority of the electoral votes. This requirement makes it unlikely that a third party can ever achieve the presidency without combining with or absorbing another major party. In addition, the states' electoral votes are allocated under a winner-take-all arrangement. All that is required to capture a state's electoral votes is a plurality of the vote in that state. Like the operation of the single-member district, this system works to the disadvantage of third parties, which have little chance of winning any state's electoral votes, let alone a sufficient number of states to elect a president.

Over and above the formidable difficulties imposed by single-member districts and the Electoral College stand an array of additional barriers to viable third parties. A particularly imposing barrier is created by the direct primary and presidential primary systems for nominating candidates. One of the consequences of these highly participatory nominating systems is to channel dissent into the major parties.[34] Unlike in other democracies, insurgents and dissidents do not need to form their own parties. Rather, they can avoid these difficulties by running candidates in the primaries of the major parties, and through this "burrowing from within" strategy often achieve major-party nominations, elective office, and intraparty influence.

In addition, the Federal Election Campaign Act (FECA) tends to benefit the major parties at the expense of minor parties. Public funding at the maximum level is available to the presidential nominees of the major parties (defined by the FECA as parties whose candidates received at least 25 percent of the vote for president in the previous election). In 2008, John McCain took advantage of this $84.1 million grant from the federal government for the general election while Barack Obama became the first candidate to turn down the money since the program began in 1976. Minor parties receive a much smaller allocation of public funds for their nominees (e.g., Reform Party candidate Pat Buchanan received $12.6 million in 2000), and only if the party received at least 5 percent of the vote in the previous presidential election. No minor party candidate has been eligible to receive funding since 2000.

Unlike the major-party presidential nominees, third-party candidates are not assured of being able to participate in the presidential debates, which provide candidates with free publicity and access to millions of voters. The rules of the nonprofit Commission on Presidential Debates exclude candidates that it deems do not have a realistic chance of being elected. Ralph Nader was thus barred from the 2000 and 2004 presidential debates.

State regulations and laws can also inhibit minor parties. The Republican and Democratic parties are assured of automatic ballot access (each party's name and candidates appearing on the general election ballot) because of their prior success in winning votes. But for new parties and independent candidates, ballot access is anything but automatic. They are required to submit petitions signed by a large number of voters just to get their candidates' names on the ballot. An unusually high hurdle to ballot access was imposed by Pennsylvania in 1997, when it enacted a law requiring a new party to secure over 99,000 signatures on a petition in a fourteen-week period. A large number of states also have "sore loser" laws that prevent candidates who lose primary elections from then running as independent candidates in the general election. All but a handful of states also ban fusion tickets, or cross-filing, under which minor parties can run candidates of the major parties under their own minor-party labels. This ban, which has been upheld by the Supreme Court, prevents minor parties from building electoral support by forming alliances with major parties and their nominees.

Minor parties at the state level are also inhibited by the widespread practice of selecting local candidates through nonpartisan elections in which candidates run without party labels. This weakens the capacity of minor parties to build a local base of support. Nonpartisan local elections were instituted as part of a late-nineteenth- and early–twentieth-century reform movement that sought to weaken corrupt local political machines. An additional motive in some states was to thwart the new Socialist parties that were electing mayors in various cities during the first decades of the twentieth century.[35] Today, approximately three-fourths of America's cities and towns hold nonpartisan elections.

Institutional barriers have clearly helped to institutionalize two-party electoral competition in the United States. However, this should not obscure a basic political truth: "No electoral system protects major political parties from the electorate."[36] This is a lesson that was forcefully brought home to Canada's Progressive Conservatives after the 1993 election, when they went from being the majority party in the national legislature to minor-party status with only two legislative seats. The Progressive Conservative Party has remained a minor party ever since, winning only twelve seats in 2000, the bare minimum required to be considered a parliamentary party. In spite of the fact that Canada, like the United States, uses single-member districts to elect its national legislature, America's neighbor to the north has a thriving multiparty system. The Republican Party's displacement of the Whigs during the 1854–1860 period demonstrates that a new party can overcome institutional barriers by changing the nation's political agenda. It is, of course, fortunate for the Republic, though unfortunate for third parties, that since the 1850s no issue as divisive as slavery has restructured American politics.

THE HISTORICAL EXPLANATION

This explanation emphasizes the impact of the special circumstances of the initial political conflicts in the new nation and the tendency for human institutions to perpetuate themselves and preserve their initial form. The initial major issue that the country faced was that of ratification of the Constitution, a yes-or-no issue that tended to divide the nation. The small farmers and debtors of the interior were pitted against the mercantile and financial interests of the coastal regions. The initial lines of cleavage thus were built upon two great complexes of interests—the agricultural interests and the financial/mercantile interests. Such a dual split was possible because the social and economic structure of society was far less complex and specialized than that of today. Partisan conflict thus began in an era when a dualist cleavage existed. The pattern of two-party politics persisted, however, even though the society changed. As V. O. Key has observed:

> The great issues changed from time to time but each party managed to renew itself as it found new followers to replace those it lost. The Civil War, thus, brought a realignment in national politics, yet it re-enforced the dual division.... As memories of the war faded new alignments gradually took shape within the matrix of the preexisting structure, with each party hierarchy struggling to maintain its position in the system.[37]

THE CULTURAL EXPLANATION

American society has not been characterized by blocs of people irreconcilably attached to a particular ideology or creed. Racial, religious, and ethnic minorities, though often encountering discrimination, have generally been able to find a niche in society and have not tended toward separatism. Religious tensions have existed, but open conflict has never been common and First Amendment rights have generally enjoyed protection. Nor has class consciousness been as common in the United States as in European nations. Labor parties have had little appeal to American working men and women. In addition, there has been widespread acceptance of the constitutional order and a capitalist economic system.

While diversity abounds within American society, the ingredients for multiparty politics have largely been lacking. No group is seeking to restore the prerogatives of the Church as a state religion; no major group is seriously advocating monarchy, socialism, or communism; a labor party would have few adherents; and serious advocates of giving over the ownership of factories and large farms to the workers are scarce. Should such groups come to exist in significant numbers, multiparty politics would be possible. But in their absence, two-party politics is feasible. It is possible for one party to be slightly to the left of center—liberal—and the other to be slightly right of center—conservative—and still gain widespread electoral support. Thus, the Democrats and the Republicans can attract divergent cores of support that have quite different policy viewpoints and still compete for the vote of the vast majority of Americans, who consider themselves to be middle-of-the-roaders.

It is difficult to assign weights to the three explanations of two-party politics that have been discussed above. Clearly, America's form of competition is the result of a combination of forces that have conspired to produce dualism.

PARTIES AS COALITIONS

Throughout their history, American parties have been broadly based coalitions. Both majority and minority parties have attracted significant support from virtually every element of society, but the core of support for each of the major parties has consistently differed. The New Deal coalition that so dominated the political scene for thirty years was composed of white southerners, blacks, blue-collar workers, urban Catholics, ethnic minorities, and Jews. By contrast, the core of GOP strength was northern white Protestants, business and professional people, small-town residents, suburbanites, and midwestern farmers. Party coalitions change over time, however, in response to new crises and issues that test the ability of party leaders to hold the diverse elements within their coalitions. For example, the challenge for today's Republican leaders involves holding together a diverse three-headed coalition composed of (1) traditional middle- and upper–middle-class economic conservatives; (2) the social conservatives of the Christian Right; and (3) former Democratic conservatives, primarily white southerners.

The coalition nature of the parties means that intraparty conflicts can be crucial in shaping the direction of governmental policy and the nature of party competition. For example, during the first part of the century, when the GOP was dominant, the struggles between the Republican Stalwarts and Progressives were in reality contests over the direction of national policy and the nature of the governing coalition. The battles between southern conservative and northern liberal Democrats for that party's soul since 1937 have heavily influenced the scope and nature of governmental actions as well as the character of interparty competition. Similarly, in the 1980s and 1990s, the struggles within the GOP between Christian Right social conservatives and traditional economic conservatives (who tend to be moderate on social issues) had a major impact upon governmental policy during the Reagan-Bush administration and also affected GOP presidential and congressional nominating politics. While American party history is clearly characterized by competition between two parties, the nature of that competition has varied considerably. Samuel J. Eldersveld has noted that there have been three types of party politics since 1800.[38] The first is relatively *balanced two-party competition* between the two major parties, such as the period of Republican-Democratic competition that has existed since the end of World War II as the parties have traded control of the presidency. There have been 100 years of such balanced two-party competition.

Some Americans tend to think of balanced two-party competition as the norm, but another prevalent pattern has been *one-party dominance*. There have been five periods of sustained one-party dominance, the most recent being the Democratic era of 1932–1946. In addition, there have been periods of *transitional pluralism* (factionalism within the dominant party). These periods of pluralist competition within the dominant party have twice preceded the emergence of a new major party. Thus, the dominant Jeffersonian coalition engaged in a series of intraparty struggles for the presidency between 1824 and 1832 before the Whig Party emerged. Similarly, schisms within the Democratic and Whig parties between 1854 and 1860 occurred as the Republican Party was taking its place as a major party. The split between the Progressives and Stalwart Republicans in 1910–1912 resulted in a three-way division of the vote in 1912 and permitted the minority Democrats to elect a president.

Eldersveld's analysis makes clear that the history of party competition is not the story of uninterrupted, balanced, two-party competition at the national level. Three patterns of competition have existed throughout the nation's history, and all three have existed during the twentieth century. The longest time span that any pattern of party politics has existed uninterrupted is the period of two-party competition which has existed since World War II—a more than fifty-year interval from 1946 to the present. Despite the turbulence of this postwar era, the party system has shown "a capacity for absorbing and containing threats to the system."[39]

THE STABILITY OF REPUBLICAN-DEMOCRATIC CONFLICT SINCE 1860

Since 1860, the Republicans and Democrats have confronted each other as the major combatants in the electoral arena. Each party has sustained dramatic swings of fortune—landslide wins, cliffhanger victories, and demoralizing defeats. These swings of electoral fortune, which can occur in a short time span, are captured in Figure 2.3, which presents data on the two parties' percentages of the popular vote for president. For example, the Democratic percentage of the vote for president went from 61.1 percent in 1964 to only 37.5 percent eight years later in 1972; the GOP share fell from 59 to 37.4 percent between 1984 and 1992 and rose to 47.9 percent in 2000. Despite the fluidity of electoral patterns both in the long run and the short term, the contest has been consistently a test of Republican-Democratic strength since 1860. The durability of this partisan division despite the potential for political dislocation caused by two world wars, depressions, waves of new immigrants, industrialization, urbanization, and changes in lifestyle deserves probing. Why haven't third-party movements emerged to challenge and replace one or both of the major parties the way they have in the United Kingdom, Western Europe, and Canada?

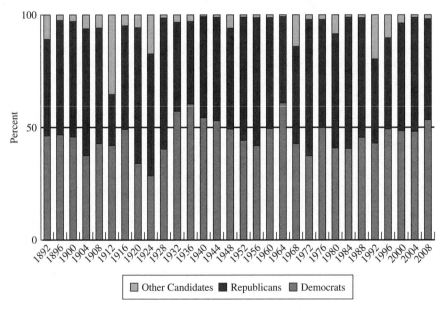

FIGURE 2.3   REPUBLICAN AND DEMOCRATIC PERCENTAGES OF THE POPULAR VOTE FOR PRESIDENT, 1892–2008

Eldersveld posits three explanations for the persistence of the equilibrium of conflict between Democrats and Republicans.[40] One reason is the parties' *capacity for absorption of protest.* Major third-party protest movements have periodically arisen since 1860, but none has been able to attract a sufficient core of voters, campaign workers, and funds to sustain themselves. Each has flowered briefly and then withered as it was absorbed into one or both of the major parties. The Populists of 1892 were taken into the Democratic Party in 1896 as the Democrats appropriated their platform and nominated William Jennings Bryan. Although Bryan never gained the presidency in three tries, he was brought into the government as Wilson's secretary of state. Similarly, Theodore Roosevelt's Bull Moose Progressives of 1912 and the Robert La Follette Progressives of 1924 were absorbed back into the GOP fold four years after their attempts to create third-party movements. Most of the Dixiecrats who bolted in 1948 and almost cost Harry Truman the election were back in the Democratic Party for the 1952 and 1956 elections against Eisenhower. Party insurgents and dissidents who are often dubbed extremists almost inevitably become members of the party establishment within a short period of time. The Gold-water conservatives, who challenged the eastern moderate establishment of the GOP in the 1960s, became a part of the establishment, as did the New Left liberals of the Democratic Party, who sought the presidential nomination for Senators Eugene McCarthy (Minn.) and George McGovern (S.Dak.) in 1968 and 1972. And after the 1992 elections, in which Ross Perot received the highest percentage (18.9 percent) of the vote polled by a third-party candidate since 1912, both the Republican and Democratic parties curried the favor of his supporters for the 1994 and 1996 elections (see Table 2.2).

Professor Leon D. Epstein has argued that one of the reasons that Republican and Democratic parties have been so successful in absorbing protest has been the existence of the direct primary to nominate candidates. This uniquely American institution permits insurgents outside the ranks of the established party leadership to use an intraparty route to power. By winning party nominations through the direct primary, insurgents gain access to the general election ballot without organizing third parties, thereby enhancing their chances of general election victories. Epstein also argues that the direct primary has institutionalized Republican and Democratic electoral dominance because voters become accustomed to participating in party primaries and choosing between groups of individuals competing for their party's label. Partisan attachments are further encouraged, he believes, by the requirement in most states that primary voters publicly declare their party affiliations or even register as Republicans or Democrats in order to participate in primary elections.[41]

The Republican-Democratic party system has also been sustained by the parties' *ideological eclecticism.* The Democrats have moved from populist radicalism in 1896, to conservatism in 1904, to progressivism in 1912, to Roosevelt's New Deal in the 1930s and 1940s, to New Left foreign and economic policy in 1972, to Jimmy Carter's moderate liberalism in 1976, to Mondale/Dukakis social and economic liberalism in the 1980s, to the Clinton/Gore centrist "New Democrat" stance and "the era of big government is over" orientation. The GOP has been equally eclectic in policy orientation—from Roosevelt's progressivism in 1904, to the conservatism of normalcy in the 1920s, to the modern moderate Republicanism of Eisenhower in the 1950s, to Reagan's economic and social conservatism of the

TABLE 2.2 | ABSORPTION OF THIRD PARTIES INTO THE MAJOR PARTIES

Third Party	Year	Percent of Popular Vote	Electoral Votes	Fate in Next Election
Anti-Masonic	1832	7.8	7	Endorsed Whig candidate
Free Soil	1848	10.1	0	Received 4.9% of vote
Whig-American	1856	21.5	8	Party dissolved
Southern Democrat	18.1	1860	72	Party dissolved
Constitutional Union	1860	12.6	39	Party dissolved
Liberal Republican and Democrats	1872	43.8	66[a]	Liberal Republicans dissolved
Populist	1892	8.5	22	Endorsed Democratic candidate
Progressive (T. Roosevelt)	1912	27.4	88	Returned to Republican Party
Socialist	1912	6.0	0	Received 3.2% of vote
Progressive (La Follette)	1924	16.6	13	Returned to Republican Party
States' Rights Democrat	1948	2.4	39	Party dissolved
Progressive (H. Wallace)	1948	2.4	0	Received 0.2% of vote
American Independent	1968	13.5	46	Received 1.4% of the vote
John B. Anderson	1980	7.1	0	Did not run in 1984
H. Ross Perot	1992	18.9	0	Received 8.4% of vote and formed the Reform Party
Reform (H. Ross Perot)	1996	8.4	0	Badly divided in 2000 and captured by former rightwing Republican Pat Buchanan, who received only 0.43% of vote

[a]Democrats also nominated the Liberal Republican candidate Andrew Greeley, who died between the general election and the casting of the electoral votes. Sixty-three of the electoral votes he won were therefore cast by presidential electors for four other persons. Three were cast for Greeley, but Congress refused to count them.

Source: Congressional Quarterly, *Guide to U.S. Elections*, 3rd ed. (Washington, D.C.: Congressional Quarterly, Inc., 1994); Federal Election Commission for 1996 and 2000 data.

1980s, to the compassionate conservatism of George W. Bush. This nondoctrinaire approach to issues and changing conditions has made it possible for the two parties to respond and adapt as circumstances seemed to dictate. This ideological flexibility has enabled the parties to tolerate within their ranks a wide variety of viewpoints.

The two parties have also exhibited *coalitional flexibility*. That is, they have demonstrated an ability to attract votes from virtually all elements of society, even from groups that are normally viewed as a part of the opposition. For example, in the 2008 presidential election, John McCain won 39 percent of the union household vote despite the support union leaders gave his Democratic opponent; and Barack Obama captured one-fourth of the Republican Party's most loyal supporters—born-again Christians. The party coalitions are not static in character. They are in a constant process of "breakup, modification, and reconstruction."[42]

THE STATE OF AMERICAN PARTIES IN THE TWENTY-FIRST CENTURY

A review of American political history reveals not only the frequency of change but also the amazing durability and resilience of political parties. Just a few decades ago, scholars were bemoaning the death of political parties in the United States. Now we live in a climate where the public sees significant differences between the parties. As I show in Chapters 7 and 8, this perceived polarization has significant implications on how citizens understand politics and participate in elections. And the discussion in Chapter 9 indicates that the public's perceptions of polarization are based on reality; elected officials have become far more divided along partisan lines during the past few decades. The increasing polarization has also served to revitalize the party organizations (see Chapter 5) and increase the stakes of winning party nominations (Chapter 6). In short, parties have consistently played a central role in American political life, and the recent partisan polarization has only served to solidify the link between parties and politics in the United States.

NOTES

1. Richard Hofstadter, *The Idea of a Party System: The Rise of Legitimate Opposition in the United States, 1780–1840* (Berkeley: University of California Press, 1969), p. 53.

2. *Washington Post*, December 27, 1998, p. A18. For a summary of data on public attitudes toward parties, see William J. Keefe, *Parties, Politics, and Public Policy in America*, 8th ed. (Washington, D.C.: CQ Press, 1998), pp. 9–17; see also Jack Dennis, "Trends in Public Support for the American Party System," *British Journal of Political Science* 5 (1975): 187–230.

3. Walter Dean Burnham, *Critical Elections and the Mainsprings of American Politics* (Cambridge: Harvard University Press, 1970).

4. Paul R. Abramson, John H. Aldrich, and David W. Rohde, *Change and Continuity in the 2000 and 2002 Elections* (Washington, D.C.: Congressional Quarterly Press, 2003).

5. Everett Carll Ladd, *American Political Parties: Social Change and Political Response* (New York: Norton, 1970), pp. 80–81.

6. Quoted in V. O. Key, Jr., *Politics, Parties, and Pressure Groups*, 5th ed. (New York: Crowell, 1964), p. 203.

7. Ladd, American Political Parties, p. 81.

8. Ibid., p. 87.

9. Ibid., p. 82.

10. Bureau of the Census, U.S. Department of Commerce, *Historical Statistics of the United States: Colonial Times to 1970* (Washington, D.C.: U.S. Government Printing Office, 1975), p. 1,072.

11. Richard L. McCormick, "Political Development and the Second Party System," in William Nisbet Chambers and W. D. Burnham, eds., *The American Party Systems: Stages of Political Development* (New York: Oxford University Press, 1967), p. 342.

12. Ladd, American Political Parties, p. 99.

13. Ibid., pp. 105–106.

14. V. O. Key, Jr., *Politics, Parties, and Pressure Groups*, 5th ed. (New York: Crowell, 1965), p. 168.

15. For a comprehensive analysis of the development of state and local party organizations, see David R. Mayhew, *Placing Parties in American Politics* (Princeton, N.J.: Princeton University Press, 1986); see especially ch. 8.

16. V. O. Key, Jr., "A Theory of Critical Elections," *Journal of Politics* 17 (February 1955): 11.

17. Key, *Politics, Parties, and Pressure Groups*, p. 186; Samuel Lubell, *The Future of American Politics*, 2nd ed., rev. (Garden City, N.Y.: Doubleday, 1956), ch. 3.

18. Ladd, American Political Parties, pp. 175–176.

19. Kristi Anderson, *After Suffrage: Women in Partisan and Electoral Politics Beyond the New Deal* (Chicago: University of Chicago Press, 1998), p. 170.

20. The impact of the direct primary on American parties is thoroughly analyzed by Leon D. Epstein, *Political Parties in the American Mold* (Madison: University of Wisconsin Press, 1986); see especially chs. 5 and 6.

21. See Mayhew, *Placing Parties in American Politics*, p. 323.

22. John H. Aldrich, *Why Parties? The Origin and Transformation of Party Politics in America* (Chicago: University of Chicago Press, 1995), pp. 241–274. For additional discussion of the changing nature of electoral politics, see Martin P. Wattenberg, *The Rise of Candidate-Centered Politics: Presidential Elections of the 1980s* (Cambridge, Mass.: Harvard University Press, 1991); and Paul R. Abramson, John H. Aldrich, and David W. Rohde, *Change and Continuity in the 1996 Elections* (Washington, D.C.: CQ Press, 1998).

23. Everett C. Ladd, "The 1996 Election and the Postindustrial Realignment," in *America at the Polls, 1996* (Storrs: Roper Center, University of Connecticut, 1997), pp. 1, 12.

24. W. Phillips Shively, "From Differential Abstention to Conversion: A Change in Electoral Change, 1864–1986," *American Journal of Political Science* 36 (May 1992): 309–330.

25. John R. Alford, and David W. Brady, "Personal and Partisan Advantage in U.S. Congressional Elections, 1946–1986," in Lawrence C. Dodd and Bruce I. Oppenheimer, eds., *Congress Reconsidered*, 4th ed. (Washington, D.C.: CQ Press, 1989), pp. 153–170.

26. Aldrich, *Why Parties?*, p. 269.

27. Earl Black and Merle Black, *The Rise of Southern Republicans* (Cambridge: Harvard University Press, 2002).

28. Key, *Politics, Parties, and Pressure Groups*, p. 279.

29. Ibid., p. 255.

30. Walter Dean Burnham, *Critical Elections and the Mainsprings of American Politics* (New York: Norton, 1970), pp. 27–31.

31. Paul Allen Beck, *Party Politics in America*, 8th ed. (New York: Longman, 1997), p. 49.

32. Ibid.

33. The impact of single-member plurality and various proportional representation is analyzed by Arend Lijphart, "The Political Consequences of Election Laws," *American Political Science Review* 84 (June 1990): 481–496; and Douglas W. Rae, *The Political Consequences of Electoral Laws* (New Haven, Conn.: Yale University Press, 1967).

34. Leon D. Epstein, *Political Parties in the American Mold* (Madison: University of Wisconsin Press, 1986), pp. 244–245.

35. Ibid., p. 127.

36. Paul R. Abramson, John H. Aldrich, Phil Paolino, and David W. Rohde, "Third Party and Independent Candidates: Wallace, Anderson, and Port," *Political Science Quarterly* 110 (Fall 1995): 366–367.

37. Key, Politics, Parties, and Pressure Groups, p. 208.

38. Samuel J. Eldersveld, *Political Parties in American Society* (New York: Basic Books, 1982), pp. 35–36.

39. Ibid., p. 36.

40. Ibid., pp. 40–43.

41. Epstein, *Political Parties in the American Mold*, pp. 131–133, 243–245. 42.

42. Eldersveld, *Political Parties*, p. 42.

CHARACTERISTICS OF THE AMERICAN PARTY SYSTEM

CHAPTER CONTENTS

The United States was the first nation to develop modern political parties that aligned the electorate around national issues and organized at the national, regional, and local levels to nominate candidates, contest elections, and organize governments. The early American parties stood in sharp contrast to the "capital factions" that passed for parties in Great Britain. However, as other nations followed the American example of extending the franchise to non-property owners, they too developed political parties capable of structuring the vote and organizing governments. Indeed, wherever elections have been conducted on a continuing basis at the national and regional levels, political parties exist. They have proved essential for organizing and mobilizing a mass electorate. As party conflict has been institutionalized in Western democracies, the party systems of these nations have come to share certain attributes: long-established parties, a limited number of parties seriously contesting for office, electoral alignments focused around national issues, and class-based patterns of electoral support. Although the American party system shares many traits with other Western democracies, its peculiar combination of characteristics makes it distinctive.

TWO-PARTY COMPETITION WITH VARIATIONS

The continuous competition between the Republicans and the Democrats for over 140 years has given the American party system a two-party character. These two parties contest for control of the presidency, Congress, governorships, and state legislatures. This sets the United States apart from most other nations, which, while having a limited number of major parties, normally have more than just two. The dominant position of the two major parties is reflected in the operation of the Federal Election Campaign Act, which bestows special benefits upon *major* parties—defined as those parties receiving 25 percent of the popular vote for president. These benefits include federal matching funds for presidential candidates seeking party nominations, federal grants for holding national conventions, and public funding at the maximum level in general election campaigns for president. Only the Republican and Democratic parties have qualified as major parties eligible for the highest level of governmental support, which gives them a substantial advantage over minor parties.

The phrase *two-party system* masks a great deal of variation in the extent and nature of interparty competition in the United States. Two-party competition aptly describes competition for selected offices in some jurisdictions, but there are also offices and regions in which the norm of strong interparty competition is not met.

PARTY COMPETITION AT THE NATIONAL LEVEL

THE PRESIDENCY   Viewed from a national perspective, presidential elections are highly competitive. In the fifteen presidential elections since World War II, the parties have alternated control, with the Republicans winning eight times and Democrats seven times. The two-party character of presidential voting is reflected in Table 3.1, which presents data on the percentages of the popular vote cast for Republican and Democratic candidates in recent elections. Note that in these elections between 1948 and 2008, the Republican-Democratic share of the popular vote dipped below 90 percent only three times (1968, 1992, and 1996) and averaged 95.6 percent. Three of the postwar presidential elections were among the most competitive in American history, including the 2000 race, in which Al Gore won the popular vote by 0.5 percentage points over George W. Bush, who gained a narrow majority of five electoral votes. The other extremely close elections were John F. Kennedy's 0.2 percent win over Richard Nixon in 1960 and Nixon's 0.7 percent win over Hubert Humphrey in 1968.

TABLE 3.1 | MAJOR-PARTY DOMINANCE OF PRESIDENTIAL VOTING, 1948–2008

	Candidates for President		Percentage of Popular Vote		
Year	Republican	Democrat	Republican	Democrat	Total
1948	Dewey	Truman	45.1	49.6	94.7
1952	Eisenhower	Stevenson	55.1	44.4	99.5
1956	Eisenhower	Stevenson	57.4	42.0	99.4
1960	Nixon	Kennedy	49.5	49.7	99.2
1964	Goldwater	Johnson	38.5	61.1	99.6
1968	Nixon	Humphrey	43.4	42.7	86.1
1972	Nixon	McGovern	60.7	37.5	98.2
1976	Ford	Carter	48.0	50.1	98.1
1980	Reagan	Carter	50.7	41.0	91.7
1984	Reagan	Mondale	58.8	40.6	99.4
1988	Bush	Dukakis	53.4	45.6	99.0
1992	Bush	Clinton	37.4	43.0	80.4
1996	Dole	Clinton	40.7	49.2	89.9
2000	Bush	Gore	47.9	48.4	96.3
2004	Bush	Kerry	50.7	48.3	99.0
2008	McCain	Obama	45.6	52.9	98.5

Source: Statistical Abstract of the United States, 2000, p. 273; Federal Election Commission data.

THE CONGRESS   By the early 1990s, the Democrats had controlled the Congress during most of the post–World War II era. Indeed, the Democrats were so dominant that until the Republican electoral sweep in the 1994 midterm elections, the Grand Old Party (GOP) had not controlled both the House and Senate for forty years. Despite the frequently lopsided nature of congressional Democratic majorities, especially in the House, the national popular vote for the House, like the vote for president, shows a high level of competition and two-party dominance. The combined Republican-Democratic share of the popular vote for the House of Representatives has exceeded 94 percent in every election since World War II. The Republican Party, which held a minority of House seats during most of the postwar era, never has had its share of the popular vote dip below 40.5 percent (1974), and it has averaged 46.6 percent in thirty elections.

PARTY COMPETITION AT THE STATE LEVEL

A measure of state-level interparty competition can be obtained by combining indicators of party voting strength: (1) percentage of votes won by each party in gubernatorial elections; (2) percentage of seats won by each party in each house of the state legislature; (3) the length of time each party controlled the governorship; and (4) the proportion of the time in which control of the governorship and the legislature has been divided between the parties.[1] When these data are combined into a single index of competitiveness for the period 2003–2006, half of the states (25) meet the test of competitiveness (see Figure 3.1), and there are no one-party Democratic or Republican states. By contrast, during the 1962–1973 period, a majority of states fell into either the one-party or modified one-party categories. The most notable change has occurred in the states of the Confederacy, where there are no longer any one-party Democratic states and only three modified one-party states. In fact, Florida, Georgia, South Carolina, and Texas are now considered modified one-party Republican states. Evidence of the shift away from the region's heritage of one-party Democratic domination was evident before the 2010 elections, when Republicans controlled eight of eleven governorships in the states of the old Confederacy. The GOP has also overcome its long-term weakness in the region's state legislatures. For example, prior to the 2010 elections it controlled at least one chamber in Georgia, Florida, South Carolina, Tennessee, Texas, and Virginia. Whereas the South has moved to two-party competitiveness, there has been a shift toward Republican control of state governments in the mountain states of the West. Thus, in five of these eights states, Republicans controlled at least one chamber of the state legislature prior to the 2006 elections.

Research comparing social and economic conditions within the states has revealed that socioeconomic diversity contributes to interparty competitiveness. A heterogeneous population permits both parties to build up support among selected groups in society because of the inevitable conflicts, tensions, and differences that socioeconomic diversity breeds. Indicators of socioeconomic diversity such as population size, educational attainment, and home ownership are each correlated with interparty competition. In states where state legislative incumbents enjoy substantial advantages, competition is depressed; competition is enhanced as the population of legislative districts increases and makes them more diverse in their makeup. In addition, the strength of the party organizations also affects partisan competition. Strong party organizations capable of mobilizing the vote tend to encourage competitive politics.[2]

Variations in Levels of Competition for Different Offices

The index of competitiveness described in the preceding section is based exclusively upon the outcome of *state* elections and gives more weight to control of state legislatures than it does to winning the governorship. As a result, this index can obscure the extent to which interparty competition exists in contests for various offices.

Statewide Elections

There is substantial evidence of a high level of interparty competition in most statewide elections. In the eleven presidential elections between 1968 and 2008, twenty of the states have been carried by the Democratic or Republican parties at least four

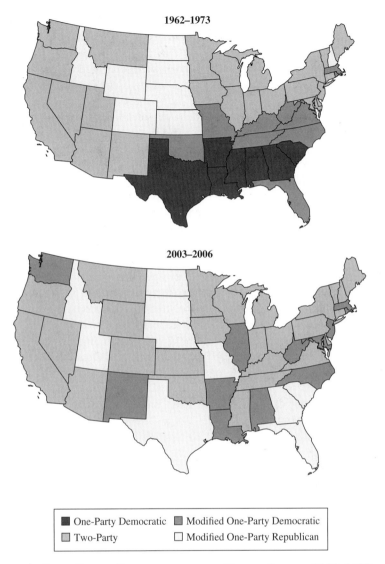

FIGURE 3.1 | INTER-PARTY COMPETITION IN THE UNITED STATES, 1962–1973 AND 2003–2006

Source: Thomas M. Holbrook and Ray La Raja, "Parties and Elections," in *Politics in the American States*, eds. Virginia Gray and Russell L. Hanson, (Washington, D.C.: Congressional Quarterly Press, 2007).

times, and twenty-six states have been won by each party at least three times. With only 539,895 popular votes separating Al Gore and George W. Bush in the tightly contested 2000 election, George W. Bush won eleven states and Al Gore eight states with 52 percent or less of the popular vote. Yet, competition in presidential elections has not been as widespread as it once was, with the two most recent presidential elections focusing on just a small number of competitive "purple states." In 2004, Bush and Kerry were separated by less than 5 percent of the vote in just eleven states and in thirty states the candidates were separated by more than 10 percent. Obama won twenty states (and the District of Columbia) with more than 55 percent of the vote in 2008 with McCain capturing fifteen states by a similar margin. Thus, the presidential contest could be considered truly competitive in just fifteen states in 2008.

Despite the fact that recent presidential elections have witnessed a narrowing of the number of competitive states, state-level elections generally invite much more inter-party competition. For instance, the Senate that convened in January 2009 contained ten members whose share of the popular vote was less than 50 percent and eighteen who won with 50–55 percent. In the elections of 2008, ten of the winners received 55 percent or less of the popular vote, including four who squeaked through with less than 50 percent.

Gubernatorial elections have also become competitive. Table 3.2 presents data on the extent of partisan change in control of governorships since 1950. During the 1950s, only 23.6 percent of gubernatorial elections resulted in a change in party control of state executive mansions. These contests have become even more competitive in the twenty-first century. In the 116 gubernatorial elections held since 2000, over one-third resulted in a change of the party controlling the governorship. In fact, both parties are often successful at winning gubernatorial elections even in states that are dominated by the opposite party in national elections. For example, prior to the 2010 elections, three of the nine states that have not been won by a Democratic presidential candidate since 1968 had Democratic governors (Kansas, Oklahoma, and Wyoming).

TABLE 3.2 | PARTY CHANGE IN CONTROL OF GOVERNORSHIPS, 1950–2008

Decade	Number of Gubernatorial Elections	Percent of Elections with a Party Change[a]
1950–1959	174	23.6 (41)
1960–1969	156	35.3 (55)
1970–1979	144	38.9 (56)
1980–1989	122	35.2 (43)
1990–1998	135	35.6 (48)
2000–2008	116	36.2 (42)

[a]An election with a party change is defined as any election in which control of the governorship shifts from one party to another.

Note: Numbers in parentheses indicate the number of party changes.

Source: Adapted from Larry Sabato, *Goodbye to Goodtime Charlie*, 2nd ed. (Washington, D.C.: CQ Press, 1983), pp. 120–121; the 1980–2008 data are derived from appropriate volumes of the *Statistical Abstract of the United States*; National Journal, November 11, 2000, p. 3622.

CONGRESSIONAL ELECTIONS   Interparty competition is increasingly the norm in state-wide competitions, but it has been relatively rare in elections to the House of Representatives. Incumbents normally win reelection easily. In the House elections since 2000, more than three-fourths of winning candidates captured over 60 percent of the vote.[3] The lack of competition in many districts reflects the difficulty the minority party has in recruiting quality candidates and an inability to raise enough funds for a meaningful race against incumbents. In 2008, the average House incumbent raised $649,285 while the average challenger $110,578.[4] Such resource advantages on the side of incumbents mean that in most districts the challenger's party is normally confronted with the task of recruiting a "sacrificial lamb" to run against the incumbent.

Incumbency has become a powerful advantage. Indeed, it is so strong that in any given congressional election, over 90 percent of the incumbents seeking reelection will normally win. As a result, the extent of party change in control of House seats has been extremely low. In the five elections since 2000, an average of only twenty-seven (6 percent) of the seats changed party control. In 2004, only thirteen seats (3 percent) switched party control. And even in 2008, a very strong year for Democratic candidates, just thirty-one seats (7 percent) changed from one party to the other (with twenty-six of those seats changing from Republican to Democratic control).

STATE LEGISLATIVE ELECTIONS   The frequent absence of meaningful two-party competition found in congressional elections is also present in elections to the state legislatures.[5] One-party domination of legislative contests is commonplace in many of the states. The Democratic Party has maintained almost total domination of state legislative elections in three southern states (Alabama, Arkansas, and Louisiana), where the party between 1953 and 2005 never held less than 60 percent of the upper- and lower-house seats and frequently controlled in excess of 80 percent. Other states characterized by one-party control of state legislatures include Maryland, Massachusetts, Rhode Island, and West Virginia for the Democrats; and Arizona, Idaho, Kansas, South Dakota, and Wyoming for the Republicans.

As is true with the U.S. House of Representatives, incumbents' advantages are substantial in state legislative races, with incumbent reelection rates in excess of 90 percent being common in three-fourths of the states, including California, Illinois, Pennsylvania, Delaware, Minnesota, Washington, Oregon, Missouri, and Wisconsin.[6]

It is clear from this brief survey of statewide, congressional, and state legislative elections that there is tremendous variability in the extent of inter-party competition depending upon which type of election is being considered. The phrase *American two-party system* accurately captures the totality of party competition, but it fails to capture the continuum of party competition found in the United States.

DECENTRALIZED POWER STRUCTURES

It is hard to overstate the extent to which American political parties are characterized by decentralized power structures. Except for a few isolated urban machines, there is almost a total absence of hierarchical relationships within American parties. Within the party in government, presidents cannot assume that representatives and senators of their party will necessarily follow their leadership on public-policy issues. Within the party organization, the national institutions of the party have a narrow range of authority over state party delegate selection procedures for national conventions, but they rarely meddle in nominations and organizational affairs of state parties. Few constraints operate upon the party in the electorate. Even incumbent presidents have found that they cannot depend upon the party's voters to give them support in bids for either renomination or reelection. Power in the American parties is fragmented and scattered among many institutions, organizations, and individuals at the national, state, and local levels.

THE IMPACT OF THE CONSTITUTION

SEPARATION OF POWERS By creating a national government composed of three branches, the Founders purposely sought to make it difficult for any individual or faction to gain control over the national government. As a result, representatives and senators are elected separately from the president and for terms of varying length. Each has a different constituency.

The looseness of the American parties is in part a response to the constitutional separation of powers. Because separation of powers permits divided control of government, political parties are free to concentrate on winning the presidency, Congress, or just one house of Congress. The minority Democrats, for example, focused their 2004 campaign on the White House since taking control of Congress seemed far less likely. When Republican presidential prospects were slight in 1996, Republicans targeted House races in an effort to retain control of Congress. With presidents, senators, and representatives each elected from separate constituencies for staggered terms, it is small wonder that these elected officials of the same party have only a minimal sense of interdependence. The highest prize of American politics—the presidency—can be gained without simultaneously having a partisan majority in Congress. In this system of separated governmental institutions, presidents can operate with a significant degree of independence from their party colleagues in Congress. Representatives and senators, each elected from a particular constituency, need not be supportive of their party's president for electoral survival. Indeed, it is often prudent for the national legislators to put some distance between themselves and their party's president.[7]

The incentives for party unity and discipline are substantially stronger in countries with parliamentary regimes. In such systems, control of the legislature is the prerequisite for achieving the prime ministership or cabinet office. Control of the executive goes to the party or coalition of parties that has a legislative majority. And when that majority is lost through electoral setbacks, the cabinet must resign and make way for the opposition. Loss of the legislative majority through defections by dissident partisans or coalition members can force a cabinet to either resign or call new elections. Neither option is a pleasant one because both threaten legislators' tenure or their chances to serve in the cabinet—the most prestigious and powerful positions in public life. The parliamentary system thus creates powerful incentives for party unity and conforming to the wishes of the party leadership. But in the United States, the institutional incentive to support party leadership and the president is lacking, and instead independent-minded behavior is encouraged.

BOX 3.1	A DEMOCRATIC SENATOR CAMPAIGNS FOR McCAIN

"What [...] is a Democrat like me doing at a Republican convention like this? The answer is simple. I'm here to support John McCain because country matters more than party."

With that line, Joseph Lieberman spurned the party that had nominated him for Vice President just eight years earlier to give his support to the Republican presidential nominee at the 2008 Republican National Convention. It is still newsworthy when a prominent member of one party endorses a presidential candidate from the opposing party. Obama enjoyed his own cross-party support from notable Republicans like former Secretary of State Colin Powell and former Rhode Island senator Lincoln Chafee. This pattern is not atypical, as the parties include officeholders of widely varying views and ideologies, particularly across different regions of the country. Democrats in Republican states like Georgia, Wyoming, and Kansas and Republicans in Democratic states such as Massachusetts and Rhode Island succeed because they match their own positions to those of their constituents and not their national party's platform. While this strategy allows the two parties to compete in states that are dominated by the opposing party in presidential elections, it often creates tension within the party. Lieberman's case was particularly notable, since he had lost the Democratic nomination for his own Senate seat in 2006, only to defeat both the Democratic and Republican nominees while running as an independent. The fact that he did not owe his Senate seat to the Democratic Party's support likely made it easier for him to endorse a Republican presidential nominee in 2008.

Because the principle of the separation of powers is embedded not just in the national Constitution but also in state constitutions, its party-fragmenting consequences are also felt at the state level. State legislators frequently operate quite independently of their party's governor and party leadership.

FEDERALISM Federalism—the constitutional division of governmental power between the national government and the states—has made it difficult for political parties to develop as centralized institutions. American parties did not antedate the writing of the Constitution, and they therefore had to organize themselves to contest state elections as well as presidential races. When the American parties were developing in the nineteenth century, there were powerful incentives to organize strong state parties because "national and state political stakes were more nearly equal than they are now."[8] Although the states are less important relative to the national government in the 2000s than they were in the nineteenth century, they continue to be potent political entities worthy of major investments by the parties. Parties organized around state as well as national elections tend to become decentralized and confederate in character. This pattern of decentralization has been strengthened by each state imposing upon its parties a unique set of statutory regulations under which the parties must operate.

Fifty semiautonomous state governments, each having a multitude of local governmental units, have created thousands of partisan elected officials, party leaders, and organizations with their own constituencies and cadres of supporters. Such localized bases of support mean that these elected officials are in a position to assert their independence from national party leaders. Often the interests of state and national party leaders and elected officials are not the same. State party leaders and candidates are likely to place a higher priority upon electing governors and state legislators than in winning control of the White House or Congress. For example, a Democratic leader of the Bronx made the following comment when asked whether he worried about presidential politics:

> It doesn't affect our life one bit. National politics—President and such—are too far removed from the bread and butter things that matter to local leaders and mayors and governor. The local leader cares about a senior citizen center, a local concern.[9]

State and national party leaders frequently come into conflict when the national and state parties compete with each other for financial contributions from party benefactors, or when national party organizations support candidates who fail to win contested primaries. Tensions are also created when state officials seek to distance themselves from national party leaders and policies that are considered political liabilities; for example, in the 2006 midterm elections some Republican candidates, particularly in the Northeast and Midwest, put as much distance as practicable between themselves and an unpopular President Bush. The distinct interests, constituencies, and bases of support that federalism creates for national, state, and local party leaders and elected officials mean that party unity is always under stress. The decentralizing forces inherent in the separation of powers system are given an encouraging boost by federalism.

THE IMPACT OF NOMINATION AND CAMPAIGN PRACTICES

Nominations and general election campaigns are not party-dominated processes in the United States. Elected officials gain nomination and election primarily through reliance on highly personalized campaign organizations, which may be supplemented by party resources. This means that parties do not control access to elective office. As a result, party leaders are not in a position to impose discipline on elected officials, who know that the party cannot assure either their electoral survival or their ascent on the political ladder.

NOMINATIONS IN THE STATES   Nominations to congressional, state, and local office, with few exceptions, are made via the direct primary. This open and participatory process makes it extremely difficult for any but the most disciplined type of party organization (e.g., the old Daley machine in Chicago) to control nominations and access to the general election ballot. The direct primary encourages candidates to build highly personal campaign organizations. Once a candidate is nominated in a primary, the local or national party leadership is obliged to accept that individual as a bona fide nominee of the party, whether the person was its preferred candidate or not.

The direct primary means that no single level—national, state, or local—of party organization is in a position to control nominations to Congress. This is in vivid contrast to most Western democracies, in which parliamentary nominations are internal party decisions made by the organizational leadership. In such systems, the party organization is in a position to impose discipline on legislators because it determines which candidates will bear the party label in elections.[10] Lacking such control over nominations, American parties are not in a position to impose discipline on representatives and senators.

PRESIDENTIAL NOMINATIONS   Presidential nominating politics of the post-1968 era is characterized by presidential primaries that determine the candidate preferences of a majority of the delegates, open and participatory state party caucuses, and intense media coverage. Party leaders no longer exercise decisive influence over the selection of presidential nominees. Influence has shifted to candidate organizations, campaign consultants, candidate- or issue-oriented activists, and the mass media—especially television. As Barack Obama demonstrated in 2008, it is even possible for a party newcomer—a person relatively inexperienced in national government and largely unknown to the party's national and state leadership—to gain a major party nomination. Even incumbent presidents are not immune from damaging renomination challenges, as Presidents Gerald Ford (1976), Jimmy Carter (1980), and George H. W. Bush (1992) discovered. Because party organizations cannot even guarantee a renomination to incumbent presidents, presidents, like senators and representatives, take office with an ambiguous relationship to their party, and their sense of party obligation is often limited.

Although party organizational control over nominations is severely limited by the widespread use of the presidential primaries to select national convention delegates, it should be noted that party organizational support remains a valuable asset. The heavy front-loading of the presidential primaries into the January–March time period, which has caused a majority of the delegates to be chosen by the end of March, has meant that having party organizations in place and actively working in support of a party-preferred candidate in the early primary states can be a critical factor in determining the outcome of the nomination process. In 2000, both George W. Bush and Al Gore were aided by the party organizational support they received against party outsiders Senator John McCain (R-Ariz.) and former senator Bill Bradley (D-N.J.).

GENERAL ELECTION CAMPAIGNS   The decentralizing forces unleashed by nomination processes are reinforced by the manner in which general election campaigns are conducted. National trends in public opinion, national media, and campaign themes do influence the outcomes of congressional, state, and local elections. Candidates, however, are aware that elections are determined to a significant degree by local factors and their ability to achieve a favorable balance of campaign resources over their opponents. With such a favorable balance of resources, the skillful campaigner can overcome adverse national swings of voter sentiment and gain election.

Congressional campaigns in particular reflect this highly individualized campaign environment. Most candidates maintain highly personalized campaign organizations and raise funds from nonparty sources, such as political action committees (PACs), which contributed over $379 million to House and Senate candidates in 2007–2008. The resourceful congressional incumbent normally uses the perquisites of office to project an image of electoral invincibility and will raise a substantial campaign war chest. These activities often scare off serious challengers. National or state parties have traditionally provided only a small percentage of the money needed to mount a reelection drive. However, recent national party initiatives have greatly expanded the parties' role in congressional campaigns. National party committees are now actively involved in candidate recruitment, direct contributions to candidates, expenditures in support of candidates, large-scale issue-advertising campaigns, and staff and technical assistance. National party involvement is especially heavy in highly competitive races and can be one of the dominating features of these contests.[11] As a result, some of the traditional diversity and independence in the conduct of congressional campaigns has been reduced. Still, most House and Senate campaigns are conducted independently.

Because national party organizations are more concerned with winning elections than with restructuring electoral politics, they have adapted their activities to a candidate-centered style of politics.[12] This campaign style encourages representatives and senators to function with considerable independence from their parties within Congress. After all, electoral survival requires cultivating trust among one's constituents and maintenance of a personal organization. Because the party cannot ensure continued congressional tenure, it is not surprising that parties often have difficulty gaining high levels of party unity on congressional roll calls. With no party to protect them, representatives and senators have created a congressional system that bestows on each member substantial resources for year-round campaigning and a committee system that enables them to build the support among constituencies that is essential for reelection.[13]

Presidential campaigns are also organized to a significant degree outside the party structure. This type of candidate-oriented campaign organization is encouraged by the Federal Election Campaign Act. Candidates who agree to accept public funding of their campaigns are required under the law to forego fund-raising activities, and the Republican and Democratic National Committees are restricted to modest levels ($19.1 million in 2008) of expenditure on behalf of their presidential and vice presidential nominees. Presidential candidates accepting public funding are also required to set up a committee to receive and expend the public funds. The law therefore creates an incentive for major-party presidential nominees to follow their natural preference for campaign organizations that are devoted exclusively to their own candidacies and that function at some distance from their national party committees. Even when candidates decline public funding, as Obama did in 2008, they still have an incentive to build their own campaign organization, over which they can exert total control.

The tie between party organizations and candidates at all levels has also been weakened by changes in the techniques of campaigning and the resulting escalation in campaign costs. The modern campaign for major office requires media experts, pollsters, computer specialists, direct mail consultants, accountants, lawyers, research specialists, and campaign consultants to perform get-out-the-vote activities and public relations functions that were once the province of party organizations. As candidates have relied increasingly upon these nonparty sources for essential services, the influence of the party over elected officials has diminished.

Candidates running for major office tend to set up shop on their own and operate as relatively independent political entrepreneurs with personalized organizations, campaign war chests, media advertising, and, once elected, a sizable staff to assist in electioneering. It is small wonder that such American politicians feel quite independent of their parties. By contrast, the British members of Parliament (M.P.s) are heavily dependent upon their parties. The party organization controls nominations; television time is allocated to parties, not individual candidates; the parties sharply limit the amount that candidates can spend on their own campaigns; and, once elected, the average M.P. has few of the staff resources and other perquisites available to members of Congress. The British M.P.s are therefore much more dependent upon their parties and much more likely to submit to party discipline.

SOME COUNTERTRENDS: NATIONALIZING INFLUENCES

Decentralization of power pervades American parties. This attribute, however, can be overemphasized. Parties have both their national and confederative aspects. Federalism fragments the parties, but national forces have always played a significant role. Leon Epstein has observed:

> However much party organizations ... have come to establish largely independent state and local bases, their electoral support originated in national and specifically presidential alignments. In other words, the party labels under which organizations could win (or lose) state and local offices derived electoral value from their national association.[14]

The nationalizing tendencies within American parties can be seen in (1) the impact of national forces on state voting patterns; (2) the expanded role played by national party organizations; and (3) the growth of national "presidential parties."

THE IMPACT OF NATIONAL TRENDS ON STATE VOTING PATTERN   State politics does not function in isolation from national political forces. Partisan loyalties are forged in the heat of presidential campaigns, and voters tend to support the same parties in both national and state elections. These national influences on voting make it difficult for third-party movements to survive at the state level. For example, two of the strongest third parties of the pre–World War II era were the Progressives of Wisconsin and the Farmer-Labor Party in Minnesota. Each was forced to merge into one of the major parties by the 1950s because the pull of national partisan alignments within the state electorates was so strong that the parties faced inevitable defeat. Even without the complications caused by third-party movements, it has become increasingly difficult for a state to maintain a party alignment of voters that is significantly different from the way they align themselves in presidential elections. The strong nationalizing influences in American life make it burdensome for a state party and its candidates to adopt policy positions significantly at odds with the national image of the party. A case in point is the Democratic Party in the South. Following the New Deal, the southern wing of the party sought to project a more conservative image than the national Democratic Party. However, the disparity between the southern Democrats and the national party has been declining since the 1960s, as fewer and fewer Democrats elected to Congress from the South can be classified as conservatives ("Boll Weevils") and more Democratic governors espouse the policies of the national party. The public's tendency to perceive a link between national Democratic policy and southern Democrats, plus the changing demography and economy of the region, made possible the Republican electoral advances in the presidential elections of 1952, 1956, and 1964. These electoral beachheads were followed by Republican victories in congressional, senatorial, and gubernatorial elections during the 1980s and early 1990s. These gains were capped by the Republicans in their sweeping 1994 victory, in which the party captured a majority of House and Senate seats in the states of the old Confederacy (including a majority in the House delegations from Florida, Georgia, North Carolina, South Carolina, and Tennessee). Clearly, the electoral alignments of the South have changed dramatically and become more like those of the rest of the country. The Democratic "solid South" no longer exists.

Like the conservative southerners within the Democratic Party, liberal and moderate Republicans from the Northeast, once a bulwark of Republicanism, have become a much diminished element of their party. With the national party having taken on a generally conservative tone due to the influx of conservative southerners and westerners, plus social conservatives, it has become more and more difficult for even liberal and moderate Republicans to win elections in the Northeast, where state congressional delegations are now heavily Democratic. Symptomatic of this situation was the early 2001 decision of Vermont Senator James Jeffords to leave the Republican Party and become an independent, thereby switching control of the Senate from the Republicans to the Democrats. Pennsylvania Senator Arlen Specter made a similar move in 2009, switching from the Republican Party to become a Democrat. And following the 2008 congressional elections, not a single U.S. House seat in New England was held by a Republican.

The impact of national electoral forces on state elections is particularly noticeable in midterm elections. Reformers have sought to insulate state elections from national tides of opinion by scheduling these elections for the midterm when the president is not on the ballot. Such timing of state elections, however, has not had the anticipated effect. In midterm elections, the normal pattern of the president's party losing House seats carries over to gubernatorial elections. In all but three midterm elections between 1950 and 2006, the president's party has suffered a net loss of governorships. The exceptions were 1962 and 1998, when there was no net change, and 1986, when the Democrats were defending twenty-seven seats, an unusually large number, and the GOP was defending only nine. The average loss was five seats. Proportionally, gubernatorial elections appear more susceptible to national trends, which normally work against the president's party, than do elections for national offices such as senator and representative. (See Chapter 8 for a more detailed discussion of state elections at midterm.)

EXPANDED ROLE OF THE NATIONAL PARTY   Both the Republican and Democratic national party organizations have achieved increased influence since the 1960s, although the two initiated the process of party nationalization in different ways. Following the divisive Democratic Convention of 1968, the national Democratic Party embarked upon major reforms of its delegate selection procedures. This reform effort took the form of an elaborate series of rules governing delegate selection procedures that the state parties were required to follow. Authority to enforce these rules was vested in the Democratic National Committee (DNC). Operating through its enforcement arm, the Compliance Review Commission, the DNC has forced state parties to comply with national party rules in delegate selection matters. Faced with this authority vested in the national party, the state parties engaged in a massive restructuring of their internal procedures to bring them into conformity with national party policy. The United States Supreme Court further strengthened the position of the national party vis-à-vis its state affiliates when it upheld the principle that national party rules take precedence over state statutes and party rules in matters pertaining to delegate selection.[15]

One of the most celebrated instances of a national party demonstrating its supremacy over state parties came in Wisconsin. National Democratic Party rules banned presidential primaries in which persons other than those publicly professing a preference for the Democratic Party participated (i.e., the DNC banned open primaries). Wisconsin has had an open presidential primary law since 1905, when it became the first state to enact a presidential primary statute. The open primary tradition of the state is a strong one, consistent with the state's independent and progressive history. Despite the clear preference of the Wisconsin Democratic Party and the Democratic-controlled state legislature for maintaining the open primary tradition, the state was forced to abandon the open presidential primary and select delegates to the Democratic convention in 1984 via a caucus system. The DNC has continued to assert its legal authority to enforce national party rules upon state parties even though it has now relented and permitted Wisconsin to operate an open presidential primary. Austin Ranney, a respected parties scholar, believes that the power conferred upon the Democratic national party organization by the rules and court decisions are so sweeping that the national party's legal authority is "at its highest peak since the 1820s."[16]

The national Republican Party also gained increased influence, but in a vastly different manner than by enforcement of nationally mandated rules. The Republicans sought to maintain the confederate character of their party by giving state parties wide latitude in matters of delegate selection and internal operation. National party power, however, has been extended through an extensive multi-million-dollar program to provide financial and technical assistance to state and local party organizations and candidates. Through these activities, the Republican National Committee (RNC) achieved an expanded role in the political system and created a relationship of interdependence between the national party and its state and local affiliates.[17] The DNC followed the RNC example of expanding its services to its state affiliates so that it too became an increasingly significant participant in state elections.

Using their considerable financial resources, the RNC and the DNC were able to achieve an unprecedented degree of intraparty integration, as the state parties have been used to implement national campaign strategies and avoid Federal Election Campaign Act restrictions on national party expenditures in federal elections. Massive transfers of funds were made by the national committees to their state party affiliates. In fact, prior to the passage of the Bipartisan Campaign Reform Act in 2002, transfers from national party committees accounted for 40 percent of state party revenue.

These transferred funds were used to pay general party overhead, finance massive get-out-the-vote drives, and cover the cost of issue advertisements designed to support presidential candidates.[18] The national parties allocate their funds to the state parties to implement a national campaign strategy geared toward winning key states in the presidential contest or maximizing the parties' seats in the House and Senate. This means that the national parties do not treat all of their state affiliates equally. Parties in key states such as California, Florida, and Ohio are normally showered with national party largess. But state parties that lack national priority status can receive virtually no national party assistance. Thus, in 2003–2004, the DNC made only token fund transfers to its state units in Rhode Island, Utah, and Wyoming, and the RNC sent only small amounts to Hawaii, Rhode Island, and Vermont.

A dramatic example of a national party using its state organizations to carry out a national strategy occurred in 2004 when the DNC and RNC combined transferred more than $32 million to state parties in three battleground states (Michigan, Ohio, and Pennsylvania).[19] As the national party organizations intensified their use of state parties to achieve national campaign goals by providing technical and financial support for state parties, financing and supervising get-out-the-vote operations, and transferring funds to pay for television advertising, state parties have suffered a loss of autonomy and have become increasingly dependent upon their national parties' largess. (For a more detailed consideration of party centralization and intraparty integration, see Chapter 4.)

The Growth of the "Presidential Party"   Prior to the 1970s, presidential nominations were dominated by the leaders of state and local party organizations—state and county party chairs, governors, senators, and mayors. They exercised their influence through the caucus system of delegate selection—the process by which two-thirds of the delegates were chosen. Few states used presidential primaries, and it was possible to win presidential nominations without even entering a single primary. The reform era of the 1970s changed all this. As presidential nominations became dominated by presidential primaries, presidential aspirants sought the nomination through direct appeals to the primary electorate. Party leaders became less important, and the personal organizations of the candidates and the media took on greater importance.

Most political scientists believed that these changes weakened political parties, but the development of candidate-centered presidential politics has included one positive party development. A new "presidential party"—the national following of activists gathered to support a candidate—has emerged. These activists have common bonds of shared attitudes—predominantly conservative in the GOP and mainly liberal in the Democratic Party. They constitute what political scientist John Kessel has called "advocacy parties"—campaign organizations dedicated to putting their policy preferences on the public agenda. These presidential parties are more ad hoc in character than the regular party organizations, but they do have substantial continuity. A sizable majority of the presidential activists in both parties were brought into politics years ago when they rallied to candidates such as Barry Goldwater, Richard Nixon, Ronald Reagan, John F. Kennedy, George McGovern, Walter Mondale, and Jimmy Carter.[20] President Obama's 2008 campaign similarly brought into the political fold a new generation of Democratic Party activists.

These networks of issue-oriented activists can have an impact above and beyond presidential elections. They can also be used to mobilize support for presidential policies. President Reagan, for example, successfully used the Reagan network to mobilize grassroots lobbying for his legislative program in Congress. President Obama called on his network of activists repeatedly during his first term in office to rally support for various causes, most notably his push for health care reform.

BROADLY BASED ELECTORAL SUPPORT

In some countries, electoral alignments closely reflect social and economic cleavages—Catholics versus Protestants, rich versus poor, city versus country, unions versus business, recent immigrants versus established groups. In such societies, parties have little meaning aside from the social groups they represent. When party allegiances closely reflect social and economic cleavages, political conflict is more likely to be bitter and unrestrained, as the tragic histories of Northern Ireland and Lebanon demonstrate. American parties, however, are quite different. Partisan loyalties cut across social and economic divisions. This results in parties that are broadly based coalitions of diverse and even conflicting elements. Such parties, because of the diversity of their followings, have difficulty maintaining unity among their elected officials and in enunciating clear statements of party policy. But coalition-type parties do provide a means of reconciling and compromising conflicts within society.

Evidence of the coalition nature of American political parties is revealed in the voting behavior of various socioeconomic groups in recent elections (see Table 7.4). Clearly, the core elements of electoral support for the two parties are quite different. Persons from labor union households, blacks, manual laborers, Hispanics, and Jews are more likely to support the Democrats than the Republicans, whereas Protestants, professional and business people, and, recently, members of the religious right tend to be Republican voters. These differences in the core constituencies of the two parties should not obscure the fact that both parties draw significant levels of support from virtually every major socioeconomic group in American life. The major exception to this generalization is black voters, who have become overwhelmingly Democratic since 1964.

The extent to which electoral support for American parties cuts across various socioeconomic divisions can be seen by examining the voting patterns of groups commonly thought of as safely in the camp of one party or the other. Persons from labor union households are usually considered to be overwhelmingly pro-Democratic. However, the Republicans can normally expect to receive the votes of at least one-third of these people, and even in a heavily Democratic year like 2008, McCain won about two of every five members of union households. Predominantly Republican groups also give substantial support to the Democrats. Thus, in 2008, Obama won about half of the vote from those with incomes over $100,000.

NONPROGRAMMATIC PARTIES

All parties have an interest in policy. Among the parties of Western nations, however, there is great diversity in the extent to which the parties are programmatic and the prime policymakers of the system. According to Leon D. Epstein, programmatic parties have policy positions that "are part of a settled long-range program to which the party is dedicated in definite enough terms to mark it off from rival parties."[21] The labor and social democratic parties of Western Europe are examples of parties with more strongly programmatic orientations than American parties, though these parties have recently been moderating their policies and accommodating themselves to market-oriented economies. They remain, however, firmly committed to a social democratic ideology of activist government, and the process of moderating their leftist orientations has been of a lengthy duration and filled with intraparty controversies. For example, the British Labour Party led by Prime Minister Tony Blair has moved away from its traditional trade union and class conflict orientation toward a more centrist position designed to appeal to mainstream, middle-class voters.

This pragmatic approach to politics, however, was resisted by many party activists, and it was not until 1995 that Labour's leaders were finally able to get the party conference to remove a provision from the party constitution calling for public ownership of major economic enterprises. The British Conservative Party, though traditionally less doctrinal than Labour, is also programmatic in the sense that it is committed to preserving capitalism and such traditional institutions as private schools and a strong military. The pursuit of its policy goals was particularly aggressive (e.g., privatization of nationalized industries and weakening trade unions) under the leadership of Prime Minister Margaret Thatcher (1979–1990). American parties are quite different. Their policy positions tend to be more ad hoc in character and adopted to meet immediate problems or electoral circumstances and not based upon long-range programs to which the parties are committed.

Neither the Democrats nor the Republicans have a clear image of the type of society they wish to foster. Neither party is committed to socialism or unfettered capitalism. Both have modified their positions frequently on such issues as governmental regulation of business, foreign policy, and the extent of government support for social welfare programs. It is even common for prominent leaders of seemingly divergent viewpoints to combine forces in the Congress. Thus, liberal Democratic Senator Tom Harkin (Iowa) and conservative Republican Orrin Hatch (Utah) were both key advocates of the Americans with Disabilities Act of 1990, which prohibited discrimination against persons with disabilities, and, in 1993, House Republican Whip Newt Gingrich worked cooperatively with President Clinton to pass the North American Free Trade Agreement (NAFTA), which was opposed by a majority of House Democrats, including Majority Leader Richard Gephardt (D-Mo.) and Chief Whip David Bonior (D-Mich.). Similarly, after a period of intense partisan confrontation between the Republican-controlled Congress and President Clinton that led to a partial shutdown of the government in 1995, the GOP leadership and the president compromised and agreed upon plans to balance the budget and reform the welfare system. And in 2001, President Bush and the Senate's most prominent liberal Democrat, Ted Kennedy, worked together to pass an education reform bill.

The broad coalition nature of the parties' electoral support makes it extremely difficult for them to make ideologically consistent and coherent policy appeals to the voters representing such a wide spectrum of interests and viewpoints. Even if the parties were inclined toward programmatic politics, their decentralized character would make enforcing party unity next to impossible. Liberals, moderates, and conservatives cohabit within both parties. Given this lack of internal policy agreement, the parties are less than reliable instruments of governmental policy making. The various constituencies of party officeholders pull them in different directions. The problem of relying upon party loyalty to implement government policies is shown in Table 3.3, which presents data on congressional support for the president's legislative program. Presidents are not able to count upon the loyalty of their

TABLE 3.3	SUPPORT FOR PRESIDENT'S POSITION ON ROLL CALL VOTES BY MEMBERS OF THE PRESIDENT'S PARTY IN CONGRESS, 1954–2009

		Average Percent of Members of President's Party Supporting His Position		
Years	President	Party	Representatives	Senators
2009	Obama	Democrat	72	79
2001–2008	Bush	Republican	64	70
1993–2000	Clinton	Democrat	76	86
1989–1992	Bush	Republican	69	77
1981–1988	Reagan	Republican	68	79
1977–1980	Carter	Democrat	69	69
1974–1976	Ford	Republican	72	65
1969–1974	Nixon	Republican	73	63
1964–1968	Johnson	Democrat	71	81
1961–1963	Kennedy	Democrat	75	83
1954–1960	Eisenhower	Republican	80	68

Source: Norman J. Ornstein, Thomas E. Mann, and Michael J. Malbin, *Vital Statistics on Congress, 1999–2000* (Washington, D.C.: AEI Press, 2000), pp. 198–199; *Congressional Quarterly Weekly.*

party's members in the Congress. The levels of defection can be significant. Even with the Congress controlled by his own party, President Obama's position on legislation during 2009 was supported by House Democrats on average only 72 percent of the time. The internal unity problems of the congressional parties are illustrated by Table 3.4, which lists Democratic senators who most frequently opposed the positions of their president, as well as Republican senators who gave President Obama support over 45 percent of the time in 2009.

Given the lack of party unity that often existed in Congress, particularly during the second half of the twentieth century, it was frequently necessary to form cross-party alliances to pass legislation; for example, the previously noted bipartisan coalition required to pass NAFTA as well as welfare reform (1996), a balanced budget agreement (1997), and major tax cut (2001). However, as conservative and moderate Democrats from the South have been replaced by conservative Republicans, and moderate Republicans from the Northeast have been replaced by liberal Democrats, both parties have become more homogeneous in terms of policy orientation. This has led to heightened party unity, intensified partisan conflict, and a decline in the frequency of bipartisan coalitions.[22] For example, when the House passed the first version of the health care reform legislation in November, 2009, just one Republican voted in the favor of the measure. In the Senate, Democrats found it impossible to attract even one Republican supporter.

The party platforms of the GOP and Democratic Party also differ substantially. Analyses of recent party platforms reveal significant differences between the two parties and consistent efforts by the officeholders of the two parties to implement

BOX 3.2	"DEAR MR. PRESIDENT... HELL NO!": WHEN THE RANK-AND-FILE REVOLT

When compared to other presidents during the past half-century, George W. Bush fared very well in winning the support of members of his own party in Congress. In fact, no president since World War II had been as successful as Bush in garnering support from his congressional partisans. However, the nonhierarchical nature of parties in the United States creates an environment where not even Bush was able to win support from his party all of the time. This fact was exceptionally clear in February 2005, when members of Congress learned that the Bush administration had approved a deal that would have given Dubai Ports World—a company located in the United Arab Emirates—control over shipping operations in several U.S. ports. Immediately, Republican and Democratic members of Congress vociferously criticized the deal and threatened to pass legislation that would prohibit it. The most highly publicized objections came from Bush's own party, best illustrated by Republican Representative Sue Myrick's (N.Y.) one-sentence letter to the White House, which read, "Dear Mr. President: In regards to selling American ports to the United Arab Emirates, not just NO but HELL NO!" Bush tried to win over his party on the issue, but he eventually was forced to acquiesce to the prevailing sentiment in both parties and agree to disallow the deal. Ultimately, the controversy over the Dubai Ports deal illustrates that presidents cannot count on support from members of their own party, and when such support is not forthcoming, presidents may not fare very well.

Source: "Republicans Split with Bush on Ports: White House Vows to Brief Lawmakers on Deal with Firm Run by Arab State," by Jim VandeHei and Jonathan Weisman, *Washington Post*, February 23, 2006, p. A01.

TABLE 3.4	DEMOCRATIC SENATORS VOTING MOST FREQUENTLY IN OPPOSITION TO THE PRESIDENT'S POSITION ON SENATE ROLL CALLS, AND REPUBLICAN SENATORS MOST FREQUENTLY VOTING IN SUPPORT OF THE PRESIDENT, 2009

Democrats	Percent of Votes Opposed	Republicans	Percent of Votes in Support
Bayh (Ind.)	23	Collins (Maine)	85
McCaskill (Mo.)	20	Snowe (Maine)	81
Feingold (Wis.)	15	Voinovich (Ohio)	78
Nelson (Neb.)	10	Bond (Mo.)	69
Begich (Alaska)	7	Alexander (Tenn.)	68
Byrd (W.Va.)	7	Lugar (Ind.)	68
Webb (Va.)	6	Gregg (N.H.)	67
Dorgan (N.D.)	5	Murkowski (Alaska)	66
Murray (Wash.)	5	Cochran (Miss.)	62

Source: Congressional Quarterly Weekly, January 11, 2010, p. 112.

those platforms. In 2004, there were sharp differences between the Democratic and Republican platforms on such issues as health care, the environment, abortion, and immigration reform. The platform is important, Gerald Pomper and Susan Lederman have observed, because

> it summarizes, crystallizes, and presents to the voters the characteristics of the party coalition.... The stands taken in the platform clarify the parties' positions on ... controversies and reveal the nature of their support and appeal.[23]

Not only are the policy positions of the parties' platforms and their elected officials different, but so are the policy positions of their rank-and-file voters and activist participants. Although both Republican and Democratic rank-and-file voters tend to be moderate in ideology, Democrats are more liberal than Republicans. The ideological orientations of party activists (e.g., national and state convention delegates, financial contributors, and campaign workers) show even greater differences between the parties. Party activists in both parties tend to be much more extreme in ideological positions, with Republican activists considering themselves much more conservative than GOP rank-and-file voters, and Democratic activists seeing themselves as more liberal than Democratic voters generally.[24]

Party activists, who are highly influential in nomination contests and in providing campaign support, are an important force in pulling the two parties apart on policy. Candidates must have the support of these party workers. The fact that in the Republican Party they are more conservative and in the Democratic Party more liberal than the parties' rank-and-file voters means that there are strong pressures within the system maintaining differences in policy between the parties. But even with these differences, American parties remain relatively nonprogrammatic and pragmatic in their approach to issues.

QUASI-PUBLIC INSTITUTIONS WITH AMBIGUOUS MEMBERSHIP

In most democracies other than the United States, political parties are considered private organizations, like the Elks, American Legion, Rotary, or American Bar Association. They make and enforce their own rules concerning qualifications for membership, organizational structure, and activities. There are few laws governing their internal decision-making processes. Membership normally involves a process of application and approval. Members are then expected to assume obligations such as paying annual dues. In return, party members are permitted to take part in party activities such as the selection of candidates.

By contrast, American parties are quasi-public institutions that are heavily regulated by statute, especially state laws. The very existence of American parties is almost mandated by state statutes that legally define parties and prescribe their organizational structure, membership criteria, leadership selection methods, and the procedures for nominating candidates. By controlling who may vote in party primaries, for example, state statutes set the qualifications for membership in American parties. In closed primary states, voters are required to state publicly their party preference before being allowed to participate in the preferred party's primary. Party membership in these circumstances is essentially a matter of self-designation. In open primary states, it is possible to vote without ever publicly professing a preference for one party over another. The voters decide in the secrecy of the voting booth in which party's primary they will vote. Austin Ranney has observed that such statutory regulation of party membership has made the Republican and Democratic parties "unique among the world's parties in that neither has effective control of its own legal membership and there is no formal distinction between member and supporter."[25]

In some jurisdictions, including Wisconsin and Minnesota, the party organizations do have modest-sized dues-paying memberships. But these formal members have few privileges that are not extended to non–dues-paying supporters of the party. Both are entitled to participate in primary elections to select the party's nominees. Party membership in the United States is therefore an ambiguous phenomenon and largely a matter of self-designation.

The extensive regulation of parties by state statutes in such matters as membership, organization, leadership selection, nominations, and campaign finance has meant that parties are not free to run their own internal affairs as they see fit. Not unlike public utilities, which provide public services in a manner prescribed by law, parties perform essential public functions under government regulations.[26] They are therefore quasi-public institutions with relatively open membership qualifications.

WEAK PARTIES, BUT SUBSTANTIAL PARTISAN INFLUENCE

Although sharing many features in common with the parties of other Western democracies, American political parties have a distinguishing set of characteristics—two-partyism, decentralized power structures, broadly based electoral coalitions, moderate policy orientations, and quasi-public status. Taken as a whole, these are features that limit party influence on governmental policy making. At the same time, party influences pervade the political system—in electoral politics, in organizing governmental institutions, and in influencing policy making. This seeming contradiction of parties being relatively weak, decentralized, and frequently lacking in unity while at the same time being an important—but not necessarily dominant—influence on electoral and governmental politics is one of the distinguishing aspects of the American political system.

NOTES

1. The index of competitiveness was developed by Austin Ranney, "Parties in State Politics," in Herbert Jacob and Kenneth Vines, eds., *Politics in the American States*, 3rd ed. (Boston: Little, Brown, 1976), pp. 59–61.

2. Samuel C. Patterson and Gregory A. Caldeira, "The Etiology of Partisan Competition," *American Political Science Review* 78 (Sept. 1984): 691–707.

See also John F. Bibby and Thomas M. Holbrook, "Parties and Elections," in Virginia Gray, Russell L. Hanson, and Herbert Jacob, eds., *Politics in the American States*, 7th ed. (Washington, D.C.: CQ Press, 1999), ch. 3.

3. Competition Results. Washington: CQ Press. Dynamically generated July 11, 2006, from CQ Electronic Library, CQ Voting and Elections Collection.

4. Center for Responsive Politics (http://opensecrets.org).

5. Ronald E. Weber, Harvey J. Tucker, and Paul Brace, "Vanishing Marginals in State Legislative Elections," *Legislative Studies Quarterly* 26 (Feb. 1991): 29–47.

6. Malcolm E. Jewell and Sarah M. Morehouse, *Political Parties and Elections in American States,* 4th ed. (Washington, D.C.: CQ Press, 2001), pp. 202–208; William E. Cassie and David A. Breaux, "Expenditures and Election Results," in Joel A. Thompson and Gary E. Moncrief, eds., *Campaign Finance in State Legislative Elections* (Washington, D.C.: Congressional Quarterly, 1998), p. 103.

7. On America's system of separated institutions, see Charles O. Jones, *The Presidency in a Separated System* (Washington, D.C.: Brookings, 1994).

8. Leon D. Epstein, *Political Parties in Western Democracies* (New York: Praeger, 1967), p. 33.

9. Maurice Carroll, "For Once, a Primary Unites a Party," *New York Times,* March 25, 1984, p. 6E.

10. For a fascinating account of how British parties can control parliamentary nominations to enforce party discipline, see Leon D. Epstein, "British M.P.s and Their Local Parties: The Suez Cases," *American Political Science Review* 54 (June 1960): 627–639; see also Anthony King, ed., *New Labor Triumphs: Britain at the Polls* (Chatham, N.J.: Chatham House, 1998), pp. 66–68.

11. For an account of national party activities in a sampling of contested races in 2000, see David B. Magleby, ed., *Election Advocacy: Soft Money and Issue Advocacy in the 2000 Congressional Elections* (Provo, Utah: Center for the Study of Elections and Democracy, Brigham Young University, 2001).

12. Gary C. Jacobson, *The Politics of Congressional Elections*, 5th ed. (New York: Longman, 2001), p. 77.

13. David Mayhew, *Congress: The Electoral Connection* (New Haven, Conn.: Yale University Press, 1974).

14. Leon D. Epstein, "Party Confederations and Political Nationalization," *Publius* 12 (Fall 1982): 71.

15. *Democratic Party of the United States of America v. Bronson C. LaFollette*, 449 U.S. 897 (1981).

16. Austin Ranney, "The Political Parties: Reform and Decline," in Anthony King, ed., *The New American Political System* (Washington, D.C.: American Enterprise Institute, 1978), p. 230.

17. John F. Bibby, "Party Renewal in the National Republican Party," in Gerald Pomper, ed., *Party Renewal in America* (New York: Praeger, 1981), pp. 102–115.

18. On the expanded role of the national party organizations and the growth of intraparty integration, see Paul S. Herrnson, "The Revitalization of National Party Organizations," in L. Sandy Maisel, ed., *The Parties Respond* (Boulder, Colo.: Westview, 1998), ch. 3; and John F. Bibby, "Party Networks: National-State Integration, Allied Groups, and Issue Activists," in John C. Green and Daniel M.Shea, eds., *The State of the Parties* (Lanham, Md.: Roman and Littlefield, 1999), ch. 5.

19. The Center for Public Integrity's Party Lines Project (http://www.publicintegrity.org/projects/entry/296/).

20. John H. Kessel, *Presidential Campaign Politics*, 4th ed. (Pacific Grove, Calif.: Brooks/Cole, 1992), pp. 113–114.

21. Epstein, *Political Parties in Western Democracies*, p. 262.

22. *Congressional Quarterly, Weekly Report*, Jan. 1999, p. 38.

23. Gerald M. Pomper and Susan S. Lederman, *Elections in America* (New York: Longman, 1980), p. 173.

24. For commentary on the consequences of activists' ideology of the political system, see Morris P. Fiorina, "Extreme Voice: A Dark Side of Civic

Engagement," in Theda Skocpol and Morris P. Fiorina, eds., *Civic Engagement in American Democracy* (Washington, D.C.: Brookings, 1999), pp. 395–425.

25. Austin Ranney, *The Governing of Men*, 4th ed. (Hinsdale, Ill.: Dryden Press, 1975), p. 199.

26. Leon D. Epstein, *Political Parties in the American Mold* (Madison: University of Wisconsin Press, 1986), ch. 6.

Party Organizations CHAPTER **4**

Party organization in the United States conjures up a variety of strikingly different images, depending upon one's perspective.

- To a ward committeeperson in Chicago, a New Jersey county chair, or a party functionary in Nassau County (Long Island), the party organization is a hierarchically run machine that dispenses jobs, social services, and help with the governmental bureaucracy in return for electoral support.
- To a Minnesota Democrat, the party organization is a group of issue-oriented liberals who take party platforms seriously, seek to control primary election outcomes through party endorsements of candidates, and work as campaign volunteers.
- To a rural southern Democrat, the party organization is a group of court-house politicians who perfunctorily fill formal positions but whose activity is limited.
- To most California activists, the real party organization is the candidate's personal following and his or her professional campaign consultants.
- To many state legislators, the party organization that really matters is the state legislative campaign committee, chaired by the party leader in the legislature, which provides money and technical assistance to candidates.
- To the staff member of the Republican National Committee, the party organization is a large bureaucracy consisting of hundreds of paid professionals using the most sophisticated techniques and operating with receipts in excess of $200 million.

As these illustrations suggest, party organization in the United States exists in an almost infinite variety of forms. The type of organization operating in any political jurisdiction depends upon a variety of factors: the level of government involved (e.g., local, state, or national), the type of governmental regulations under which it must operate, the extent of interparty competition that exists, the clientele or bases of party support, regional and local traditions, and the nature of the electorate. Generally, however, American political party organizations are *cadre* parties rather than *mass membership* parties. Cadre parties are characterized by a small number of leaders and activists who maintain the organization, recruit candidates, seek to influence nominations, and campaign for the party's nominees. The party organization is active mainly during the election season, and the party in the electorate has little impact on the organization or control over its elected officials. By contrast, a mass membership party is characterized by a large dues-paying membership that plays an active role in selecting party leadership and in developing policy positions. The mass membership party tends to be active the year around and exerts substantial influence over the party's governmental officeholders.

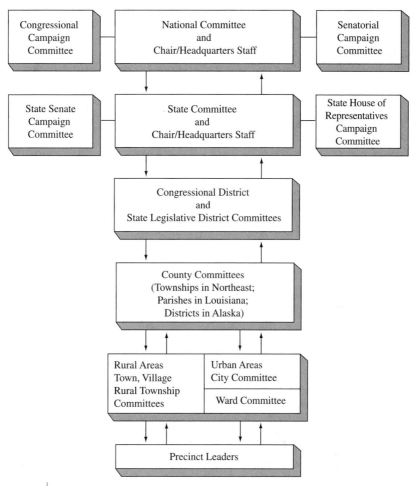

FIGURE 4.1 | LAYERS OF PARTY ORGANIZATIONS IN THE UNITED STATES

The American cadre type of party structure is based upon a complex set of inter-locking national party rules, state and federal statutes, and state and local party rules. It is organized to carry out its primary task—the winning of elections. Party organization, therefore, is built around geographic election districts, starting with the basic unit of election administration, the precinct. Above that in ascending order are city/village/town committees, county or township committees, legislative district committees, congressional district committees, state central committees, and, at the national level, the national committee (see Figure 4.1). Although the party organization builds from the local precinct to the national committee, this structure should not be viewed as a hierarchy. As V. O. Key, Jr., observed, party organization "may be more accurately described as a system of layers of organization."[1] Each separate layer focuses its efforts on the elections within its particular jurisdiction. Thus county parties are concerned primarily with control of the courthouse offices, state committees with the governorship, and the national committees with control of the presidency. At the same time, each level of party organization normally needs to obtain the collaboration of other layers of organization to achieve its objectives. But as Key noted, "that collaboration comes about, to the extent that it does come about, through a sense of common cause rather than by the exercise of command."[2]

This layered organizational structure characterizing American parties is called *stratarchy,* "an organization with layers, or strata, of control rather than centralized leadership from the top down."[3] Each stratum has its own organization and functions to perform, and each is quite autonomous within its own sphere while maintaining contact with party units above and below. Samuel Eldersveld has noted that a special component of stratarchy is *reciprocal deference.* That is, between the layers of organization "there is a tolerance of autonomy, of each layer's status and its right to initiative, as well as tolerance of inertia."[4] This tolerance stems from the lack of effective sanctions that higher levels of the party can exercise over lower-level units and the fact that each stratum needs the assistance of the other for such activities as fund-raising and mobilizing the vote. The spirit of tolerance for autonomy was captured by a midwestern state party chair who commented about his relationship with the county party organizations in his state: "At best we are a loose confederation. I have no jurisdiction over county chairmen. I'd have resented a state chairman telling me what to do when I was county chairman."

The party organizational structure suffers further fragmentation due to the existence at the national level of congressional and senatorial campaign committees in each party, which operate with substantial autonomy from the national committees. There is similar organizational structure at the state level, where state legislative campaign committees function independently of the state committees of the party.

Supplementing and at times dominating the loosely structured system of formal party organization are thousands of organizations formed by individual candidates seeking both their party's nomination and general election victory. These personal candidate organizations are focused upon winning elections for a single individual for one office. Often, especially in the case of presidential candidate organizations, they command greater financial resources, professional staff, and volunteer workers than regular party organizations. Never was this more evident than in 2008, when Barack Obama's campaign organization dwarfed that of the Democratic National Committee. These candidate organizations are, however, less permanent and less encompassing in their electioneering activities.[5] Also operating within the orbit of party organizations are party-allied groups that assist the parties and their candidates with fund-raising, voter mobilization, and issue development. Although legally autonomous from the parties, these groups' activities are often crucial to Republican and Democratic candidates; for example, organized labor's massive get-out-the-vote activities and advertising campaigns on behalf of Democrats and the voter guides distributed by the Christian Coalition for the benefit of Republicans. Another element in party organizations is professional campaign consultants, political "hired guns" whose skills are now deemed absolutely essential for any major campaign. These specialists in the various campaign arts—media advertising, direct mail, polling, campaign management, fund-raising—tend to work exclusively for one party or the other and hence must be considered a part of each parties' resource base. The party organization, therefore, is in reality a *network* that extends beyond the regular and legally constituted party structure to include candidate organizations, party-allied groups, and campaign consultants.[6]

THE NATIONAL PARTIES

THE NATIONAL COMMITTEES

Traditionally, the national party committees have been cited as classic examples of the decentralized character of American parties. These bodies, composed of delegates from the respective state parties, were created in the mid-1800s to serve as the interim agents of the party conventions. Because their principal function during the post–Civil War era was managing the presidential campaign, the committees were active for only a few months during a four-year period. It was not until the chairmanship of Will Hayes (1918–1921) that the Republican National Committee (RNC) established a year-round headquarters with full-time paid staff; and the Democratic National Committee (DNC) did not do so until 1928. The ad hoc character of national committee staffing extended well into the twentieth century, with the campaigns of 1928 and 1932 conducted largely by members of Congress, senators, governors, and other party notables with the assistance of borrowed professionals.

The national committees gradually became more institutionalized, with expanded full-time staff, elaborate division of labor, heightened professionalism, and larger budgets (see Figure 4.2).[7] Thus since 1950, the size of the DNC staff has never dipped below forty persons, and the RNC has exceeded eighty. These personnel perform fund-raising, public relations, voter mobilization, national convention management, campaign management and training, research, and policy development functions. Although the budgets and staff increased and the functions of the committees have been extended from an exclusive concern with presidential elections, the committees traditionally exercised little power. The leading study of the RNC and DNC, published in 1964, characterized national committee politics as "politics without power."[8] Although this was something of an exaggeration, the phrase did aptly capture the inability of the national committees to exert significant influence upon the behavior of state and local party leaders and elected officials. Yet national committees are the most inclusive organization within the parties. Only the national committee represents the party organizations of the fifty states plus ex officio representation for important elected officials and organized interests. Active and aggressive leadership of the national committee is capable of generating publicity for the party, raising campaign funds, mobilizing voters, and providing financial and technical assistance to candidates and state and local party units. The national committee can be an effective catalyst for stimulating the party organization, even though its formal powers are limited. This has been especially true for the party that does not hold the White House. For the out-party, the national committee is normally a major arena of party activity and struggles for power.[9]

NATIONAL COMMITTEE MEMBERSHIP   For most of their history, the RNC and the DNC had roughly comparable bases for committee membership. Each state party organization selected a national committeeman and committeewoman to serve on the

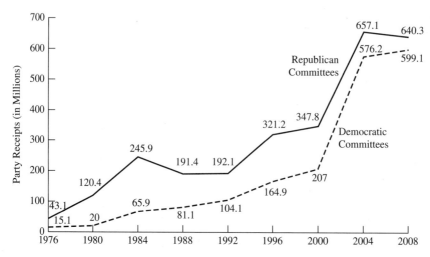

FIGURE 4.2 | NATIONAL PARTY RECEIPTS, 1976–2004 (COMBINED RECEIPTS OF NATIONAL, CONGRESSIONAL, AND SENATORIAL COMMITTEES IN MILLIONS)

Source: Federal Election Commission.

committee. State party chairs were made members of the RNC in the 1960s, and the Democrats adopted this policy in the 1970s. The committees' membership reflected the confederate nature of the national parties, with each state having equal representation and its national committee members serving essentially as party ambassadors from their states.

As a part of a series of major party reforms, the Democrats significantly changed the basis for representation on the DNC in 1974. These changes involved a major expansion of the size of the committee, representation for elected officials and various party auxiliaries, and equal representation of the sexes. The principle of state equality was abandoned in favor of a formula that took into account the population of the state and its record of support for Democratic candidates. The Republicans have not moved to change their representational scheme and maintain the principle of state equality and a confederate party system. The large number of people serving on the national committees, especially the DNC, has meant that deliberative action is almost impossible at national committee meetings. Instead, the locus for decision making is with the national chair and the executive committee, who meet prior to national committee meetings. The full national committees normally ratify the recommendations of the chair and executive committee.

An observer of DNC and RNC meetings is immediately struck by the fact that the differences between the two committees go well beyond their respective sizes. (See Table 4.1 for the composition of the two national committees.) Differences in style of operation and party constituencies are apparent.[10] RNC meetings are extremely well organized, structured, and professionally staffed. There is an air of formality and relative order about the conduct of the meetings. DNC meetings are less well organized, are more informal, and have a rather ad hoc character. The major subunits of RNC gatherings are meetings of the state chairs and regional associations.

| BOX 4.1 | PARTY ORGANIZATIONS ON THE WEB |

Political parties have proved to be good at adapting to new environments throughout American history. Recently, these organizations have had to work to adjust to technological advances that have made the Internet an important medium. But not all party organizations adapted as quickly to these changes. Rick Farmer and Rich Fender conducted a study of state party Web sites in 2000, and their findings revealed a tremendous amount of variation in the sophistication of party Web sites. Remarkably, three state parties did not even have an operational Web site as recently as 2001—the Republican and Democratic parties in Rhode Island and the Mississippi Democratic Party. Among the organizations who did maintain sites, the authors found that party Web sites often lacked technical sophistication and frequently included only minimal content. While most included basic contact information and links to candidate Web sites, they tended to lag behind in offering items such as streaming audio and video.

While there continues to be a great deal of variation in the Web sites operated by state parties, the national parties appear to be keeping current on Internet trends. Both the DNC and RNC maintain blogs on their Web sites and incorporate content from their sites on YouTube, Facebook, and Twitter (the RNC had 125,000 fans on Facebook in March 2010 compared to 75,000 for the DNC). The party sites also offer easy ways for activists to become involved by signing up for e-mail distribution lists, contributing money, creating and managing local events with other party supporters, and creating and managing personalized Web sites. While ordinary citizens do not necessarily frequent these Web sites, they have become a critical tool used by party organizations to organize and mobilize party activists, as well as an important portal through which money is raised.

Source: Rick Farmer and Rich Fender, "Casting a Weak Net: Political Party Web Sites in 2000," in John C. Green and Rick Farmer, eds., *The State of the Parties* (Lanham, Md.: Rowman & Littlefield, 2003).

There are also informal meetings of various ideological and candidate factions. The DNC has all of these types of subunits and factions, but in addition has active caucuses for blacks, Hispanics, and women that have played a major role in DNC meetings. Through the efforts of Chairman Paul Kirk (1985–1989), these caucuses lost official recognition in 1985. Kirk believed that the prominence of the caucuses was conveying an image of the party as a collection of special interests. The caucuses continue to exist on an informal basis, however, and the black, women's, and Hispanic caucuses retained ex officio representation on the DNC Executive Committee.[11] There is no comparable specialized representational structure—formal or informal—within the RNC. This no doubt reflects the important role that organized groups have traditionally played within the Democratic coalition. By contrast, the Republicans, with their more homogeneous constituency and middle-class orientation, have had a less extensive and explicit relationship with organized groups.

THE NATIONAL CHAIR

Because the national committees are unwieldy in size and meet but twice a year, the national chair plays a key role in determining how the committee will operate. The

TABLE 4.1 | COMPOSITION OF THE REPUBLICAN AND DEMOCRATIC NATIONAL COMMITTEES

Republican National Committee	Number	Democratic National Committee	Number
One national committeeman for each state, D.C., Guam, Puerto Rico, American Samoa, and Virgin Islands	55	National committee members—apportioned among the states on the same basis as national convention delegates (at least two per state)	212
One national committeewoman for each state, D.C., and territory	55	State party chair and next highest official of the opposite sex from each state, D.C., Puerto Rico, American Samoa, Guam, Virgin Islands, and Democrats abroad	112
State chair from each state, D.C., and territory (Republican rules provide ex officio membership on the RNC executive committee for representatives of the following: Republican Finance Committee, National Federation of Republican Women, Republican State Chairmen's Advisory Committee, Budget Committee, and other Republican groups that may be granted membership by the Executive Committee.)	55	Chair of Democratic Governors Association, plus two additional governors	3
		Two Democratic leaders from the House and Senate	4
		Chair of Democratic Mayors Conference, plus two additional mayors	3
		Chair of National Conference of Democratic Lieutenant Governors, plus one additional lieutenant governor	2
		Chair of National Conference of Democratic Secretaries of State, plus one additional secretary of state	2
		Chair of National Association of Democratic State Treasurers, plus one additional state treasurer	2
		Chair of Democratic County Officials Conference, plus two additional officials	3
		Chair of Democratic State Legislative Leaders Association, plus two legislators	3
		Chair of National Democratic Municipal Officials Conference, plus two officials	3
		President of Young Democrats and two members	2
		Chair of College Democrats of America, plus one additional member	3
		President of National Federation of Democratic Women, plus two members DNC officers	2
		Not more than 75 additional members	75
Total	165		441

chair's policies and programs, in turn, are implemented by the headquarters staff. Republican and Democratic rules now require that the chair serve on a full-time basis. This prevents elected officials like United States senators and representatives from becoming national chairs. Incumbent presidents designate who will serve as their party's chair. Until the 1980s, it was customary at national conventions for the presidential nominee to designate a national chair for the upcoming campaign. This designation was then ratified by the national committee. In the interest of party unity, recent presidential nominees have allowed national chairs to serve out their terms, which run until the January after presidential elections. The presidential nominees, however, do install their own campaign personnel in key national committee positions to make certain that the national committee and presidential campaign are working in concert. For example, in the summer of 2008, the DNC's political operations staff moved from Washington, D.C. to Chicago to be integrated into Obama's campaign headquarters for the duration of the campaign.

For the party that does not control the presidency—the out-party—control of the national chairpersonship is an important element in the struggle for intraparty ascendancy. Losing presidential campaigns inevitably breed struggles for control of the national committee. Often this takes the form of attempts to depose the national chair. Following the Republican Party's loss of the White House and dozens of congressional seats in 2008, incumbent RNC chair Mike Duncan faced four challengers for his post. It took six ballots before former Maryland lieutenant governor Michael Steele gained the 85 votes necessary to win the election and become the party's next chair.

Traditionally, there have been two basic styles of national committee leadership. One was the speaking chair, who saw the role as one of acting as spokesperson on behalf of the party, generating publicity, and criticizing the opposition. In 2001 President Bush selected Virginia Governor James Gilmore to be his RNC chairman and party spokesperson, with the expectation he would take his cues from senior White House political advisor Karl Rove. There were, however, tensions between the independent-minded Gilmore and the White House staff. This tension and 2001 off-year election losses of key governorships led to Gilmore being allowed to resign and the president designating former Montana governor Marc Racicot to be his replacement. The role of party spokesperson is often easier to fill for the chair of the party that does not hold the White House. Michael Steele has generated a great deal of publicity with his public statements about Democrats and the Obama administration during his time in the position.

The growing institutionalization of the national committees, with their enlarged staffs and budgets, and the rules requirement that chairs serve on a full-time basis, has meant that national chairs have increasingly emphasized their role as organizational leaders. Their job is to create a headquarters capable of providing the services needed to win elections. The classic example of a chair who emphasized building an effective party organization (a "nuts and bolts" chair) was Ray C. Bliss (1965–1969), who headed the RNC after the 1964 electoral disaster. Bliss seldom spoke in public and devoted his energies toward rebuilding the Grand Old Party (GOP) organizations—especially in metropolitan areas.[12] Although recent national chairs have generally been effective party spokespersons, their principal qualification for the job has been extensive experience as party organizational and campaign leaders. After losing the

2004 presidential election, Howard Dean, Democratic presidential candidate in the 2004 election, was tapped for the job of DNC chair because of his proven effectiveness at grassroots organizing and his success at raising funds through many small donations.

Frequently, a major responsibility of the national chair is maintaining or restoring a sense of party unity. The national chair, therefore, must give recognition to the various factions (congressional, gubernatorial, candidate, racial, ideological, and regional), mediate disputes, and negotiate compromises on party rules and policy positions. Such a challenge may have never been more pronounced than it was for DNC Chair Howard Dean following the epic contest between Hillary Clinton and Barack Obama for the Democratic Party's presidential nomination. Dean worked hard over the summer to help bridge the divide between Obama and Clinton supporters and his efforts culminated in a party convention that featured a united Democratic Party heading into the fall campaign.

The national chairs who have been considered the most effective have generally been those leading the out-party. Out-party chairs have considerable flexibility and can exert an independent influence on their party because they normally have personally campaigned for the post and developed a core of supporters among party leaders. For example, the RNC's Haley Barbour played a critical role in the GOP winning control of Congress for the first time in forty years by borrowing large sums and providing unprecedented national committee support for the 1994 congressional campaigns. After he took office in 2005, Howard Dean assumed a very active and visible role as the chair for the DNC. In fact, during the fifteen months after Dean first took office, he received seven times more coverage in major news papers than RNC chairman Ken Mehlman.[13] He also implemented his 50-state strategy, where the DNC worked to contest campaigns in all fifty states rather than conceding large blocks of states to the Republicans. While this strategy angered many Democratic members of Congress, Dean had considerably more leeway to ignore those complaints than would have been the case if he was serving at the pleasure of a Democratic president.

The chair of the party that controls the White House—the in-party—generally has little flexibility or independence. In fact, Senator Robert Kerrey (D-Neb.) complained in 1998 that the DNC was a "wholly owned subsidiary of the [Clinton] White House."[14] The power of the White House staff over the party's national chair was again demonstrated in late 2001, when RNC Chairman James Gilmore was forced to relinquish his post amid reports of tensions and disagreements between Gilmore and President George W. Bush's senior political advisor, Karl Rove. The *New York Times* quoted a prominent GOP leader as commenting, "I haven't seen anybody win in a clash with Karl Rove. The party is being run out of the White House and that's not Jim's [Gilmore] style."[15] The president designated former Montana governor Marc Racicot, a close and long-time ally, to replace Gilmore.

As David Wilhelm's fate illustrates, the White House staff and its Office of Political Affairs has characteristically emerged since the 1960s as the central institution for presidential party management. In the current era of candidate-centered politics, national committees no longer manage presidential campaigns. Nor do the national committees any longer dispense federal patronage. That role is now performed by the White House Personnel Office. In terms of its relations with the president, the in-party national committee provides backup political support and implements the political strategies of the president. Thus, during the Clinton administration, the DNC paid the retainer fees of professional campaign consultants who advised the president, including multimillion-dollar fees annually to presidential pollsters.[16] The Bush presidency, too, used its national committee to further its goals. In 2001, the RNC "brought twenty-one 'tax families' to the White House to illustrate the benefits of his tax cuts," paid their travel expenses, and arranged for seven of them to conduct satellite interviews with their hometown television stations.[17]

Although most presidents from Reagan through George W. Bush have been supportive of their national committees and worked closely with them, particularly on fund-raising, some recent presidents have sought to weaken the national committee because they wished to concentrate party leadership in the hands of White House staffers. The Nixon administration tended to downplay the role of the RNC as a campaign mechanism to help all GOP candidates and instead emphasized the chair's role as a publicist for the president. Another notable example of White House neglect of the national party machinery occurred during the Carter administration, when the president and his staff, through inattention to the party organization, left the DNC unprepared for the 1978 midterm elections.[18] Then, as the 1980 elections approached, the Carter White House used the meager financial resources of the DNC to fund presidential polls by the president's pollster, Pat Caddell. Even Bill Clinton, traditionally an assiduous fund-raiser for his party, was criticized because he and White House consultants diverted DNC efforts away from electoral support activities into television campaigns for the president's embattled legislative program during 1993–1994.[19]

COMMITTEE ACTIVITIES   The actual work of the national committees is done by their professional staffs, which operate out of permanent party headquarters buildings on Capitol Hill. These facilities are packed with high-tech equipment, including state-of-the-art television studios. Although the titles of the administrative divisions of the RNC and DNC vary slightly, both have staff specialists for fund-raising, political operations (assistance to candidates and party organizations), communications, voter mobilization, liaison with voter groups, convention and meeting arrangements, and administration. The in-party also has an office that liaisons with the White House and the administration.

- *Fund-Raising.* Both national committees have the capacity to raise large sums of "hard money"—funds raised in accordance with Federal Election Campaign Act (FECA) restrictions; for example, the RNC's $427.6 million and the DNC's $260.1 million during the 2007–2008 election cycle. Most of this money is raised from individual donors, often in contributions of less than $100 made online. Both committees also operate extensive large-giver programs (e.g., fund-raising dinners and receptions). From the mid-1990s through 2002, amassing "soft money" was a significant aspect of the RNC and DNC fund-raising operations. "Soft money" was raised outside the restrictions of the FECA and was collected in large denominations from individuals, corporations, unions, and other interest groups. While it was not supposed to be used for direct support of federal candidates, both parties discovered ways to use this money in ways that technically were not interpreted as direct support for federal candidates but did in fact provide significant aid to them. For example, soft money was used extensively to fund major get-out-the-vote drives and "issue-advocacy" advertising—media advertising that portrays a party's candidates favorably while not explicitly calling for their election or the defeat of opponents. However, "soft money" contributions were banned following the 2002 election by the Bipartisan Campaign Reform Act (BCRA). As noted later in this chapter, the banning of "soft money" has had a major impact on how national and state parties raise and spend money.

- *Assistance to State and Local Party Organizations.* Under the leadership of chair Bill Brock after the 1976 elections, the RNC initiated a massive effort to strengthen its state and local parties and assist state-level candidates. Among the programs Brock developed that have been continued and expanded by his successors are (1) assistance in developing a professionalized fund-raising operation; (2) grants to hire professional staff members; (3) computer/data processing assistance; (4) campaign schools for candidates and their managers; (5) financial and technical assistance to gubernatorial and state legislative candidates; (6) issues research; (7) assistance with redistricting; (8) campaign management training; and (9) national committee field staff to provide on-the-spot counseling and assistance to party leaders. Because the DNC has lagged behind the RNC in fund-raising, it was not until the mid-1980s that it was able to follow the Republican example and implement programs of assistance to state and local party units. The DNC's major effort is assisting state parties in operating "coordinated campaign" organizations that are jointly funded by the DNC, state parties, allied interest groups such as organized labor, and Democratic candidates. These organizations are geared toward providing a broad range of services to candidates, including voter registration, voter-list development, get-out-the-vote drives, polling, targeting, press relations, scheduling, and media purchases.

- *Campaign Activities.* Federal law permits the national committees to spend a fixed amount, which is adjusted for inflation every four years, to support their presidential nominees' campaigns ($19.1 million in 2008). Another major presidential campaign activity is financing state-level get-out-the-vote drives, media advertising, and other party-building activities in accordance with the strategies of the presidential candidates.

- *Communications.* Each national committee has a series of specialized publications for state leaders, county leaders, and party rank and file. Both have also created extensive e-mail networks, Facebook group sites, and Twitter accounts that allow them to easily reach activists throughout the nation. They sponsor major campaign advertising efforts. Advertisements aired by the DNC in 2005 that sought to undermine President Bush's attempt to reform Social Security are a recent notable example. Similarly, the RNC ran advertisements to criticize Democratic efforts to reform health care in 2009.

- *Conventions.* The national committees are responsible for planning, arranging, and managing the national conventions.

- *Research*. The research operations of the committees provide issue background to candidates and party leaders, engage in research designed to expose the weaknesses of opposition party candidates, and commission polls to gauge public opinion.

REVITALIZATION AND PARTY CENTRALIZATION   As noted previously, until the 1970s, national committees had been viewed as so weak and lacking in political clout that a landmark study in 1964 characterized them as "politics without power."[20] They were largely the creatures of and financed by state party organizations. Today, no informed observer would describe the national committees as "weak." Indeed, the entire relationship between the national committees and their state affiliates has been transformed. American parties are still decentralized, but power and influence have increasingly been flowing toward the national party organizations. This process of power centralization has occurred through the enforcement of national party rules and the provision of funds and services to state parties.

For its part, the DNC achieved increased power within the Democratic Party through its role as the initiator and enforcer of national party rules governing delegate selection to the national convention. This power was gained through a series of party reform commissions starting with the McGovern-Fraser Commission, appointed after the divisive 1968 convention. This commission and its successor commissions recommended to the DNC a detailed and codified set of party rules governing delegate selection.

The DNC used this newfound legal authority to compel state Democratic parties to bring their delegate selection procedures into compliance with national party rules. Failure to comply can result in a state's national convention delegation not being seated at the convention. Faced with this type of national party sanction, the state parties embarked upon a massive restructuring of their internal procedures. This impressive display of national party legal authority over party organizations culminated in a series of U.S. Supreme Court decisions upholding the principle that national party rules take precedence over state party rules and state statutes in matters of delegate selection.[21]

Although these Supreme Court decisions confer similar authority upon the national Republican Party, the Republicans did not follow the Democratic route of imposing restrictions on state parties. Indeed, it has followed a conscious policy of refraining from exercising this authority and has sought to maintain the confederate character of the party organization. This GOP reluctance to extend its rule-enforcement authority should not be interpreted as indicative of an absence of centralizing tendencies within the party. Within the Republican Party, centralization has moved forward since the 1960s through a series of RNC programs designed to strengthen state and local organizations and to assist federal, state, and local candidates. Through its extensive programs of assistance to party organizations and candidates, the RNC has significantly increased its influence over state parties because most are anxious to participate in RNC-initiated programs and share in their benefits. As one midwestern Republican state chair commented, "I figure that I should go along with the National Committee as much as possible because I want as much of their money as I can get." By using its ample financial resources to aid state parties and candidates, the RNC has achieved an enlarged role in the political process and increased the functional interdependence of the national and state Republican parties.[22]

As the DNC has followed the Republican example of extending significant amounts of aid to its state affiliates, it, too, has achieved enhanced influence. Because of programs of support for state parties and candidates that were initiated on a large scale first by the RNC and recently on a more limited scale by the DNC, the traditional flow of intraparty funds has been reversed. Since the 1980s, the flow in both parties has been from the national party to the state party organizations. The national committees are therefore no longer dependent upon their state organizations and have achieved substantial autonomy as well as enhanced leverage over their state party organizations because of their superior financial and technical resources. A by-product of this revolution in intraparty patterns has been an unprecedented level of party integration.[23]

PARTY INTEGRATION IN FEDERAL ELECTION CAMPAIGNS   Large-scale transfers of party funds from the national committees to state parties were previously encouraged by provisions of the FECA. The act imposed strict limits on the amount of money national parties can contribute or expend on behalf of candidates for the presidency and Congress but permitted state and local parties to spend without limit on party-building activities such as voter registration and get-out-the-vote drives. As a result, both national parties collected large sums of money that they transferred to state and local party organizations to support party-building activities and issue-advocacy advertising which assisted candidates for the presidency and Congress (see Figure 4.3). With the FECA encouraging the national party organizations to

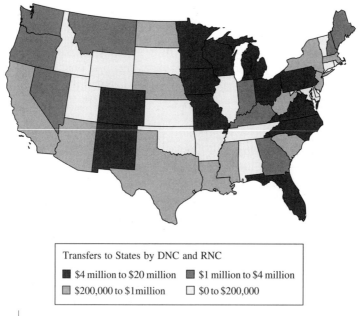

Transfers to States by DNC and RNC

■ $4 million to $20 million   ■ $1 million to $4 million
■ $200,000 to $1 million   □ $0 to $200,000

FIGURE 4.3 | NATIONAL-TO-STATE PARTY TRANSFERS, 2007–2008

Source: Federal Election Commission.

channel funds and campaign activities through the state parties in an effort to influence the outcome of federal elections, the state parties became an integral part of presidential, Senate, and House campaigns. Fund transfers from the national party organizations to state parties, joint national–state party campaign activities, and national party technical assistance to state affiliates all resulted in a nationalizing of party campaign efforts and substantially heightened levels of integration between the two strata of party organization. Thanks to the assistance provided by the national party committees, many state parties were strengthened, but they also grew increasingly dependent upon the national party organization and lost some of their former autonomy.

PARTY ACTIVITIES AFTER THE BCRA   Passed in 2002, the BCRA first took effect during the 2003–2004 election cycle. One of the primary goals of the new campaign finance rules was to eliminate the role of unregulated "soft money" in party spending. Before BCRA, "soft money" was exempt from federal laws, and this allowed individuals to give unlimited amounts to the party organizations even though their contribution to individual candidates was capped at $1,000. As noted in previous sections, this money was often transferred to state party organizations where it was then used to fund get-out-the-vote efforts and extensive advertising campaigns. The BCRA, however, prohibited the national party committees from raising or spending "soft money" of any kind and greatly limited the extent to which state parties could do so. This change profoundly affected party organizations:[24]

- *National Parties Raised More Hard Money.* The 2004 presidential campaign was the first in which the national party committees could raise and spend only regulated "hard money." The new campaign finance regulations did not keep the DNC and RNC from raising large amounts of money. In fact, the national committees raised $797 million in "hard money" contributions for the 2004 elections, and $688 million for the 2008 campaign.[25]
- *Transfers to State Parties Declined.* While the national committees were undeterred in their fundraising, the new regulations no longer encouraged the massive transfers of money to state parties that had previously been routine. Under the old regulations in 2000, the national parties transferred over $400 million to state parties, but in 2004, that amount dropped to approximately $117 million. In 2008, the amount transferred increased slightly to $123 million.
- *State Parties Did Not Advertise.* How did state parties cope with the definitive decline in financial support in 2004? Figure 4.4 presents how state parties spent their money in 2000 compared to 2004. Interestingly, the state parties actually spent more on grassroots efforts, mobilization, and administration in 2004. However, the notable difference in the post-BCRA election is the almost complete cessation of advertising by state parties. Previously, national party committees would transfer "soft money" to state parties that was to be used to air "issue ads" aimed at influencing congressional and presidential elections. The ban on "soft money" eliminated these transfers to the state parties and the advertisements that they paid for.

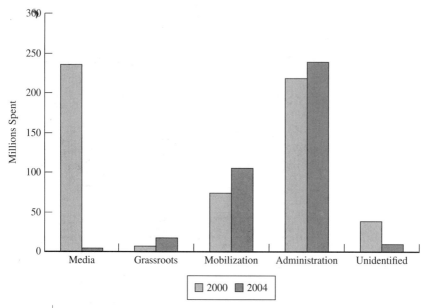

FIGURE 4.4 | STATE PARTY EXPENDITURES, 2000 AND 2004

Source: Raymond J. LaRaja, "State and Local Parties," in Michael J. Malbin, ed., *Election After Reform: Money, Politics, and the Bipartisan Campaign Reform Act* (Lanham, Md.: Rowman & Littlefield, 2006).

- *Parties Continued to Make Strategic Transfers.* While the national parties greatly reduced the extent to which they transferred funds to state party committees, they did continue to transfer some money, and they did so very strategically. Figure 4.4 demonstrates how the RNC and the DNC allocated the money they transferred to state parties in 2004. They sent money to states where it was most likely to have an impact. Thus, in 2004, there were large-scale transfers by the RNC, and the DNC made large-scale transfers to battleground states in the presidential election, most notably Florida, Michigan, Ohio, and Pennsylvania, while states having a low priority in the campaign received only token or small transfers of funds. This trend continued during the 2008 campaign, when the DNC and RNC transferred a combined $11.8 million to Pennsylvania state party organizations, $13.9 million to Ohio state parties, and nearly $20 million to the state party organizations in Florida. However, new battleground states also received significant transfers in 2008, including North Carolina ($7.5 million), Colorado ($6.6 million), Virginia ($5.9 million), and Indiana ($4.0 million).

Overall, while the BCRA has not prevented the DNC and RNC from raising and spending massive amounts of money, it has changed the relationship between the national and state parties by decreasing the amount of money transferred between those levels of the party organization. I will discuss additional changes brought about by the BCRA in later chapters.

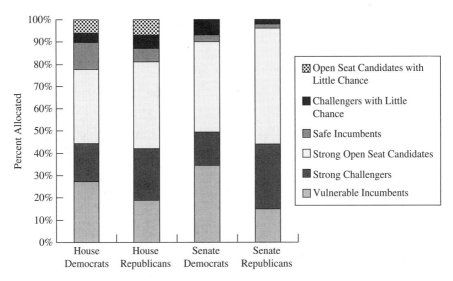

FIGURE 4.5 | ALLOCATIONS OF NATIONAL PARTY FUNDS IN U.S. HOUSE AND SENATE ELECTIONS, 2002: CONCENTRATING ON COMPETITIVE RACES WHERE THERE IS A CHANCE TO WIN

Source: Adapted from Federal Election Commission data analyzed by Paul S. Herrnson, *Congressional Elections: Campaigning at Home and in Washington,* 4th ed. (Washington, D.C.: CQ Press, 2004), p. 101.

THE HILL COMMITTEES

Increasingly important elements of the national party are the congressional and senatorial campaign committees. These organizations—whose official names are the Democratic Congressional Campaign Committee (DCCC), National Republican Congressional Committee (NRCC), Democratic Senatorial Campaign Committee (DSCC), and the National Republican Senatorial Committee (NRSC)—are organizationally autonomous from the national committees and operate quite independently. The members of these Capitol Hill committees are members of the House and Senate. These committees concentrate their efforts on holding their parties' marginal seats and on assisting challengers and open seat candidates with a reasonable chance of success against opposition party members. As a result, safe incumbents as well as challengers and open seat candidates with no realistic likelihood of winning receive little in the way of party assistance (see Figure 4.5).

Campaign finance regulations impose severe restrictions on the amount of money party committees can contribute to congressional and senatorial candidates ($5,000 per election to House candidates or $10,000 for the primary and general election combined, and $37,300 combined for senatorial candidates). Such restrictions mean that national party committees can have only minimal impact on congressional campaigns through direct contributions to candidates. However, in addition to being authorized to make limited contributions directly to candidates, the party organizations are also permitted by the FECA to make expenditures in support of their parties' candidates. These monies are called *coordinated expenditures* and are normally used for polling, producing campaign advertising, and buying media time—major expenses that involve technical expertise. The limits on coordinated expenditures, unlike those on the direct contribution limits, are adjusted at each election for inflation. In 2010, the coordinated expenditure limit for party committees is $43,500 for each House race. The congressional campaign committees also engage in candidate recruitment and training.

The senatorial campaign committees are in a position to play a substantially more prominent role than the congressional committees. The FECA permits coordinated expenditures on behalf of senatorial candidates at a level of two cents times the voting-age population of the state, with the amount adjusted for inflation since 1974. Under this formula, the amount of money that a party committee may spend in populous states can be significant. For example, the 2010 limit was over $2.4 million in California. This limit can be doubled by a device first developed by the Republicans and approved by the courts. Through a technique called an "agency agreement," the NRSC has assumed the spending quota of state party committees and thus been able to double the national party spending limit in selected states. As a result of this device, both the Republican and Democratic senatorial campaign committees have been able to pump large sums into key races.

In addition to making direct contributions and coordinated expenditures, the Hill committees also encourage *party-connected* funds to flow to their candidates. These are contributions from the political action committees (PACs) operated by House and Senate party leaders as well as individual members and former members (these are sometimes referred to as leadership PACs). In 2008, 381 leadership PACs contributed nearly $40 million to candidates for federal offices, including over $1 million contributed by PACs run by Democrat Steny Hoyer and Republicans John Boehner and Eric Cantor. Recently, the Hill committees have also solicited contributions from these leadership PACs. Faced with the prohibition of "soft money" after the BCRA passed, the DCCC identified 186 incumbents who were sure to win reelection but were sitting on over $80 million combined in their leadership PACs. The DCCC called up on each of these incumbents to transfer between $70,000 and $400,000 to the Hill committee, an effort that eventually amounted to $18.3 million in transfers from the members' committees. Similarly, the NRCC raised $19.4 million in transfers from its members' PACs. The Hill committees used these funds to contribute and spend on behalf of congressional candidates involved in competitive campaigns.

Not only do the Hill committees make contributions and steer party-connected funds to their candidates, but they also assist candidates with fund-raising; for example, by providing lists of contributors, having party leaders attend candidates' fund-raising events, and steering contributions from wealthy individuals and PACs to candidates.

Despite the substantial role that the congressional and senatorial campaign committees play in helping to fund candidates, it is important to keep in mind that the party-based money constitutes a relatively small proportion of candidates' total receipts, usually less than 10 percent of all money raised. The bulk of campaign money comes from nonparty sources (individuals are the largest source, followed by PACs). As a result, the ability of the party leadership to affect their colleagues' roll call voting behavior and increase party unity by either granting or withholding party funds is extremely limited. And as long as party funds are allocated strategically rather than on the basis of candidates' ideology, Hill committee resources are not likely to be an effective tool for congressional leaders to use in trying to impose discipline upon their colleagues.

There is also evidence that the national party committees are affecting the way House and Senate campaigns are run. Party-favored candidates have found that there is no "free lunch" in politics. In exchange for national party funds, candidates are often required to agree to certain conditions; for example, to conduct polls, to air their television ads at a predetermined stage of the campaign, and to surrender contributor lists in return for party fund-raising help.

PARTY-ALLIED GROUPS

A party's organizational resources, in their totality, involve more than the formal, legally constituted party organizations such as the national or the Senate and House campaign committees. The organizational resource base of the parties also includes other organizations on which the parties rely for electoral services. One of the earliest manifestations of allied groups being integrated into the party structure was the emergence during the 1940s of labor unions as a source of support upon which the Democratic Party came to rely. Led by the Congress of Industrialized Organizations (CIO), unions provided campaign funds to candidates, mobilized voters, and sought to influence public opinion. Unions were such an integral part of the Democratic Party that Yale political scientist David R. Mayhew concluded after an exhaustive analysis that the "Democratic Party in the 1940s and 1950s [was] made up largely of machines and unions."[26] At the same time, most corporations had GOP leanings.

Although close ties between organized interests and parties are hardly a new phenomenon, there has been a dramatic increase in the involvement of party-allied groups in recent elections. Indeed, allied-group support for party candidates and interaction between these groups and the party organizations has become so heavy that the concept of party organization requires a broad definition.

Recent elections are replete with evidence of extensive involvement by allied groups in partisan campaigns and of close linkages between the parties and these groups. For example, RNC and Republican House and Senate campaign committee personnel often work closely with the leaders of Americans for Tax Reform, the Christian Coalition, the National Federation of Independent Business, and the National Rifle Association on electoral strategy and campaign activities. A similar pattern has been evident between the Democrats and their allied groups. Pro-Democratic groups—the AFL-CIO, EMILY's List, the National Education Association (NEA), the Sierra Club, NARAL Pro-Choice America, the National Committee for an Effective Congress, the NAACP, and the League of Conservation Voters—have worked together and with Democratic leaders on recent campaigns. Interest groups, such as the ones just listed, often pick up the tab on some of the most expensive elements of a campaign, such as direct mailings and radio and television advertisements.

During the 2004 campaign, "527" organizations—named for the section of the tax code that governs their activities—became an important source of party-allied activity. While they cannot expressly advocate the election or defeat of a particular candidate, the major 527 organizations were closely tied to one party or the other during the 2004 campaign, and they spent nearly $479 million to influence campaigns for president and congress. Much of this spending, as in the case of the Republican-affiliated Swift Boat Vets for Truth, was dedicated to advertising or, as in the case of Democratic-affiliated America Coming Together, on get-out-the-vote efforts. (For more information on 527 groups, see Box 4.2.)

Even though party-allied groups have become an increasingly important campaign resource of the parties and their candidates, it must be kept in mind that these partisan allies have their own agendas and maintain an autonomous organizational structure. When groups advertise on behalf of individual candidates, they are also articulating their own positions on the issues they care about. And although the ties between parties and allied groups may be close, these groups do not necessarily coordinate all their activities with either candidates or parties. In addition, they are not above voicing loud, public criticisms of their preferred party's actions on occasion.

Additional Components of the Party Network: "Think Tanks" and Consultants

In addition to prominent party-allied groups such as the AFL-CIO or Citizens for Tax Reform, the party organizational networks extend to the proliferation of Washington public-policy research organizations (dubbed "think tanks"). A prime example is the Progressive Policy Institute, an affiliate of an unofficial Democratic group with centrist leanings, the Democratic Policy Council. The Progressive Policy Institute has been a source of policy proposals used by Democratic candidates from Bill Clinton to Barack Obama. Republicans also have research institutes to assist them, notably the conservative Heritage Foundation, whose mission is to formulate and promote conservative public policies.

Political consultants have also become a prominent element in the infrastructure of candidates' campaigns for major offices and the parties' organizational networks. A substantial share (41 percent in a recent survey) of campaign consultants serve an apprenticeship within party organizations before moving out into the private sector. And once out on their own, they normally reinvent a relationship with the party that helped to train them.[27] Because trust and loyalty are important to politicians, consultants normally work exclusively for only one party.

To win elections, party organizations need the technical/professional skills and the personalized and comprehensive candidate services that consultants can provide. The parties, therefore, seek to retain the talents of their former employees, who are familiar with the party organizations and its network. National and Hill committees of both Republicans and Democrats regularly purchase the services of consultants for polling, research, and candidate consulting. Not only do the party committees hire consultants for specialized work, but they (especially the Hill committees) also provide their candidates with lists of approved and reliable consultants. Hiring a consultant off the approved list can at times be a requirement for the candidate to receive party funding. Clearly, consultants add essential resources to the parties' organizational infrastructure.

| BOX 4.2 | 527s: Here One Day, Gone the Next? |

During the 2004 campaign, 527 committees spent over a half-billion dollars. These organizations provided a unique opportunity for wealthy individuals, corporations, and unions to avoid the limits on giving established for contributions to candidates, parties, and PACs. The five 527 committees that spent the most in 2004 spent nearly half of the total amount spent by all 527 committees. However, four year later, each of these 527 organizations was entirely absent from the political scene, indicating the amorphous nature of these groups:

- *America Coming Together* (Spent $76.3 million). Funded by long-time Democratic donors such as George Soros as well as Democratic-affiliated groups such as labor unions and the Sierra Club, America Coming Together was largely aimed at get-out-the-vote efforts in battleground states. They used inventive fundraising and publicity strategies, including a series of concerts in battleground states that were headlined by acts such as Bruce Springsteen, The Dave Matthews Band, and the Dixie Chicks. However, the organization was disbanded following the 2004 election.
- *Media Fund* (Spent $54.4 million). This organization was largely supported by transfers from other Democratically affiliated 527s such as Joint Victory Campaign 2004. The committee was headed by Harold Ickes, a top advisor in the Clinton Administration, and focused largely on airing advertisements criticizing President Bush's record during the first term of his presidency. Like America Coming Together, Media Fund also disbanded following the 2004 presidential election.
- *Progress for America Fund* (Spent $35.4 million). A Republican-affiliated organization funded by loyal supporters of President Bush. This group focused largely on airing "issue advertisements" that promoted Bush's reelection or attacked John Kerry. The most famous advertisement run by this organization criticized Kerry as a "flip-flopper" while showing awkward video of Kerry windsurfing. The Fund helped promote Bush's push to privatize Social Security in 2005 and support his Supreme Court nominees that same year. But by 2008, this 527 had also ceased operations.
- *Swift Boat Veterans for Truth* (Spent $22.4 million). This organization was created exclusively to criticize Kerry's record as a Vietnam War veteran as well as his protests against that war after leaving the armed services. Most notably, the organization aired a series of advertisements that called into question the legitimacy of Kerry's war medals. Despite its apparent influence in the 2004 campaign, was disbanded in 2006.
- *Moveon.org Voter Fund* (Spent $21.2 million). Moveon.org was founded in 1998 in opposition to attempts to impeach President Clinton. In 2004, the organization used its 527 committee to air anti-Bush advertisements throughout the campaign. Known for its innovative (and sometimes controversial) advertising methods, Moveon.org held a contest asking supporters to submit their own anti-Bush ads. The winning advertisement, which was aired nationally by the group in January 2004, showed children doing blue collar jobs and asked, "Guess who's going to pay off President Bush's $1 trillion deficit?". While Moveon.org continues to thrive, the organization decided in 2008 to permanently deactivate its 527 arm.

Source: Center for Public Integrity and the Center for Responsive Politics.

STATE PARTIES

STATE PARTIES AND THE LAW

As noted in Chapter 3, there is a tendency in the United States for extensive statutory regulation of parties by the states. These regulations take an almost infinite variety of forms. Some states engage in only a minimal amount of regulation, while others have extensive party regulatory statutes. Most states regulate party membership (which voters may participate in primary elections), organizational structure, access to the general election ballot, methods of nomination, and campaign finance. There is, however, a great deal of variation among the states in the extent and manner of regulation.

Data collected by the Advisory Commission on Intergovernmental Relations demonstrates both the pervasiveness and the variety of state regulation: thirty-six states regulate the procedures used to select state committee members; thirty-two states stipulate the composition of state committees; twenty-two states specify when these committees must meet; twenty-seven states regulate their internal rules and procedures. Only five states (Alaska, Delaware, Hawaii, Kentucky, and North Carolina) do not specify some aspect of the parties' organizational structure, procedures, and composition.[28]

A major factor in the proliferation of party-regulatory statutes in the United States was the spread of the direct primary as the principal nominating device for state and congressional office. Requiring parties to nominate candidates via the primary meant that the states had to enact laws that defined parties, fixed eligibility to vote in party primaries, regulated the conduct of primary elections, and assured general election ballot access to primary winners. Regulations such as these almost mandate the existence of political parties and have made state parties quasi-public agencies. Their legal position has much in common with that of public utilities. Both the party and the utilities perform essential public functions under the protection of the law.[29] Both, however, must submit to extensive statutory regulation.

Although most state parties have a status similar to that of public utilities, the legal position of the parties is in the process of modification as a result of a series of recent Supreme Court decisions holding that political parties have First and Fourteenth Amendment rights of free political association. In the case of *Tashjian v. Connecticut* (1986), the Court ruled that Connecticut could not constitutionally ban voters who registered as independents from voting in the Republican primary after the state GOP had authorized both registered Republicans and independents to vote in a Republican primary. The Court also struck down (*Eu, Secretary of State of California v. San Francisco County Democratic Central Committee,* 1989) a series of unusually restrictive provisions in the California statutes that had banned party endorsements in primary elections, limited state chairs' terms to two years, and required the state chairpersonship to be rotated between residents of northern and southern regions of the state. The *Eu* and *Tashjian* decisions caused some to speculate about the possibility of state parties being "privatized" and freed from being treated as quasi-state agencies. However, such an outcome is highly unlikely, as it would require the abandonment by the states of primary elections as the principal means of nominating partisan candidates for public office. Because the states are not likely to take such an unpopular step and the Supreme Court is not apt to require it, continued extensive state regulation of parties will probably continue into the foreseeable future.[30]

In 1996, the Supreme Court expanded the doctrine that parties have freedom of association rights to the realm of campaign finance law. In *Colorado Republican Party v. FEC*, the Court freed parties from the spending restrictions imposed by the FECA and allowed them to engage in independent expenditures (spending not coordinated with candidates). This decision opened the way for major increases in spending by state and national parties in federal elections.

The most recent instance of the Court limiting state regulatory powers came in 2000, when the Republican and Democratic parties of California, plus several minor parties, challenged the constitutionality of the state's blanket primary law, which had been adopted by referendum in 1996. Under a blanket primary, voters are allowed to vote for candidates of different parties as long as they vote for only one candidate per office. Thus, under the blanket primary, a voter could vote in the Republican primary for governor and then vote in the Democratic primary for U.S. senator. The Supreme Court in *California Democratic Party v. Jones* (2000) struck down the blanket primary law. It declared that the blanket primary constituted a "stark repudiation of the political association" that denied parties the power to control their own nomination processes and define their identities. This decision left open the question of whether or not open primaries (primaries in which voters are not required to declare party affiliation in order to participate) are constitutional. However, the Supreme Court's recent ruling in *Washington State Grange v. Washington State Republican Party* (2008) quieted such concerns. In this decision, the Supreme Court rejected the Washington State Republican Party's claim that an open primary election (where candidates from both parties run in the same primary) would violate the parties' rights to determine which candidates it would be associated with on the ballot. The *Washington State Grange* case demonstrates that although the Court has been willing to relieve state parties of excessively burdensome regulations, it has also demonstrated that it will allow states considerable leeway in determining the nature of their electoral and party systems.

THE STATE COMMITTEES

In each of the states there is a Republican and Democratic state committee. The actual title varies, but a common title is Republican or Democratic State Central Committee. State statutes and party by-laws determine the basis for membership on the state committee. Committee members may be elected to represent counties, congressional districts, legislative districts, major municipalities, or party auxiliary groups like the Federation of Republican Women, Young Republicans, and Young Democrats. The size of these bodies varies from about twenty persons in Iowa to over a thousand in California. As the size of state committees is often unwieldy and their meetings infrequent, many state parties rely heavily upon an executive committee to carry out state committee functions between meetings. The responsibilities of the state committees include overseeing the work of the state chair and the headquarters staff, calling of state conventions, adopting party policies, supervising platform drafting, fund-raising, and assisting candidates and local organizations.

THE STATE CHAIR

With state committees composed of part-time volunteers, the person responsible for directing the activities of the state party is the state chair. Most state chairs are elected by the state committee (73 percent), although 27 percent are chosen by state party conventions. Approximately three-quarters of the state chairs are elected to two-year terms, with the balance chosen for four years. The turnover, however, is high, with tenure averaging less than three years. State parties are thus plagued with a lack of continuity in their leadership. Each chair faces a unique set of circumstances, but the main duties of the chair include supervising the headquarters staff, conducting fund-raising, recruiting candidates, serving as a party spokesperson and liaison with elected officials, and strengthening local organizations. In addition, state chairs serve as members of their parties' national committees.

THE ROLE OF THE GOVERNOR

It is an unusual governor who actively seeks to direct the affairs of the state central committee the way that presidents hold sway over the national party committees. In a nationwide study, less than 50 percent of the state party chairs reported that they believed it necessary to have the governor's approval before taking action. Most considered the governor's role in party affairs to be advisory rather than controlling.[31] And, just as governors do not exert day-by-day control over their state party organizations, such organizations play only a supportive or supplementary role in gubernatorial campaigns. In this era of candidate-centered politics, governors rely primarily upon their own personal campaign organizations.

Governors do normally seek to influence and can even control the selection of their party's state chair, lest the party machinery falls into unfriendly hands. New York and New Jersey, for example, have long traditions of governors handpicking the party chairs and expecting the designees to follow the governors' instructions. Nevertheless, because the interests of the governor and the state party are seldom identical, conflicts are not uncommon.

The actual pattern of governor–state party relations varies from those in which the state party organization is dominated by the governor and closely tied to his or her political fortunes to those exhibiting the type of outright hostility described above. A New England Democratic chair described a tightly linked governor–state party relationship as follows:

> I'm the governor's agent. My job is to work with him. If I look good, he looks good, because I'm his man. I don't bother him with messy stuff. He expects me to handle it my way. I meet with the [local] leaders on his behalf. I'm liaison to city and town leaders. (Personal interview)

Generally, this is a relationship of coordinate responsibility: The governor and state chair consult on appointments, candidate recruitments, fund-raising, and other major party activities. The governor assists the party with fund-raising and candidate recruitment, but neither the governor nor his or her staff runs the state central committee and headquarters. Likewise, the state party chair does not seek to manage the governor's campaign organization or determine gubernatorial policy.

A Republican chair in a midwestern state with a long tradition of professionalized party leadership summarized his relationship with a governor of his party as follows: "I don't go to his office and he doesn't come over here…. A lot of people think he isn't interested in the party. But that's just not true. He cares and he helps me. His attitude is, 'What can I do to help?'" The governor corroborated these comments by saying that his state party chair "doesn't want to be governor and I don't want to be party chair" (Personal interviews).

THE DEMISE OF THE TRADITIONAL STATE ORGANIZATION

Although state parties underwent revitalization in the 1970s through the 1990s, they bear scant similarity to the old-style organizations that dominated politics in the Middle Atlantic, New England, and lower Great Lakes states at the beginning of the twentieth century. These patronage-based organizations, which controlled nominations and ran their candidates' campaigns, had largely passed from the scene by the mid-1980s. Unlike their predecessor organizations, the modern-day state parties do not control nominations or run campaigns. In this new candidate-centered environment, state parties are instead service agencies for candidates and local parties, as well as the vehicles through which national parties pursue their campaign strategies.

Patronage as a basis for party organizations has been severely weakened by civil service laws, strengthened public-employee unions, and a critical public. These anti-patronage forces have been augmented by a series of Supreme Court decisions that have undermined large-scale patronage operations in both parties. In *Eldrod v. Burns* (1976), the Court ruled that the Cook County Democrats could no longer fire people on the basis of their party affiliation. This decision was followed by one declaring that the Illinois GOP could not use "party affiliation and support" as the basis for filling state jobs unless party affiliation was an "appropriate requirement" for the position (*Rutan v. Republican Party*, 1990). In once patronage-rich Illinois, the Democratic state chair has lamented that "the party no longer functions as an employment agency. More and more, we must rely on a spirit of volunteerism."[32]

Even though patronage jobs no longer provide a basis for building a strong organization, there are other forms of patronage that can be used. Gubernatorial appointments to state boards and commissions controlling gambling, licensing, hospitals, state investments, higher education, environmental and recreation policy, and cultural activities are much sought after by persons seeking policy influence, recognition, and material gain. Partisan considerations can affect state decisions regarding state contracts, bank deposits, economic development, and the purchase of professional services. These types of preferments, however, are useful to the party primarily for fund-raising, and they do not provide campaign workers the way large-scale patronage operations did.

THE SERVICE-ORIENTED STATE ORGANIZATION OF THE 2000s

To survive and perform a meaningful role in current state politics, the parties have had to adapt to an environment characterized by

- An absence of large-scale patronage

- Candidate-centered campaigns often staffed by professional consultants and funded in significant degree by PACs
- Heightened interparty competition for statewide offices
- Strengthened national party organizations

In adapting to these conditions, the state party organizations have become service agencies to their candidates and local affiliates. The institutionalization of state parties as campaign service organizations parallels the resurgence of party organizations at the national level, where a massive fund-raising capacity has transformed the once weak RNC and DNC into major service agencies to candidates and state/local parties. There are also parallels between the major campaign roles played at the national level by the senatorial and congressional campaign committees and state legislative campaign committees, which have emerged as the principal party campaign resource for state legislative candidates.

Among the indicators of the evolution of most state parties into organizations capable of providing significant services to candidates and local parties are (1) permanent headquarters; (2) professional leadership and staffing; (3) adequate budgets; and (4) programs to maintain the organization, support candidates and officeholders, and assist local party units.[33]

- *Permanent Headquarters.* As late as the 1970s, state parties frequently were ad hoc operations run out of the offices or homes of the state chairs. This type of operation has now largely ceased to exist as the parties have established permanent headquarters in the state capital. These headquarters are increasingly located in modern office buildings stocked with high-tech equipment for data processing, fund-raising, communications, and printing. For example, the Wisconsin GOP has a three-story building well stocked with high-tech equipment. It contains a telemarketing center capable of contacting 400,000 persons per day, computers that link up with every media outlet in the state (with reporters' names listed by legislative and congressional district), a computer-based research facility, a finance center, and office space for political operatives. The degree to which headquarters use up-to-date technology depends upon the parties' financial resources, but almost all have some form of computerized voter database that is used for fund-raising, mailings, voter registration, voter contact, and recruitment of volunteers. In creating these databases, the national party organizations frequently provided technical assistance. In terms of utilization, there are party differences. Republican organizations have emphasized fund-raising, whereas the Democrats have found the databases most useful for contacting voters, providing election-day reminders and information to voters, and recruiting volunteers. The state parties also operate sophisticated Web sites and maintain extensive social networking platforms that allow them to mobilize supporters during a hotly contested campaign or policy debate.
- *Professional Staffing.* In the 1960s, most state party headquarters operated with a minimal staff—often only an executive director, a secretary, and a few volunteers. However, twenty-first-century campaigning and party building require extensive and professionalized staffing, and therefore full-time professional leadership is now the norm. In 2000, 54 percent of the state chairs

worked full time in their positions, compared to approximately one-third in 1984. Nearly every state organization has a full-time executive director, and a majority also have a field staff, public relations director, research staff, comptroller, and fund-raiser.[34] The average headquarters has a staff of nine in election years, plus seven part-time employees. The Florida parties, for example, have well-developed staffs. The state GOP headquarters has regularly had a staff of twenty-five, plus several part-time employees, and the Democrats have had a staff of sixteen, with four part-time workers.[35] In spite of the progress the state parties have made in professionalized staffing, they constantly have to confront the problem of high turnover in staff leadership positions. The tenure of state chairs averages only two years, and senior political operatives tend to be transients who move about the country from job to job with party organizations, candidates, and consulting firms, often following leads provided by national party organizations.

- *Finances.* Operating a professionalized headquarters, of course, requires an ability to raise significant amounts of money on a continuing basis. Nearly every state party is now equipped with the technology to operate direct-mail fund-raising in addition to more traditional methods such as dinners, large-contributor programs, and contributions from allied groups. John H. Aldrich's 1999 survey found that the average state party's election-year budget was $2.8 million.[36] National averages, however, mask the extent to which some state parties are capable of raising prodigious amounts of money. For example, the New York State GOP has demonstrated the ability to raise over $20 million.[37] It should also be noted that state parties receive and spend large sums that are transferred to them from the national party organizations.

- *Party Programs for Support of Candidates and Party Building.* Since the 1960s, state parties have expanded their activities in the areas of candidate support and party building. In terms of support for candidates, over 80 percent make financial contributions to gubernatorial, state constitutional, congressional, and legislative candidates.[38] State parties also provide a variety of campaign services—polling, fund-raising assistance, media consulting, and campaign seminars. Most also operate large-scale voter mobilization programs that include registration drives, voter identification and voter-list maintenance, phone banks, and assistance with absentee ballots. State parties also engaged in such party-building activities as publishing newsletters, conducting leadership-training sessions, conducting polls, recruiting candidates, sharing mailing lists with local units, and conducting joint county-state fund-raisers and get-out-the-vote drives.

Although the state parties have become organizationally stronger and capable of providing a broader array of campaign services than in the past, the key to understanding their role in campaigns is to recognize that they play a supplementary role to that of the candidates' own personal organizations. The parties can help with money, voter-mobilization activities, some technical services (e.g., polling, consulting), and volunteers. Campaigning in the American states is not party centered. Instead, it is candidate centered, and therefore the party organizations rarely control nominations and they do not run campaigns. Rather, candidates create their own personal organizations to secure party nominations in the primaries and contest the general elections.

STATE LEGISLATIVE CAMPAIGN COMMITTEES

Increasingly important elements of the state party organizational structure are the legislative campaign committees. These organizations are fashioned after the congressional and senatorial campaign committees at the national level. They are composed of incumbent legislators who raise funds and hire staff to assist their parties' legislative candidates. In some states, these committees have become substantially more important than the regular state party as a source of support for legislative candidates. Indeed, legislative campaign committees have emerged in most states as the principal party support mechanism for legislative candidates.[39] The most active legislative campaign committees are found in states with high levels of interparty competition, high campaign costs (candidate expenditures exceeding $500,000 are no longer unusual), and weak state central committees. The development of strong legislative campaign committees is also associated with high levels of legislative professionalism—full-time legislators who are paid a reasonable salary and are supported by ample staff. As legislative service has increased in value and competition for control of legislative chambers has intensified, legislative leaders have created campaign committees to protect their own interests as well as those of the party and individual legislators.

Legislative campaign committees in many of the states have become full-service campaign organizations that closely resemble regular party organizations in that they provide candidates with money, campaign staff, and technical services (media consulting and, in some instances, polls), and in some states they even get involved in voter-mobilization activities. In Pennsylvania, for example, the Republican legislative committees in the House and Senate raised a combined $10.7 million in 2008, while Democratic legislative committees reported receipts of $9 million.[40]

Legislative campaign committees follow a strategy of concentrating their resources on close races in an effort to either maintain or win control of legislative chambers. Minority parties therefore tend to support challengers to a greater extent than do majority parties. As is true of the national House and Senate campaign committees, their state-level counterparts target their resources on competitive races—those of vulnerable incumbents, strong challengers, and open seat candidates. A recent survey of party funding of legislative candidates found that 80 percent of Republican funds and 50 percent of Democratic money went to nonincumbents. This interparty difference reflects the fact that the Democrats have been the majority party and the Republicans the minority party in most state legislatures in recent decades.[41]

Although shared goals, party loyalty, and personal associations encourage an element of cooperation and coordination between legislative campaign committees and state central committees, legislative campaign committees tend to operate independently. They are run by legislative leaders and they service primarily the agendas and priorities of legislative partisans. This gives them autonomy and freedom from the agendas of state central committees and both presidential and gubernatorial campaign organizations.[42]

| BOX 4.3 | CONVICTIONS REVEAL THE PREVALENCE OF MACHINE POLITICS IN CHICAGO |

In July, 2006, several high-level Chicago officials in Mayor Richard Daley's (D-Ill.) administration were convicted on several counts of mail fraud for their role in arranging for particular applicants to receive city jobs as political patronage. The federal government's case against Daley's aides also unveiled the strength and pervasiveness of Daley's Democratic Party machine. During the trial, city officials testified that the defendants held phony job interviews and falsified ratings forms to assure that candidates preferred by the party machine received city positions. Former city officials from departments such as Streets and Sanitation testified during the trial that they hired and promoted employees based on lists of names they received from Daley's assistants, names of people who were being rewarded for supporting and working for the election of Democratic machine politicians. As one of the prosecuting attorneys said after the guilty verdict, "This case was about the creation of a new machine, a corrupt jobs machine, a machine that stole jobs that should have gone to qualified applicants without political favor and instead went to fuel the political armies."

But the machine corruption revealed in 2006 was hardly new. Even as recently as 1997, several *Chicago Tribune* reporters spent months trying to untangle what happened at a single city council meeting. During that meeting, the elected officials, all part of the Daley machine, made approximately 21 decisions per minute without real debate, decisions that mostly involved the extension of political favors to machine supporters. Past convictions of high-level Chicago officials for similar offenses did little to prevent the present-day abuses. As *Tribune* reporter Patrick T. Reardon noted during the 2006 trial, "News stories and criminal trials won't really make a dent ... as long as one party dominates Chicago government so completely, corruption will never disappear."

Source: Patrick T. Reardon, "The Price of Our City's Efficiency: Corruption," *Chicago Tribune*, July 2, 2006; Rudolph Bush and Dan Mihalopolous, "Daley Jobs Chief Guilty," *Chicago Tribune*, July 7, 2006.

COUNTY AND LOCAL PARTIES

THE PARTY MACHINE

The most familiar type of local party organization is the big city machine, best exemplified by the Cook County Democratic Organization during the era of Mayor Richard J. Daley.[43] Urban machines were most prevalent in the late 1800s and into the mid-1900s. This organization was run as a hierarchy by the mayor, who worked through his ward leaders and their precinct captains. The organization was sustained by patronage. Ten thousand city jobs were distributed on the basis of patronage. A single ward leader could have as many as 500 jobs to distribute to his followers. The organization's ward and precinct leaders also served as ombudsmen, assisting residents with their problems in dealing with governmental agencies. Loyalty to the organization and its candidates was achieved through the material or tangible rewards that the organization provided; issues and ideology were secondary.

Urban party machines were in many ways an enigma. At their core, they were inherently undemocratic, as votes were routinely bought with favors, jobs, or money. Machine politicians were often ruthless in their pursuit of support, willing to pay whatever it would take to stay in power and then make staying in power pay off for them. Yet machines are often remembered fondly for their attention to poor citizens and immigrants for whom the machines were an important source of aid; after all, these citizens often provided the "cheapest" source of votes for the party machine. But much of the rewards that machines were able to distribute to supporters came from big businesses that benefited greatly from a machine's ability to steer favorable contracts their way. In addition, urban machines often avoided dealing with important issues since doing so was unnecessary for winning elections.

LOCAL PARTIES TODAY

Traditional organizations still function in a few places such as Chicago, Philadelphia, and Albany. One of the most professional and effective party organizations is the Republican Party of Nassau County (Long Island), New York. Most members of the party executive committee hold patronage positions in county government; the county chair is a full-time salaried leader; the party raises more money than the GOP state committee, owns a three-story headquarters building, operates its own printing plant and artist's studio, and makes extensive use of pollsters.[44] Indeed, this organization has emerged as the strongest force in New York state Republican politics. Yet urban machines have largely faded from the political landscape, the casualties of progressive reforms such as the Australian (secret) Ballot, which prevents party leaders from knowing who someone voted for; the party primary, which removes the control that party leaders have over the party nomination; and civil service reform, which prohibits machines from using government jobs as rewards to supporters.

There are well-funded and professionalized local parties based upon volunteers rather than patronage. One of the most effective is the GOP of Santa Clara County, California. It has a paid executive director, a headquarters complete with computerized volunteer and voter lists, and a sophisticated targeting system for reaching voters.[45] Such organizations, however, are not the norm for American local politics.

Most county parties are not bureaucratic or hierarchically run organizations. Their leaders and workers are part-time volunteers; there is no permanent headquarters or paid staff; and activity is not a year-round phenomenon, but rather cyclical and concentrated around campaign season. Although it has been commonplace to assert that parties are in a state of decline and may even be dying, case studies of local parties and national surveys reveal substantial party activity at the county level. A force that may cause county parties to become more effective is the increased interest in local parties being demonstrated by the national party committees. As their fund-raising capacity has increased, the Republicans, in particular, have been providing financial and technical assistance to county parties.

DOES PARTY ORGANIZATION MAKE A DIFFERENCE?

A key question concerning party organizations is whether or not they can make a difference in determining election outcomes. Journalistic reports and scholarly case studies provide evidence that the party organization can have a critical impact. The benefits of having a party organizational strength advantage over the opposition party were dramatically demonstrated during the hotly contested post-election recount and challenge phase of the Florida presidential election in 2000. The well-organized and amply funded Florida State Republican Party was turned overnight into a full-fledged operative arm of the Bush campaign. The three-story party headquarters was turned over to Bush lawyers and strategists; thirty employees scheduled for after-election layoff were put at round-the-clock service to the Bush organization; party workers observed every court clerk's office to act as an early warning system for surprise motions and orders; and state Republicans handed out disposable cameras to document questionable vote counting and evidence bags to gather disputed chads.[46]

Recent studies by political scientists also document the impact of party organizational strength and electoral activity. Thus analyses of gubernatorial elections show that the party with an organizational strength advantage gains increments of voters over the opposition party.[47] The relationship between party organizational strength and electoral success is complex, and the organization's impact is often indirect in character. A strong party organization can provide the infrastructure for candidates and activists (1) to continue the battle in the face of short-term defeats and enduring minority status; and (2) to take advantage of favorable circumstances when they arise (e.g., the retirement of a popular opposition party incumbent, divisiveness within the dominant party, or low approval ratings for an incumbent president). In spite of commentaries in the media about the decline of parties, political science research reveals vibrant campaign activity at the local grass roots.[48]

THE PARTY ACTIVISTS

Party organizations require officers, workers, and volunteers—political activists willing to give their time, talents, and treasure for the success of the party and its candidates. There are a variety of incentives that cause people to become actively involved in political activity.

INCENTIVES TO PARTICIPATE

PATRONAGE AND PREFERMENTS Some people become involved in politics because of direct material rewards. Patronage—awarding government jobs to the supporters of the winning candidate—has a long tradition in American politics, dating at least to the era of Jacksonian democracy. Andrew Jackson believed that "to the victor belong the spoils" and that the average citizen was qualified to hold appointive governmental office.[49] Patronage appointees traditionally have been a major source of party workers. Civil service laws (appointment on the basis of merit, using competitive examinations), reform movements, and court decisions have reduced the number of patronage positions available for the parties to fill. At the federal level, for example, the number of positions available for distribution to presidential supporters is extremely limited due to civil service laws. Out of a total federal civilian workforce of 2.7 million persons, only about 3,000 full-time federal jobs are open to political appointees. Even in Chicago, the once-vast patronage army (10,000 jobs were once at the disposal of the mayor, aldermen, ward committeemen, and the heads of various agencies) that maintained Mayor Richard J. Daley's

Democratic machine is now only a shadow of its former self. Daley's son, who became mayor in 1989, has not sought to base his power on a revival of the old patronage system. Today Chicago's patronage is primarily of the "pinstripe" variety. That is, city business is funneled to firms that assist candidates in raising the big money needed for advertising and computerized mailings, which have, to a large degree, replaced the armies of patronage workers. For example, in the year after Richard M. Daley's election, over half of the legal business of the city was channeled to a firm that had raised more money for Daley than any other city law firm. Other businesses that aided the mayor's campaign also were rewarded with city contracts.[50]

There remain state governments (e.g., New Jersey, Pennsylvania, Illinois, and Indiana) in which patronage continues to thrive. For example, in New Jersey, the governor appoints all department heads, plus state judges, state and county prosecutors, tax officials, and many salaried and unsalaried commission, board, and authority members. However, even in states with long traditions of patronage-based policies, patronage is on the decline. Thus, Indiana discontinued the practice of giving lucrative franchises for dispensing auto and driver's licenses to county party leaders, who in turn were expected to kick back part of the proceeds to the state party.

Not all patronage is dispensed by governmental executives. Members of Congress, state legislators, and city council members normally hire their staffs on the basis of political loyalty. These officials may also exert heavy influence on the appointments made by the executive branch. Some executive appointments are actually controlled by legislators, as in the case of senatorial influence over the appointment of federal judges, marshals, and attorneys. In spite of its organization-building potential, patronage poses problems for party leaders. As noted above, the pool of available patronage jobs is shrinking due to civil service laws, strong public employee unions, tight budgets, privatization of governmental functions, and court decisions. A further problem for the parties in making patronage appointments is that governmental jobs may carry with them qualifications that deserving party workers cannot meet—such as legal training or skill in operating sophisticated equipment. In addition, most available patronage positions have little appeal to the educated, middle-class persons that the parties are seeking to enlist in their ranks. Traditionally, patronage has been most appealing to the disadvantaged. A final problem for party leaders is the fact that elected officials may seek to use their appointing power to build a personal following rather than to strengthen the more inclusive party organization.

Patronage jobs are not the only material incentive available to political leaders. Governmental officials can give preferential treatment ("preferments") to persons they are seeking to recruit into party service or reward for past service. Preference in the awarding of government contracts has been a traditional way of rewarding business leaders who supported the winning candidate. The importance of government contracts to the construction industry has been a major reason for the industry's involvement in campaign finance. Preference can also be extended through administrative decisions and leniency in the enforcement of governmental regulations. Heavily regulated businesses (e.g., liquor, transportation) are normally involved in politics in a major way.

ELECTED OFFICE   Holding major elected office carries with it prestige and power not found in most patronage positions. Party involvement can provide a stepping-stone to elective office. There are today few party organizations that are so strong that they can guarantee a party nomination to a preferred candidate. At the same time, party involvement and the support derived from party workers can be an essential ingredient in securing the nomination to a key office. The allure of public office, for example, is quite strong among state party chairs, who frequently run for high-status offices such as governor or senator. Because parties play a significant role in nominations and have control over important campaign resources, incumbent officeholders frequently play an active part in party affairs. This involvement helps them hold their existing positions secure and provides a basis for moving up the ladder of elected positions.

SOCIAL BENEFITS   Not all the benefits of political participation are based upon material rewards. There are also solidary or social benefits. The friendships and camaraderie of the organization can be a strong force that binds individuals to the party. Similarly, the sense of recognition that an individual feels when a prominent elected official calls him or her by name in a crowd, personally acknowledges letters or phone calls, or extends an invitation to a social gathering can cause individuals to engage in political work on a continuing basis. Studies of party activists in a number of cities such as Houston, Los Angeles, and Chicago have consistently shown that important reasons for participation in party politics include "social contacts and friendships," "personal recognition," and the "fun and excitement of campaigns." And the longer people participate in party work, the more important such personal motivations become. Although many first engaged in political activity out of concern for issues or ideology, the longer they participated the less important these concerns became as group solidarity incentives took a greater prominence.[51] Parties have recently tried to capitalize on these incentives by using social networking sites to organize activists and encouraging campaign work among small groups of friends and family.

ISSUES AND IDEOLOGY   Politics ultimately involves determining the direction that governmental policy will take. It is thus not surprising that an important motivational force for participation is concern for issues and ideology. Concern for public policy is especially important in creating a stimulus for entry into party work. Persons anxious about health care, schools, abortion, civil rights, women's rights, the environment, and the scope of government activity can be stimulated to take part in politics. A variety of studies focusing upon party activists operating in different settings—from local party organizations to national conventions—indicate that issue-oriented incentives have become more common in American politics. The trend toward advocacy parties has also been revealed in studies of county-level leaders of presidential campaigns as well as Republican and Democratic county chairs. These party leadership corps tend to contain a large proportion of "true believers"—persons driven by a commitment to enact specific policies or ideology. These activists may also be viewed as "purists": they want to win elections, but they are prepared to lose if unable to convince the electorate to endorse their policies.[52]

THE DISTINCTIVENESS OF ACTIVISTS

Most Americans' political involvement seldom extends beyond the minimal act of periodically voting. Political activists are therefore set apart from the average citizen by their high levels of political participation. They also have other distinctive characteristics. First, activists tend to come from families that are active and interested in politics. Second, party activists are generally of relatively high socioeconomic status. Politics takes time, knowledge, and financial resources. These commodities tend to be concentrated among the middle and upper middle classes. The party leadership corps are not, therefore, necessarily representative demographically of their party's voters. Analysis of the social backgrounds of state party chairs demonstrates this tendency of political leaders to come from upper middle-class backgrounds. In 2008, 66 percent of Republican national convention delegates had incomes in excess of $75,000 compared to 39 percent of rank-and-file Republican voters, while 70 percent of Democratic delegates had that level of income compared to 26 percent of Democratic voters generally.[53]

Party activists are also distinguishable from ordinary voters in terms of ideological orientation. Activists are much more likely to view the world from an ideological perspective and to adopt a liberal or conservative position on issues. As would be expected, Democratic and Republican activists tend to see politics from differing ideological vantage points, with Democrats being significantly more liberal than Republicans. Studies of national convention delegates have consistently documented the substantial ideological differences between Republicans and Democrats. As can be seen in Table 4.2, Democratic and Republican delegates are further apart ideologically than are rank-and-file voters of the two parties. There is also an ideology gap between each party's activists and its party voters. Table 4.2 also illustrates this pattern by comparing the ideology of national convention delegates with that of party voters. Republican activists are much more conservative than GOP voters, whereas Democratic leaders were somewhat closer to their party's voters in 2008.

TABLE 4.2 | THE IDEOLOGY OF NATIONAL CONVENTION DELEGATES, PARTY VOTERS, AND ALL VOTERS: A COMPARISON, 2008 (IN PERCENT)

Political Views	Democratic Delegates	Democratic Voters	All Voters	Republican Voters	Republican Delegates
Very liberal	19	15	8	2	*
Somewhat liberal	22	34	18	4	*
Moderate	50	34	36	30	26
Somewhat conservative	2	10	20	33	28
Very conservative	1	6	15	30	40

*Less than 1 percent.

Source: *New York Times*/CBS Poll.

BOX 4.4 | WHY PARTIES POLARIZE: THE ROLE OF PARTY ACTIVISTS

Political scientists have long sought to understand why parties take the positions they do on issues. Anthony Downs popularized the idea of the median voter theorem, which states that in a two-party winner-take-all system (the type of system that exists in the United States) the two parties should take very similar positions near the center of the ideological spectrum. Yet, as noted in previous chapters, the Democrats and Republicans do not exactly follow the median voter theorem. In fact, they take distinct positions on many issues and in recent decades have become increasingly polarized. But why is this the case?

One explanation is that parties seek more than simply votes. The important point to remember about parties is that votes are not the only goods that they are seeking. Other resources are also critical, including financial contributions and personnel. Even if a party took the most strategic positions on the issues to win the maximum number of votes, without money (to pay for all forms of advertising) and personnel (to go door-to-door, make phone calls, etc.) they may not be able to inform the electorate about those positions. As Table 4.2 indicates, party activists—those giving their time and their money to the party's cause—tend to hold positions that are more polarized than the mass electorate. As a result, to court the help and support of these activists, parties must take positions on the issues that may not be optimal for winning the general election. John Kerry faced this dilemma when he found it necessary to vote against a budget authorization for the Iraq War even though he had previously voted in favor of the military intervention. The vote against the authorization was largely attributed to his need to appeal to Democratic activists prior to the campaign for the Democratic presidential nomination. Thus, one way to understand why politicians and parties do not always take centrist positions is to recall the influence of the more ideological party activists.

Source: John H. Aldrich, *Why Parties?* (Chicago: University of Chicago Press, 1995).

PARTY ORGANIZATIONS AS NETWORKS OF ISSUE-ORIENTED ACTIVISTS

Issue and ideological concerns have become so important as a motivation for participation that party organizations are increasingly becoming "issue-based networks of participatory activists."[54] The influence of the Christian Right within the Republican Party is one manifestation of this pattern; the influence of pro-choice, gay rights, environmental, and affirmative action supporters in the Democratic Party is another. The source of this trend toward party organizations based upon issue-oriented activists "can be traced to a series of complex interacting forces: the emergence of a range of culture/social issues such as abortion, school prayer, women's rights, law and order, gay rights, and environmentalism; broad socioeconomic trends, such as rising levels of educational attainment, a shrinking blue-collar workforce, and increased white-collar employment; plus, the decline in the availability of patronage as an incentive to participate in politics."[55]

The ideological orientations of party activists have profound implications for the functioning of the American political system, because these are the individuals

BOX 4.5	TALK RADIO FOR LIBERALS? THE INTERNET GIVES LIBERAL ACTIVISTS A VOICE WITH INFLUENCE IN THE DEMOCRATIC PARTY

During the 1990s, talk radio gave a voice to conservative Republicans frustrated with the direction of the federal government. Most famously, Rush Limbaugh's program became so popular with conservative Americans that Limbaugh himself gained a great deal of influence within the Republican Party. Since Bill Clinton left the White House, the Internet has played an increasingly similar role for liberal activists in the Democratic Party. Moveon.org, an organization that began as a Web site in 1998, has built what many view as the most important non-union activist and financial force in the Democratic Party. The liberal blog DailyKos has become so widely read among liberal activists that candidates now actively court its creator, Markos Moulitsas. In fact, Moulitsas gained such an important profile in the party that he appeared in campaign ads for Democratic congressional candidates in 2006. These and other Internet sites provide the party with easily mobilized resources, but they also create a more difficult balancing act for Democrats seeking to balance the party's liberal wing with members who are more moderate. For example, both Moveon.org and Moulitsas openly campaigned against Senator Joe Lieberman (D-Conn.) in his 2006 reelection campaign because they viewed Lieberman as too accommodating to Republicans.

While Republicans have also used the Internet as a resource, it has been more critical for Democratic activists, who are more than twice as likely as Republicans to volunteer online and five times more likely than Republicans to contribute money online. The continuing popularity of conservative talk shows hosted by Limbaugh, Sean Hannity, and others gives Republican activities an outlet that Democrats have now found on the Web. But this venue for liberal Democrats also worries some moderates in the party such as Representative Tim Roemer (D-Ind.), who warns, "The Internet is certainly a generator of some very positive factors for Democrats. But it's also a very small slice of our party, and if that slice dominates the entire pie, we're in serious trouble."

Source: "The Internet and Democrats," Ronald Brownstein, National Journal, July 1, 2005.

---

who have influence over nominations, party policy positions, and campaign strategy. In fact, party activists are one force driving the recent polarization of the Democratic and Republican parties. There is substantial evidence that the party activists of both parties have become more ideologically polarized in recent years.[56] This increasing polarization has provided a foundation of support for candidates taking more extreme positions on issues, support that has become more crucial to winning party nominations. For example, early in his first term as president, George W. Bush took action to restrict the amount of stem cell research that the government would fund. While the move was widely unpopular among the general public, it appealed to many ideological activists within the Republican Party. Bush's move demonstrated how politicians often choose to go against a majority of the public in order to appeal to party activists, the result of which is an increasing polarization of political elites in both parties.

Although there is an overall tendency for Republican activists to be conservative and Democratic leaders to be liberal, neither party's activists constitute a monolithic bloc. As a result, there is constant tension within each party between the "true believers," who reject compromise and want party policy to reflect their policy views, and those activists of a more moderate persuasion, who are willing to compromise on ideology in order to attract a wider spectrum of voters and win elections. Nowhere is this tension more apparent than in presidential nominating politics, where ideologically committed activists exert a powerful influence over the delegate selection process and occasionally even the nominee's vice presidential selection. John McCain's choice of Sarah Palin as his running mate in 2008 was at least partly driven by the candidate's need to appeal to the more socially conservative activists in the Republican Party.

In addition, activists are an important constituency of candidates. Candidates need campaign workers and financial contributors, and they need them before they make their appeals to the mass electorate in the general election. Winning elections first requires putting together a campaign organization, obtaining adequate financing, and securing a party nomination. In these endeavors, party activists are especially important. But these middle-class activists are not apt to be attracted by material rewards like patronage. It is therefore necessary to motivate them through intangible rewards—such as participation in a just cause. Because of the need to appeal to an activist constituency that is more liberal in the Democratic Party and more conservative in the Republican Party than rank-and-file party voters, it is often difficult for centrist candidates to secure their parties' presidential nomination. A candidate for the Republican presidential nomination needs strong conservative credentials to appeal to the activist constituency that plays a dominant role in nominations, whereas Democratic presidential aspirants need to demonstrate their liberal credentials.

PARTY ORGANIZATIONS: ADAPTABLE AND DURABLE

As voters during the 1960s and 1970s were shown to be less influenced by partisan considerations and as competing types of organizations like PACs, campaign/media consulting firms, and candidate organizations gained heightened prominence, there were dire predictions about the future of party organizations. One prominent journalist who espoused the thesis of party decline even wrote a book entitled *The Party's Over*.[57] This chapter's survey of party organizations in America demonstrates that parties have shown qualities of adaptiveness and durability in a changing political environment. In fact, there is undoubtedly evidence of increased organizational strength, especially among national party organizations and party activist networks. It has also been shown that party organizations can have an impact on a party's capacity to win elections. American parties, however, are characterized by a complex set of power relationships with both diffused and hierarchical elements. They function under unusually restrictive statutory regulations, and they exist in a wide variety of forms with differing levels of effectiveness.

POLITICAL PARTY WEB SITES

Democratic National Committee:
http://www.democrats.org

DNC Facebook Page:
http://www.facebook.com/democrats

DNC Twitter Account:
http://twitter.com/democratsdotorg

Democratic Congressional Campaign Committee:
http://www.dccc.org

Democratic Senatorial Campaign Committee:
http://www.dscc.org

Republican National Committee:
http://www.gop.com

RNC Facebook Page:
http://www.facebook.com/GOP

RNC Twitter Account:
http://twitter.com/rnc

National Republican Congressional Committee:
http://www.nrcc.org

National Republican Senatorial Committee:
http://www.nrsc.org

All state Democratic and Republican parties also maintain Web sites that can be accessed through the DNC and RNC sites.

Green Party:
http://www.gp.org

Libertarian Party:
http://www.lp.org

Reform Party:
http://www.reformparty.org

NOTES

1. V. O. Key, Jr., *Politics, Parties, and Pressure Groups*, 5th ed. (New York: Crowell, 1964), p. 316.
2. Ibid.
3. Samuel J. Eldersveld and Hanes Walton, Jr., *Political Parties in American Society*, 2nd ed. (New York: Bedford/St. Martin's, 2000), p. 106.
4. Ibid.
5. Joseph S. Schlesinger argues that these candidate organizations are basic units of the party. See his "The New American Political Party," *American Political Science Review* 79 (Dec. 1985): 1152–1169.
6. Mildred A. Schwartz, *The Party Network: The Robust Organizations of Illinois Republicans* (Madison: University of Wisconsin Press, 1990).
7. The development of the national committees into institutionalized bureaucracies is described in Cornelius P. Cotter and John F. Bibby, "Institutional Development of Parties and the Thesis of Party Decline," *Political Science Quarterly* 95 (Spring 1980): 1–27.
8. Cornelius P. Cotter and Bernard C. Hennessy, *Politics without Power: The National Party Committees* (New York: Atherton, 1964).

9. For an in-depth analysis of out-party national committees, see Philip A. Klinkner, *The Losing Parties: Out-Party National Committee, 1956–1993* (New Haven, Conn.: Yale University Press, 1994).

10. For an insightful analysis of the differing political cultures of the Republican and Democratic parties, see Jo Freeman, "The Political Culture of the Democrats and Republicans," *Political Science Quarterly* 101, no. 3(1986): 327–356; see also Klinkner, *The Losing Parties*, ch. 10.

11. James R. Dickenson, "DNC Withdraws Recognition of 7 Caucuses," *Washington Post*, May 18, 1985, p. A7; Peter Bragdon, "DNC Approves Kirk's Plan to Alter Democrats' Image," *Congressional Quarterly Weekly Report* (June 29, 1985), p. 1287.

12. John F. Bibby and Robert J. Huckshorn, "Out-Party Strategy: Republican National Committee Rebuilding Politics, 1964–66," in Bernard Cosman and Robert J. Huckshorn, eds., *Republican Politics: The 1964 Campaign and Its Aftermath for the Party* (New York: Praeger, 1968), pp. 205–233.

13. Based on a Lexis-Nexis search of major newspapers conducted by the author from February 15, 2005 through May 15, 2006.

14. *Wall Street Journal*, May 1, 1998, p. A1.

15. Richard L. Berke, "GOP's National Chairman Resigning after a Brief Term," *New York Times* (national edition), Dec. 1, 2001, p. A11.

16. "The Vote Processor," *The Economist*, Aug. 13, 1994, p. 30. On DNC payments to Clinton's consultants, see Elizabeth Drew, *On the Edge: The Clinton Presidency* (New York: Simon and Schuster, 1994), p. 124.

17. Howard Kurtz, "Bush Using End Run around Capital Media," *Washington Post*, Feb. 16, 2001, p. A4.

18. David S. Broder, "A Neglected Democratic Party," *Washington Post*, June 14, 1978; David S. Broder, "A.K.A. Difficult Circumstances," *Washington Post*, March 4, 1981; David Adamany, "Political Parties in the 1980s," in Michael J. Malbin, ed., *Money and Politics in the United States* (Chatham, N.J.: Chatham House, 1984), p. 86. For a historical account of White House–national committee relations, see James W. Davis, *The President as Party Leader* (New York: Greenwood, 1993), ch. 5.

19. David S. Broder, "The Road Back," *The Washington Post*, Jan. 20, 1994, C7.

20. Cornelius P. Cotter and Bernard Hennessy, *Politics without Power* (New York: Atherton, 1964).

21. *Democratic Party of the United States of America v. Bronson C. LaFollette*, 449 U.S. 897 (1981), and *Cousins v. Wigoda*, 419 U.S. 477 (1975).

22. The contrasting patterns of party centralization are discussed more fully in John F. Bibby, "Party Renewal in the National Republican Party," in Gerald Pomper, ed., *Party Renewal in America: Theory and Practice* (New York: Praeger, 1981), pp. 102–115.

23. See John F. Bibby, "State Party Organizations: Coping and Adapting to Candidate-Centered Politics and Nationalization," in Maisel, *The Parties Respond*, pp. 41–46; John F. Bibby, "Party Networks: National–State Integration, Allied Groups and Issue Activists," in John G. Green and Daniel M. Shea, eds., *The State of the Parties: The Changing Role of Contemporary American Parties*, 3rd ed. (Lanham, Md.: Rowman & Lit-tlefield, 1999), ch. 5.

24. Raymond J. LaRaja, "State and Local Parties," in Michael J. Malbin, ed., *Election After Reform: Money, Politics, and the Bipartisan Campaign Reform Act* (Lanham, Md.: Rowman & Littlefield, 2006).

25. Based on Federal Election Commission resources.

26. David R. Mayhew, *Placing Parties in American Politics* (Princeton, N.J.: Princeton University Press, 1986), p. 324.

27. Robin Kolodny and Angela Logan, "Political Consultants and the Extension

of Party Goals," *P.S.* 31 (June 1998): 156.

28. For a detailed analysis of state regulation of parties, see *The Transformation of American Politics: Implications for Federalism* (Washington, D.C.: Advisory Commission in Intergovernmental Relations, 1986), pp. 123–160.

29. For an insightful consideration of political parties as public utilities, see Leon D. Epstein, *Political Parties in the American Mold* (Madison: University of Wisconsin Press, 1986), ch. 6.

30. For informed commentary on Supreme Court decisions affecting state parties, see Jack W. Peltason, "The Constitutional Law of Parties," in Nelson W. Polsby and Raymond E. Wolfinger, eds., *On Parties: Essays Honoring Austin Ranney* (Berkeley: Institute of Government Press, University of California, Berkeley, 1999), pp. 16–18; and Leon D. Epstein, "The American Party Primary," in Nelson W. Polsby and Raymond E. Wolfinger, eds., *On Parties: Essays Honoring Austin Ranney* (Berkeley: Institute of Government Press, University of California, Berkeley, 1999), pp. 189–199.

31. Cornelius P. Cotter, James L. Gibson, John F. Bibby, and Robert J. Huckshorn, *Party Organizations in American Politics* (New York: Praeger, 1984), pp. 111–112.

32. A. James Reichley, The Life of the Parties: A History of American Political Parties (New York: Free Press, 1992), p. 385.

33. Cotter et al., *Party Organizations in American Politics*, pp. 13–40; Reichley, *The Life of the Parties*, pp. 386–391; John H. Aldrich, "Southern Politics in State and Nation," *Journal of Politics* 62 (August 2000): 643–670; Andrew M. Appleton and Daniel S. Ward, eds., *State Party Profiles: A 50-State Guide to the Development, Organization, and Resources* (Washington, D.C.: CQ Press, 1996); and Reichley, *The Life of the Parties*, pp. 386–391.

34. Aldrich, "Southern Politics," p. 656.

35. Appleton and Ward, *State Party Profiles*, p. 62.

36. Aldrich, "Southern Politics," p. 665.

37. Center for Public Integrity Party Lines Project (http://www.publicintegrity.org/projects/entry/296/)

38. Aldrich, "Southern Politics," p. 659.

39. For a detailed analysis of legislative campaign committees, see Anthony Gierzynski, *Legislative Party Campaign Committees in the American States* (Lexington: University of Kentucky Press, 1992); and Daniel M. Shea, *Transforming Democracy: Legislative Campaign Committees and Political Parties* (Albany: State University Press of New York, 1995).

40. National Institute on Money in State Politics (http://www.followthemoney.org/).

41. Anthony Gierzynski and David A. Breaux, "The Financing Role of Parties," in Joel A. Thompson and Gary F. Moncrief, eds., *Campaign Finance in State Legislative Elections* (Washington, D.C.: CQ Press, 1998), pp. 195–196.

42. Frank J. Sorauf, *Inside Campaign Finance: Myths and Realities* (New Haven, Conn.: Yale University Press, 1992), p. 120. See also Daniel M. Shea, "The Development of Legislative Campaign Committees: A Second Look," *American Review of Politics* 15 (Summer 1994): 213–234.

43. For a complete survey of traditional party organizations, see David R. Mayhew, *Placing Parties in American Politics* (Princeton, N.J.: Princeton University Press, 1986).

44. Tom Watson, "All Powerful Machine of Yore Endures in New York's Nassau," *Congressional Quarterly Weekly Report*, Aug. 17, 1985, pp. 1623–1625.

45. David S. Broder, "Ground War Heating Up in California," *Washington Post*, Sept. 18, 1988, p. A16.

46. Adam Nagourney and David Barstow, "G.O.P.'s Depth Outdid Gore's Team in Florida," *New York Times* (national edition), Dec. 22, 2000, pp. A1, A22.

47. Cotter et al., *Party Organizations in American Politics*, ch. 5.

48. Paul Allen Beck, Audrey Haynes, Russell J. Dalton, and Robert Huckfeldt, "Party Effort at the Grass Roots: Local Presidential Campaigning in 1992," paper delivered at the annual meeting of the Midwest Political Science Association, Chicago, April 1994. On local party activities acting as a catalyst to stimulate political activists, see Robert Huckfeldt and John Sprague, "Political Parties and Electoral Mobilization: Political Structure, Social Structure, and the Party Canvass," *American Political Science Review* 84 (March 1992): 70–86.

49. The phrase was actually uttered by New York senator William Marcy in defense of Andrew Jackson.

50. Anne Freedman, *Patronage: An American Tradition* (Chicago: Nelson-Hall, 1994), p. 70.

51. For the four-city study, see William Crotty, ed., *Political Parties in Local Areas* (Knoxville: University of Tennessee Press, 1986); and Eldersveld, *Political Parties in American Society*, p. 178.

52. See John M. Bruce, John A. Clark, and John H. Kessel, "Advocacy Politics in Presidential Parties," *American Political Science Review* 85 (Dec. 1991): 1089–1106. On the ideology of national convention delegates, see Herbert McCluskey, Paul J. Hoffman, and Rosemary O'Hara, "Issue Conflicts and Consensus among Party Leaders and Followers," *American Political Science Review* 54 (June 1960): 406–427; Aaron Wildavsky, "The Goldwater Phenomenon: Purists, Politicians, and the Two Party System," *Review of Politics* 27 (July 1965): 386–413; and Warren E. Miller and M. Kent Jennings, *Without Consent: Mass-Elite Linkages in Presidential Politics* (Lexington: University of Kentucky Press, 1988).

53. "Convention Delegates: Who They Are... And How They Compare on Issues," *New York Times* (national edition), Aug. 14, 2000, p. A17.

54. Byron E. Shafer, ed., *Postwar Politics in the G-7: Orders and Eras in Comparative Perspective* (Madison: University of Wisconsin Press, 1996), p. 36.

55. Ibid., p. 34.

56. Geoffrey C. Layman, Thomas M. Carsey, and Juliana Menasce Horowitz, "Party Polarization in American Politics: Characteristics, Causes, and Consequences," *Annual Review of Political Science* (Vol. 9, 2006), pp. 83–110.

57. David S. Broder, *The Party's Over: The Failure of Politics in America* (New York: Harper and Row, 1971); for a scholarly discussion of the possibility of partyless politics, see Walter Dean Burnham, *Critical Elections and the Mainsprings of American Politics* (New York: Norton, 1970).

NOMINATIONS FOR STATE AND CONGRESSIONAL OFFICES

Voter Turnout in Primaries

- Personal Characteristics and Turnout

- Party-Polarizing Potential of Unrepresentative Primary Electorates

- Political/Institutional Influences on Turnout

The National Party Organizations and Nominations in the States

The Direct Primary and the General Election

The Direct Primary and Political Parties

Although Americans pride themselves on having operated with free elections for over two hundred years, the voter's choice in general elections is severely limited. In most elections, citizens are faced with choosing between Republican and Democratic nominees, or "wasting" their vote on a third-party candidate who has only the remotest chance of winning. The functioning of American democracy, therefore, is affected in critical ways by the decisions the two major parties make in selecting persons to bear their labels in the general election. As a result, controversy has surrounded the parties' nomination decisions since the advent of political parties in the United States. For the party, the nomination process is a crucial part of its activities. It is this activity more than any other that distinguishes the political party from other political organizations such as the AFL-CIO, Americans for Democratic Action, Common Cause, the Chamber of Commerce, or Farm Bureau. Only political parties nominate candidates on their own labels and present them to the voters as their official representatives. The nomination is also critical for the parties because selecting the "right" candidate can determine whether a party will win or lose the general election. A candidate lacking in appeal to the party's traditional voters and independents, or one who divides rather than unites the party's electorate and workers, is not likely to gain public office. Finally, the nomination process is important to the party because control of the party is at stake. Influence over the selection of party nominees goes a long way toward determining which party factions will gain ascendancy in terms of the policy direction of the party and the rewards that elected officials bestow upon their supporters. The critical character of the nomination process for the parties was aptly summarized by the late E. E. Schattschneider:

> Unless the party makes authoritative and effective nominations, it cannot stay in business.... The nature of the nomination procedure determines the nature of the party; he who can make nominations is the owner of the party....[1]

In most Western democracies, the selection of candidates rests in the hands of the party organization—the party officers and activists. Operating largely without government regulation, these leaders designate the party's candidates, and there is no appeal to the party-in-the-electorate of their decisions. The average voter participates only in the general election—a contest between the parties—and not in the intraparty contest to select nominees. Nominating processes in the United States, by contrast, not only involve party activists but also permit extensive participation by rank-and-file voters. Indeed, a persistent trend in the evolution of nominating practices in the United States has been toward increasing the opportunities for popular participation and weakening the capacity of party organizational hierarchies to control candidate selection for local, state, and national offices. The American nomination process is unique not only for the amount of popular participation that it permits but also for the wide variety and high level of statutory regulation that governs it.

THE EVOLUTION OF THE DIRECT PRIMARY

FROM LEGISLATIVE CAUCUS TO PARTY CONVENTION

After the American Revolution, the legislative caucus evolved as the principal means of making nominations for state offices. The legislative caucus was an informal meeting of all the party's elected members of the state senate and house of representatives. A similar method of nomination—the congressional caucus—was used to select presidential candidates. The legislative caucus was not a particularly representative institution, because it not only left citizens out of the process but also left unrepresented those districts that had elected opposition party legislators. To correct this problem, some of the states used a "mixed caucus" system, which permitted special delegates, representing districts held by the opposition party, to participate in the caucus to nominate candidates.

Andrew Jackson's failure to gain the presidential nomination from the oligarchs of the congressional caucus in 1824 and the subsequent defeat of the caucus nominee, William H. Crawford, contributed in a significant way to the demise of the caucus system. Jackson was a popular figure—the hero of the Battle of New Orleans and a symbol of democracy and egalitarianism. His backers sought to discredit the caucus system. It was replaced by a convention system of nomination.

The convention process normally started with local or precinct caucuses that selected delegates to attend county conventions. The county conventions then selected delegates to a state party convention. The state conventions nominated the party's candidates for statewide office, such as governor, attorney general, and secretary of state. Courthouse candidates were nominated by the county conventions, and there were also congressional district conventions to select candidates for the United States House. Its supporters considered the convention system to be a democratic reform designed to permit greater popular participation and improved representation for party rank-and-file voters. Like the legislative caucus, the convention nominating process fell into disrepute. The convention process was susceptible to manipulation and domination by party leaders and "bosses," who were often under the influence of well-financed interests anxious to gain favorable concessions from state governments. It was charged that conventions too often selected candidates who were not the popular choice of party voters. There was also the further problem of convention nominations being tantamount to election in one-party areas so that, in effect, the actual choice of public officials was being made at party conventions and not by the voters at the general election.

THE DIRECT PRIMARY

Early in the twentieth century, the convention system was replaced in most states by the direct primary—nomination of party candidates by the voters directly.

The direct primary took power away from the party organization, thereby lessening the power of party leaders over elected officials. The primary permitted direct expression of voter preferences and struck down "the intermediate links between rank and file of the party and would-be candidates."[2]

V. O. Key has concluded that despite the oratory about democracy, citizen participation, corrupt party machines, and special interests during the time when the direct primary was being adopted, the primary was "at bottom an escape from one-partyism."[3] The Civil War and Reconstruction made the South a one-party Democratic area. The direct primary, therefore, evolved in the South as a means to permit popular government where interparty competition of a meaningful nature had ceased. The importance of a lack of interparty competition as an impetus to adoption of the direct primary is illustrated in Virginia and North Carolina, the southern states that held out the longest against instituting primaries. These were also the southern states with the highest level of interparty competition during the 1880s and 1890s, the decades preceding widespread adoption of the primary.[4]

The electoral realignments of the 1890s solidified Democratic one-party dominance of the South, but they also created one-party Republican areas in the Northeast, Midwest, and West. The primary thus spread through these states as interparty competition diminished and GOP state convention nominations became tantamount to election. In 1903, Wisconsin was the first state to enact a comprehensive direct primary law. In states with more established party systems and real two-party competition, such as New York, Delaware, Connecticut, and Rhode Island, the primary was adopted more slowly.

Although one of the reasons for instituting the direct primary was to deal with the problems created by one-partyism, there is evidence that the introduction of the direct primary frustrated and delayed the development of two-party competition. The primary weakened the minority party because it focused public attention upon contests within the dominant party. Voters were channeled into the primary of the dominant party because that was where the election was actually being decided. Persons with political ambitions also gravitated into the majority party because they saw little future in the minority party. In view of these patterns of behavior, V. O. Key concluded that "primary competition tended to be substituted for general election competition; competition within parties for competition between parties."[5] He believed that without the direct primary, interparty competition would have come sooner to one-party areas of the North and South.

THE DIRECT PRIMARY AND PROGRESSIVISM

The direct primary embodied an essential belief of the reformist Progressive movement of the early twentieth century. The Progressives believed intermediaries between the people and their government should be removed and that the voters should be able to choose nominees for office without encroachments on their sovereignty by party leaders. Robert M. La Follette, Sr., the leader of the Wisconsin Progressives, stated the case for the direct primary:

> Under our form of government the entire structure rests upon the nomination of candidates for office. This is the foundation of representative government. If bad men control nominations we cannot have good government....

> [We] must abolish the caucus and convention by law, place nominations in the hands of the people, and make all nominations by direct vote at a primary election.
>
> With nominations of all candidates absolutely in the control of the people... the public official who desires re-nomination will not dare to seek it, if he has served the machine and the lobby and betrayed the public trust.[6]

The Progressives fought for the direct primary not only because it was consistent with their democratic faith, but because it provided a means of challenging the power of established party leaders, achieving political power, and fulfilling personal ambition. La Follette in Wisconsin, Hiram Johnson in California, and other Progressive leaders used the primary to strengthen their faction's influence within the dominant Republican Party of their states.

The Direct Primary in the South

Whereas the direct primary in the North was designed to provide a forum for electoral competition and to advance the fortunes of the Progressive faction of the GOP, in the South the direct primary was designed to unify the Democratic Party under conservative leadership, weaken the Republican opposition, and prevent black voters from having electoral influence. Use of the primary to select Democratic candidates, it was thought, would give greater legitimacy to the nominee than would selection by party conventions, and the party might thereby be unified. It was hoped that settling intraparty differences in the primary and presenting a united front in the general election would reduce the influence of the opposition parties and their voters—mainly blacks, who up until the Depression of the 1930s were overwhelmingly Republican. Southern Democratic parties also adopted rules barring blacks from voting in party primaries in order to prevent any candidate or faction from making appeals to black voters in order to gain a party nomination.[7]

The advocates of the primary in the South were largely successful in achieving their goals. The Democratic primary became the only significant election; only in states with concentrations of Republicans in mountain areas was the GOP a force of modest significance (e.g., Tennessee, Kentucky, Virginia, North Carolina); and the white primary effectively excluded blacks from the electoral process.

Post–World War II Trends

During the years after World War II, the primary was instituted in those states that had been holdouts. In 1976, Indiana adopted the primary for nominating statewide candidates and became the last of the holdout states to accept the primary. Other states that became primary states were Rhode Island (1947), Connecticut (1955), and New York (statewide offices, 1967). In enacting the primary laws, Rhode Island, Connecticut, and New York also made provision for preprimary endorsement of candidates by the party organizations.[8]

The nature of southern primaries has also changed with the demise of the whites-only primary, the enfranchisement of blacks, and the emergence of strong Republican parties. Blacks are now an increasingly larger proportion of the southern Democratic Party's supporters and active participants in the primaries as both voters and candidates. While it was only a minor force in southern state politics, the Republican Party frequently opted to take advantage of a provision in state law that permitted nominations via conventions. As the party has gained electoral strength in the region, it has shifted to use of the primary to nominate its candidates.[9]

STATE REGULATION OF THE DIRECT PRIMARY

There is tremendous diversity among the states in the operation of the direct primary. The constitutional principle of federalism permits the states wide latitude in tailoring their election laws to fit state traditions, political conditions, and the preferences of state leaders and voters.

NOMINATION BY CONVENTION

Although the direct primary is the predominant method of nominating candidates, thirteen states either permit or require a role for party conventions. In Connecticut, for example, the winner of the party's endorsement at the state convention automatically becomes the nominee unless challenged in the primary by a candidate who received at least 15 percent of the convention votes. Several of the southern states (Alabama, Georgia, South Carolina, and Virginia) permit the parties to nominate either by primary or by convention. This option permits state parties to determine which method of nomination they wish to use based upon strategic considerations. For example, the Virginia Republicans have frequently opted for the convention method as a means of strengthening the influence of party leaders and conservative activists, who tend to dominate their party's conventions. The convention method of nomination, of course, enhances the influence that party leaders have over the nominating process because candidates cannot appeal effectively over the heads of party leaders to rank-and-file voters, as in a primary. The convention system also gives an advantage to candidates with strong organizations capable of mobilizing party activists.

PARTY AFFILIATION REQUIREMENTS FOR VOTING

There is wide variation among the states in terms of the party affiliation requirements imposed in order for a voter to participate in primaries. The states array themselves along a continuum regarding the severity of their party affiliation requirements from those that restrict participation to registered partisans to others with no restrictions (see Table 5.1).

CLOSED PRIMARIES Fourteen states and the District of Columbia have closed primaries. In these states, voters must register as party affiliates in order to vote in a party primary. Participation is thus restricted to those who are willing to register publicly as partisans; those who register as independents are barred from voting. A voter who wishes to switch party registration must do so in advance of the primary, normally twenty to thirty days prior to the primary. New York is particularly

TABLE 5.1 | PARTY AFFILIATION REQUIREMENTS FOR VOTING IN DIRECT PRIMARIES

Closed: Party registration required; changes permitted within a fixed time period	Semi-Closed: Unaffiliated voters permitted to vote in a party primary; or voters may change their party registration at the polls	Semi-Open: Voters must publicly declare their choice of party ballot at polling place on Election Day	Open: Voter decides in which party primary to vote in privacy of voting booth	"Nonpartisan": Top two primary votegetters, regardless of party, are nominated for general election
Connecticut[a]	Arizona[c]	Alabama[j]	Hawaii	Louisiana
DC	California[d]	Arkansas[j]	Idaho	Washington
Delaware	Colorado[e]	Georgia[j]	Michigan	
Florida	Iowa[f]	Illinois[j]	Minnesota	
Kentucky	Kansas[g]	Indiana[j]	Missouri	
Maine	Massachusetts[g]	Mississippi[j]	Montana	
Maryland[b]	New Hampshire[g]	Ohio[j]	North Dakota	
Nebraska[b]	New Jersey[g]	South Carolina[j]	Texas	
Nevada	North Carolina[h]	Tennessee[k]	Virginia	
New Mexico	Rhode Island[g]		Vermont	
New York	Utah[g]		Wisconsin	
Oregon[d]	West Virginia[i]			
Oklahoma	Wyoming[l]			
Pennsylvania				
South Dakota				

[a]Unaffiliated voters can register with a party a day before the primary election.

[b]Parties have the option to permit unaffiliated voters to participate in their party primary. The parties generally do not exercise this option.

[c]Independent voters may choose either party ballot, which registers them.

[d]Unaffiliated voters may vote in primaries, if permitted by party rule.

[e]Voters may declare party affiliation at the polls, which enrolls them.

[f]Voters may change party registration or declare party affiliation at the polls.

[g]Unaffiliated voters may select a party ballot at the polls and choice automatically registers them with that party.

[h]Unaffiliated voters may vote in either party primary and choice is recorded.

[i]Independent voters may vote in Republican primary.

[j]Voter's choice of party ballot is recorded and parties have access to the lists.

[k]No record kept of voter's choice of a party ballot.

[l]Same-day registration permits voter to declare or change party affiliation at the polls and reverse the change after voting.

Source: Federal Election Commission, "Party Affiliation and Primary Voting 2000," Malcolm E. Jewell and Sarah M. Morehouse, *Political Parties and Elections in American States* (Washington, D.C.: CQ Press, 2001), p. 103.

restrictive about changes in party registration. It requires that changes be made one year before the primary.

Thirteen states have created *semi-closed* primary systems. These states have loopholes in their closed primary laws that permit unaffiliated or independent voters to vote in party primaries. The ability of unaffiliated voters to participate in partisan primaries may be granted either by state law or by state party rules. In some states (e.g., Arizona, Colorado, Kansas, New Hampshire, and Rhode Island), independents who choose to vote in a party primary are then automatically registered with that party, whereas in Utah no record is kept of the party primary in which an independent voted. Because the right of independents to vote in primaries is determined in some states by party rules, it is possible for one party to grant the right to participate while the other party operates a completely closed primary. Thus, in West Virginia, only the Republicans permit unaffiliated voters to take part in their primaries. This reflects the fact the Republicans are the state's minority party and therefore are in search of new adherents.

States may also operate semi-closed primaries by allowing unaffiliated voters to vote or by permitting voters to change their party registration on Election Day (e.g., Iowa, Kansas, and Utah). Wyoming is less restrictive. It allows election-day registration, and voters may change their party registration at the polls and then reverse the change after voting.

The justification for the closed primary is that because primaries are the process through which party nominees are chosen, only party affiliates with a reasonably stable commitment to the party should be permitted to vote. It is argued that the selection of a nominee is one of the most important decisions that a party makes and it should not be turned over to nonparty members or made vulnerable to "raiding" from outsiders who lack a long-term commitment to the party. Party organization leaders have traditionally preferred the closed primary system because it prevents "cross-overs" by voters from the opposition party, creates a known constituency to whom appeals for support can be made, and facilitates control of the nomination process.

Public Statement of Party Preference Required   Nine states (mainly in the South) operate *semi-open* primary systems, in which voters are not required to register as party affiliates, but they are required to declare publicly in which party's primary they wish to participate. In most of these states a record is kept of the primary in which a person has voted and the parties have access to these lists. Voters are free to change their party preference at each primary. Some states require voters to submit their preference in writing, and a few states require voters to swear that they support the party if their participation in a primary is challenged. By requiring voters to publicly declare a party preference, the semi-open primary system denies voters the anonymity of their party preference that is provided by open primary systems.

Open Primary   Eleven states have the open primary, in which no requirements concerning party affiliations are imposed upon persons voting in the primary. In open primary states, the voters decide in the privacy of the voting booth in which party's primary they wish to vote. As in the previously described types of primaries,

| BOX 5.1 | PRIMARY RULES AND POLARIZATION |

Primaries are an important polarizing force in American politics, and different types of primaries may exacerbate or reduce this effect. While candidates in general elections compete for votes among the entire electorate, in primaries they are competing over a smaller and more ideological group of voters. Strategically, candidates must take more extreme positions to win primaries than would be desirable for succeeding in the general election. However, the extent to which primaries cause candidates to take polarizing positions differs depending on the type of primary used by a state. In open primaries, candidates taking more moderate positions can still win by capturing the votes of independents and supporters of the other party. However, in closed primaries, more polarizing position-taking is necessary. Research conducted by Elisabeth Gerber and Rebecca Morton demonstrates the effect that this has on the ideologies of members of Congress. Their study found that House members from states with closed primary laws were more extreme on congressional roll call votes relative to the districts that they represented. Members representing districts in states with semi-closed and open primary laws were more moderate. Thus, the authors conclude that closed primaries contribute to greater polarization among officeholders.

Source: "Primary Election Systems and Representation," Elisabeth R. Gerber and Rebecca B. Morton, *Journal of Law, Economics, & Organization*, vol. 14 (2).

voters in open primary states are restricted to voting in only one party's primary. Particularly open primaries occur in states such as Wisconsin and Minnesota, which combine open primary laws with election-day registration at the polls. In these states, a voter need not be registered prior to the primary in order to vote, since registration is permitted at the polls on primary Election Day. And North Dakota does not require voter registration in any form.

The basic rationale for the open primary is that all voters should be permitted to participate in the crucial process of selecting nominees for public office and that such participation should not be restricted to those who publicly acknowledge a partisan preference. In addition, the advocates of the open primary stress that it protects the privacy of party preference and electoral choice.

"NONPARTISAN"/TOP TWO PRIMARY   An unusual variation on the open primary was instituted in Louisiana in 1975. This process, instituted for every elected office in the state, calls for an initial "primary" in which all candidates run on the same ballot regardless of their party affiliation (the election is not truly nonpartisan since the party affiliations of the candidates do appear on the ballot). If a candidate receives a majority of the votes cast in the open primary, then that candidate is elected and no general election is held for that office. If no candidate wins a majority of the vote in the first election, then a runoff is held between the top two finishers. Since all candidates run on the same ballot, two candidates from the same party could face each other in this runoff election and neither party is guaranteed a spot in the runoff.

This reform was introduced by Governor Edwin Edwards; despite other rationalizations for the reform, the true reason for Edwards's proposal was electoral expediency. Democrats in Louisiana were annoyed with having to run in a party primary and, often, a runoff before facing a Republican candidate in the general election. This reform would cut back on at least one election in which a Democrat would have to compete, presumably lowering the costs of having to wage three separate campaigns. Democrats assumed that the first election would eliminate any Republican competition and that the runoff would decide which Democrat would take office. However, Republicans have gained strength in Louisiana, and runoff elections typically pit Democrats against Republicans. Washington passed a similar primary system in 2004, but because of a court challenge, the system was not used by the state until 2008. The impact of the law on party strength in Washington is not yet clear.

Since neither party holds its own primary, the procedure has resulted in a weakening of the state's political parties. Some argue that another consequence of this rule change has been the tendency of the system to generate runoff elections between candidates that take issue positions more ideologically extreme than most voters. The clearest example of this was in the 1991 gubernatorial election, when former Ku Klux Klan leader David Duke made the runoff election against Edwards.

THE CONSTITUTIONALITY OF PRIMARY LAWS   Prior to its being declared unconstitutional by the Supreme Court in 2000, Alaska, California, and Washington used a blanket primary to nominate candidates. The blanket primary permits voters to take part in more than one party's primary by switching back and forth between parties from office to office. Under this system, it was possible for an elector to vote in the Republican primary for governor, the Democratic primary for United States senator, the Republican primary for a member of the House of Representatives, and then go back to the Democratic primary for state legislative candidates.

California's blanket primary was challenged by the Republican and Democratic parties, as well as by several minor parties, on the grounds that it violated the parties' First Amendment rights of free political association. In the case of *California Democratic Party v. Jones* (2000), the Supreme Court declared that the state's blanket primary constituted a "stark repudiation of political association" that denied the parties the power to control their own nomination processes and define their own identities. California and the other states with blanket primaries were then forced to change their primary statutes to bring them into conformity with the Court's decision.

The California blanket primary case left open the question of whether or not open primaries are constitutional, since they also limit the ability of the parties to control their own nomination processes. This issue was not before the Court in the California case, but two dissenting justices stated that they believed that the decision cast doubt on the constitutionality of other forms of open primaries. However, a 2008 ruling by the Supreme Court in *Washington State Grange v. Washington State Republican Party* suggested that the court was not likely to rule against open primary laws in general. In that case, the state parties asked the court to strike down the "top two" primary law because they claimed it violated their First Amendment rights to determine which candidates represented them on the ballot. But the court dismissed this view and upheld the law, which had been supported by 60 percent of the public when it passed by initiative in 2004.

Regulation of Candidacies and Cross-Filing

In addition to regulating which persons may vote in a party primary, states decide the qualifications a candidate must meet in order to run. Most of the states permit a person to run in only one party's primary and only the most minimal tests of party membership are required. However, nine states permit candidates to be endorsed by more than one party. An interesting case of cross-filing exists in New York, where this system operates to encourage minor parties and to facilitate coalitions of the Democratic Party with the Liberal Party and the Republicans with the Conservative Party. New York permits parties that nominate candidates by convention—the Liberals and Conservatives—to nominate the same candidate as the major parties. It is therefore common for Democratic nominees to appear on the general election ballot in both the Democratic Party and Liberal Party columns, and for GOP nominees also to be listed as Conservative Party candidates. Thus, in 1994, Republican George Pataki upset Democratic Governor Mario Cuomo, even though Cuomo received more votes on the Democratic line than Pataki did on the GOP line. However, Pataki's 328,000 votes on the Conservative Party line and 54,000 on the Freedom Party line gave him a narrow 173,798-vote margin of victory. Interestingly, the Freedom Party was the creation of the state Republican Party and was designed to provide a means for non-Republicans to vote for Pataki without having to vote for him in either the Republican or Conservative columns.

The provision for cross-filing, or fusion tickets, in New York has created a powerful incentive for the creation and maintenance of minor parties and made them a critical element of the state's electoral politics. At the same time, the possibility of these parties refusing to nominate their coalition partner's candidate and instead running their own candidate, or even nominating the other major party's nominee, can pose a serious threat to their coalition partner's electoral prospects. The Liberal and Conservative parties are therefore in a position to exert leverage on the major parties to nominate candidates acceptable to the third parties. These maneuverings frequently have a major impact on the outcome of general elections.[10] Thus, Rudolph Giuliani, the Republican nominee for mayor of New York City, was aided in winning the 1993 and 1997 mayoral elections by receiving the Liberal Party nomination. The Liberal Party nomination of Giuliani demonstrates an important feature of minor parties. That is, their primary goal is maximizing their influence and not supplanting one of the major parties. In the case of Giuliani's election, the Liberal Party reaped substantial patronage rewards from the mayor and Republicans found themselves in competition with Liberal Party members for patronage positions in the city.[11]

Unlike New York, most of the states forbid fusion tickets, in which a candidate can become the nominee of more than one party. These anti-fusion laws were adopted as a means of disadvantaging third parties seeking leverage in the manner of New York's minor parties by nominating selected major-party candidates. Minnesota's ban on fusion tickets was challenged by a left-of-center third party that sought to nominate an incumbent Democratic Farmer-Labor legislator. In the case of *Timmons v. Twin Cities Area New Party* (1997), the Supreme Court upheld Minnesota's effort to strengthen the two-party system, noting that although a state may not "completely insulate the two-party system from minor parties or independent candidates' competition … states may enact reasonable election regulations that favor the traditional two-party system."

REGULATION OF THE PROPORTION OF THE VOTE REQUIRED FOR NOMINATION: THE RUNOFF PRIMARY

The normal practice in the states is for the nomination to go to the candidate who receives the most votes (a plurality) in the primary, even if that individual receives less than a majority of the votes cast. Consider the example of the 2010 Illinois Republican primary for governor, which included seven candidates. Bill Brady earned the party's nomination with just 20 percent of the primary vote, barely edging out Kirk Dillard (who also received 20 percent) by less than 400 votes. Thus, Brady won the Republican nomination despite the fact that four of every five Republican primary voters cast a ballot for somebody else.

In ten southern and border states plus South Dakota, a majority of the vote in the primary is required for nomination, and in North Carolina, 40 percent of the primary vote is required for nomination. If no candidate receives a majority, then a second or runoff primary is held between the top two finishers in the first primary. This system was instituted in the South during an era when the Democratic Party was dominant and its nomination was tantamount to election. To assure that the person nominated (and thus "elected") in the Democratic primary had the support of a majority of Democratic voters, the runoff primary was instituted. The potential for a second primary diminishes the internal party pressures for preprimary coalition formation and therefore tends to increase the number of candidates in the initial primary. The runoff can also result in a different candidate winning the nomination than led in the first primary.

REGULATION OF ACCESS TO THE GENERAL ELECTION BALLOT: "SORE LOSER" LAWS

The importance of a party nomination is enhanced if a candidate who loses a primary is not permitted to run in the general election as an independent. In twenty-seven of the states, the legislatures have enacted "sore loser" statutes that prevent independent candidacies by persons who lost a primary nomination. The lack of such a law became important in Connecticut's 2006 Senate race, when Senator Joseph Lieberman (D-Conn.) lost in the Democratic primary but won the general election as a third-party candidate. Such statutes are party-protective measures in that they limit the extent to which intraparty factional struggles can be carried over into the general election. Critics charge that these laws unduly limit candidacy. The Supreme Court, however, has upheld the constitutionality of "sore loser" statutes (*Storer v. Brown*, 1974).

REGULATING THE TIMING OF PRIMARIES

Because party primaries are administered by state governments, each state sets the date for those primaries. There is a remarkable amount of variation in when states hold their party primaries (see Figure 5.1). For instance, in 2010, Illinois held its

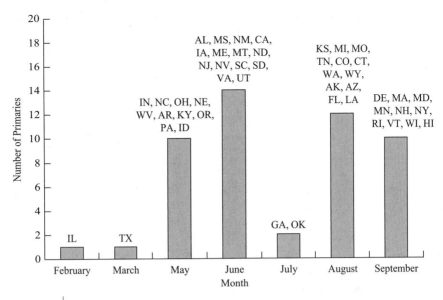

FIGURE 5.1 | TIMING OF CONGRESSIONAL PRIMARIES IN 2010

primary on February 2nd, nine months before the general election. On the other hand, Hawaii held its primary on September 18th, only six weeks before the general election. When a primary occurs it may have important consequences for voters and candidates. Some argue that late primaries will increase turnout in the general election by focusing the electorate's attention for a shorter time period and that late primaries reduce campaign costs by compressing the electoral calendar. However, research commissioned by the Pennsylvania state legislature determined that these claims were not supported by evidence from the states. Rather, the commission found that officials in states that held late primaries generally found them to be problematic. These officials cited the lack of time for citizens to get to know the candidates before the general election and the potential benefit that this had for incumbents running for reelection. Related to this point was the concern that there was no time for candidates to "regroup their campaigns" for the general election. For many of these reasons, Washington's traditional late-September primary was moved to mid-August after 2006.[12]

PREPRIMARY ENDORSEMENTS

Clearly, the intent of the Progressive reformers and one of the consequences of the direct primary has been to reduce party organization control over nominations. Party organizational influence has not, however, been totally removed from the process, and this is especially true in those states that use preprimary endorsements by the party organizational leadership. Endorsements can be statutory mandates, informal practices of the party organization, or a practice of party-affiliated organizations.

STATE STATUTORY REQUIREMENTS FOR ENDORSEMENT

In seven states (Colorado, Connecticut, New Mexico, New York, North Dakota, Rhode Island, and Utah), state law provides for preprimary endorsement by party conventions. The existence of these statutory requirements for endorsing conventions reflects the ability of the party organizations in these states to retain a significant role in the nomination process even while the state legislatures were succumbing to the pressures for the direct primary. Endorsement frequently carries with it the right to have one's name placed on the primary ballot or to be listed first on the ballot. In Rhode Island, for example, endorsed candidates have an automatic right to a place on the primary ballot, but other candidates must qualify by circulating petitions. Access to the ballot may also be restricted by requiring that a candidate receive a fixed percentage of the convention delegate votes in order to enter the primary. The minimum convention vote required for getting one's name on the primary ballot is 30 percent in Colorado, 25 percent in New York, 20 percent in New Mexico, and 15 percent in Connecticut. These requirements have frequently prevented challenges to the party organizations' preferred candidates. New Mexico's endorsing conventions have been used to achieve slates balanced between Hispanic and Anglo candidates.[13] In Utah, the convention designates for each office two candidates, whose names are placed on the primary ballot. However, if one candidate receives 70 percent of the convention vote, that individual is automatically declared the party nominee. A candidate in Colorado can avoid a primary and become the party's nominee if he or she receives the support of 50 percent of the convention delegates. It is possible in several of the states with statutory requirements for preprimary endorsement of candidates to get on the primary ballot by securing the requisite number of signatures on a petition.

EXTRALEGAL ENDORSEMENTS

In fifteen states, endorsements by one or both parties are allowed by party rules, with the endorsing done either by party conventions or by committees. For example, both parties in Illinois, Massachusetts, and Minnesota regularly endorse candidates, and California recently joined the list of states with endorsement permitted under state party rules. Other states that use party endorsement are Delaware, Michigan, Pennsylvania, Ohio, Virginia, and Wisconsin. In New Jersey, county party organizations frequently endorse candidates in an effort to influence who will enter and win the primary. Behind the scenes, it is not unusual for party leaders to assist a favored candidate while discouraging others from getting into the race. There are also unofficial party endorsements by party-affiliated groups in California. These unofficial party affiliates, including the Republican Assembly and the California Democratic Council, seek to influence nominations through their group endorsements.

Extralegal endorsement practices often reflect a desire on the part of party activists to select candidates committed to a particular political faith or faction. In Minnesota, for example, ideological concerns have played a major role in endorsement politics, as the Democratic Farmer-Labor Party has utilized endorsement to maintain a liberal policy orientation. The state Republicans, in their efforts to further a conservative agenda, even went so far as to deny endorsement in 1994 to its moderate, pro-choice incumbent governor, Arne Carlson. Not all endorsement activities are motivated solely out of ideological concerns, however. An interest in maintaining political control, not ideology, has been a major motivation of the Illinois Democratic State Central Committee in its slate making. Other party interests that can be advanced through endorsement are selecting the strongest candidate and avoiding a divisive primary that could split the party for the general election.

CONSEQUENCES OF PREPRIMARY ENDORSEMENTS

REDUCED PRIMARY COMPETITION   Preprimary endorsement reduces the amount of competition in primaries. Candidates who fail to gain endorsements often withdraw from the race and do not enter the primary. There is frequently competition in gubernatorial primaries, but it is much less common in states having party endorsement processes.[14] In states having endorsement processes, there was competition in only one-half of the gubernatorial primaries between 1968 and 1998, whereas there was competition in three-fourths of the primaries in states without endorsement procedures.[15] Preprimary endorsements have their greatest impact in reducing primary competition through the elimination of minor candidates. Major challengers, however, can normally mount effective primary campaigns even without endorsements.

Incumbent governors typically win renomination and face little or no meaningful opposition. For incumbent governors, party endorsements significantly reduce the likelihood of their being challenged in primaries. Between 1968 and 1998, endorsed Democratic incumbents were unchallenged in the primaries in 37 percent of the cases, whereas nonendorsed incumbents faced challenges 68 percent of the time. The pattern was similar for Republicans. Endorsed GOP incumbents faced primary opposition 27 percent of the time, whereas 56 percent of nonendorsed incumbents had primary opponents.[16]

DECLINING EFFECTIVENESS OF PREPRIMARY ENDORSEMENTS   The ability of party organizational endorsements to give the winning edge to their candidates has declined in recent years. Thus, endorsed candidates in states with both legally mandated and informal endorsement procedures won contested gubernatorial primaries in at least 80 percent of the cases from 1960 to 1980, but those winning percentages dropped to 53 percent between 1982 and 1998.[17] Even in traditionally strong party organization states such as Connecticut, a party endorsement is no longer tantamount to winning the nomination. While Lieberman easily captured the majority of votes that were necessary to win the state party' endorsement in 2006, he eventually lost the Democratic primary to the wealthy challenger, Ned Lamont. In that same year, the candidate who won the Connecticut Democratic Party's endorsement for governor also lost the Democratic primary.

Although the impact of preprimary endorsements on primary outcomes appears to have declined in recent years, a comprehensive study conducted by Sarah McCally Morehouse found that preprimary endorsements do tend to lessen the impact of campaign spending. Endorsed candidates usually succeed in getting themselves as well known as their challengers because the endorsement process requires

| BOX 5.2 | AN OHIO WRITE-IN CANDIDATE BECOMES THE CENTER OF ATTENTION FOR BOTH PARTIES |

When Representative Ted Strickland (D-Ohio) vacated his seat to run for governor in 2006, Democrats turned to state Senator Charlie Wilson to try to keep the seat in Democratic hands. There was only one problem: Wilson's name did not appear on the ballot for the Democratic primary. To appear on the primary ballot in Ohio, a congressional candidate need only collect 50 signatures from registered voters in his or her district, but Wilson did not clear even that low hurdle. His campaign collected only 98 signatures, 50 of which came from outside the district, leaving him 2 signatures shy of the requirement. Had his name appeared on the ballot, Wilson would likely have won easily without spending much money on the campaign for the nomination. But as a write-in candidate, things suddenly became much more expensive. The DCCC got involved in the race to help Wilson's campaign instruct voters on how to write his name in on the ballot. Altogether, more than $1 million was spent on behalf of Wilson's write-in candidacy for the nomination.

But Democrats were not the only party getting involved. Since the two Democrats who were on the ballot were political amateurs, Republicans knew that they would win the seat easily if Wilson did not receive the nomination. The NRCC's campaign to keep Wilson from receiving the Democratic nomination culminated with its advertisement attacking Bob Carr, one of the unknown Democratic candidates on the ballot. The logic behind this effort was to increase the visibility of Carr, which would lead more Democrats to vote for him. In fact, the ad attacked the candidate for being too liberal to work with Republicans in Congress, favoring environmental regulations, and opposing the extension of President Bush's tax cuts, "attacks" that publicized positions that Democratic primary voters would find desirable. Despite the involvement from the NRCC, Wilson won the nomination by receiving 44,367 write-in votes in the primary, twice as many votes as the two candidates whose names actually appeared on the ballot. But the episode demonstrated that both parties are likely to become very involved in primary campaigns when the stakes are high and the outcome is uncertain.

Source: Stephen Koff, "Ohio Democrats Spell Mistake W-I-L-S-O-N," *The Plain Dealer*, April 20, 2006.

them to engage in extensive face-to-face meetings with at least a thousand party activist delegates from across the state. The public visibility gained through the endorsement process thus helps to compensate for any campaign spending advantage their challengers may have. Further offsetting the impact of challenger spending in gubernatorial primaries are the resources of time and effort poured into the race by the party organizations on behalf of their endorsed candidates. By contrast, in states that do not use preprimary endorsing conventions, the candidates spending the most money normally have the best chance of winning the primary.[18]

COMPETITION IN PRIMARIES

It was the expectation of the reformers that the direct primary would stimulate competition among candidates for party nominations. This hope has not been fulfilled, however. In a substantial percentage of the primaries, nominations either go uncontested or involve only nominal challenges to the front-runner. The two key determinants of intraparty competition in the primaries are the extent of the inter-party competition and incumbency.

THE IMPACT OF INTERPARTY COMPETITION

V. O. Key first demonstrated that competition in primaries is significantly influ-enced by the pattern of two-party competition that exists within a state or district. Competition in primaries is greatest where a party's prospects in the general elec-tion are the highest.[19] The impact of general election prospects on primary compe-tition is evident in nominations for the U.S. House. In districts that are generally considered safe for one party, the dominant party normally has a contested primary—often with more than two candidates—when the incumbent is not seeking reelection. Of course, when the prospects of victory in the general election are dis-mal, there is little or no competition for party nominations. Indeed, in congressional districts that heavily favor the incumbent's party, it is frequently impossible for the minority party to induce anyone to enter the primaries. For example, in 2006 there was no major-party challenger for fifty-six House incumbents. Incumbency is a distinct advantage in nominating contests, and the presence of an incumbent in a primary is usually enough to ward off serious opposition. Because incumbents tend to scare off strong competitors in the primaries, they of course win renomination in overwhelming proportions. Between 2000 and 2008, sixty-seven incumbent governors sought renomination and sixty-three (94 percent) were successful. When no incumbent is running, however, the competition in the primary can be intense. For example, in Michigan in 2010, when the incumbent Democratic governor was facing term limits and the Democrats were facing a difficult political environment, more than a half-dozen candidates entered the primary for the GOP nomination.

The advantages of incumbency are particularly striking in nominations for the U.S. House of Representatives. Between 1980 and 2008, the percentage of incum-bent representatives renominated never dipped below 95 percent. The incidence of primary victories for incumbent senators was also high—consistently above 90 per-cent (see Table 5.2). The tendency of incumbents to discourage strong primary opposition and win renomination is also prevalent in state legislative elections. Thus, for most members of Congress and state legislators, the primary is not unlike the common cold. It is a nuisance, but seldom fatal.

THE IMPACT OF NOMINATING PROCEDURES

The type of nominating procedures used within a state also affects the extent of pri-mary competition. As noted previously, states that use preprimary endorsement procedures have lower levels of competition because of the ability of party organi-zations to restrict candidacies in these states. Runoff primaries tend to multiply the number of candidates in the initial primary, as do blanket primaries.[20] Interestingly, studies of competition for nominations for governor and senator have not demon-strated that open primaries encourage a higher level of competition than closed pri-mary systems. Apparently, the absence of a requirement for party registration by voters is not a sufficient condition to produce intraparty nominating contests.

TABLE 5.2 | RENOMINATION RATES OF INCUMBENT UNITED STATES REPRESENTATIVES AND SENATORS, 1980–2008

	Incumbent Representatives			Incumbent Senators		
Year	Seeking Renomination	Renom-inated	Percent	Seeking Renomination	Renom-inated	Percent
2008	390	387	99.2	29	29	100.0
2006	403	402	99.8	28	27	96.4
2004	401	401	100.0	26	26	100.0
2002	392	384	98.0	29	28	96.6
2000	403	400	99.3	28	28	100.0
1998	403	402	99.8	30	30	100.0
1996	384	382	99.5	21	20	95.2
1994	386	382	99.0	26	26	100.0
1992	368	349	94.8	28	27	96.4
1990	406	405	99.8	31	31	100.0
1988	408	407	99.8	27	27	100.0
1986	393	391	99.5	28	28	100.0
1984	395	392	99.2	26	26	100.0
1982	393	383	97.5	31	30	96.8
1980	398	392	98.5	27	25	92.6
Total	4,337	4,285	98.8 (Mean)	303	298	98.3 (Mean)

Source: CQ Voting and Elections Database.

VOTER TURNOUT IN PRIMARIES

Just as the reformers' high hopes for competition in primaries have been largely unfulfilled, so too have their expectations concerning voter participation. An average of only about 30 percent of the voting-age population votes in gubernatorial primaries in years when both parties have contested primaries. If only one party has a major primary contest, voter participation is often substantially lower. When turnout is measured as a percentage of the voting-age population in all the states holding primaries, the turnout rate is often quite low—an average of 24 percent in midterm elections from 1962 to 1994. It was only 18.22 percent in 1994 and 17 percent in 1998.[21]

There are regional variations in turnout rates, with several of the western states (e.g., Montana and Wyoming) having some of the highest levels of voter participation. These are states that also have high turnout rates in general elections. Traditionally, the primary turnout has been high in southern Democratic primaries. Indeed, because historically the Democratic primary was the real election in the South, there was a pattern of higher turnout in primaries than in the general election. However, as general elections have become increasingly competitive between the Democrats and Republicans, the pattern of participation in southern primaries has changed dramatically. Overall, the percentage of the electorate participating in gubernatorial primaries has declined, the Democratic share of the popular vote in primaries has gone down, and the level of participation in Republican primaries has increased. With the frequently low level of turnout that prevails in primary elections, questions naturally arise about the representativeness of primary voters.

Personal Characteristics and Turnout

The same sorts of personal characteristics that are associated with voting in general elections are operative in primaries. Primary voters tend to be better educated and older than nonvoters. They are also more knowledgeable concerning politics, more interested in campaigns, and have a greater sense of civic duty. Primary voters rank even higher than voters in general elections in these characteristics. Primary turnout is also strongly affected by the strength of a person's party identification (i.e., one's psychological attachment to a political party). Political scientists have consistently demonstrated that the stronger an individual's party identification (e.g., being a strong Republican versus a weak Republican), the more likely that person is to vote. Jewell's study of primary voting has shown that party identification has an even stronger and more consistent impact on primary turnout than it does in general elections. He also found that party identification was especially important in determining which younger and less-interested voters will vote in primaries.[22]

BOX 5.3   When is the Primary?

Party primaries generally suffer from low turnout for a variety of reasons. Among these is the fact that different states hold their primaries at different times, making it less likely that citizens will be aware of when their own state primaries are to be held. Generally, individuals only start paying close attention a few weeks before the primary election date. This fact was clear when a survey firm asked Washington State voters if they knew when the state and congressional primaries would be held in their state. The survey was fielded in mid-July, but the primary was not to be held until August 19th. Despite the fact that respondents were given just three options to choose from in a multiple choice format, just 13 percent knew the date of the primary. That means that respondents did worse than if they had just guessed randomly! Forty-six percent chose one of the other two date options and 41 percent said that they were not sure when the primary was. Fortunately, more citizens in Washington state appeared to learn about the date of the primary as it approached, which was evidenced by the fact that 31 percent of the voting age population turned out to vote in the election.

Source: Survey USA.

PARTY-POLARIZING POTENTIAL OF UNREPRESENTATIVE PRIMARY ELECTORATES

The tendency of party activists to have higher rates of turnout in primaries and also to have stronger ideological orientations than rank-and-file voters has caused political scientists to consider whether patterns of voter turnout bias the outcomes of a primary.[23] That is, do the patterns of primary turnout introduce a bias into the results of primaries, which in the Republican Party favors conservative candidates and in the Democratic Party helps liberal candidates?

There is evidence from recent political science research that suggests that because turnout in primaries is low and primary voters in both parties are more extreme in their views than are general election voters on the whole, members of Congress find that to protect their flanks they may have to play to noncentrist elements in their constituencies. It is therefore believed that the primary election system is contributing to a polarization of the parties in Congress. In understanding this party-polarizing consequence of primaries, it is important to keep in mind that primaries are *intraparty* competitions, whereas general elections are *interparty* competitions. Intraparty competition, or the potential for an intraparty challenger, means that those seeking party nominations must be attentive to the electorates they are likely to face in primaries—electorates that are apt to be non-centrist on the whole.[24]

Because Republican primary voters are more conservative than general election Republican voters or independents, and Democratic primary voters are slightly more liberal than are their general election counterparts, candidates in competitive primaries find it necessary to adopt either highly conservative or highly liberal policy positions. A candidate may also adopt relatively extreme policy positions to ward off potential challengers in the primary. Party activists, who are often motivated by their strong noncentrist views, constitute an additional force pushing primary candidates to adopt highly conservative or liberal views. These activists are influential because they contribute money, run campaigns, and support candidates. Ideological interest groups play a similar role by supporting primary candidates with relatively polarized views. In addition, the candidates themselves tend to have views that are noncentrist. Although candidates tend to diverge from centrist positions in part because of their primary electorates, there is also the potential for substantial variability across the states and congressional districts in the extent to which primary electorates are unrepresentative. Turnout is likely to be affected by the particular mix of candidates on the ballot in any given state's primary. If a liberal Democratic incumbent is running against token opposition, moderate and conservative partisans may have little incentive to vote, whereas a contest for an open seat between clearly identified liberal and conservative candidates could stimulate these people to vote in larger numbers.

POLITICAL/INSTITUTIONAL INFLUENCES ON TURNOUT

There are a variety of political/institutional variables that affect turnout. These variables relate to the statutory regulations surrounding the primary, the nature of the party system, and the levels of competition that exist in primary contests.

MAJORITY VERSUS MINORITY PARTY STATUS   Turnout tends to be highest in the primary of the party that has the greatest likelihood of winning the general election, precisely because that party's contest is more likely to determine which person will eventually hold public office.

COMPETITION   Competition for a party's nomination spurs voters to participate in primaries. In the absence of a real contest for a nomination, voter turnout diminishes. A party's share of the primary electorate may vary dramatically depending upon whether or not it has a red-hot contest in a given year. The extent of competition is influenced by such factors as *endorsement* and *incumbency*, both of which operate to depress competition and thus indirectly reduce turnout. Traditions of competition in state primaries, as in the one-party South, can have the effect of stimulating turnout.

CLOSED VERSUS OPEN PRIMARIES   Because open primaries do not require voters to publicly disclose a partisan preference, open primaries tend to have higher levels of turnout than do closed primaries. Independents can be precluded from participation in closed primary states.

THE NATIONAL PARTY ORGANIZATIONS AND NOMINATIONS IN THE STATES

The recruitment and nomination processes within the states illustrate the traditionally decentralized character of the American party system. Despite the importance of congressional and senatorial nominations for the functioning of the national-level parties, the national party organizations traditionally played only a minor role in candidate recruitment and nomination. Recruitment was a matter of self-selection, with aspiring members of Congress determining on their own when the time was ripe for them to move from careers in statehouses, city halls, courthouses, or the private sector to the Congress. Aspiring representatives and senators put together personal organizations to contest first the primary and then the general election. Party leaders in Congress and occasionally the president sometimes gave informal encouragement to promising candidates, but it was traditional for the national party leadership to stay aloof from state nomination contests.

A classic example of national party weakness in influencing congressional nominations occurred in 1938, when President Franklin D. Roosevelt sought to purge dissident conservatives in the primaries. Despite the fact that Roosevelt was at the zenith of his popularity during this period, his intervention in the primaries against incumbent senators in Oklahoma, Georgia, South Carolina, and Maryland failed. His inability to influence primary election outcomes paralleled the experience of President William Howard Taft and Senate Republican Leader Nelson Aldrich (R.I.), who sought to oust western Progressives in the Republican primaries of 1910. Usually, however, the president and national party leaders remained silent, even when their loyal supporters had been challenged in the primaries.

The traditional hands-off policy of national parties toward congressional and senatorial nominations changed in the late 1970s and early 1980s because of the realization that candidate quality is a major determinant of electoral success.

| BOX 5.4 | THE RISE OF PARTY PURITY GROUPS |

In 2009 and 2010, scores of conservative activists organized themselves into something called the Tea Party Movement and worked to challenge Republicans who they thought were too moderate. While the movement attracted a great deal of attention from the news media, it was just the most recent example of what Michael H. Murakami has dubbed "party purity groups." As he notes:

> These organizations side ideologically with one [of] the two major political parties, but are frustrated with moderates, who seem to betray core party values by siding with the opposition, even if only on a narrow range of issues. Changes in communication technology enable these groups to act on these growing frustrations stoked by the polarized political milieu. With the ability to garner large memberships, raise hundreds of millions of dollars, air attack ads, and recruit candidates, party purity groups are able to heavily influence party primary processes.

Murakami makes note of several recent examples where more ideologically extreme challengers have challenged incumbents in primary elections with the help of party purity groups like MoveOn.org and the Club for Growth. These efforts have met with some notable successes. For example, Senator Joseph Lieberman was defeated in the 2006 Connecticut Democratic primary by a challenger sponsored by MoveOn.org. And two incumbent members of the House of Representatives lost their renomination attempts to challengers supported by party purity groups in 2008. Even when these efforts fail and the incumbent is able to defeat these ideological challenges, the experience can still have a lasting impact. In 2004, Senator Arlen Specter narrowly defeated a conservative challenger in the Republican primary who was backed by the Club for Growth. Facing the near certainty of another such challenge in his 2010 re-election bid, Specter chose instead to switch parties and run for re-election as a Democrat.

Source: Michael H. Murakami. "Divisive Primaries: Party Organizations, Ideological Groups, and the Battle over Party Purity," *PS: Political Science & Politics* (2008) 918–923.

The national party committees now aggressively recruit candidates to enter primaries and, just as aggressively, discourage others. These candidate recruitment efforts are concentrated in competitive constituencies. However, there are also attempts to find candidates in districts considered safe for the opposition party, in order to prevent the general election from going uncontested and to build a base of support for future elections when conditions may be more favorable (e.g., after an incumbent retires).[25]

National and regional party staff meet with state and local party officials to identify and encourage candidates to run. To entice potentially attractive candidates into the primaries, promises of campaign money and services, polls, and the persuasive talents of party leaders, House and Senate members, and even presidents are used. The parties' staffs also serve as liaison persons with PACs and campaign consultants, who have the financial resources and skills needed to run effective congressional campaigns. Despite these enticements, parties are not always successful in their efforts to convince quality candidates to run for office. For example, in 2008, the Republican Party found it difficult to recruit candidates to challenge Democratic members of Congress who had won their seats in 2006. This lack of quality challengers allowed the Democratic Party to target more Republican-held seats rather than worry about defending seats they had picked up in 2006. As the Democratic Congressional Campaign Committee Chair noted at the time, "The fact that [Republicans] have not been able to field candidates in a lot of these districts means we have not had to circle the wagons and play defense."

National party candidate recruitment activity is not without its risks. Conflicts can arise between national and state party leaders, and bitter resentments can build up among supporters of a candidate not favored by national party officials. These problems can damage the chances of the eventual nominee. As a result, the national party tends to stay neutral if there is more than one candidate in the primary. The major exceptions to the rule of neutrality in primaries tend to occur when an incumbent representative or senator is being seriously challenged. Thus, in 2002, with partisan control of the House of Representatives likely to be decided in just a handful of congressional districts, Representative Tom Davis (R-Va.), the chairman of the Republican congressional campaign committee, with the blessing of the White House, took the unusual step of taking sides in contested GOP primaries in Ohio and Kansas. Davis considered securing the strongest candidates in these races so important that he was willing to accept infuriating the local Republican leaders in Ohio and Kansas.[26]

The heavy involvement of the national parties in candidate recruitment in recent years is clearly a departure from past practices, but it has not done away with the dominant pattern of self-selected candidacies. However, the national parties' continuing involvement in recruitment and high levels of candidate support in general elections may create a pool of successful candidates with strong ties to national party and congressional leaders. To the extent that these officeholders perceive national party support to have been a critical factor in their nomination and election, they may feel a sense of obligation to the leaders who helped them in their hour of need. That sense of obligation is a potential lever of influence for the congressional leaders in seeking to affect the voting of representatives and senators in the halls of Congress. To date, however, the new activism of the congressional and senatorial campaign committees has not been used by party leaders in Congress to enforce discipline and unity. An aggressive future leader, however, could seek to expand influence over colleagues on the basis of campaign support that has been provided. Such a leader might also threaten to withhold it from dissident members.

THE DIRECT PRIMARY AND THE GENERAL ELECTION

The primary, of course, has significant implications for the general election. It narrows the field of candidates and choice available to the voter. The outcome of a primary may also affect a party's general election prospects—enhancing those prospects if a strong candidate wins and diminishing the chances of winning if a weak candidate is nominated. Party leaders are frequently concerned about the potential divisiveness of a contested primary. They fear that a hotly contested primary will leave the party disunited for the general election. Preprimary endorsements are one method of seeking to prevent divisive primaries. Others include channeling financial and campaign support to a preferred candidate in an effort to discourage opposition. There are many frequently cited examples of divisive primaries that have resulted in the party's nominee going down in defeat, but there is no consistent pattern demonstrating that contested primaries are necessarily damaging. Of course, one reason that primary contests do not consistently result in general election losses is that primary competition is most frequent within the stronger of a state's two parties.[27] There are also circumstances when a contested primary may help the nominee. Battling for a party nomination normally generates substantial publicity for the candidates and keeps their names before the public. A tough primary fight may even enhance the image of the winning candidate as an attractive personality, skilled campaigner, and person who is knowledgeable about critical issues. The absence of a primary fight can push a candidate off the evening news programs and front pages of the papers in the crucial months of the spring and summer before an election. Such lack of publicity and testing of the candidate in a primary can be a serious liability in the general election.

Furthermore, candidates who have been tested in tough primary battles are apt to be improved campaigners, more able fund-raisers, and generally stronger candidates for the experience. Their organizations are more likely to be well established and ready to contest the general election than those of the candidates who ran unopposed in the primaries. Candidates learn valuable lessons about what works and what does not work in the course of campaigning, and candidates who have survived intense primary fights are likely to have learned more than those who had no significant primary opposition.

THE DIRECT PRIMARY AND POLITICAL PARTIES

The institutionalization of the direct primary as the principal method of nominating state and congressional candidates in the United States is part of a long-term trend toward shifting power away from party leaders toward rank-and-file voters. In their effort to weaken the capacity of parties to control the selection of candidates for major elective office, the reformers of the Progressive Era were largely successful. In only a handful of jurisdictions are party organizations sufficiently strong that they can bestow their endorsement upon a candidate and assure the individual's nomination in a primary. Even the much-vaunted Cook County (Illinois) Democratic organization can no longer control even mayoral nominations in Chicago. As Leon D. Epstein has observed, a distinct disadvantage flows from party organizations' loss of the power to select candidates. "There is less incentive to be a member of such an organization, in the usual dues-paying sense, if one can become a candidate selector merely by voting in a party primary." This is perhaps one of the reasons it has been harder for American than for European parties to build mass membership organizations.[28]

As the impact of preprimary endorsements and the influence of the national congressional campaign committees illustrates, however, party support can be helpful to a candidate in gaining a nomination. Party organizational support is not irrelevant in the primary process, but it is seldom sufficient to secure a nomination. Rather, the candidate must build a personal organization and following among the voters as well as a substantial war chest if the hurdle of the primary is to be cleared successfully. The direct primary has therefore contributed to a candidate-centered type of politics in America, in contrast to the more party-centered politics of most Western-style democracies that do not utilize the primary for nominations.

Although the direct primary has contributed to a weakening of political parties organizationally, Leon D. Epstein believes that the primary helps to account for the extraordinary and continued *electoral dominance* of the Republican and Democratic parties. He believes that the direct primary institutionalized the Republican and Democratic labels in electoral politics and encouraged a two-party system. The primary provides unusual opportunities for insurgents to win major-party nominations and thereby forego the normally self-defeating process of running as third-party candidates. Challengers to established party organizational leadership are thus encouraged to seek intraparty avenues to power, and voters become accustomed to choosing from among individuals and factions that are competing for a party label.

Epstein's argument, of course, is paradoxical. It asserts that while strengthening the parties electorally, the primary has weakened the party organization and the party in the government. The primary has thus by statute institutionalized the electoral looseness of American parties but in the process also has acted as a party preservative. But just as preservatives in food processing change the nature and quality of what is being preserved, the direct primary has left the parties as persistent electoral labels whose importance is frequently questioned after Election Day.[29]

Notes

1. E. E. Schattschneider, *Party Government* (New York: Farrar and Rinehart, 1942), p. 64.
2. V. O. Key, Jr., *American State Politics: An Introduction* (New York: Knopf, 1956), pp. 87–88.
3. Ibid., p. 88.
4. Ibid., p. 91.
5. Ibid., p. 117.
6. Ellen Torelle, ed., *The Political Philosophy of Robert M. La Follette* (Madison, Wis.: Robert M. La Follette Co., 1920), pp. 29–31.
7. Malcolm E. Jewell, *Parties and Primaries: Nominating State Governors* (New York: Praeger, 1984), pp. 9–11.
8. Ibid., pp. 11–12.
9. Malcolm E. Jewell and Sarah M. Morehouse, *Political Parties and Elections in American States*, 4th ed. (Washington, D.C.: CQ Press, 2001), p. 102.
10. For an analysis of the operation of New York's cross-filing system, see Howard A. Scarrow, *Parties, Elections, and*

Representation in the State of New York (New York: New York University Press, 1983), pp. 55–80; and Robert J. Spitzer, "Multiparty Politics in New York," in Paul S. Herrnson and John C. Green, eds., *Multiparty Politics in America* (Lanham, Md.: Rowman and Little-field, 1997), pp. 125–137.
11. Spitzer, "Multiparty Politics in New York," p. 133.
12. "Primary Election Dates in Pennsylvania: An Analysis of Proposals for Change," Report of the Task Force and Advisory Committee on Primary Election Dates, November, 2000.
13. Sarah McCally Morehouse, *The Governor as Party Leader: Campaigning and Governing* (Ann Arbor, University of Michigan Press, 1998) pp. 22–23.
14. Jewell and Morehouse, *Political Parties*, pp. 109–110. For evidence of endorsements helping candidates with primaries, see James P. Melcher, "The Party's Still Lively: New Findings about Statewide Preprimary Endorsements,"

American Review of Politics 19 (Spring 1998): 53–56. See also Andrew D. McNitt, "The Effect of Endorsement on Competition for Nominations: An Explanation of Different Nominating Systems," *Journal of Politics* 42 (Feb. 1980): 257–266; and Tom W. Rice, "Gubernatorial and Senatorial Primary Elections: Determinants and Consequences," *American Politics Quarterly* 13 (Oct. 1985): 434–435.

15. Jewell and Morehouse, *Political Parties*, p. 120.

16. Ibid., p. 119.

17. Ibid., p. 109–110.

18. Morehouse, *The Governor as Party Leader*, pp. 121, 181–200.

19. Key, *Politics, Parties and Pressure Groups*, pp. 379–380; Key, *American State Politics*, pp. 107–111.

20. Rice, "Gubernatorial and Senatorial Primary Elections," pp. 435–437; and Berry and Canon, "Explaining Competitiveness," pp. 459–471.

21. Committee for the Study of the American Electorate, press release, Sept. 23, 1995; Terry M. Neal, "Primary Turnout Continues to Decline," *Washington Post*, Sept. 29, 1998, p. A4.

22. Jewell, *Parties and Primaries*, p. 176.

23. V. O. Key considered the consequences of unrepresentative primary electorates in his *American State Politics*, pp. 153–165.

24. Barry C. Burden, "The Polarizing Effects of Congressional Primaries," in Peter F. Galderisi, Michael Lyons, and Marni Ezra, eds., *Congress Primaries in the Politics of Representation* (Lanham, Md.: Rowman and Littlefield, 2001); David Brady and Morris Fiorina, "Congress in the Era of the Permanent Campaign," in Norman J. Ornstein and Thomas E. Mann, eds., *The Permanent Campaign and Its Future* (Washington, D.C.: AEI and Brookings, 2000),

pp. 134–161; David Brady and Edward Schwartz, "Ideology and Interests in Congressional Voting: The Politics of Abortion in the U.S. Senate," *Public Choice* 84 (1995): 25–48.

25. On national party recruitment activities, see the publications of Paul S. Herrnson, *Congressional Elections: Campaigns at Home and in Washington*, 3rd ed. (Washington, D.C.: CQ Press, 2000), pp. 47–48; and *Party Campaigning in the 1980s* (Cambridge: Harvard University Press, 1988), pp. 48–54.

26. Richard L. Berke, "G.O.P. Giving House Hopefuls Primary Help," *New York Times* (national edition), March 3, 2002, pp. 1, 22.

27. Jewell and Morehouse, *Political Parties*, pp. 138–139; see also Patrick J. Kenny, "Sorting Out the Effects of Divisiveness in Congressional and Senatorial Elections," *Western Political Quarterly* 41 (1988): 756–777; Patrick J. Kenny and Tom W. Rice, "The Relationship between Divisive Primaries and General Election Outcomes," *American Political Science Review* 31 (1987): 31–44; and Donald B. Johnson and James L. Gibson, "The Divisive Primary Revisited: Party Activists in Iowa," *American Political Science Review* 68 (1974): 67–77.

28. Leon D. Epstein, "The American Party Primary," in Nelson W. Polsby and Raymond E. Wolfinger, eds., *On Parties: Essays Honoring Austin Ranney* (Berkeley: Institute of Government Press, University of California–Berkeley, 1999), p. 50.

29. For a full exposition of Epstein's intriguing argument concerning the impact of the direct primary on parties, see Leon D. Epstein, *Political Parties in the American Mold* (Madison: University of Wisconsin Press, 1986), pp. 244–245; and his "The American Party Primary," pp. 52–53.

PRESIDENTIAL NOMINATING POLITICS

CHAPTER CONTENTS

Media Politics in Presidential Nominations

A Lengthy, Candidate-Centered, Primary-Focused, Participatory, and
Media-Oriented Process

Vice President Hubert H. Humphrey won the 1968 Democratic presidential nomination even though he did not open his campaign until March of that year or enter
a single presidential primary. Instead, he depended upon his support among party
leaders. If 2008 had been like 1968, there is little doubt that Hillary Clinton would
have been the Democratic Party's nominee for president. Indeed, as early as 2004, it
was clear that Hillary Clinton would compete for the presidential nomination in
2008 and she spent the next two years quietly building a sizeable campaign organization that raised enormous sums of money and attracted widespread support from
party leaders. By the end of 2007, Clinton was well ahead of the field in the polls
and even farther ahead when it came to endorsements from the Democratic Party
elite. But it was first-term Senator Barack Obama who would accept the Democratic
Party's nomination at the national convention in Colorado nine months later.

Such is the nature of the modern presidential nomination system. A process once
heavily dominated by party leaders, who influenced the selection of national convention delegates, is now more candidate centered. A process that once relied upon internal party procedures to select delegates through caucuses and conventions now relies
primarily upon presidential primaries to determine the allocation of delegates among
contenders for a party's nomination. Participation was once restricted to party regulars in the caucus and convention states and to primary voters in a few primary states.
Today, the competition for the presidential nomination is an open and participatory
process characterized by mass citizen involvement in primaries and open access to
party caucuses. Now that the presidential primaries and some caucuses receive saturation media coverage, the media has far-reaching influence concerning who ultimately
wins a nomination. Presidential nominating politics of the twenty-first century is candidate centered, primary focused, participatory, and media intensive.

METHODS OF DELEGATE SELECTION

The national nominating conventions held in the summer of presidential election
years are the culmination of a long season of campaigning to select national convention delegates. The delegates, meeting in convention, nominate the party's candidates for president and vice president, adopt a platform, and approve rules that will
govern the party. The composition of the convention, of course, determines the
nature of the decisions the convention will make on the nominations, platform,
and rules. The processes of delegate selection, therefore, are critical to the outcomes
of the convention.

There are three principal methods of delegate selection: (1) the presidential primary; (2) the party caucus/convention process; and (3) automatic selection by virtue
of the party or elected position an individual holds. Both parties use the presidential
primary and caucus/convention selection processes, but only the Democrats have
automatic delegates (see Figure 6.1). The various states are free to devise their

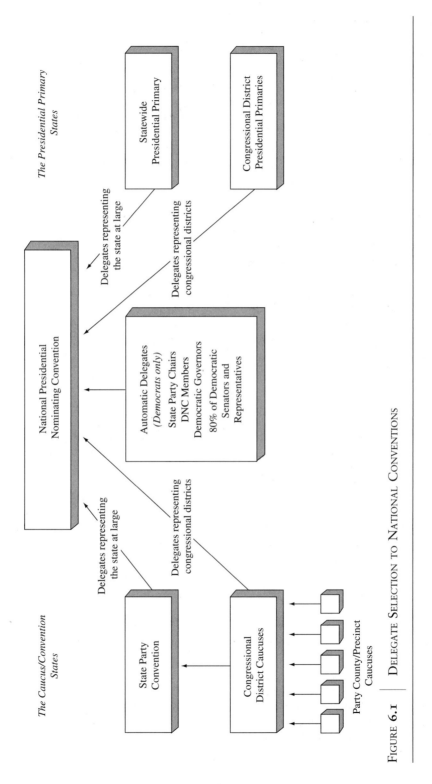

The Presidential Primary States

Statewide Presidential Primary

Congressional District Presidential Primaries

Delegates representing the state at large

Delegates representing congressional districts

National Presidential Nominating Convention

Automatic Delegates
(Democrats only)
State Party Chairs
DNC Members
Democratic Governors
80% of Democratic Senators and Representatives

The Caucus/Convention States

Delegates representing the state at large

Delegates representing congressional districts

State Party Convention

Congressional District Caucuses

Party County/Precinct Caucuses

FIGURE 6.1 | DELEGATE SELECTION TO NATIONAL CONVENTIONS

own methods of delegate selection as long as those methods conform to guidelines contained in the rules of the national Republican and Democratic parties. The procedures for selection of delegates are frequently set forth in state statutes, which may be supplemented by state party rules. In the absence of state statutes governing delegate selection, state parties may adopt rules to determine how delegates will be chosen. Because each state legislature and/or state party organization is involved in devising the procedures for delegate selection, practices followed within the states vary widely.

STATE DELEGATE SELECTION PROCEDURES MUST CONFORM TO NATIONAL PARTY RULES

Although the states have some latitude in determining how their delegates to national conventions will be chosen, the procedures they devise must be in strict conformity with national party rules. In other words, national party rules take precedence over state statutes and state party rules in matters of delegate selection. A state delegation that is not chosen in conformity with national party rules runs the risk of not having its delegation seated at the national convention—a severe sanction that the national party can impose.

The most celebrated instance of conflict between a state party and its national organization over the delegate selection procedures took place in Wisconsin. In 1903, Wisconsin was the first state to adopt a presidential primary law, but it was a law that also provided for conducting the presidential primary under open primary procedures. After 1974, Democratic national party rules forbad selecting delegates through open primary procedures, and thus Wisconsin's law was out of conformity with national party rules. Wisconsin sought to maintain its open primary, but the U.S. Supreme Court upheld the right of a national party organization to determine delegate selection procedures.[1] Wisconsin Democrats, therefore, were forced in 1984 to abandon the open presidential primary for selecting their convention delegates and adopt caucus procedures that satisfied the national Democratic Party. In an effort to put this often bitter controversy behind it and prepare for the 1988 elections, the Democratic National Committee in 1986 agreed to permit states with open primary traditions (Wisconsin and Montana) to use open presidential primaries. While making this accommodation to Wisconsin, the DNC continued to assert its power to regulate delegate selection procedures.

PRESIDENTIAL PRIMARIES

The largest share of convention delegates is chosen through procedures that involve presidential primaries. In 2008, thirty-six Democratic presidential primaries were used to allocate delegates among presidential candidates while the Republicans used primaries in 38 states. These primaries determined the allocation of over two-thirds of the delegates selected to either convention. The number of states and territories using the presidential primaries has increased significantly since 1968, when fifteen Republican and Democratic primaries were used in the selection of 39.1 percent of the delegates (see Figure 6.2). However, the number of primaries held in any

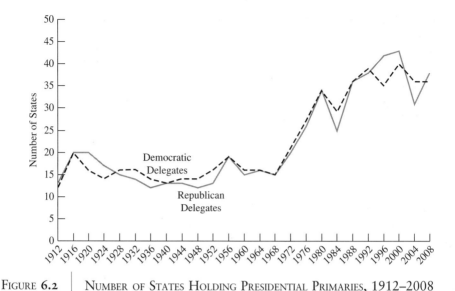

FIGURE 6.2 | NUMBER OF STATES HOLDING PRESIDENTIAL PRIMARIES, 1912–2008

Source: C. C. Euchner, J. Maltese, and M. Nelson (2002). *Development of the Presidential Electoral Process: The Primary System.* In *Guide to the Presidency* (vol. 1). Washington: CQ Press. Information for 2004 and 2008 comes from DNC and RNC.

given presidential election year has been subject to considerable variation depending on political conditions. For example, in 2004, there were only thirty-one primaries used to select Republican delegates due to the fact that George W. Bush was unopposed for his party's nomination.

Most presidential primaries are funded and operated by the state governments. However, facing budget shortfalls in 2004, seven states that had previously funded presidential primaries passed legislation canceling that funding for the 2004 campaign. Parties in these states were forced to either fund and operate their own primaries (as the state Democratic parties in Michigan, Utah, and South Carolina do) or change their process to a caucus system (which happened in Colorado, Kansas, Maine, and North Dakota). Therefore, despite having a highly competitive nomination campaign in 2004, there were fewer Democratic presidential primaries compared to 2000.

With the largest share of the delegates selected through procedures that involve presidential primaries, it has become imperative for presidential candidates to enter virtually all of the primaries in order to win sufficient delegates to gain a convention majority. The importance of the primaries, however, goes beyond the number of delegates that are at stake in these contests. The results of primaries constitute an ostensibly objective indicator of a candidate's ability to win the election. Primaries are thus particularly important because of the image of candidate popularity, electability, and momentum they can convey.

The mechanics of the presidential primaries vary from state to state depending upon applicable state laws and party rules. For example, in some states the names of

BOX 6.1	MICHIGAN AND ARIZONA TAKE PRESIDENTIAL PRIMARIES ONLINE

In 2004, the Michigan State Democratic Party invited citizens to cast their ballots for the party-run presidential primary in person, by mail, or over the Internet. It was only the second time that Internet voting had been offered in a binding statewide primary, the first being the Arizona Democratic primary in 2000, which was not competitive since it was held after Bill Bradley left the race. While Howard Dean and Wesley Clark embraced Internet voting in Michigan, many of the other candidates opposed the option, at least partly because they believed it favored Dean, whose campaign was considered the most Internet-savvy. Yet once the DNC agreed to allow Michigan to offer the Internet option, the candidates did their best to take advantage of it. Some candidates arranged to have laptops brought to the workplaces of their union supporters to have them apply for Internet ballots during their lunch breaks. Most of the contenders included links on their Web sites to allow supporters to easily apply for their Internet ballots. Voters casting ballots by mail or online could cast their ballots at any time before the official primary date on February 7.

Ultimately, 46,543 voters cast their ballots online, which was over one-fourth of the total electorate for the primary. This was nearly twice as many voters as those who cast their ballots by mail, though more than half of all votes were cast in person. While the experiment in Internet voting was largely viewed as a success because of the lack of any serious reported problems, some detractors continued to question the fairness of the method. These concerns largely relate to the "digital divide" in the United States—poorer citizens are less likely to have access to the Internet than those who are more wealthy. As Al Sharpton explained prior to the Michigan primary, "If someone can vote in the warmth of their living room, but a grandmother has to go down four flights of stairs and out into the cold, that's not an even playing field." The Michigan Democratic Party scrapped its online voting program for the 2008 primary, leaving the fate of Internet voting in doubt for the near future.

Source: Katharine Q. Seelye, "Michigan's Online Ballot Spurs New Strategies for Democrats," **New York Times***, January 10, 2004.*

individuals who are running for delegate positions are on the ballot and voters vote directly for delegates. In other states, the names of the presidential candidates are on the ballot, but the names of persons seeking to be delegates are not. There is normally a contest for delegates in each congressional district and an additional contest to determine how the delegates who will represent the state at large will be allocated among the presidential candidates. A presidential candidate, therefore, can lose the statewide vote and fail to win any at-large delegates and still pick up delegates by making a strong showing in the primaries of individual congressional districts within a state.

Depending upon state laws and party rules, the states also vary in terms of which voters are allowed to participate in the primaries. These rules governing primary participation can affect the outcome of primaries. National Democratic rules mandate that Democratic primaries must be closed (only registered Democrats can vote) or semi-open (only Democrats or those registered as independents can vote). National Republican rules impose no such limitations on participation, and states are free to use open (any registered voter can vote), closed, or semi-open primaries. In 2008, the fact that New Hampshire has a semi-open primary had a significant effect on the Republican contest. Senator John McCain (Ariz.) needed a victory in New Hampshire to sustain his campaign and build momentum. Exit polls indicated that McCain was able to defeat Mitt Romney in the primary largely because independents made up more than one-third of the electorate and he easily carried that group. Romney appeared to narrowly win among self-identified Republicans, indicating that McCain may have lost if the state held a closed primary.

STATE PARTY CAUCUSES AND CONVENTIONS

Until the 1972 conventions, a majority of the states used state party caucuses and conventions to select delegates. For example, in 1968 almost two-thirds of the delegates to national conventions were chosen via party caucuses and conventions. This procedure involves a relatively small proportion of the electorate. It is party members and activists who normally have the interest, motivation, and knowledge to participate in the series of party meetings that culminate in the congressional district and state party meetings to choose delegates.

In caucus/convention states, the process of delegate selection involves a progression of party meetings starting at the local level, running through the congressional district, and culminating in a state party convention. The process normally begins with local caucuses at either the precinct or county level. Party members and activists attend these meetings, often after having been mobilized by presidential candidate organizations or interest groups. Local caucus participants register their candidate preferences and also elect representatives to the congressional district caucus, the next level of party meetings in the process. At the congressional district caucus, representatives chosen by the various local caucuses meet to (1) register their preference for the party's presidential nominee; (2) elect delegates to the national convention to represent the congressional district; and (3) elect delegates to the state party convention. The national convention delegates selected to represent the congressional district at the national convention are chosen to reflect the extent of support candidates for the presidency have among the congressional district caucus participants. Delegates from the various congressional districts in a state then meet in a state party convention to elect national convention delegates to represent the state at large.

Because the caucus system is an internal party process, it places a premium on a candidate having dedicated supporters—the type of people who are willing to spend evenings and weekends taking part in lengthy party meetings. It also requires an effective organization to mobilize people to turn out and support the candidate at each stage in the process. It is essential that a presidential candidate's organization have intimate knowledge of the state laws and party rules for delegate selection and of intraparty politics. Whereas presidential primaries are media oriented in order to appeal to a mass electorate, the caucus/convention process is more of an intraparty affair that requires an efficient organization.

COMBINATION PRESIDENTIAL PRIMARY AND CAUCUS SYSTEMS

Some states use a combination of the presidential primary and party caucus to choose their national convention delegates. In 2008, the Texas Democrats held a presidential primary during the day on March 4th, and then party caucuses that evening. Approximately two-thirds of the delegates were allocated according to the results of the primary, which Hillary Clinton narrowly won. An additional one-third of the delegates were allocated according to the results of the caucuses, which Barack Obama captured. Occasionally, states hold presidential primaries that are purely popularity contests and that have no binding effect on delegate selection, because the delegates are actually chosen in party caucuses and conventions. In 2004, the District of Columbia held the first primary of the presidential campaign on January 13th, but it was purely non-binding and had no effect on the selection of delegates.

AUTOMATIC UNPLEDGED DELEGATES

In an effort to increase convention participation by party leaders and elected officials, the Democrats for their 1984 convention made provision in their rules for granting automatic delegate status to major party leaders and elected officials. These delegates are not officially pledged to any presidential candidate, though they may choose to informally announce their intention to vote for a particular candidate. Under Democratic rules, national committee members, state party chairs and vice chairs, and Democratic governors are automatically convention delegates, as are Democratic members of the U.S. House and Senate. Designation of the congressional delegates is made by the House and Senate Democratic caucuses. In 2008, about one-fifth of the Democratic delegates were such "super delegates." There are no automatic delegates to Republican national conventions. Republican Party leaders and elected officials must go through the regular primary and caucus procedures in order to become delegates.

Reporter Roger Simon wrote in 2008 that "At the beginning of the 2008 campaign, very few people even knew what a super delegate was. It was like the Electoral College before the 2000 election. Who cared?"[2] Of course, the 2008 Democratic nomination campaign changed all of that. As I discuss later in this chapter, neither Barack Obama nor Hillary Clinton was able to win enough elected delegates in primaries and caucuses to clinch a majority of Democratic delegates. Thus, automatic delegates were ultimately responsible for breaking the stalemate, with most pledging their support for Obama, who had won a majority of the elected delegates. While these automatic delegates played a decisive role in the 2008 campaign, few relished having to publicly decide between two prominent figures in the party. The Democratic rank-and-file were no more happy about a system that gave party leaders such influence. Thus, in 2009, the Democratic National Committee began the process of revising their rules to remove the voting rights of automatic delegates. Automatic delegates may continue to be invited to Democratic conventions in future presidential election years, but their role will be to watch the voting, not to take part in it.

PHASES OF THE NOMINATION PROCESS

Achieving a presidential nomination has become a full-time, often four-year, endeavor. The lengthy and often intense schedule of the presidential nominating process can be broken down into a series of phases that culminate with the national convention.[3]

BOX 6.2	ATTENTION TO DETAIL: HOW UNDERSTANDING THE RULES HELPED OBAMA WIN THE NOMINATION IN 2008

One of the important stories of the 2008 race for the Democratic nomination was the ability of the Obama campaign to develop a sophisticated strategy for maximizing the number of delegates he would win in every state. This excerpt from Roger Simon's review of the campaign tells part of that story:

> [Obama advisors Jeffrey] Berman, and [David] Plouffe [had] been making very spe-cific plans since April 2007 about winning delegates. They both knew the media would concentrate on states won: Who would win Iowa? Who would win New Hampshire? That often determined the outcome right there. "One candidate wins and knocks out the others, who run out of money," Berman said. "But you don't know in advance if there will be a knockout." By the end of January 2008, there was going to be no early knockout. The candidates were splitting victories and defeats (though some were more dramatic than others), and the status of Michigan and Florida was going to remain in limbo.
>
> [...]
>
> The Obama campaign decided it would not contest every state at stake on Super Tuesday. It saw no point in making an effort in Bill Clinton's home state of Arkansas, for example. But in one of the most crucial decisions of the campaign, the Obama forces decided winning wasn't everything. "We determined how to contest the states we expected to lose," Berman said. [...] "We took a look at the congres-sional districts, projected winning margins and competed where we thought we could limit her margins to what we could live with," Berman said. "We wanted to hold Hillary's margin to the smallest number of delegates possible. She would win a state, but not achieve a large delegate advantage."
>
> Illinois and New York, the two home states of the candidates, were a good test of this strategy. Both candidates would, of course, win their home states. New York had 232 delegates at stake and Illinois had 153 delegates at stake, which meant that Hillary had what seemed to be a 79-delegate advantage going into Feb. 5. But that's not how it came out. "We got 197 delegates out of the two states, and she got 188," Berman said. "This was quite an accomplishment."
>
> Now take two other Feb. 5 states, Idaho and New Jersey. Idaho? Did the Clinton campaign care from Idaho? It did not. To the Clinton campaign, Idaho was an odd place that had more potatoes than people, and it was also a caucus state, which the Clintons hated. New Jersey was a different matter. It bordered New York, it was a primary state and it was Clinton Country. But the Obama campaign targeted key congressional districts in New Jersey to keep Hillary's victory margin there as small as possible. "In Idaho, we had a 15-3 win in terms of delegates, and in New Jersey, she had a 59-48 win," Berman said. Do the math. Obama gets a 12-delegate net win out of Idaho—tiny, weird, potato-infested Idaho—and Hillary gets only an 11-delegate net win out of New Jersey. "So we got a greater net gain out of Idaho than she got in New Jersey," Berman said.

Source: Roger Simon, "Relentless" *Politico* (August 25, 2008): http://www.politico.com/news/stories/0808/12732.html

Phase 1: Laying the Groundwork and Preliminary Skirmishing: The "Invisible Primary"

During the period following a presidential election, prospective candidates for a presidential nomination four years hence begin the planning and preparations for their campaigns. This frequently involves recruiting a professional staff experienced in national politics, creating a political action committee (PAC) and tax-exempt foundation to fund candidate activities, and developing a campaign plan. Candidates crisscross the nation making appearances before the state party conventions, civic groups, trade associations, unions, and other candidates' fund-raisers in an attempt to gain media attention and make contacts with party leaders. Iowa and New Hampshire are inevitable and are frequent stops on the campaign itinerary of presidential candidates, because these states hold critical early events in the national convention delegate selection process.

The extent of early campaign preparations and activity were already evident as early as 2005 among prospective candidates for the nominations in 2008.[4] Since his loss to Bush in 2000, John McCain had been targeting 2008 as his opportunity to emerge as the front-runner for the Republican nomination. He was a constant presence on television in 2005 and 2006, appearing more than any other potential presidential candidate. McCain also gave the commencement speech at Reverend Jerry Falwell's Liberty University in 2006, an act seemingly aimed at courting religious conservatives in the Republican Party. Massachusetts Governor Mitt Romney, also considered a contender for the 2008 Republican nomination, spent 2005 and 2006 traveling extensively to the three states thought to be most pivotal for securing the nomination—New Hampshire, Iowa, and South Carolina.

On the Democratic side, the early assumed front-runner was Senator Hillary Clinton (D-N.Y.). Clinton's first task was to win an easy reelection as New York's senator in 2006; a tough reelection campaign would signal weakness for her presidential aspirations. To accomplish this, however, she had to avoid any overt indications that she was campaigning for the Democratic nomination; thus, she carefully avoided traveling to Iowa and New Hampshire in 2005 and 2006. In the meantime, however, she concentrated on raising massive amounts of money for her reelection campaign—over $50 million—despite the fact that her Senate race was not expected to be competitive. Any money not spent on her reelection could be transferred and used for her presidential campaign, a fact that put her well ahead of other potential candidates for the nomination in fund-raising. John Edwards also sought to capitalize on his good showing in the 2004 Democratic primaries and his presence on the 2004 Democratic ticket by becoming a frequent visitor to New Hampshire and Iowa during 2005 and 2006.

The pace of presidential campaigning intensifies during the year of the midterm elections, as the candidates seek to play a prominent role in assisting their parties in congressional, senatorial, and state elections. There are appearances at fund-raisers for party candidates from Maine to California. Most of the major contenders have their own personal PACs, which fund their campaign forays and provide contributions to state and congressional candidates. Hillary Clinton's HILLPAC donated over $100,000 to thirty-one Democratic House candidates and $170,000 to twenty-one Senate candidates in 2006. The strategy is to create a sense of obligation among officeholders that can be converted later into commitments of support for the presidential nomination.

During the year preceding the presidential election, the pace of campaigning accelerates, with frequent visits to key primary states. One of the staples of this phase of the campaign has been appearances at state party conventions, which occasionally conduct straw polls—informal votes—of candidate popularity among the delegates. These tests of popularity among party activists are used by the candidates to demonstrate support for the nomination. Of course, they carry little real value when it comes to judging the prospects of a candidate. After all, Ron Paul fared quite well in many straw polls held before the 2008 Republican nomination race; yet, he flopped when actual votes were cast, winning just thirty-five delegates.

It is also essential in the year before the presidential primaries begin for candidates to raise serious money for their nomination campaigns. Two types of candidates have special advantages in raising campaign war chests—candidates with national stature and those who can compensate for a lack of national stature through access to well-heeled constituencies. For example, Hillary Clinton's visibility and status as former first lady and the senator of one of the largest states gave her a fundraising advantage in the run-up to the 2008 Democratic nomination battle, and of course President Obama can be expected to take full advantage of his position to harvest early money for his renomination and reelection campaigns in 2012.

The importance of early fund-raising is clear: From 1980 to 2000, no candidate that had led their competitors in fund-raising on December 31 of the year before the presidential election failed to go on to win the nomination. Yet, while raising large sums of money is still important, recent history suggests that it might not be critical to lead in fund-raising. Howard Dean led the fund-raising race among Democrats at the end of 2003, but ended up losing the nomination to John Kerry in 2004. At the end of 2007, Hillary Clinton led all Democrats in money raised while Mitt Romney was ahead of the Republican field. Neither candidate won his or her party's nomination.

It appears as though raising large sums of money is a necessity for mounting a serious campaign for the party's nomination, but it is no guarantee of success. Clinton built a substantial war chest prior to entering the presidential race in 2007 and continued to add substantial sums through the rest of the year. But Obama was raising large sums as well, albeit in a very different way. While Clinton was relying mostly on traditional Democratic donors who could give the maximum contribution to her campaign ($2,300 per donor for the primary campaign), Obama was attracting large numbers of small donors. When the first campaign finance reports were filed in April, 2007, the *Washington Post* reported that Obama had "stunned political observers" by keeping pace with Clinton's fund-raising during the first three months of the invisible primary. Obama's early fund-raising success did not fade either. In fact, Obama continued to keep pace with Clinton throughout the year and by the fall it was clear that the Democratic nomination would effectively be a two candidate race, with both candidates boasting tremendous war chests. Despite their own credentials, John Edwards and Bill Richardson were simply not able to keep up with Obama and Clinton, which served to diminish the seriousness of their candidacies (see Figure 6.3).

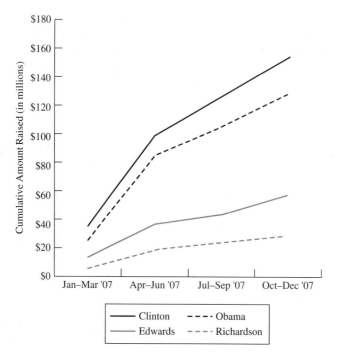

FIGURE 6.3 | FUNDRAISING BY CANDIDATES FOR THE DEMOCRATIC PRESIDENTIAL NOMINATION IN 2007

Source: Federal Election Commission.

PHASE 2: DELEGATE SELECTION: THE EARLY CONTESTS AND THE CONSEQUENCES OF FRONT-LOADING

The early contests for delegates are important not only because of the number of delegates at stake but also because of the benefits that attach to doing well in these events. Events of critical importance are the Iowa caucuses, the first major delegate selection event of the season, and the New Hampshire primary, which is by state statute the first in the nation. Each normally receives saturation news coverage. The results of these early contests establish front-runners for the nomination and begin the process of narrowing the field of candidates. Those who do well in these events gain publicity, standing in the polls, increased fund-raising capacity, and support from influential party leaders. Those who falter in the early contests find that their poll ratings, fund-raising, and support from prominent leaders all diminish, and many are forced to drop out of the race.

The early stage of the primary and caucus season has been described as the "media fishbowl" phase of the presidential nominating campaign.[5] It is a time when the electronic and print media have their greatest impact through their allocation of coverage to the candidates and their assessments of who won and who lost delegate selection contests. These assessments help to winnow the field of candidates. What matters most in the early contests is how the results of the primaries and caucuses are interpreted. Specifically, candidates seek to meet or exceed the expectations that have been set by the news media. In 2004, Howard Dean's campaign never recovered from his failure to meet the media's high expectations for him in Iowa. Alternatively, John Kerry and John Edwards exceeded expectations in Iowa by finishing first and second in the caucuses, and, accordingly, they became front-runners for the Democratic nomination. In 2008, the failure of either Hillary Clinton or Barack Obama to meet the news media's expectations in Iowa and New Hampshire, respectively, led to a protracted six-month nomination struggle.

THE IOWA CAUCUSES AND NEW HAMPSHIRE PRIMARY In the lore of presidential nominating politics, the Iowa caucuses and the New Hampshire primary, normally the opening events of the delegate selection season in a presidential election year, are seen as an opportunity for candidates to establish momentum for winning their party's nomination. These events have also been viewed as an opportunity for underdog and lesser-known candidates to focus resources on small states and, if they are successful, to use the media attention and jump in their poll standings to gain the support needed to win future primaries. The classic example of a little-known, underdog candidate who used the momentum gained from his early successes in Iowa and New Hampshire to win future primaries and his party's 1976 nomination was the then-former Georgia Governor Jimmy Carter. More recently, however, winning the Iowa caucuses and/or the New Hampshire primary has not necessarily been the ticket to a presidential nomination. Indeed, Hillary Clinton won the New Hampshire primary in 2008, but eventually lost her bid for the Democratic nomination. The decline in importance of the Iowa caucuses, and especially the New Hampshire primary, is attributable mostly to *front-loading*—the concentrating of state presidential primaries and caucuses that select the bulk of the convention delegates during February and March of presidential election years.

The concentration of primaries and caucuses resulting from front-loading means that candidates must be equipped to compete in quick succession in a series of multistate primaries across the country after the New Hampshire primary. It is no longer possible to use the momentum of a win in Iowa and New Hampshire to create the support needed to win a nomination. The organizational and financial resources essential to compete in a primary-packed schedule from February through March must already be in place before the New Hampshire primary. (See the discussion of front-loading and its effects later.) Thus, Barack Obama's 2008 victory in Iowa was critical to eventually propelling him to the Democratic nomination, but he was only able to fully capitalize on his caucus victory because he already had significant financial resources and a well-developed campaign organization.

Instead of predicting the winner of a nomination, the New Hampshire primary, as well as other early primaries, has played a role in winnowing the number of candidates in the race; those who do poorly drop out for lack of support.[6] Former Arkansas Governor Mike Huckabee's surprise victory in Iowa in 2008 vaulted him into prominence and allowed him to finish second for the Republican Party's nomination. At the same time, Mitt Romney's failure to win either Iowa or New Hampshire effectively toppled him the frontrunner position he had earned during the invisible primary period. And on the Democratic side, John Edwards' chances of winning the nomination in 2008 were also thwarted when he failed to finish first in Iowa.

Iowa also played a pivotal role in the 2004 nomination campaign. Howard Dean entered the Iowa caucuses as the clear front-runner in public opinion polls, fund-raising, endorsements, and media coverage. On the other hand, John Kerry's campaign was struggling, and he concentrated his resources in Iowa in hopes of making a strong showing there. Kerry succeeded in scoring an unexpected victory by capturing 38 percent of the vote. Dean finished a disappointing third and made a bad night worse when the television stations kept replaying an awkward "scream" that he unleashed during his concession speech. The consequences of the result in Iowa were clear in New Hampshire, where Kerry's prospects for victory quickly improved and Dean's diminished. Dean held an 8 percent lead over Kerry on the day of the Iowa caucuses, but three days later he trailed Kerry by 13 points. Ultimately, Kerry won the New Hampshire primary and eventually secured the nomination by defeating Dean and John Edwards, who had also benefited by finishing second in Iowa. But the effect that Iowa had on the campaign in 2004 was clear: Kerry won a majority of convention delegates, followed by Edwards and Dean; the same order the candidates finished when the first votes were cast in Iowa on January 19th.

FRONT-LOADING THE PRESIDENTIAL PRIMARIES   In 2008, more and more states engaged in a competition to move ahead the dates of their primaries in an effort to give their states' electorates greater influence over the selection of presidential nominees. This process of bunching the primaries early in a presidential year has been dubbed "front-loading." Thus, in 2008, following fast after New Hampshire's first-in-the-nation primary on January 8th, a series of single-state and multistate primaries followed in quick succession, so that less than a month after the New Hampshire primary more than 50 percent of the delegates had been selected (Table 6.1 shows the high level of front-loading in 2008). This front-loading has become far more pronounced during recent decades. Figure 6.4 presents the percentage of Democratic Party delegates decided with each successive week after the New Hampshire primary in 1976, 2000, and 2004. Note that in 1976, the increase in delegates was gradual and a majority of delegates had not been chosen until ten weeks after the New Hampshire primary. In 2000 and 2004, a majority of the delegates were decided in half that time.

TABLE **6.1** | FRONT-LOADING OF THE PRESIDENTIAL PRIMARIES, 2008

Date	State Primary	Number of Delegates at Stake
January 8	New Hampshire	23
January 15	Michigan	78.5
January 26	South Carolina	46
	Florida	105.5
——— *John Edwards Withdraws* ———		
February 5 "Super Tuesday"	Alabama	53
	Arizona	57
	Arkansas	36

continued

TABLE **6.1** | FRONT-LOADING OF THE PRESIDENTIAL PRIMARIES, 2008 *continued*

Date	State Primary	Number of Delegates at Stake
	California	375
	Connecticut	49
	Delaware	16
	Georgia	89
	Illinois	156
	Massachusetts	95
	Missouri	74
	New Jersey	109
	New York	236
	Oklahoma	39
	Tennessee	70
	Utah	24

———— *Majority of Convention Delegates Were Chosen by February 5* ————

Date	State Primary	Number of Delegates at Stake
February 9	Louisiana	57
February 12	Maryland	72
	Virginia	85
February 19	Wisconsin	76
March 4	Ohio	143
	Rhode Island	22
	Texas	198
	Vermont	16
March 11	Mississippi	34
April 22	Pennsylvania	161
May 6	Indiana	74
	North Carolina	117
May 13	West Virginia	29
May 20	Kentucky	52
	Oregon	53
June 3	Montana	17
	South Dakota	16

REPUBLICAN PRIMARIES

Date	State Primary	Number of Delegates at Stake
January 8	New Hampshire	12
January 15	Michigan	30
January 19	South Carolina	24
January 29	Florida	57

continued

TABLE **6.1** | FRONT-LOADING OF THE PRESIDENTIAL PRIMARIES, 2008 *continued*

Date	State Primary	Number of Delegates at Stake
——— *Rudolph Giuliani Withdraws* ———		
February 5 "Super Tuesday"	Alabama	48
	Arizona	53
	Arkansas	34
	California	173
	Connecticut	30
	Delaware	18
	Georgia	72
	Illinois	70
	Massachusetts	43
	Missouri	58
	New Jersey	52
	New York	101
	Oklahoma	41
	Tennessee	55
	Utah	36
——— *Majority of Convention Delegates Were Chosen by February 5* ———		
——— *Mitt Romney Withdraws* ———		
February 9	Louisiana	47
February 12	Maryland	37
	Virginia	63
February 19	Wisconsin	40
	Washington	40
March 4	Ohio	88
	Rhode Island	20
	Texas	140
	Vermont	17
——— *Mike Huckabee Withdraws* ———		
——— *McCain Wins a Majority of Convention Delegates* ———		
March 11	Mississippi	39
April 22	Pennsylvania	74
May 6	Indiana	57
	North Carolina	69
May 13	West Virginia	30
May 20	Kentucky	45
	Oregon	30
May 27	Idaho	32
June 3	New Mexico	32
	South Dakota	27

Note: Only primaries are listed.

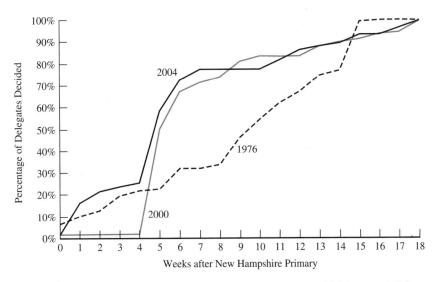

FIGURE **6.4** | COMPARISON OF FRONT-LOADING IN THE 1976, 2000, AND 2004 DEMOCRATIC NOMINATION CAMPAIGNS

Source: Democratic National Committee.

Front-loading of the primary process has the effect of favoring candidates who have the following characteristics:

- They have public visibility and name recognition.
- They are well organized on a nationwide basis and thus are capable of mounting primary campaigns in a number of states simultaneously and in quick succession.
- They have ample financial resources.

The importance of these traits was clearly evident in 2008, when both Obama (on the Democratic side) and Huckabee (on the Republican side) finished better than expected in Iowa. But it was Obama who was able to capitalize on this success, largely because he possessed far greater financial resources and national organization than Huckabee did.

The Iowa caucuses and the New Hampshire primary feature "retail politics"— direct selling of candidates through extensive personal contact with voters. But after New Hampshire's primary, the nominating terrain changes dramatically, and the style of campaigning becomes "wholesale politics"—reaching the mass electorate through heavy reliance on media advertising in a number of states simultaneously as groups of states hold their primaries in rapid succession. Candidates with limited resources who focus their efforts on a single early contest such as Iowa's caucuses can at times achieve victories (e.g., Mike Huckabee in 2008). But in a heavily front-loaded system, these victories can seldom be sustained, because the candidates are not equipped to compete on a nationwide basis against their better organized and financed opponents.

TABLE 6.2 | TREND TOWARD EARLY CAPTURE OF PRESIDENTIAL NOMINATIONS: THE DATES ON WHICH PRESIDENTIAL NOMINEES GAINED A MAJORITY OF THE NATIONAL CONVENTION DELEGATES, 1972–2008

Year	Candidate and Party	Date
2008	John McCain (Rep.)	March 4
	Barack Obama (Dem.)	June 3
2000	George W. Bush (Rep.)	March 14
	Al Gore (Dem.)	March 14
1996	Bill Clinton (Dem.)	March 12
	Bob Dole (Rep.)	March 26
1992	George H. W. Bush (Rep.)	April 28
	Bill Clinton (Dem.)	June 2
1988	George H. W. Bush (Rep.)	April 26
	Michael Dukakis (Dem.)	June 7
1984	Ronald Reagan (Rep.)	May 8
	Walter Mondale (Dem.)	June 5
1980	Ronald Reagan (Rep.)	May 26
	Jimmy Carter (Dem.)	June 3
1976	Jimmy Carter (Dem.)	July 14 (at the convention)
	Gerald Ford (Rep.)	August 19 (at the convention)
1972	George McGovern (Dem.)	July 12 (at the convention)
	Richard Nixon (Rep.)	August 22 (at the convention)

Sources: Associated Press, "Dates on Which Candidates Clinched the Nomination for the Presidency in Their Parties," March 15, 2000 (Lexis-Nexis); Ceci Connolly, "Bush, Gore Clinch Nominations," *Washington Post*, March 15, 2000, p. A6; Adam Nagourney, "Texas and Ohio to Clinton; McCain Is In as Choice for the G.O.P.," *New York Times*, March 5, 2008, p. A1; Dan Balz and Anne E. Kornblut, "Obama Claims Nomination," *Washington Post*, June 4, 2008, p. A1.

The 2004 Democratic nomination campaign demonstrated that front-loading has often caused nominations to be decided early in the delegate selection process. Despite having several qualified candidates in the field, it took only five weeks after the New Hampshire primary for Kerry to force his only serious competitors out of the race. Indeed, the race was decided before more than twenty states had even held either primaries or caucuses to select national convention delegates. Similarly, the 1996 and 2000 nominations were clinched by the eventual nominees before mid-March. As Table 6.2 shows, there has been a trend toward early clinching of nominations as front-loading of the primaries and caucuses has intensified. But Table 6.2 also points to the anomaly of the 2008 Democratic nomination, which was not decided until the final states cast their votes in June.

In 2008, the national parties paid a great deal of consideration to the issue of their nomination calendars. The Democratic National Committee ruled that their nomination calendar would begin on February 5, but they made exceptions to allow Iowa and New Hampshire to hold their elections in January. The DNC also allowed

BOX 6.3 | WHAT'S SO HARD ABOUT SCHEDULING PRIMARIES AND CAUCUSES?

After almost every presidential election year, both parties consider a variety of proposals about how to reform the way that primaries and caucuses are scheduled. But how easy is it for either party to influence when states hold their primaries? The answer to this question reveals the extent to which political parties are nonhierarchical entities and subject to regulations imposed by state governments. Consider the following factors that must be considered:

- Primaries and caucuses are run by the state government in some states and by the state parties in others.
- The DNC and RNC can penalize a state party by reducing the size of its delegation if those delegates were decided outside of the "window" (the period during which states are allowed to hold primaries or caucuses). But state parties may be less concerned with the size of their delegation than their ordering on the calendar. Iowa and New Hampshire comprise fewer than 5 percent of either party's delegates; their influence has little to do with the size of their delegation at the convention.
- In 2008, the DNC allowed Iowa and New Hampshire to hold their events before February 5, but the RNC threatened to penalize either state's delegation if their events were held prior to February 5. Therefore, the DNC and RNC calendars were inconsistent.
- Iowa state law mandates that both parties' caucuses be held on the same day. The law also stipulates that the Iowa caucuses are to be held eight days before any other state's primary or caucus. New Hampshire state law mandates that its primary must be held seven days before any other state's primary. These laws essentially force the Iowa and New Hampshire Republican parties to break the rules set by the RNC.
- In 2008, the DNC allowed Nevada and South Carolina to hold their primaries or caucuses earlier than February 5, a move that violated state laws in Iowa and New Hampshire and forced those states to move their events ever earlier. The Iowa caucuses were ultimately held on January 3rd, the earliest date yet for a delegate selection event.

Source: Democratic National Committee's Commission on Presidential Nomination Timing and Scheduling.

Nevada and South Carolina to hold their events before February 5th to address concerns about the regional and racial/ethnic representativeness of the early state electorates. South Carolina has a large African American population while Nevada has a significant proportion of Hispanics. While this action quelled some complaints about the nomination calendar, it also upset party leaders in other states who were not sanctioned by the DNC to hold earlier primaries or caucuses. In a brazen challenge to the national party, both Michigan and Florida moved their primaries into January essentially daring the DNC to penalize two crucially important swing states.

The DNC held its ground and announced that neither state would receive any delegates at the national convention. Most of the candidates for the nomination agreed not to campaign in either state and several, including John Edwards and Barack Obama, even took their names off of the ballot in Michigan. Neither the DNC nor the states' party leaders could have foreseen the ramifications that their decisions would ultimately have on the race for the nomination. Clinton won both primaries and ultimately advocated for both states' delegates to be given full voting rights at the convention. The Obama campaign vigorously opposed such a plan, particularly given that Obama's name had not even appeared on the ballot in Michigan. In June, before either candidate had received a majority of delegates, the DNC rules committee agreed to allow each state to bring their full delegations to the convention, but each of the delegates received only a half vote. However, when it became clear that Obama would become the nominee, he pushed for both state's delegations to receive full voting rights at the convention, a move that the convention's credentials committee ratified.

Phase 3: Delegate Selection: The Later Primaries and Caucuses

While Michigan and Florida ultimately received full voting rights at the Democratic convention, it seems clear that by violating DNC rules the state's party leaders forfeited a great deal of influence for their states in the 2008 nomination process. The early primaries and caucuses traditionally establish who is the front-runner, which candidates are still serious contenders, and even indicate who is going to be the nominee. In John Kessel's phrase, a "mist clearing" occurs after these initial contests.[7] This generally means that primaries held after mid-March are little more than formalities, since the front-runners had already amassed enough delegates to be assured of winning their parties' nominations.

However, 2008 proved a significant exception to this rule. Over half of the states had held Democratic primaries or caucuses by the end of Super Tuesday in 2008, yet Obama and Clinton finished the day nearly even in the delegate count and neither candidate was close to clinching a majority of the delegates. As a result, states holding their contests later in the calendar received enormous amounts of attention from the candidates. In particular, states like Pennsylvania (April 22nd), Indiana, and North Carolina (both on May 6th) received inordinate attention because they were the only populated states left on the calendar after early March. And even small states like Montana and South Dakota, which held the final primaries on June 3rd, made it into the limelight as they provided the necessary delegates for Obama to finally clinch the nomination.

Although it usually becomes clear who the presidential nominees will be during the later primaries and caucuses, this stage in the nominating process can have crucial and long-term implications for the outcome of the general election. Lengthy, contentious, acrimonious primary campaigns cost the eventual nominee valuable time and money needed for intraparty fencemending, media advertising, and planning of general election campaign strategy. However, the theory that divisive presidential primaries cause general election defeats is open to serious doubt. For example, vulnerable incumbents (e.g., Ford in 1976, Carter in 1980, and Bush in 1992) almost inevitably engender serious challengers for renomination. But these vulnerable incumbents were in serious electoral trouble even before they faced intraparty challenges for the nomination. And no nomination contest in recent memory was more prolonged or acrimonious than the 2008 campaign for the Democratic nomination; yet, Obama still had plenty of time to win back most disgruntled Clinton supporters in time for a relatively easy general election victory.

PHASE 4: THE CONVENTION: RATIFYING THE DECISION OF THE PRIMARIES AND KICKING OFF THE GENERAL ELECTION CAMPAIGN

National conventions are no longer deliberative bodies whose delegates weigh the competing claims of rival candidates for the nomination. Conventions ratify the decisions of the preconvention campaign fought out in presidential primaries and caucuses. The principal significance of the modern-day national convention, therefore, is that it is the kickoff of the general election campaign. It is an opportunity for the party and its nominee to set the themes of the campaign and to project a favorable candidate image during a period when the party will have a virtual monopoly on television news coverage. The *Washington Post*'s respected national politics reporter Dave Broder summarized the significance of conventions as follows: "Convention week is important, not because it marks the end of the nominating period, but because it is the start of the general election. It is the time when most voters take their first serious look at the candidates and their parties and begin to focus on the choice they will make in November."[8]

The nominations now are made on the first ballot. No convention has gone beyond the first ballot in selecting a nominee since the 1952 Democratic convention, which chose Adlai Stevenson on the third ballot. Even though the actual nomination may have been decided well in advance of the convention, what happens at the convention and how it is presented in the news media can have important implications for the campaign.

During the first two days of a convention, the major items on the agenda are the reports of the convention committees—Credentials, Permanent Organization, Rules, and Resolutions (Platform). The full convention must consider these reports and then adopt or amend them before the convention can proceed to the nomination stage of its schedule.

- The Credentials Committee makes recommendations to the full convention concerning which delegates from a given state should be seated in those instances where there is a dispute about who are the bona fide and properly chosen delegates. In 2008, it was the Democratic Credentials Committee which restored the full voting rights of Michigan and Florida's delegations.
- The Committee on Permanent Organization, now largely a pro forma group, nominates persons to serve as the permanent officers (e.g., permanent chair, secretary, parliamentarian, sergeant at arms).
- The Rules Committee recommends the procedures under which the convention will operate.
- The Resolutions Committee drafts the party platform.

In the past, the tone of a convention was heavily influenced by the strength of the coalitions supporting the various candidates for the nomination. A convention where the candidates were relatively close in delegate strength was apt to be contentious and potentially divisive (e.g., Republicans in 1976). But even under these conditions, divisive conventions appear to be a thing of the past. Even following the long and occasionally acrimonious nomination campaign experienced by Democrats in 2008, the Democratic National Convention put forward a unified front in supporting the nominee. Both Hillary and Bill Clinton gave rousing speeches to rally support for Obama at the convention and it was Hillary Clinton who, in a moment staged for television, called for the convention to halt the ceremonial roll call and instead accept Obama as the nominee by acclamation. Thus, the 2008 Democratic convention demonstrated that in the modern era of presidential nominations, a convention following an extended hard-fought nomination campaign is difficult to distinguish from one nominating a candidate whose nomination was not even contested.

Nevertheless, the convention provides the nominee with an opportunity to unify the party by making overtures to the various factions of the party, especially those that lost the presidential nomination. In 2008, Obama did this by supporting the full seating of the Michigan and Florida delegations at the convention and allowing a roll call vote to proceed so that some ballots could be cast in Clinton's favor.

The vice-presidential nomination is also often used to unify the party and broaden the presidential nominee's electoral support. In 2004, John Kerry's selection of John Edwards was an attempt to appeal to moderate Democrats, especially southerners, who may have been more uneasy with a nominee from Massachusetts. Four years later, John McCain picked little-known Alaskan Governor Sarah Palin in an attempt to appeal to both women and social conservatives within his own party.

The vice-presidential choice can also be used to reinforce campaign themes of the presidential nominee or to address specific problems facing the nominee. For example, one of Obama's potential weaknesses in the general election was his inexperience, particularly on matters of national security. This inexperience was particularly noticeable when contrasted with John McCain, a candidate with impeccable credentials on foreign policy. Thus, many onlookers speculated that Obama's selection of Senator Joseph Biden was made at least partly to mitigate any concerns that voters might have about Obama's experience.

While candidates can occasionally be upstaged at their convention by another speaker (i.e., Sarah Palin in 2008), the climax of the convention is the nominee's acceptance speech, a major media event that provides an opportunity to bind up wounds within the party, portray the candidate in a highly favorable manner, and present the themes of the campaign. This was perhaps best captured at the 2008 Democratic National Convention, when the final night's proceedings were taken out of the convention hall and over to Invesco Field where 84,000 onlookers watched Obama accept his party's nomination. Generally, nominees have received a postconvention "bounce" in the polls. Since 1964, the Gallup Poll has found that presidential nominees on average receive a 6–percentage-point "bounce" from the conventions (see Table 6.3).[9] In 2008, both Obama and McCain received post-convention bounces, though an unconventional vice presidential choice led McCain's "bounce" to be a bit bigger.

THE ONGOING PROCESS OF PARTY REFORM

Political rules are never neutral. They always benefit some and disadvantage others. Nowhere is this truism more apparent than in the rules governing presidential nomination politics. These rules, therefore, have been and continue to be points of contention among the various party factions struggling to control presidential nominations. The immediate causes of the latest surge of nomination reforms were the divisive 1968 and 1972 Democratic conventions and the Watergate scandal of the early 1970s. These events, plus attempts to remedy problems

TABLE 6.3	PRESIDENTIAL NOMINEES' POSTCONVENTION "BOUNCE" IN THE GALLUP POLL OF VOTERS' CANDIDATE PREFERENCES (PERCENTAGE OF POINTS GAINED IN THE GALLUP POLL)

	Candidate's Party	
Year/Candidates	Dem.	Rep.
2008 Obama vs. McCain	+4	+6
2004 Kerry vs. Bush	±0	+2
2000 Gore vs. Bush	+8	+4
1996 Clinton vs. Dole	+5	+11
1992 Clinton vs. Bush	+16	+5
1988 Dukakis vs. Bush	+7	+6
1984 Mondale vs. Reagan	+9	+4
1980 Carter vs. Reagan	+10	+8
1976 Carter vs. Ford	+9	+5
1972 McGovern vs. Nixon	±0	+7
1968 Humphrey vs. Nixon	+2	+5
1964 Johnson vs. Goldwater	+3	+5
1960 Kennedy vs. Nixon	+6	+14
Average, 1960–2008:	+6	+6

Source: Gallup Poll Monthly, Aug. 2000 and Sept. 2004; Stephen J. Wayne, *The Road to the White House 2000* (New York: Bedford/St. Martin's, 2000), p. 181; *Gallup Daily,* "McCain's Bounce Gives Him 5-Point Lead," September 8, 2008.

in the nominating process that were perceived to have contributed to the Democrats losing five of six presidential elections between 1968 and 1988, created a powerful impetus for an ongoing process of reform within the Democratic Party.

THE REFORMED DEMOCRATS

The 1968 Democratic Convention was widely held to have been unrepresentative of the sentiments of Democratic voters. Many believed that party leaders had used unfair tactics in securing the nomination for Hubert Humphrey. In an effort to placate the dissidents and confident that a mainline Democrat, Senator Edmund Muskie (Maine), would be the nominee in 1972, party regulars readily agreed to the reformers' demand for a commission to overhaul Democratic rules of delegate selection. This commission came to be known as the McGovern-Fraser Commission after the men who served as its chairs, Senator George McGovern (S. Dak.) and Representative Donald Fraser (Minn.). The commission proceeded to propose a series of major changes in the Democrats' nomination process that were put into effect for 1972. Successive reform commissions and the DNC continued to reformulate and refine the rules governing the party's nominating process so that today they constitute an elaborate and codified set of procedures that are rigorously enforced by the DNC.[10] Among the most salient features of these reformed rules are the following:

- *Openness.* State parties must have written rules of delegate selection, give public notice of all meetings, and have uniform statewide times and dates for meetings; mandatory assessments of delegates are banned; and requirements that a state party can impose in order for a person to become a candidate (e.g., the number of signatures on a petition) for delegate have been eased.
- *Proportional Representation.* Delegates must be chosen through presidential primaries, and party caucuses must be allocated among the candidates based upon their share of the vote. A minimum threshold of 15 percent of the vote in a primary or caucus is required before a candidate can be awarded delegates. All types of winner-take-all primaries are banned.
- *Ban on Open Primaries.* Open presidential primaries are banned, with special exemptions granted to Wisconsin and Montana because of their open primary traditions.
- *Automatic (Super) Delegates.* Automatic, unpledged (uncommitted) delegate status is granted to the following Democratic Party officials and public officeholders: the president and vice president; members of the House and Senate; members of the Democratic National Committee; Democratic governors; and former presidents, vice presidents, speakers of the House, Senate majority leaders, and former DNC chairs.
- *Affirmative Action.* State parties are required to encourage participation and representation of minorities and traditionally underrepresented groups.
- *Equal Division.* State delegations must be composed of an equal number of men and women.
- *Three-fourths of a state's delegates must be selected through either primaries or caucuses at the congressional district level*; that is, all of a state's delegates cannot be selected on the basis of a statewide primary.

These rules changes have transformed the nomination process most significantly by reducing the ability of party leaders to influence or control the delegate selection process. Traditional party-dominated systems of delegate selection were abolished. Caucus systems that involved party officials coming together to start the process of delegate selection were banned or replaced by participatory caucuses in which any professed Democrat could participate. Also prohibited were the "delegate primaries" used in Pennsylvania and New York. In these primaries, party notables ran for delegate under their own names without indicating on the ballot their preferred presidential candidate. Both the party-official-dominated caucuses and delegate primaries had assured party leaders of a dominant voice in delegate selection within their states. Byron Shafer, a leading analyst of Democratic reforms, has noted that these changes put party officeholders at "an active disadvantage" and meant that "the guaranteed role of the regular party has been discarded."[11]

The Democratic reforms also encouraged the proliferation of presidential primaries and thereby made the nomination process highly participatory, candidate centered, and media oriented. Rather than risk using caucus/convention procedures that might run afoul of vigorously enforced national Democratic Party rules and result in a state's delegates not being seated at the convention, many of the states opted for the presidential primary as a safe alternative. The presidential primary also had widespread appeal because of its participatory nature and seemingly representative character. Thus, between 1968 and 1976 the number of Democratic primaries jumped from fifteen to twenty-seven.

Although the immediate impetus for changes in delegate selection procedures occurred within the Democratic Party, the Democratic reforms had a spillover effect on the GOP. State legislatures, in revising their statutes to make them conform to national Democratic rules, frequently adopted the same or similar rules for both the Democrats and Republicans. The number of Republican primaries, therefore, also increased after 1968.

The influence of party leaders has been enhanced by the trend since 1992 toward heavy front-loading of the primary and caucus schedule. The support of party officials, donors, and officeholders has become increasingly important in determining nomination contests because candidates require the resources they can provide when confronted with the daunting task of running in a series of multistate primaries that occur in quick succession during February and March of the delegate selection season. Although one perceptive observer described the 2000 nomination process as "The Return of the Party Leaders," their influence remains substantially reduced from what it was in the prereform era.[12]

Kamark and Goldstein argue that in addition to making the nomination process more open and participatory, less party centered and more candidate centered, and more media oriented, the reform process has had two disadvantageous consequences for the Democratic Party.[13] First, proportional representation encourages a "predisposition of the Democratic Party to break down into factions" because various elements of the party can be assured of winning delegates for their standard bearer under a proportional system. Second, proportional representation is apt to prolong the divisiveness of the nomination battle and make achieving party unity more difficult. That is, second- and third-place finishers in the primaries—some of whom may be leaders of the more ideologically extreme elements in the party—may be encouraged to stay in the race because proportional representation enables them to keep on acquiring delegates in the primaries. This is less of a problem for the Republican Party, which relies primarily upon winner-take-all primaries rather than proportional representation.

The 2008 nomination contests provide a useful case in support of this point. On Super Tuesday, McCain won six states with less than 50 percent of the vote; yet, he took nearly all of the delegates from those states. Because Democrats allocate their delegates proportionally, there is little difference between winning a state by a few percentage points or losing it by a few. For example, in California, McCain won just 42 percent of the primary vote, but because of the Republican rules, he received 158 of the 170 Republican delegates (or 93 percent) at stake in the state. Clinton won 51 percent of the vote in California's Democratic primary, but that gave her just 204 of the 370 (or 55 percent) Democratic delegates up for grabs. Figure 6.5 presents the rates at which candidates for each party's nomination accumulated delegates in 2008. Because of the Republican's winner-take-all rules, McCain was able to clinch a majority of Republican delegates by March 3rd. Obama's victory was not secure until the final votes were cast in Montana and South Dakota on June 3rd.

Democratic Race

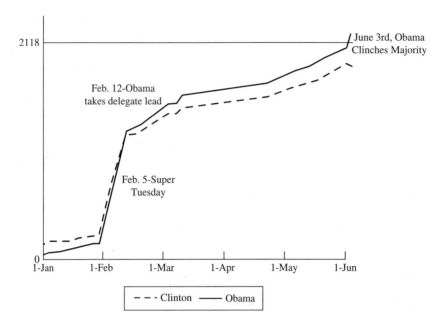

Republican Race

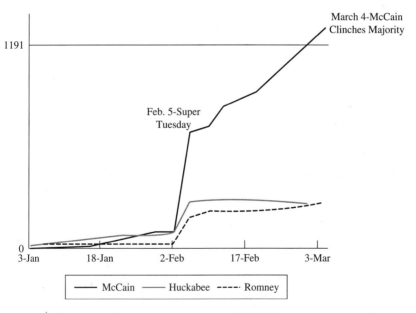

FIGURE 6.5 | DELEGATE ACCUMULATION IN THE 2008 DEMOCRATIC AND REPUBLICAN NOMINATION RACES

Source: CNN Delegate Tracker. Democratic tally includes automatic ("super") delegates.

Understanding that their proportional rules would allow for extended (and potentially divisive) nomination contests, Democrats created an additional class of automatic delegates that are commonly referred to as "super delegates." This delegate pool is comprised of all Democratic members of Congress, every Democratic governor, all members of the Democratic National Committee, former Democratic presidents and vice presidents, former Democratic House and Senate leaders, and ex-DNC chairs. In 2008, there were more than 800 Democratic super delegates; this is more than the number of elected delegates that were at stake in California, New York, and Illinois combined.

Part of the impetus for creating these automatic delegates was to allow party leaders to bring a nomination race to a relatively quick conclusion once a clear frontrunner had been established. However, in 2008, super delegates created more confusion among Democratic voters and activists than they did clarity. Because the race between Obama and Clinton was so close, it eventually became clear that neither candidate would be able to clinch the nomination based on elected delegates alone. Due to her prominence in the party, Hillary Clinton was able to attract support from over one-hundred super delegates before the Iowa caucuses. Thus, Obama trailed far behind Clinton in super delegate endorsements for much of the campaign. However, as Obama started winning, he also started accumulating super delegate support. At the same time, super delegates were no longer eager to endorse Clinton once it seemed as though she would not become the party's nominee. After Obama won an impressive victory over Clinton in North Carolina on May 6th, he overtook her in super delegate support and on the day of the last two primaries in Montana and South Dakota, super delegates flocked to Obama's side to give him the delegate total he needed to clinch the Democratic nomination.

While super delegates did eventually put Obama over the top, they did not help to prevent a protracted nomination campaign. Instead, they became a lightning rod for criticism about the party's nomination process as many wondered how such a close nomination contest could ultimately be decided by the party elites. For their part, most super delegates did not relish their influential positions as evidenced by the fact that many held off endorsing either candidate for as long as possible for fear of alienating the person who might become the eventual nominee. By April, DNC Chair Howard Dean had to publicly urge super delegates to make their preferences known and even then, hundreds maintained their silence.

The Democratic Party's 2008 nomination experience is sure to provide the impetus for even more reforms of the nomination system. By the end of 2009, the party was already beginning the process of formally eliminating the voting rights of super delegates, a reform that seems almost certain to pass. There were also renewed discussions about determining how to discourage the substantial front-loading and calendar violations (i.e., Florida and Michigan) that occurred in 2008.

THE UNREFORMED REPUBLICANS

Reform of party rules has been an almost quadrennial activity and frequent source of intense controversy within the Democratic Party, as contending interests, factions, and candidates seek to shape the rules for the next nominating contest to their advantage. The Republicans have followed a quite different strategy and have sought to maintain the basic party structure and rules that evolved prior to the era of the McGovern-Fraser Commission.[14] Party rules of delegate selection have not been a major source of controversy within the GOP the way they have been for the Democrats. In fact, the intense ideological element of the Republican Party has not found the rules a barrier to party influence and ascendancy. As far back as 1964, the conservative wing of the party demonstrated the permeability of the party structure and succeeded in nominating its candidate, Senator Barry Goldwater (Ariz.).

Republican rules differ from those used by the Democrats in several ways:

- *Republican Rules Are Harder to Change.* It is not possible under Republican rules for the RNC to promulgate rules changes affecting an upcoming national convention in the way the DNC can.[15] The normal method of rules change in the GOP is for the RNC Rules Committee to recommend changes to the full national committee, which in turn makes recommendations to the national convention rules committee. The committee then makes a report to the convention, which must give final approval to a proposed rules change. This lengthy procedure imposes major obstacles to any major revisions of GOP rules and prevents tampering with the rules between conventions. There are also significant substantive differences between the rules of the two parties.
- *Delegate Apportionment.* The GOP uses a significantly different formula to apportion delegates among the states. The Republican formula is weighted to reflect the electoral votes and the extent of Republican voting strength in the state. It does not reflect population to the extent that the Democratic formula does. Republican conventions are also somewhat smaller in terms of total delegates than Democratic conventions. In 2008, there were 4,418 Democratic delegates and 2,380 Republican delegates.
- *Maintaining the Confederate Character of the Party.* The Democratic rules changes that culminated in the adoption of the party charter in 1974 significantly strengthened the national party organization at the expense of the state parties in matters of delegate selection. The national Democratic Party has an elaborate set of rules governing these matters that it vigorously enforces upon the state parties. By contrast, the Republican rules give the state parties wide latitude in matters of delegate selection, and the RNC has adopted a permissive attitude toward its state parties. Republican rules contain no mandates banning open primaries, requiring affirmative action programs or equal division of the sexes in state delegations, setting threshold requirements or provisions for proportional representation, or stipulating the percentage of state delegations that must be selected at the congressional district level. Further evidence of the party's commitment to maintenance of its confederate character is the requirement of equal state representation on all convention committees. One man and one woman delegate from each state, regardless of state size, are required for each convention committee. The Democrats, by contrast, allocate committee seats in accordance with a more complicated formula that takes into account state population and support for the Democratic ticket.

BOX 6.4	IN 2008, PEOPLE FLOCKED TO GOOGLE TO FIND OUT "WHAT'S A SUPER DELEGATE?"

The extended race for the Democratic presidential nomination in 2008 exposed citizens to the inner workings of Democratic Party rules governing delegate selection. Of course, most citizens were unfamiliar with these rules and went to the Internet to find some answers. Consider the case of Democratic super delegates. The figure below shows the frequency with which people searched for the terms "super delegate" or "superdelegate" during 2008 relative to how frequently they had done so in 2004. The first large spike in the chart shows that following Super Tuesday, people searched for information on super delegates about sixteen times more frequently than they had in 2004. Searches on the topic continued to significantly out-pace the 2004 traffic until the first week in June, when Hillary Clinton conceded the nomination to Obama.

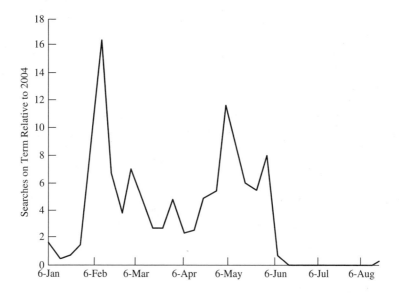

Source: Google Trends.

- *No Automatic Delegates.* The Democrats have sought to increase the participation in their conventions by party and elected officials by granting them
  automatic delegate status, but the Republicans have consistently resisted such
  proposals. The provision for automatic delegates by the Democrats was believed to be necessary because the reforms caused the number of party and
  elected official delegates to fall off dramatically. The highly structured Democratic rules frequently required such officials to run against their own constituents if they wished to become delegates. This was an undertaking in which few
  wished to engage. The less restrictive GOP rules governing delegate selection by
  state parties have meant that it has been easier within the Republican Party to

designate party leaders as delegates. As a result, there is no strong pressure in the GOP for giving party leaders automatic delegate status.

The differences between the largely unreformed GOP and the reformed Democratic Party, however, should not obscure the basic similarities in the nomination process as it operates within both parties. In both parties, the bulk of the delegates are selected through presidential primaries, and it is the early primaries for both Republicans and Democrats that have disproportionate influence upon the choice of a nominee. The process is highly participatory, even in caucus/convention states, because party rules and state laws permit participation by even the most nominal of partisans. The media play a major role in screening the candidates and in interpreting the results of caucuses and primaries. Party organizations and leaders are no longer as dominant as in the prereform era. Their place has been taken by the organizations of the candidates and the media.

Campaign Finance: The Federal Election Campaign Act

The Watergate revelations of campaign finance irregularities in 1972 led the Congress to enact campaign finance reforms, the Federal Election Campaign Act (FECA) Amendments of 1974. The key provision of the act, as it pertains to presidential nominating campaigns, is that relating to public funding. In 2002, Congress enacted the Bipartisan Campaign Reform Act (BCRA), which left in place the FECA's provisions for public funding but amended contribution limits. Candidates for major-party nominations are eligible to receive federal matching funds for their campaigns, provided they comply with the following conditions:

- Raise at least $5,000 in individual contributions of $250 or less in each of twenty states. Only individual contributions of up to $2,000 can be accepted, and only the first $250 counts toward the federal match.
- Abide by an overall expenditure limit that is adjusted prior to each election to account for inflation. In 2004, the overall expenditure limit was $37 million, plus an additional 20 percent to cover fund-raising costs.
- Abide by individual state expenditure limits based upon a formula of $0.16 cents per voter, plus an inflation adjustment.
- Disclose all contributions and expenditures of $200 or more to the Federal Election Commission.

Candidates for presidential nominations are not required to accept federal matching funds for their campaigns, and candidates who decline public funding need not abide by the FECA expenditures limits. Between 1976 and 1996, only two serious candidates, former Governor John Connally of Texas in 1980 and multimillionaire publisher Malcolm (Steve) Forbes in 1996, declined federal funding. However, refusing public funding has become so common in recent years that some have asked whether the era of public financing is over. George W. Bush refused public funding in both 2000 and 2004, Howard Dean and John Kerry did so in 2004, and John Edwards was the only major candidate from either party to accept public funds in 2008. The decisions of recent contenders to forego public funding and the spending restrictions that went with it were based upon the following considerations:

- Successful early fund-raising that made matching funds unnecessary.
- The expectation that other candidates would also forego the limits and spend well above the spending limits in key states.
- Foregoing public funding would project strength to the press strong during the invisible primary.
- The fact that front-loading required high levels of early expenditure and the FECA's overall expenditure limits for candidates accepting public funding could leave his campaign hitting the overall limit in the middle of the primaries, or worse, out of money before crucial primaries in large states.
- Finally, candidates were also concerned about what would happen *after* they secured their party's nomination. In 1996, Bob Dole accepted public funding and sewed up the GOP nomination early, but he had been forced to spend heavily in the process. This caused him to hit the overall spending limit in April, months in advance of the Republican convention. The Republican National Committee tried to fill this financial void by running issue ads featuring Dole, but this was not sufficient to compete with the Clinton-Gore ad campaign, which helped give the Democrats a substantial and enduring lead in the polls.[16] As Bush noted, "I'm mindful of what happened in 1996 and I'm not going to let it happen to me."[17] Similar difficulties faced Al Gore in 2000, since he accepted public funding while Bush did not.

Because of these considerations, it is unlikely that serious future contenders for either party's nomination will elect to accept matching funds. The restrictions for accepting public funding are simply too limiting for the realities of present-day campaigns. While individual contribution limits have doubled after the BCRA, matching funds have not, and spending limits have also increased only with inflation. Candidates particularly complain that state spending limits based on population size do not accurately reflect the importance of states in the nomination process. For example, in 2008, the spending limit for New Hampshire was just $841,000, a paltry amount given the importance of this primary. Although state-by-state spending limits have been breached through candidate machinations and FEC implementation of the FECA, the relatively low national spending limits are enforced for candidates who accept federal matching funds. In 2008, the national spending limit for the nomination period was $42.1 million. By comparison, Hillary Clinton and Barack Obama spent more than twice that amount in 2007 alone. In addition, a candidate is put at a serious disadvantage, both with regard to spending and perception of strength, when his or her opponent declines public funding. Thus, any candidate accepting public funding in the future is unlikely to be considered a serious contender by the media, activists, or potential contributors. As campaign finance expert Michael Malbin wrote after the election, "The public funding system for presidential elections collapsed in 2008. The policy question for the future will be whether to revive it at all and, if so, how."[18]

PARTICIPATION IN PRESIDENTIAL NOMINATING POLITICS

The extent of popular participation in candidate selection has been a continuing concern of those who have shaped the rules governing presidential nominating politics. A basic tenet of the Progressives, who developed the presidential primary early in this century, was a belief that the citizenry should make presidential nominating decisions, not party leaders. The presidential primary was, therefore, an element in the Progressive reform agenda. Latter-day reformers, who pushed for the McGovern-Fraser Commission reforms and for greater use of the presidential primary, were also committed to participatory democracy. These reformers believed that more participation in the process would result in more representative conventions, nominees who would have a higher level of legitimacy with the public, and more public support for the political system.[19] In practice, however, participation rates in presidential nominating politics remain quite low.

VOTER TURNOUT IN PRESIDENTIAL PRIMARIES

Voter turnout in primaries has consistently lagged substantially below that in general elections. The proliferation of primaries since 1968 has meant that in absolute terms the number of people voting in presidential primaries has increased significantly. In 1968, there were fifteen Republican and Democratic primaries in which 12 million voters participated. With thirty-eight Republican and thirty-six Democratic primaries in 2008, the total turnout was over 58 million people, an all-time high. As the case of 2008 illustrates, the number of persons voting in presidential primaries is subject to considerable variation from one election year to another depending upon the number of primaries being held and whether one or both parties' nominations are hotly contested.[20] Thus, Democratic primary turnout was twice as high in 2008 as it had been in 2004.

A major point of contention between proponents and opponents of presidential primaries relates to the representativeness of the primary voters. That is, do they distort the choice of nominees because they are not representative of party rank-and-file voters? All studies of primary turnout demonstrate that the actual voting electorate in presidential primaries tends to be weighted in favor of those who are older, better educated, and more well-to-do. These findings concerning the demographic unrepresentativeness of presidential primary voters are similar to those for general elections and gubernatorial and congressional primaries.

Those who do participate in presidential primaries tend to be more partisan (i.e., have a strong commitment to their party) than nonvoters, irrespective of their party preferences. Regarding the ideological representativeness of presidential primary voters, political scientists have produced conflicting conclusions depending upon the methodology employed. When primary voters were compared to all eligible voters[21] or general election voters,[22] they were shown to be ideologically unrepresentative; that is, Republican primary voters were more conservative and Democratic primary voters were more liberal. However, when voters in Democratic and Republican primaries were compared to their respective party followings (general election voters who identified with the party or voted for its nominee), primary voters were not shown to be unrepresentative.[23] Nonetheless, the distinctive partisan and ideological orientations of Republican and Democratic primary voters do have a profound impact upon presidential nominating politics. With Republican primary voters tending to be conservative and Democratic primary voters weighted on the liberal side, candidates' strategies are affected. Indeed, all successful Republican nominees since 1964 have sought to demonstrate that they had strong conservative credentials, and no candidate who has campaigned openly as a moderate or liberal has been successful. The Democratic picture is almost a mirror image of the Republicans. Successful Democrats in the modern era have generally sought to demonstrate their liberal credentials.

PARTICIPATION IN CAUCUSES/CONVENTIONS

Because caucuses require participants to attend meetings that are often lengthy, contentious, and, in many states, held in the midst of winter, citizen participation in caucuses is substantially low—commonly around 2 percent of the eligible voters.[24] However, because of their special importance as the major presidential nominating event prior to the New Hampshire primary, the Iowa caucuses do normally attract higher levels of turnout—14 to 20 percent of the registered voters.[25] Like turnout in primaries, the Iowa caucus turnout is affected by whether or not there is a contest for the nomination in one or both parties and whether the candidates' strategies involve targeting Iowa.

Caucus participants, like primary voters, tend to be middle class and upper-middle class, better educated than average, and older. They also tend to be strongly partisan and often have intense ideological commitments. More ideologically extreme candidates, therefore, normally do better in caucuses than in primaries. For example, Mike Huckabee, whose background as an ordained Baptist minister endeared him to many religious conservatives, was able to claim a surprising victory in the Iowa caucuses. McCain, whose occasional ideological moderation generated skepticism among the religious right, performed twice as well in primaries than he did in caucuses.

Candidates with strong organizations capable of mobilizing their supporters to turn out at the caucuses also tend to do well. Barack Obama used his impressive campaign organization to consistently out-perform Hillary Clinton in Democratic caucuses in 2008. While Clinton narrowly edged Obama in the total primary vote, Obama won more than two-thirds of the delegates selected at caucuses. On Super Tuesday, Hillary Clinton won the primary states with the most delegates, such as California and New York. On the other hand, Obama won with much bigger margins in smaller caucus states like Alaska, Idaho, and North Dakota. Thanks to Obama's ability to carry caucuses by wide margins, Super Tuesday was essentially a draw, which ultimately benefited Obama.

NATIONAL CONVENTION DELEGATES

National convention delegates are not a representative cross-section of either their parties' rank-and-file voters or the adult population (see Table 6.4). Status as a convention delegate is a reward that is given to only the most intensely involved candidate supporters and party workers. Reflecting the general American patterns of participation in party politics, national convention delegates are drawn primarily from well-educated, middle- and upper-middle-class strata of society. It is these people who have the time, leisure, money, and interest to participate actively in politics. There are, however, differences in the composition of Republican and Democratic conventions, with the Democrats having higher proportions of blacks, Hispanics, Catholics, and union members.

TABLE 6.4 | 2008 DEMOCRATIC AND REPUBLICAN NATIONAL CONVENTION DELEGATES AND VOTERS COMPARED (PERCENTAGE)

	Democratic Delegates	Democratic Voters	All Voters	G.O.P. Voters	G.O.P. Delegates
Men	51	42	46	44	68
Women	49	58	54	56	32
White	65	72	83	93	93
Black	23	23	12	2	2
Asian American	3	3	2	2	2
Hispanic (may be of any race)	11	9	8	10	5
Political ideology					
Very liberal	19	15	8	2	*
Somewhat liberal	22	34	18	4	*
Moderate	50	34	36	30	26
Somewhat conservative	2	10	20	33	28
Very conservative	*	6	15	30	40
Member of a labor union	24	10	10	6	5
College graduate	26	17	21	28	31
Postgraduate	55	13	12	11	50
Family income					
Under $50,000	10	43	39	31	5
$50,000–$75,000	17	21	23	22	22
Over $75,000	70	26	31	39	66

*Less than 1 percent.

Source: New York Times/CBS Poll.

The most striking differences between Republican and Democratic delegates are not in their socioeconomic characteristics but in their political philosophies and positions on public-policy issues (see Table 6.4). Republican delegates are strongly conservative in their orientation, whereas the Democrats tend toward a liberal position. It is also clear that the delegates from both parties are somewhat ideologically unrepresentative of both their own party's rank-and-file voters and the total adult population. Democratic delegates are more liberal than their party rank-and-file and the general public, whereas Republican delegates are more conservative than their party's voters and the general public. These are the inevitable consequences of the tendency of party activists to be drawn from the most politically committed elements of society and the processes through which delegates are chosen. Participation is skewed toward the extreme ends of each party's dominant ideological tendency, and the convention delegates reflect this bias.

MEDIA POLITICS IN PRESIDENTIAL NOMINATIONS

The media have always played a significant role in presidential nominating politics because reporters and commentators are inevitably forced to make decisions about which candidates deserve extensive coverage, which candidates did well or poorly in the primaries and caucuses, which candidates are the front-runners, and which candidates are surging or fading. The decisions that the media make on such issues have significant effects on the nominating campaign and can influence how the field of candidates is narrowed to a small number of serious contenders. With the opening up of the caucuses and the proliferation of the primaries, the role of party leaders as the arbiters of presidential nominations has declined, while the role of the media has been expanded.

The media's crucial role in influencing the public's perception of the candidates was evident in the 2004 Democratic nominating contest. In the 2004 campaign, Howard Dean at first benefited but ultimately suffered from media attention. During 2003, Dean was the favorite of the national media because of his fund-raising prowess and the distinction of being the anti-war candidate among the Democratic field. Appearing on the cover of news magazines helped propel Dean into front-runner status, but this status also put him under a more critical lens. Prior to the Iowa caucuses, Dean's coverage on network newscasts was far more critical than that of the competitors who were trailing him. After Dean's poor showing in Iowa and his "scream" captured on television at his campaign rally that evening, the news media were especially critical of Dean, continuously replaying the unflattering footage of his "scream" and criticizing his campaign in general. As Dean himself explained, "[The media] played a role in the rise and they played a role in the fall. They defined me as the front-runner, and then their idea was to attack the front-runner as much as possible."[26] Less than 40 percent of his coverage on network news programs was positive following the Iowa caucuses, while John Kerry (71 percent positive) and John Edwards (86 positive) became media favorites, helping to make them the new front-runners for the Democratic nomination.[27]

Barack Obama and Hillary Clinton both experienced the fickle nature of the news media during the 2008 campaign. As the upstart challenger, Obama received wildly positive coverage following his early victories while the narrative about Clinton focused largely on negative themes about how she had mismanaged her campaign. The perceived disparity in coverage was so significant at one point that a *Saturday Night Live* skit portrayed reporters grilling Clinton (played by Amy Poehler) with tough questions during a debate while Obama (played by Fred Armisen) was asked "Are you comfortable? Can we get you anything?" However, a study of primary coverage conducted by the Project for Excellence in Journalism concluded that while Obama initially received more favorable coverage than Clinton, he eventually took his lumps from the media as well and both candidates received relatively similar proportions of negative and positive coverage during the campaign.

| BOX 6.5 | DID THE DIVISIVE PRIMARY COST BARACK OBAMA VOTES? |

As the Democrats' long nomination campaign dragged on, many in the party were concerned that the hard-fought race would hurt the eventual nominee in the general election. Prominent Democratic strategist Donna Brazile noted during the campaign that "People were excited; now they're exhausted. [...] In the beginning, they liked one candidate and respected the other; now they love one and hate the other." Indeed, a Gallup poll conducted in the midst of the nomination campaign found that 28 percent of Clinton supporters said they would vote for McCain if Obama won the nomination while 19 percent of Obama supporters said they would defect if Clinton prevailed. But did the campaign really hurt Obama's chances in November?

On one hand, general election exit polls found that only 14 percent of those voting in November claimed to have wanted Clinton to win the nomination, and 83 percent of that group ultimately voted for Obama. On the other hand, the real effects of the nomination campaign may have been in diminishing the extent to which Clinton supporters participated in the general election campaign. Indeed, in their study of voters in Franklin County, Ohio, Todd Maske and Anand E. Sokhey found that, "To different degrees (and in different ways), Clinton supporters in Franklin County, Ohio, defected, stayed home from the polls, and participated less vigorously in the campaign relative to their fellow Democrats." Ultimately, the divisive nomination race did not keep Obama from winning the presidency, but it may have diminished the size of his victory

Source: Katharine Q. Seelye and Julie Bosman, "Carrying Primacy Scars Into the General Election," *New York Times*, April 1, 2008; Todd Makse and Anand E. Sokhey, "Revisiting the Divisive Primary Hypothesis: 2008 and the Clinton-Obama Nomination Battle," *American Politics Research* 38 (2010).

In recent campaigns, the Internet has become an increasingly important part of the campaign for the nomination. In 2004, during the period between the New Hampshire primary and Super Tuesday (March 2), one-fourth of all Democratic primary voters reported going online to get information about the campaign. Of these voters who used the Web for information, nearly three-quarters went to news Web sites for that information, while one-fourth accessed the candidates' Web sites.[28] Howard Dean's campaign, specifically, was largely supported by liberal bloggers who viewed the candidate favorably largely because of his willingness to oppose the war in Iraq. Ironically, however, Dean became a punchline when the video of his scream in Iowa was circulated widely and synchronized with music.

The Internet played an even greater role in the 2008 nomination campaigns. Hillary Clinton announced her candidacy with a video posted to her Web site. And nearly one in four Americans reported that they received frequent e-mails asking them to support a candidate during the campaign.[29] But Obama clearly out-paced the efforts of other candidates in using the Internet as an innovative grassroots organizing tool. The candidate's custom built site, my.barackobama.com, allowed users to easily build their own communities and network with other Obama supporters. Obama used the platform to raise enormous sums of money during the primary (over $500 million raised online, according to some estimates), to organize supporters so efficiently that he dominated caucus events, and to create a loyal block of activists who could be mobilized cheaply and efficiently. As Arianna Huffington noted, "Were it not for the Internet, Barack Obama would not have been the nominee."[30]

A LENGTHY, CANDIDATE-CENTERED, PRIMARY-FOCUSED, PARTICIPATORY, AND MEDIA-ORIENTED PROCESS

The American system for nominating presidents is primary focused, open and participatory, candidate centered, and media oriented. It is a process that confounds most European observers, who are accustomed to a leadership selection process that is dominated by party leaders. The leaders of political parties in most Western-style democracies except the United States are chosen by their parties' members in the lower house of the national legislature. The remarkable 2008 campaign for the Democratic nomination highlighted all of the characteristics that make the American system unique. Clinton and Obama officially announced their candidacies in early 2007, but the eventual nominee did not become clear until June of the following year. During that period, the candidates combined to spend over half a billion dollars and more than 32 million citizens participated in the process by voting in caucuses and primaries. Clinton began the campaign with the support of much of the party's leaders, but Obama was able to win the nomination anyway. And despite the fact that both candidates developed large bases of energetic and loyal followers, the factions ultimately joined together to support the party's nominee in the general election. Never has it been clearer that the modern-day presidential nomination campaign is a lengthy, costly process that is generally won on mass appeal rather than the support of the party establishment.

PRESIDENTIAL NOMINATING POLITICS WEB SITES

The Federal Election Commission provides information on campaign finance regulations and information on candidate fund-raising and expenditures.
http://www.fec.gov

The Note is ABC News' daily political update. They track potential presidential candidates closely and, in the past, have maintained an Invisible Primary ranking of the contenders.
http://blogs.abcnews.com/thenote/

National Journal's Hotline On Call is a blog used by the Hotline staff to post political news of interest, with an emphasis on tracking presidential contenders.
http://hotlineblog.nationaljournal.com/

Similar to The Note, MSNBC's First Read also tracks politics on a daily basis, and focuses particularly on presidential nominating campaigns from the Invisible Primary through the conventions.
http://firstread.msnbc.msn.com/

The Polling Report compiles public opinion surveys tracking support for the 2012 presidential candidates.
http://www.pollingreport.com/2012.htm

NOTES

1. *Democratic Party of the United States of America v. Bronson C. LaFollette*, 449 U.S. 897 (1981). For a detailed account of the efforts of the national Democratic Party to close the Wisconsin primary, see Gary D. Wekkin, *Democrat versus Democrat* (Columbia: University of Missouri Press, 1984).

2. Roger Simon, "Why Believe the Super-delegates?" *Politico* (August 25, 2008): http://www.politico.com/news/stories/0808/12732.html.

3. For a detailed analysis of presidential nominating politics, see Stephen J. Wayne, *The Road to the White House, 2000* (New York: Bedford/St. Martin's, 1997), pp. 103–186.

4. For perspective accounts of the early activities in the 2000 nominating process, see Harold W. Stanley, "The Nominations: The Return of Party Leaders," in Michael Nelson, ed., *Elections 2000* (Washington, D.C.: CQ Press, 2001), ch. 2; and William G. Mayer, "The Presidential Nominations," in Gerald M. Pomper, ed., *The Election of 2000* (New York: Chatham House, 2001), ch. 2.

5. Rhodes Cook, "The Nomination Process," in Michael Nelson, ed., *The Elections of 1988*, Washington: CQ Press, 1989, pp. 45–46.

6. Barbara Norrander, "The End Game in Post-Reform Presidential Nominations," *Journal of Politics* 62 (Nov. 2000): 999–1011.

7. John Kessel, *Presidential Campaign Politics*, 4th ed. (Pacific Grove, Calif.: Brooks/Cole, 1992), p. 34.

8. David S. Broder, "A Chance to Be 'Presidential,'" *Washington Post*, July 15, 1984, p. 8.

9. Gallup Daily, "McCain's Bounce Gives Him 5-Point Lead," September 8, 2008. http://www.gallup.com/poll/110110/Gallup-Daily-McCains-Bounce-Gives-Him-5Point-Lead.aspx

10. On Democratic reforms, see David E. Price, *Bringing Back the Parties* (Washington, D.C.: CQ Press, 1984), chs. 6 and 7. On the postreform nomination process, see Leon D. Epstein, "Presidential Nominations since Party Reform," *American Review of Politics* 14 (Summer 1993): 149–162.

11. Byron E. Shafer, Quiet Revolution: *The Struggle for the Democratic Party and the Shaping of Post-Reform Politics* (New York: Russell Sage Foundation, 1983), p. 526.

12. Stanley, "The Nominations," p. 27.

13. Elaine Ciulla Kamarck and Kenneth M. Goldstein, "The Rules Do Matter: Post-Reform Presidential Nominating Politics," in The Parties Respond, 2nd ed., ed. L. Sandy Maisel (Boulder, Colo.: Westview, 1994)," pp. 186–189.

14. The differing approaches of the Republican and Democratic parties to party reform are described in John F. Bibby, "Party Renewal in the National Republican Party," in Gerald Pomper, ed., *Party Renewal in America: Theory and Practice* (New York: Praeger, 1980), pp. 102–115.

15. The differences between Republican and Democratic Party rules are described in more detail in Robert J. Huckshorn and John F. Bibby, "National Party Rules and Delegate Selection in the Republican Party," *P.S.* 16 (Fall 1983): 656–666.

16. Stanley, "The Nominations," pp. 31–32.

17. Don Van Natta, Jr., "Bush Foregoes Federal Funds and Has No Spending Limits," *New York Times*, July 16, 1999.

18. Michael Malbin, "Small Donors, Large Donors and the Internet: The Case for Public Financing after Obama," Campaign Finance Institute Working Papers, April 22, 2009.

19. Austin Ranney, *Participation in American Presidential Nominations, 1976* (Washington, D.C.: American Enterprise Institute, 1977), p. 14.

20. For an analysis of the factors affecting voter turnout in presidential primaries, see Barbara Norrander and Greg Smith, "Type of Contest, Candidate Strategy, and Turnout in Presidential Primaries," *American Politics Quarterly* 13 (Jan. 1985): 28–50; and Barbara Norrander, "Selective Participation: Presidential Primary Voters as a Subset of General Election Voters," *American Politics Quarterly* 14 (Jan. 1986): 35–53.

21. William Crotty and John S. Jackson, *Presidential Primaries and Nominations* (Washington, D.C.: CQ Press, 1985), pp. 91–93.

22. Kamark and Goldstein, "The Rules Do Matter," p. 184.

23. John C. Geer, "Assessing the Representativeness of Electorates in Primary Elections," *American Journal of Political Science* 32 (Nov. 1988): 929–945; see also Barbara Norrander, "Ideological Representativeness of Presidential Primary Voters," *American Journal of Political Science* 33 (Aug. 1989): 570–587; and Larry M. Bartels, *Presidential Primaries and the Dynamics of Public Choice* (Princeton, N.J.: Princeton University Press, 1988), pp. 140–148.

24. Ranney, *Participation in American Presidential Nominations*, 1977, p. 15.

25. Walter J. Stone, Alan I. Abramowitz, and Ronald B. Rapoport, "How Representative Are the Iowa Caucuses?" in Peverill Squire, ed., *The Iowa Caucuses and the Presidential Nominating Process* (Boulder, Colo.: Westview, 1989), pp. 11–12.

26. Jane Hall, "Burned by the Spotlight," *Columbia Journalism Review*, September/October, 2004.

27. Center for Media and Public Affairs News Release, "Network News Focus: Flubs, Fluff—Not Functional," February 9, 2004.

28. Kenneth Winneg and Talia Jomini, "The Internet as a Source of Campaign Information: An Analysis of Its Use in the 2004 Democratic Primary Campaign," Paper presented to the 59th Annual Conference of the American Association of Public Opinion Research, May 15, 2004.

29. Lee Rainie and Aaron Smith, "The Internet and the 2008 Election," Pew Internet and American Life Project, June 15, 2008.

30. Claire Cain Miller, "How Obama's Internet Campaign Changed Politics," *New York Times*, BITS Blog, November 7, 2008: http://bits.blogs.nytimes.com/2008/11/07/how-obamas-internet-campaign-changed-politics/.

POLITICAL PARTIES AND THE VOTERS

CHAPTER 7

CHAPTER CONTENTS

When the party nominating processes have narrowed the list of candidates and the campaign maneuverings have ended on election eve, it is the voter who decides the fate of the parties and their candidates. Parties cannot survive or exercise significant influence on the affairs of state without substantial voter support, because modern democratic governments derive their legitimacy through free elections. The nature of the party-in-the-electorate, therefore, is crucial to understanding the parties' role in the political process. Which voters will actually turn out and go to the polls on Election Day? How strong is the pull of partisanship in determining voter choices? Which party will benefit from the short-term influences of current issues and candidates' images? The electoral fate of the parties is tied up in the answers to these questions, which are the focus of this chapter.

VOTER TURNOUT

Although free elections are critical to the functioning of the republic, less than two out of every three citizens who were eligible to vote did so in 2008; 61.7 percent of the voting-eligible population cast presidential ballots. This figure was higher than in any election since the 1960s.

When deciding whether to vote, you might consider several factors:

- What benefits do I receive by voting?
- Do I feel strongly about the candidates?
- Is my vote likely to make a difference?
- Does casting a vote fulfill my civic duty?
- What are the costs of voting?
- Is the polling place difficult to travel to and is there likely to be a wait to vote?
- Have I learned enough about the candidates to cast an informed vote?
- Am I even registered to vote?

The answers to questions such as these often separate voters from nonvoters and help us understand why turnout varies so much in the United States.

Voter turnout often depends upon the timing of the election and the offices being contested. There is also substantial variation among the states in their rates of voter turnout. Figure 7.1 demonstrates that voter turnout is substantially higher in presidential election years than it is in midterm elections for the House of Representatives. Presidential elections are characterized by saturation news coverage and intense campaigns. As a result, voters receive more information about the candidates than they do in midterm congressional elections. Since 1960, the fall-off in turnout from presidential elections to the next midterm congressional election has averaged 17.5 percent. Turnout also varies between offices being contested. As is shown in Figure 7.1, there is a fall-off in voter participation between presidential balloting and voting for the House of Representatives in presidential election years.

Among the states, there are major differences in rates of turnout (see Figure 7.2), with southern and southwestern states having the lowest levels of voter participation. Political scientists have found that these varied turnout rates are related to both the political and the demographic characteristics of the states. Interparty competition is highly correlated with turnout: as the chances that either party may win go up, the

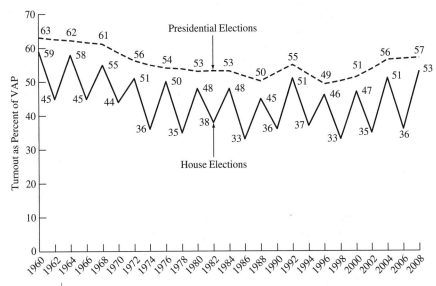

FIGURE 7.1 | VOTER TURNOUT IN PRESIDENTIAL AND HOUSE ELECTIONS, 1960–2008

Source: Statistical Abstract of the United States, 2000, p. 291; Data from 2000 to 2008 compiled by authors.

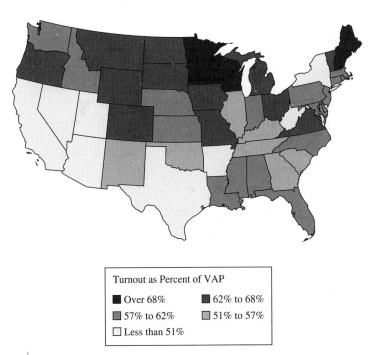

FIGURE 7.2 | TURNOUT IN THE AMERICAN STATES, 2008

Source: Created by the author using turnout data provided by Michael P. McDonald. Data available at http://elections.gmu.edu.

people are more likely to vote.[1] Campaign spending can also increase turnout because as more money is spent, voters are provided with more information about the candidates, which increases the likelihood that they will vote.[2]

Turnout is also affected by the socioeconomic makeup of the state population. The following characteristics are associated with higher levels of Election Day turnout: high incomes, high-status occupations, high levels of educational achievement, middle age, Jewish heritage, Catholicism, and being white. Citizens of higher socioeconomic status tend to be better able to bear the costs of voting; more than half of the variation among the states in voter turnout was caused by differences in race, age, income, and educational level.[3] Differences in state registration requirements can also cause differential turnout rates. The restrictiveness of these regulations varies tremendously. For example, North Dakota has no registration requirements; Wisconsin requires registration only in urban areas; Idaho, Maine, Minnesota, New Hampshire, Oregon, Wisconsin, and Wyoming permit registration at the polls. It has been estimated that if every state had registration laws as permissive as those in the most permissive states, turnout would rise by 9 percent.[4] Such permissive regulations lower the costs of voting for citizens.

With passage of the so-called Motor Voter law in 1993 by Congress, states are now required to implement a series of measures designed to make registration easier: registration of individuals applying for driver's licenses; registration by mail; and registration at designated government agencies, for example, public assistance offices and state-funded agencies serving persons with disabilities. The Federal Election Commission reported that the act has been successful in increasing voter registration numbers. In states covered by the law, voter registration increased 3.7 percent between 1994 and 1998. However, the actual impact of the law in terms of increasing turnout at the polls has been less than impressive.[5]

To facilitate the process of voting, an increasing number of states now have liberalized their absentee voting procedures to provide absentee ballots to any voter who requests that option. Oregon conducts elections entirely by mail. This procedure, which individualizes and extends the voting process over a number of weeks, has been shown to have considerable popular appeal. In 2008, almost 39 million voters, or 30 percent of the total electorate, cast their ballots early. However, there is limited evidence that it is also increasing turnout. The people most likely to choose to vote early are already highly motivated to participate in the political process.[6]

WHO VOTES?

DEMOGRAPHIC CHARACTERISTICS The two personal characteristics that are most closely related to voter turnout are *age* and *education* (see Table 7.1). As age increases, so does turnout. Young people tend to have a low rate of turnout compared to those in the over-sixty age bracket. The low rate of turnout among eighteen- to twenty-year-olds has undoubtedly contributed to the decline in overall turnout that occurred in the 1970s, because the extension of the franchise to these persons significantly expanded the pool of eligible voters. This pattern of abstaining from voting reflects the unsettled character and mobility of young people's lives. Registration requirements, residency rules, military service, and moving all create hurdles to political participation among the young. It should be noted, however, that by age thirty-five, most

TABLE 7.1 | PARTICIPATION IN NATIONAL ELECTIONS, 2008

Characteristic	Percentage of Persons Reporting That They Voted in 2008
Male	55.7
Female	60.4
White	59.6
Black	60.8
Hispanic	31.6
Age	
18–20	41.0
21–24	46.6
25–34	48.5
35–44	55.2
45–64	65.0
65 and over	68.1
School years completed	
8 years or less	23.4
High school	
1–3 years	33.7
4 years	50.9
College	
1–3 years	65.0
4 years or more	73.3
Employed	60.1
Unemployed	48.8
Not in labor force	55.5

Source: Statistical Abstract of the United States, 2010, Table 406.

people have become at least occasional voters and that only a small portion of the middle-aged and older public remain outside the voting public. It is estimated that only 5 percent of the electorate could be classified as habitual nonvoters.[7]

Education is the most important influence on voter turnout. The higher the level of educational attainment, the greater the likelihood of voting. Better-educated persons are more likely to vote because they tend to be better able to see the relevance of politics in their lives and the things they care about, are more interested in politics, and are more skilled in dealing with registration requirements. Adding to this is the fact that the political and policy agenda may not address the issues and needs of less-educated

| BOX 7.1 | WAS 2008 "THE YEAR OF THE YOUTH VOTE"? |

Historically, America's youth does not vote nearly as frequently as their older counterparts. But in the past two elections, turnout among the 18–29 age group has increased markedly. While just 41 percent of 18–29-year olds voted in the 2000 election, an estimated 52 percent did so in 2008. Obama won this age group by a stunning 2-to-1 margin over McCain in November, making it one of the most loyally Democratic groups. But 2008 was already being described by *Time* magazine as "The Year of the Youth Vote" well before the general election campaign. In fact, Obama owed his surprising victory in the Iowa caucuses to a much larger than normal turnout among young Democrats who gave him overwhelming support. The youth vote also helped propel him to victory in many other states. Overall, 60 percent of Democrats who were 18–29-years old voted for Obama in the primaries, compared to just 38 percent who supported Clinton.

Despite Obama's success among young voters in both the primaries and the general election, it is important to keep in mind that nearly half of the under-30 population still did not cast a vote in 2008. One of the challenges faced by this age group is voting for the first time, since young citizens do not always understand the registration process. This is particularly problematic for an age group that is often in geographical transition. In 2004, one of every three nonvoters among this age group said that they had not yet registered in their new hometown. Thus, many young citizens who wanted to participate may have been unable to do so.

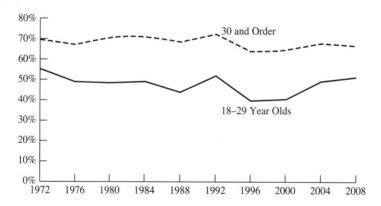

Source: The Center for Information and Research on Civic Learning and Engagement.

Source: Emily Hoban Kirby and Kei Kawashima-Ginsberg, "The Youth Vote in 2008," The Center for Information and Research on Civic Learning and Engagement, August 17, 2008.

citizens. In addition, higher levels of educational attainment are associated with better-paying jobs. However, income has only slight impact on turnout when other factors such as education, age, race, sex, and region are held constant.

There are also racial differences in turnout races. In the past, a higher proportion of whites than blacks voted; however, in the first presidential election featuring an African American candidate, black turnout was comparable to that among whites. Hispanics, on the other hand, continue to be much less likely to vote than either whites or blacks, though much of this difference is due to their lower levels of education and income. Beginning in the 1980s, women began to have slightly higher turnout rates than men, reversing the traditional pattern of higher male turnout. Political scientists have not developed a widely accepted theoretical reason for women voting at a higher rate than men, but it is clear that women can be expected to remain a majority of the American electorate.

THE ROLE OF PERSONAL ATTITUDES

Legal impediments, such as restrictive registration laws, can hold down participation in elections. To make voting easier and more convenient, some have even suggested making Election Day a national holiday as it is in other nations. Although 50 percent of nonvoters in one survey reported that they would be likely to vote if it were done on a holiday, there is reason to doubt their good intentions. If these persons are not now sufficiently interested in politics to vote, there is every reason to believe that they would take a holiday from both work and voting if given the opportunity. Nonvoting is not primarily a matter of legal impediments; it is more influenced by personal attitudes—a lack of interest, low sense of civic obligation, and weak feelings of partisan affiliation. Nonvoters are also more likely than voters to believe that elections do not make a difference. The importance of personal attitudes can be seen in Figure 7.3. Likely voters are more apt to be partisans and to see a difference between the parties. They also have a sense of civic obligation and feel guilty if they do not participate in elections. Likely voters also have a greater sense of confidence in their ability to understand politics and the willingness of public officials to pay attention to the wishes of the people.

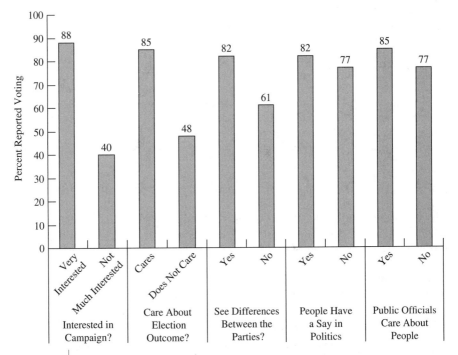

FIGURE 7.3 | ATTITUDES TOWARD VOTING AND POLITICS, 2008

Source: National Election Study.

POLITICAL PARTIES AND TURNOUT

Voters are generally of a higher socioeconomic level than nonvoters; they are also more apt to be better educated, middle aged, and white. In partisan terms, this pattern of turnout means that Republicans are slightly more likely to turn out and vote than are Democratic voters. As a result, get-out-the-vote campaigns aimed at maximizing turnout have traditionally been an emphasis of Democratic campaigns. Increased voter turnout, however, is not necessarily the key to Democratic electoral success. Abramson, Aldrich, and Rohde have shown, for example, that under any reasonable scenario increased turnout would not have led to Democratic victories in 1980, 1984, and 1988. In those elections, the Democrats' problem was not low turnout but high levels of defection to the GOP. Turnout may have made a modest contribution to Clinton's victory, because the 1992 increase in turnout was somewhat greater among Democrats than Republicans. However, just as the Democrats were damaged more by defections than low turnout in the 1980s, so was their 1992 victory attributable more to conversions (one in six Clinton voters voted for Bush in 1988) than to increases in turnout.[8] In 1996 and 2000, voters who considered themselves Democrats had lower turnout rates than did Republicans. Had Democrats turned out at the same level as Republicans and supported their party's ticket at the same level as voting Democrats, Al Gore's share of the popular vote would have increased an estimated 1.8 percentage points.[9] This small increase in Gore's share of the vote might have given him an electoral vote majority.

| BOX 7.2 | A CATALIST FOR DEMOCRATIC VICTORY? |

Following the 2004 election, Democrats were left scratching their heads wondering how Republicans had, once again, done a better job of mobilizing their voters than they had. Borne out of this frustration was a new company called Catalist, which would collect data on every single person in the United States with the goal of allowing Democratic candidates to more efficiently target their get-out-the-vote (GOTV) appeals. As *Atlantic* reporter Marc Ambinder notes in this excerpt, the sophisticated operation appeared to make a major difference in 2008:

> Get-out-the-vote operations mounted by the Obama campaign, the Democratic Party and progressive organizations mobilized more than one million dedicated volunteers on Election Day. But it was buttressed by a year-long, psychographic voter targeting and contact operation, the likes of which Democrats had never before participated in. In 2008, the principal repository of Democratic data was Catalist, a for-profit company that acted as the conductor for a data-driven symphony of more than 90 liberal groups, like the Service Employees Union—and the DNC—and the Obama campaign.

> [...]

> According to the analysis, those registered voters contacted by Catalist member groups turned out at a rate of 74.6%; the voters who weren't turned out in proportions roughly equivalent to the national average—about 60.4%. In four states, the

continued

| BOX 7.2 | A CATALIST FOR DEMOCRATIC VICTORY? *continued* |

number of new votes cast by liberals exceeded Obama's victory margin: in Ohio, Florida, Indiana and North Carolina. If you assume that only 60% of these voters chose Obama, the margin was still greater than Obama's in North Carolina and Indiana, both essential to his victory. With the caveat that correlation does not equal causation, the report provides convincing, if not absolute, evidence that the progressive/Democratic data-mining and targeting operation measurably helped elect Barack Obama.

[...]

Until the 2008 cycle, it was hard to get Democratic groups, and even Democratic state parties, to share technology and data. Democrats relied on static and easily obtainable information, like voter files and party registration data, to find other Democrats. Pollsters were often able to target particular messages to particular groups of people, but it was not until 2008 that targeting, for Democrats, increased its magnification to the level of the individual. Perhaps even more importantly, the type of targeting and voter contact activities was less effective. When Democrats identified a likely voter or a potential voter based on telephone contact, they lacked the resources and know-how to follow up in a way that increased the likelihood that the voter in question would actually turn out to vote. Republicans, by contrast, had pretty much mastered this process.

[...]

So did it work?

"The data tells us that the volume of contact was extraordinarily large; it was orders of magnitude larger than in 2004," said Laura Quinn, Catalist's chief executive officer. But it all might have been noise had the Obama campaign not embraced a methodology that used the data effectively, she said. "They really religiously built relationships and kept up person to person contact. This was an extraordinary candidate, and it was an extraordinary election, and that opened the door to places that progressives hadn't been before. It really looms large in the data."

Source: Marc Ambinder, "Exclusive: How Democrats Won the Data War in 2008," *The Atlantic*, October 5, 2009. Reprinted by permission of the author.

An important role that parties play in the political system is to mobilize voters and increase turnout. They do this in several ways:

- Parties provide labels for candidates to run under. Party labels appear on ballots for most high-profile elections, such as those for president, Congress, and governor, and it provides voters with important information about the general ideological beliefs of the candidates. In fact, in elections where the party label is not used, turnout tends to decline significantly, and many voters who go to the polls to cast votes in other contests skip those for which no party labels are provided. Thus, the party label itself helps to increase turnout in American elections.

- One reason that voters do not turn out to vote is that they often find it difficult to learn as much as they would like about all the candidates running in all of the elections. In addition to providing a party label that conveys some of this information, parties also spend a great deal of money providing citizens with information about candidates they favor and oppose. This information often comes in the form of phone calls, direct mail, email, or advertising.
- Parties also focus much of their attention on explicit get-out-the-vote (GOTV) efforts as well. These efforts are largely aimed at those who are likely to support the party's cause if they do end up voting. Parties attempt to mobilize these voters by registering them to vote, persuading them to vote early, making phone calls on Election Day to remind them to vote, or even providing transportation to polling sites for those citizens who need it. In 2008, over 60 percent of Americans claimed that they had been contacted by at least one of the two major parties.[10] Overall, Obama and the Democrats held an advantage over Republicans when it came to contacting Americans—78 percent of Americans reported being contacted by the Democratic side while just 65 percent were contacted by the Republicans. According to exit polls, Obama held some of the biggest advantages in GOTV efforts in states that he turned from red to blue, including Nevada, Colorado, Indiana, Virginia, and Iowa.

BOX 7.3	WHAT DO BOWLING AND FACEBOOK HAVE TO DO WITH VOTING?

In 1995, Robert Putnam observed that present-day Americans join bowling leagues less and bowl alone more than their predecessors. People are today more disconnected from each other than in previous generations. As social "norms and networks" (or "social capital") weaken, Putnam argues, communities and nations suffer a broad range of consequences, including declining political and civic participation, lowered levels of trust in one's neighbor as well as in one's government, increased crime, and even hampered economic progress. In this view, the fact that turnout has declined since the 1950s may be linked to the fact that we spend less time with our families, friends, and neighbors in social and civic settings.

The explosion in the use of the Internet in every area of social and civic life raises the question of whether this technology can mitigate or reverse the ill effects of our thinner "networks of interaction." Proponents of the Internet claim that it facilitates communication with community members and political leaders at every level of government as well as the ability to join, contribute to, and participate in a wide variety of organizations. The social networks created by Internet sites like Facebook.com may help reconnect young people with their larger community, yielding social, political, and economic benefits in years to come. Putnam and other scholars are not entirely convinced that the Internet revolution can significantly bolster our stock of social capital, however. For one thing, they argue, it is face-to-face interaction that builds trust and the capacity and interest in cooperation among community members. The anonymity of the Internet and the ease of interacting or withdrawing from online discussions and relationships may encourage not social connectedness but "drive-by" relationships. Further, the Internet may actually fracture American's sense of community by making it easy for people to interact only around the single, often quite narrow, issues that interest them.

Source: Robert D. Putnam, "Bowling Alone: America's Declining Social Capital," *Journal of Democracy* 6(1) (1995): 65–78.

An indicator of the intensity of a campaign is the level of spending in which the parties and candidates engage to mobilize voters. Studies of campaign spending in gubernatorial and state legislative races have demonstrated that spending increases electoral involvement, but after a certain threshold is reached, additional increments of spending produce increasingly smaller payoffs in terms of voter turnout.[11] Research on the success of partisan GOTV efforts indicates that personal contact with a citizen increases the likelihood that he or she will vote by 8–10 percent. Direct mail and phone calls to the public result in smaller increases in turnout. Many close elections in the United States are determined by which party is better able to get its supporters to the polls.

IS NONVOTING A SOCIAL PROBLEM?

A commonly expressed view is that America's seemingly high rate of nonvoting is symptomatic of a civic disorder that endangers the Republic. Unfavorable comparisons between turnout rates in the United States and other Western democracies are frequently cited as evidence of decay in the American body politics (see Table 7.2). It is necessary, however, when considering these cross-national comparisons, to keep in mind that other nations compute turnout rates as a percentage of registered voters going to the polls. By contrast, American turnout rates are normally calculated as a percentage of the voting-age population. As a result, most of the free

TABLE 7.2 | PERCENTAGE TURNOUT OF REGISTERED VOTERS: SOME INTERNATIONAL COMPARISONS

Country	Year	Type of Election	Percentage of Turnout Registered Voters
United States	2008	Presidential	57.1
Austria	2004	Presidential	71.6
Belgium	2007	Parliamentary	91.1
Canada	2008	Parliamentary	59.5
Greece	2007	Parliamentary	74.1
India	2004	Parliamentary	57.75
Italy	2008	Parliamentary	80.5
Ireland	2007	Parliamentary	67.0
Hungary	2007	Legislative	64.4
Israel	2009	Parliamentary	64.7
Russia	2008	Presidential	69.7
South Africa	2009	National Assembly	77.3
Sweden	2006	Parliamentary	82.0
Turkey	2007	Parliamentary	84.2

Source: International Institute for Democracy and Electoral Assistance.

world can boast of higher turnout rates than the United States. However, when turnout in the United States is computed on the basis of registered voters, instead of voting-age population, the rate is more respectable (89.7 percent in 2008). In addition, Americans have more opportunities to vote than do citizens of other democracies because of the frequency and varied types of elections in the United States— primaries and general elections for national, state, and local offices; state and local referenda; and recall elections. British political scientist Ivor Crewe emphasized this point when he observed that

> Turnout rates provide only a limited perspective on the amount of electoral participation. Turnout cannot measure the frequency of elections. Although turnout in the United States is below that of most other democracies, American citizens do not necessarily do less voting; in fact, they probably do more. No country can approach the United States in frequency and variety of elections. Only one other country— Switzerland—can compete in the number and variety of local referendums. Only Belgium and Turkey hold party "primaries" in most parts of the country.[12]

There is no compelling evidence to indicate that America's relatively low rate of turnout results in distortions of the citizenry's will. In general, nonvoters have candidate preferences much like those of voters.[13] A study of voters' and nonvoters' candidate preferences and policy views in the 1992 and 1996 elections underscores the fact that, taken as a whole, nonvoters appear well represented by those who vote. Benjamin Highton and Raymond E. Wolfinger estimate that if nonvoters had actually voted, Bill Clinton's victory margins would have been increased—an additional 1.3 percent in 1992 and more than doubled in 1996. The election outcome, however, would not have changed. Nor did Highton and Wolfinger find evidence that an electorate that included the nonvoters would have provided the constituency needed to support more liberal governmental policies. This is because the "party of nonvoters" is an extremely diverse group. The most prevalent characteristics of nonvoters were residential mobility and youth. Fully 43 percent of nonvoters in 1992 and 1996 had moved within the previous two years, and one-third were under the age of thirty. These are not characteristics that suggest political distinctiveness in terms of policy preferences.[14]

Nonvoting in America may not be indicative of an ailing polity, yet reasons for concern still exist. With educated, affluent, and influential groups having the highest turnout rates, universal suffrage does not necessarily provide a counterweight to power and wealth, for example. Indeed, the research of Hill and Leighley has shown that where the poor have higher levels of turnout, welfare benefits are more generous than in states with low turnout among the poor.[15] A high incidence of nonvoting can also threaten the legitimacy of democratic government and cause people to withdraw their support from the government. Large blocs of nonvoters with weak ties to established political leaders and parties could, therefore, pose a threat to political stability.

PARTY IDENTIFICATION

Voters' electoral choices are a product of the interaction between their enduring attitudes and beliefs and more transitory factors such as current issues and candidate images. The most important long-term influence is *party identification*—a feeling of

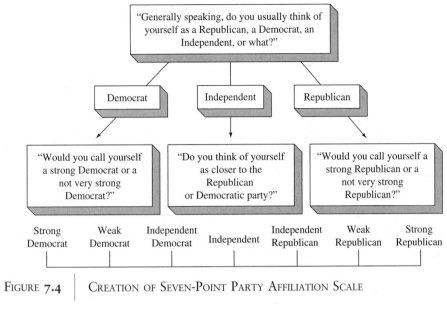

FIGURE **7.4** | CREATION OF SEVEN-POINT PARTY AFFILIATION SCALE

Source: Based on National Election Study.

attachment to and sympathy for a political party.[16] It is considered a long-term and continuing influence on voter choice because one's party identification is not likely to undergo frequent changes in response to changing events or life circumstances. Unlike issues and candidate images, which vary from year to year, a voter's party identification is quite stable.

Party identification is measured either with a three-point or seven-point scale in public opinion surveys. Figure 7.4 explains that this scale is created by first asking citizens whether they think of themselves as a "Republican, Democrat, Independent, or what," and then asking citizens to clarify the strength of their initial answer. The first question provides information about which party a citizen identifies with, and the follow-up question provides more detail about the strength of that attachment. Figure 7.5 shows that between 1952 and 2008, approximately three-fourths to two-thirds of the American electorate held a partisan identification, with the Democrats maintaining a consistent advantage over the GOP. It is also interesting to note that the percentage of citizens identifying as independent-leaners has increased, suggesting that citizens are less willing to identify themselves with a party now than in the past, though they still admit to leaning toward one party or the other.

Party identification tends to be acquired at an early age. Studies of gradeschool children have shown that by fourth grade most students have a partisan preference.[17] This sense of partisanship is usually devoid of an informational or policy content—that is, young children know little about the candidates and issue differences between the parties. Children's sense of partisan affiliation is usually acquired through their families; they tend to imitate the behavior of their parents even when the adults are not actively seeking to persuade their children to adopt their viewpoints. Learning party identification is not, therefore, a conscious activity; it is an

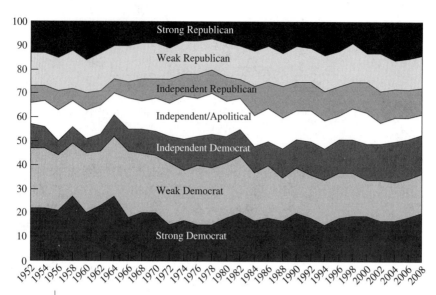

FIGURE 7.5 | PARTY IDENTIFICATION IN THE UNITED STATES, 1952–2008

Source: National Election Study.

informal, family-centered process. As Herbert Asher has noted, "One reason why the family is so crucial is that other agents of political learning, such as teachers and school curricula, studiously avoid getting enmeshed in partisan questions."[18]

Although partisanship is normally learned in childhood, there is substantial stability in most people's party affiliations. However, changing life circumstances and real-world events, as well as policy preferences, can cause some voters to change their party preference.[19] For example, party identification is often changeable in early adulthood, when many people leave their hometowns and families for the first time and are exposed to different viewpoints and life experiences. Sometimes partisan shifts occur during a shorter time frame. In 2000, the Pew Research Center interviewed people in September and then again in November after the election. They found that 18 percent of those they interviewed changed their answer to the party affiliation question when they asked it again in November. However, these party switchers were mostly made up of Republicans and Democrats who later stated that they were independents, as well as some independents who later claimed that they identified with one of the two major parties. Very few citizens changed their party identification from Democratic to Republican or vice versa during that short time period.[20]

CHARACTERISTICS OF PARTY IDENTIFIERS

Citizens who affiliate with political parties tend to be more interested in and knowledgeable about politics and more politically active than others (see Figure 7.6). Partisans are also more likely to see important differences between the parties and to care more about electoral outcomes. It is difficult to disentangle whether identifying with a party causes these traits or is caused by them, but they do reinforce each other.

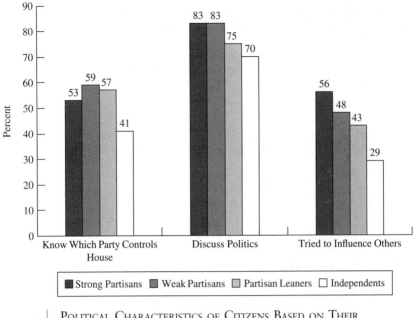

FIGURE 7.6 | POLITICAL CHARACTERISTICS OF CITIZENS BASED ON THEIR PARTISANSHIP, 2008

Source: National Election Study.

For instance, because they see greater differences between the parties, identifiers become increasingly less open to the other party's positions and more convinced of the importance of their party winning. This commitment leads them to become more involved in the political process, which further reinforces their partisan attachment.

Strong partisans show the highest levels of political knowledge, interest, and activity. They are commonly found displaying yard signs for their favored candidates, attending political rallies, volunteering for a candidate's campaign, or contributing money. Independents, on the other hand, are only occasionally interested in politics. They are less likely to discuss politics with friends or family. In 2004, one of every three independents could not even indicate which position Dick Cheney held in the national government. Indeed, some independents do not affiliate with a party because they do not know enough about politics to do so confidently. Other independents may follow politics more but still see few differences between the parties and thus care less about which party wins elections. They are more likely to think that both parties are corrupt or out of touch with normal citizens and may feel as though they are choosing between the lesser of two evils in elections.

PARTISANSHIP AS A POLITICAL FILTER

Once a citizen has an attachment to a particular political party, that attachment tends to influence how that person makes sense of politics. Partisans tend to seek political information from sources that share their opinions, and they are more likely to believe information received from fellow partisans. In 2000, approximately two-thirds of those surveyed said that they had not spoken to a single person about the election who was going to vote for the other party's candidate.[21] Similar filtering takes place when an individual decides where to get political news. Surveys indicate that Republicans are much more likely to watch Fox News regularly compared to Democrats. Fox News is widely viewed as a conservative-leaning news outlet. Republicans are also more likely than Democrats to listen to conservative talk shows hosted by conservative commentators such as Bill O'Reilly and Rush Limbaugh, while Democrats more frequently listen to National Public Radio.[22] Jon Stewart's *Daily Show*, which regularly satirizes Republicans, has an audience that is far more Democratic than Republican.[23]

Even when partisans do encounter those with opposing views, they tend to discount them to a greater extent. For example, Republicans not only watch Fox News more than Democrats, but they also view it as the most credible news outlet while Democrats rank it as one of the least credible. Partisans are more open to being persuaded by other members of their party, and they tend to discount arguments made by those from the opposite party. For example, during the Monica Lewinsky scandal, Hillary Clinton made news by suggesting that a "vast right wing conspiracy" was out to bring down her husband's presidency. A survey of Americans conducted following those remarks found that 73 percent of Democrats agreed with her assessment while only 23 percent of Republicans did.[24] Surveys during the first year of Obama's presidency showed that 44 percent of Democrats thought that Fox News' coverage of Obama was too critical, while only 18 percent of Republicans said the same.

Partisanship also affects the types of traits and beliefs that citizens attribute to politicians they know little about. When partisans do not know where a politician from their party stands on an issue, they project their own beliefs on the politician, assuming that he or she shares their view. Similarly, if the politician belongs to the opposite party, the partisan will tend to think that he or she disagrees with them. This type of projection serves to reinforce the partisanship of respondents.

PARTISANSHIP AND VOTE CHOICE

The strength of party identification is related to both voters' patterns of turnout and loyalty to their parties. As the strength of commitment to a party increases, so does the likelihood that a person will turn out and vote. Strong partisans, therefore, have higher rates of turnout than weak partisans, who in turn are more likely to vote than independents. As would be expected, independents and weak partisans are less likely to support one party consistently than are strong Republicans and strong Democrats, who have a high degree of party loyalty.

In most post–World War II presidential elections, Republican voters have exhibited a higher degree of loyalty than Democrats, although the degree of party loyalty is heavily influenced by such factors as the appeal of the candidates in a given election. One of the major explanations for Democratic defections during this period was the existence of conservative southern Democrats who often abandoned the party in presidential elections to vote for Republicans like Ronald Reagan. The pattern of Democratic presidential candidates being hit hardest by partisan defections became less pronounced in the 1990s since most conservative

TABLE 7.3	PRESIDENTIAL VOTING OF PARTY IDENTIFIERS, 2004 AND 2008 (PERCENT)			
	2004		2008	
	Bush	Kerry	McCain	Obama
Strong Democrat	3	97	5	95
Weak Democrat	17	83	14	86
Leaning Democrat	12	87	10	90
Independent	47	53	44	56
Leaning Republican	89	11	81	19
Weak Republican	89	11	88	12
Strong Republican	98	2	96	4

Source: National Election Study, 2004 and 2008.

southern Democrats had become independents or Republicans by that decade. As Table 7.3 shows, party loyalty was high for both parties in 2004 and 2008. However, Obama fared better than Kerry among independents and Republican leaners, which helped provide the margin of his victory. Obama was also aided by the fact that there were more Democratic Party identifiers in 2008 and fewer Republicans.

DEALIGNMENT OR POLARIZATION?

Studies consistently have demonstrated that party identification is the major determinant of how people vote. However, during previous decades there was substantial evidence that partisanship was having a reduced impact on voters' decisions. Voters were engaging in ticket splitting with increased frequency—that is, voting for one party's candidate in one race but voting for the other party's candidates in contests for different offices. Figure 7.7 shows that at the turn of the century, ticket splitting between presidential and congressional candidates was unusual, but that by the 1960s and through the 1980s, it was commonplace for almost one-third of the nation's congressional districts to have split outcomes between the presidential and congressional outcomes.

In studying the shifts in party identification that occurred during and after presidential campaigns, Seymour Martin Lipset found that voters were shifting their party identification to bring it into harmony with their vote preference. The fact that voters shift in response to candidate preference, together with the sizable proportion of citizens claiming to be independents, demonstrates "that a large part of [the electorate] can be easily moved from one party to another."[25] Morris Fiorina has suggested that because voters' partisanship responds to political events and conditions, party identification should be considered a sort of "running tally" of past experiences—a summary expression of political memory.[26] With voters becoming less than permanently wedded to a particular party, the electorate has become increasingly susceptible to mobilization by either party and subject to the impact of short-term influence like candidate appeal and issues.

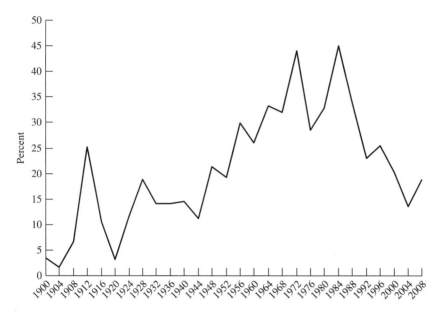

<figure>
FIGURE 7.7 | DISTRICTS WITH SPLIT OUTCOMES (CARRIED BY PRESIDENT OF ONE PARTY AND HOUSE MEMBER OF ANOTHER), 1900–2008
</figure>

Source: Norman J. Ornstein, Thomas E. Mann, and Michael J. Malbin, *Vital Statistics on Congress, 1997–1998* (Washington, D.C.: Congressional Quarterly, Inc., 1998), p. 71. Used by permission; 2000–2008 data from Congressional Quarterly Voting and Elections Database.

Paul Allen Beck has observed that American electoral politics involves the confluence of realignment (e.g., southern whites in the Republican Party; blacks being overwhelmingly identified with the Democrats) and dealignment (i.e., a decline in party identification among a large percentage of voters), concluding that current electoral politics is "a tale of two electorates":

> One is partisan and ideologically polarized, the product of considerable reshuffling of old party coalitions. The other is independent and nonpartisan, sometimes even antipartisan. In the partisan electorate, there is near parity of party strength, which makes election outcomes depend more than before on short-term factors involving candidates and their campaigns. The substantial size of the dealigned portion of the electorate further magnifies the impact of the short-term forces by leaving a large pool of potential voters available for temporary mobilization on behalf of either major party candidate or a third party or independent candidate—or for demobilization into nonvoting.[27]

However, recent elections have indicated a potential resurgence in the importance of party identification as the incidence of split-ticket voting has subsided. In 2004, the number of congressional districts in which there was a split outcome in the presidential and congressional voting dropped to 13.6 percent, the lowest level of split outcomes since 1944 (see Figure 7.7). Figure 7.8 reveals a similar pattern in presenting the percentage of respondents to national surveys who reported splitting

FIGURE **7.8** | REPORTED SPLIT TICKET VOTING, 1952–2004

Source: National Election Study.

their votes for President and Congress. Split-ticket voting reached a high level in the 1970s and 1980s, but has been on the decline ever since.

It should be noted that when voters were asked in 2004 whether they considered themselves Democrats, Republicans, or independents, more voters chose independent than Democrat or Republican. In 2008, the percentage of Democrats and independents were nearly equal. Even though partisan dealignment seems to have been concentrated mainly in the late 1960s and early 1970s and a large majority of voters continue to consider themselves Democrats or Republicans, there is still a larger proportion of the electorate that consider themselves nonpartisans than perhaps ever before. Yet this high percentage of independents may mask an important distinction between behavioral independents and attitudinal independents. Behavioral independents are those citizens who express their independence through their political activity, by supporting candidates of different parties on a frequent basis. Attitudinal independents are those who do not feel as though they are tied to a specific party, even if they vote consistently for that party's candidates. Survey results appear to indicate that more citizens claim they are independents than actually behave that way. In 2008, 35 percent of voters surveyed claimed they were independents, yet only 16 percent split their tickets. In addition, while 35 percent initially claimed they were independents, only 8 percent said that they did not lean toward one party or the other. Political scientists have discovered that the so-called independent leaners behave as much like partisans as those who say they weakly affiliate with one party or the other. For example, Table 7.3 shows that weak Democrats were less likely to vote for Obama than independents who admitted that they leaned toward the Democratic Party (though the pattern was reversed for Republicans). Thus, while the percentage of independents in the electorate continues to remain high, this is not reflected in the behavior of the electorate, which appears to be growing increasingly partisan in recent decades.

PARTIES, CITIZENS, AND ISSUES

Party identification has been a long-term and enduring influence upon voter choices, but its impact can be modified by the short-term and changing influences of candidates and issues.

CANDIDATE IMAGE

Candidate images are especially important when the candidates' personalities, political styles, backgrounds, and physical appearances are given a high level of media coverage, as in presidential elections. For example, in 2000 and 2004, the candidates' personal qualities appear to have helped the Republicans. Pew surveys administered during the 2004 campaign revealed that voters were more likely to see George W. Bush as a "strong leader" and "honest and truthful" compared to John Kerry, traits that were considered particularly important in the first presidential election after 9/11. In 2008, Obama was described by a large majority of voters as "inspiring," and his relative youth and inexperience in Washington became pluses in an election where many Americans were looking for a significant change from the unpopular President Bush.

In some elections, a candidate gains a major advantage over an opponent because the opponent has a particularly unfavorable image with the voters. In 2004, Kerry was harmed by the view that he was a "flip-flopper" who would not take a consistent position. John McCain's fumbled handling of the financial crisis in 2008, coupled with his selection of Sarah Palin as the vice presidential nominee, led many voters to begin questioning whether he had the proper judgment to be president. In early August, McCain had held a significant advantage over Obama on the question of judgment; but by October, 41 percent of voters questioned McCain's judgment, compared to just 29 percent who did the same for Obama.[28] Normally, candidate image has a reduced impact upon voter choice the farther down one goes on the ballot to less visible and less well-known candidates. A candidate's personal qualities may still be important in terms of obtaining a nomination, winning party or interest group endorsements, and putting together a campaign staff, but they are apt to have limited influence on voter decisions simply because the voter is less likely to be aware of them.[29]

IMPACT OF ISSUES

The impact of issues on voter choice varies depending upon conditions and candidates. In the 1964–1972 period—a time of controversial candidates, the civil rights movement, and the Vietnam War—there was an increased correlation between attitudes on issues and vote choice.[30] In the 1980s and up through 1996, however, the issue positions of presidential candidates had a lesser impact on voters. For example, aside from the improved state of the economy, there were no issues in 1996 that were particularly influential. However, in recent presidential elections, issues have become far

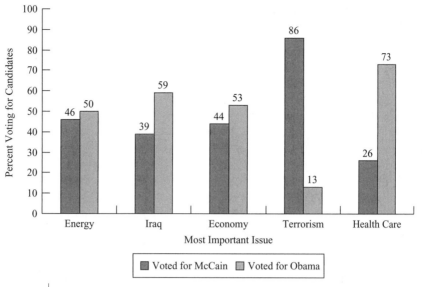

FIGURE **7.9** | IMPACT OF ISSUES ON VOTE CHOICE, 2008

Source: National Election Pool Exit Survey.

more significant. In 2004, issues appeared to strongly determine citizens' vote choices. Voters choosing terrorism (19 percent of those voting) and moral values (22 percent) as their most important issues voted overwhelmingly for Bush; those who placed primary importance on the war in Iraq (15 percent), education (4 percent), health care (8 percent), or the economy (20 percent) voted for Kerry by a wide margin. In 2008, the single dominant issue was the economy; over 60 percent of voters noted that this issue was most important to their decisions. Obama carried 53 percent of these voters, nearly identical to the percentage of the national vote he won (see Figure 7.9).

There are several factors that need to be present for issues to have an impact on voters: (1) voters must be informed and concerned about an issue; (2) the candidates must be distinguishable from each other on this issue; and (3) the voters must perceive the candidates' stands in relationship to their own issue position.[31] Generally speaking, voters are ill-informed about these positions. Some voters, therefore, project on their favored candidate their own personal issue positions, irrespective of the actual position of the candidate. Other voters may adopt an issue position because their preferred candidate has taken that position. In addition, voters may not feel intensely about some issues, even though they are subject to substantial debate during the campaign. Voters' ability to cast their ballots based upon issues is also affected by the campaign strategies of the candidates, who may or may not engage in issue-oriented campaigns.

The conditions for issue voting are most likely to be met when voters are suffering or perceive a threat, as this is when voters tend to care most intensely about an issue. Economic threats are the easiest for voters to understand. Aside from such wrenching events as wars or terrorist attacks like those on New York City and the

Pentagon on September 11, 2001, foreign policy threats are usually more difficult to comprehend. The higher salience and hence electoral payoff attached to economic issues lay behind the well-publicized reminder, "It's the economy, stupid," which was tacked to the wall of Clinton's campaign headquarters in 1992. In 2008, a failing economy was the dominant issue for most voters.

RETROSPECTIVE VOTING   Another way of viewing issue voting is in terms of voters rendering a verdict on the past performance of the candidates and their parties, rather than in terms of candidates' promises for the future. Retrospective voting is especially important when an incumbent is running for reelection.[32] In 1992, when George H. W. Bush was running for reelection, only about two voters in five approved of his performance, and he was ousted from the White House. By contrast, in 1996, Bill Clinton, as the incumbent president, was given a generally positive performance evaluation by the voters. This, combined with the absence of any advantage for the Republicans in terms of their being perceived as better able to deal with the voters' concern, helped Clinton gain reelection.[33] In 2000, Vice President Gore's campaign did not fully exploit the public's generally positive retrospective judgment on the Clinton presidency, especially its handling of the economy. Instead, Gore ran a mainly prospective campaign that stressed what he would do as president. This strategy was dictated by concerns that too close an association with Clinton, whose personal behavior was a liability among voters, would hurt Gore's candidacy. However, post-election critiques of the campaign noted that he had failed to take full advantage of the prolonged economic expansion that had occurred during the Clinton administration. In 2004, evaluations of Bush's first term were largely mixed, contributing to the closeness of that election.

The impact of retrospective voting was clearly felt by John McCain in 2008. Economic conditions quickly deteriorated in 2007 and by the beginning of 2008, 40 percent of Americans said that they were worse off economically than they had been a year earlier while only 35 percent said that they were better off. It was the first time that more Americans felt "worse off" than "better off" economically since the early 1990s. Given that Republicans had held the White House for the eight previous years, Republicans received most of the blame for the economy. As a result, when voters went to the polls in November, 49 percent said that economic conditions were "poor" and 50 percent said that they were "very worried" about the economy. Obama won 66 percent of the first group and 60 percent of the second.

With a faltering economy also came dissatisfaction with the incumbent Republican president. Approval of Bush was already on the decline as a result of the public's unhappiness with America's continued presence in Iraq. A flailing economy did little to help Bush's approval ratings; fewer than one-in-three Americans approved of the job he was doing as president in 2008. Only Richard Nixon had consistently reached such low levels of presidential approval, and that was in the final months of the Watergate scandal before he resigned his office. Despite the fact that McCain did not have particularly close ties to President Bush (in fact, they had been bitter rivals in 2000), the Democrats were successful in linking McCain to Bush during the campaign. According to exit polls, half of the electorate thought that McCain would continue Bush's policies if he won the election. This was a problem for McCain since 51 percent of voters strongly disapproved of the job Bush had done as president; Obama was supported by more than 80 percent of these voters.

ISSUE OWNERSHIP Parties also develop reputations in particular issue areas that help them win support from voters. For example, Democrats are generally trusted more by the public to handle social welfare issues such as health care, social security, and education, largely because they established government programs in those areas and continue to be more concerned with providing such services. On the other hand, Republicans have established a favorable reputation on foreign policy, taxes, and crime, based largely on the success of Republican presidents in dealing with these issues during their presidencies. When voters are more concerned with issues owned by one of the parties, they are more likely to vote for that party's candidates.[34] Thus, the parties often work hard to shift the electorate's attention to issues they own. In 2000, Al Gore focused much of his campaign on health care and social security, whereas George W. Bush campaigned on tax cuts.

While the issue reputations of the parties are generally stable over long periods of time, citizens may eventually come to update how they view the parties on some issues. For example, between the first and second terms of George W. Bush's administration, citizens changed which party they trusted more to deal with issues of terrorism, the war in Iraq, and taxes (see Figure 7.10). In 2002, Republicans were trusted more on terrorism and Iraq and trusted as much as Democrats on taxes. However, dissatisfaction with Iraq and the Republican-controlled government more generally led to substantial changes in terms of which party was favored on these issues in 2006 and 2008, with Democrats gaining an edge in all three areas. Thus, while parties can benefit from their reputations on particular issues, they must also work to maintain their advantages on those issues when they control government.

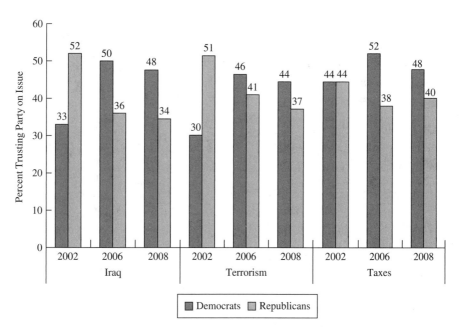

FIGURE 7.10 PERCENTAGE OF PUBLIC TRUSTING PARTIES ON IRAQ, TERRORISM, AND TAXES, 2002–2008

Source: ABC News/Washington Post Surveys.

SOCIAL AND ECONOMIC BASES OF PARTISANSHIP AND VOTING

In the United States, lines of partisan conflict tend to cross-cut social and economic cleavages in society. The parties tend, therefore, to be broad coalitions embracing a wide variety of interests. Indeed, both parties draw significant levels of electoral support from virtually every major socioeconomic group in society. The only significant exception is black voters, who since 1964 have voted Democratic in overwhelming proportions (88 percent in 2004 and 95 percent in 2008). Although both parties can expect at least some backing from just about every socioeconomic group, the two parties do not gain equal proportions of support from each group. There are distinctive patterns in the voting behavior of various groups, and the Republicans and Democrats have different bases of support.

ECONOMIC AND CLASS DIFFERENCES

As income, education, and occupational status go up, the likelihood of an individual voting Republican increases (see Table 7.4). Lower-income persons, blue-collar workers, and people from labor union households have constituted a traditional base of Democratic support, whereas professional/managerial personnel and college-educated, nonunion household members have tended to be Republicans. Although

TABLE 7.4	PRESIDENTIAL VOTING PATTERNS OF POLITICAL AND SOCIOECONOMIC GROUPS, 2008 (PERCENT OF VOTE)	
	Obama (Dem.)	McCain (Rep.)
Democrats	89	10
Republicans	9	90
Independents	52	44
Liberals	89	10
Moderates	60	39
Conservatives	20	78
First-time voters	69	30
Whites	43	55
African Americans	95	4
Hispanics	67	31
Asian Americans	62	35
Men	49	48
Women	56	43
Age		
18–29	66	32
30–44	52	46

continued

TABLE 7.4 | PRESIDENTIAL VOTING PATTERNS OF POLITICAL AND SOCIOECONOMIC GROUPS, 2008 (PERCENT OF VOTE) *continued*

	Obama (Dem.)	McCain (Rep.)
45–64	50	49
65+	45	53
Region of residence		
East	59	40
Midwest	54	44
South	45	54
West	57	40
Family income		
Under $15,000	73	25
$15,000–29,999	60	37
$30,000–49,999	55	43
$50,000–74,999	48	49
$75,000–99,999	51	48
over $100,000	49	49
Union household	59	39
Education		
Less than high school	63	35
High school graduate	52	46
Some college	51	47
College graduate	50	48
Postgraduate	58	40
Protestant	45	54
Catholic	54	45
Jewish	78	21
Married	47	52
Not married	65	33

Note: Percentages may not add to 100 because of rounding or votes for third-party candidates/non-answers.

Source: National Election Pool exit polls.

these patterns have been present in presidential elections since the New Deal realignment of the 1930s, it is important to note that a significant proportion of the voters in each of these categories consistently depart from their group's normal partisan inclination. For example, Republicans can typically expect to receive about 35–40 percent of the labor union household vote, and Democrats customarily gain a similar share of the professional/managerial voters and the college educated.

Since 1952, analysts have observed a decline in class-based differences between the parties. Indeed, the United States is regarded as unusual among Western-style democracies for the relatively low impact that social class has upon voting behavior. In most European democracies, social class is much more significant. The relatively weak impact of social class on voting in the United States is attributable in significant degree to American cultural values of freedom and individualism, which stress getting ahead based upon ability and hard work rather than through class solidarity. Successful candidates, therefore, normally do not seek to exploit class-based issues.

Although class-based voting in the United States is not strong, since the 1930s the Democrats have done better than the Republicans among voters with lower incomes and education levels, as well as among union members. Table 7.4 shows that Obama clearly fared better in 2008 among the poor than among the affluent. Interestingly, the Democrats do well at both the upper and lower socioeconomic levels even though their economic policies appeal more to less–well-off Americans. And those with advanced degrees—especially well-educated women—seem to reject the Republican emphasis in recent campaigns on traditional values. At the same time, Republican appeals to traditional values may have attracted working-class support. The downward trend in class-based voting is dampened when the analysis is expanded to include African Americans, because they are disproportionately working class and overwhelmingly Democratic. However, blacks vote Democratic mainly because they are black, not because they are working class. In other words, their support for the Democratic Party is driven more because of the party's position on civil rights issues. Thus, both working- and middle-class blacks voted overwhelmingly Democratic in the last four presidential elections.

Although class-based voting seems to be on the decline in the nation as a whole, this is not true in the South, where a very different pattern is emerging. Through the 1950s, virtually all southerners, irrespective of their socioeconomic status, were Democrats. Since that time, the middle class have become increasingly Republican, while the working class, especially the black working class, have remained strongly Democratic. As a result, class-based voter alignments in the South have been intensified, whereas they have been reduced in the North. In both regions, however, class-based voting is still relatively weak compared to other Western industrialized nations.[35]

RELIGIOUS DIFFERENCES

Religion, like class, has constituted a traditional basis of partisan alignment since the New Deal period. Catholics tended to be Democrats, and white Protestants tended to be Republicans. At the beginning of the twenty-first century, religious politics revolve more around the importance of religion in one's life than it does in Catholic-versus-Protestant conflict. As Figure 7.11 shows, a relationship exists between the frequency of church attendance and voting behavior. The Republican John McCain fared better among regular church attendees than did Democrat Barack Obama, a pattern also present in previous presidential elections.

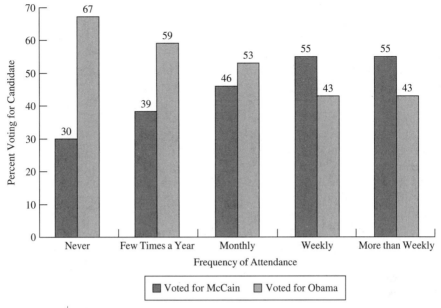

FIGURE 7.11 | PRESIDENTIAL VOTE AND FREQUENCY OF CHURCH ATTENDANCE, 2008

Source: National Election Poll Exit Survey.

Jewish voters have been overwhelmingly Democratic since the New Deal era. The allegiance of Jewish voters to the Democratic Party has held firm even though substantial proportions of the Jewish population have achieved middle-and upper-middle-class status. Anti-Semitism and discrimination against Jews have tended to cause them to identify with the less advantaged and to be supportive of liberal social welfare policies. This type of policy orientation has made them pro-Democratic, irrespective of income, class, or educational attainment. Since the 1980s, Jewish voters' Democratic proclivities have been further encouraged by the appeals made by Republicans to fundamentalist Christian groups and their endorsement of these groups' positions on issues of social policy (e.g., support for prayer in public schools).

GENDER DIFFERENCES

Although eleven states gave women the right to vote by 1918, it was not until the ratification of the Nineteenth Amendment in 1920 that women achieved the constitutional right to vote. This amendment almost doubled the voting-age population in a single stroke. It did not, however, result in any significant changes in the conduct of elections, which party won, or the direction of national policy. Women's voting patterns tended to be quite similar to those of men. In fact, gender was not a source of partisan division in the United States until fairly recently. Beginning in 1980, however, a new pattern emerged: women became less likely to vote Republican than men, and the term "gender gap" entered the political vocabulary. The gender gap reflects the fact that since the 1960s women have encountered new types of problems as they have entered the workforce in expanded numbers and as the number of single-parent, female-headed households has increased. The impact of these changes can be seen in the fact that family status has now become a variable influencing voting behavior. In 2004, married voters favored the Republican nominee John McCain, whereas those who were single, divorced or separated, or widowed, all strongly backed Barack Obama by a substantial margin (see Table 7.4).

In 2000, Gore was a clear beneficiary of the gender gap. The Voter Research and Surveys exit polls show that he lost to Bush among men (53–42 percent) but had a 54 to 43 percent advantage among women. John Kerry did not fare as well among women in 2004, a fact that many believe contributed to his defeat. He only won 51 percent of the women's vote and only 44 percent of the vote among white women. In 2008, Obama performed 7 percentage points better among women than he did among men (56 percent among women, 49 percent among men). These recent results underscore an important point—the size of the gender gap varies widely from election to election. The gap was as small as 4 percent in the 1992 election that brought Bill Clinton to office, but it was as large as 15 percent in his re-election campaign in 1996. One reason for the discrepancy may be the importance of issues during campaigns—while the economy was the dominant issue in 1992, Clinton's 1996 campaign reached out to women by addressing issues such as family leave. Scholarly research indicates that when so-called women's issues become a more prominent part of the campaign, the tendency of women to vote for Democratic candidates increases.[36]

Although most discussion has focused upon the movement of women in the Democratic direction, the gender gap has always had another important component—the movement of men toward the Republicans. This movement of men toward the Republican Party has largely occurred in the South, where conservative white men have changed their allegiance from the Democrats to Republicans. Indeed, except for 1992 and 2008, men have given GOP presidential candidates a higher percent of their vote in every election since 1980, with the margin reaching a high of 25 percent when Reagan topped Mondale 62 to 37 percent in 1984.[37]

REGIONAL DIFFERENCES

Periodically, major issues have emerged in American political history that have pitted one section of the country against another. These conflicts have had a lasting impact on party loyalties and voting habits. Because the first Republican president led the Union during the Civil War and a Republican Congress forced Reconstruction upon the South, the region became overwhelmingly Democratic in its political sympathies after the Civil War and up until the latter half of the twentieth century.

In the South, the small-town, white, Protestant, middle-class conservatives that in other regions could have been expected to provide the core of support for the Republican Party were Democrats. They elected Democrats to Congress and supported virtually every Democratic presidential nominee from the post–Reconstruction period until the 1950s. Starting in the 1950s, however, the GOP began to win significant proportions of the southern vote for president, and the Republicans have won a plurality of the white southern vote in every presidential election since 1968.

A major factor causing partisan change in the South was civil rights: as the national Democratic Party came to reject southern autonomy on matters of race policy in the 1960s and to champion civil rights for southern blacks, conservative white southerners began to desert the party. Lyndon Johnson's promotion and passage of civil rights legislation at the federal level was a turning point for the South. Southern Democrats filibustered the 1964 civil rights bill for three months, but eventually Johnson was able to push the legislation through Congress with the support of a coalition of northern senators from both parties. That same year, Johnson easily defeated Senator Barry Goldwater (R-Ariz.), who was one of only five senators from outside the South to vote against the bill. While the election resulted in a lopsided victory for Johnson, Goldwater won a majority of the southern white vote, a sign of the South's anger at the Johnson administration. As southern politics experts Earl Black and Merle Black explain:

> Many racially conservative white southerners felt betrayed by the national Democratic party and began to reassess their partisan options. Some whites who had been trained from childhood to hate Republicans and revere Democrats now saw in the Goldwater wing of the Republican Party an alternative to the Democratic Party.[38]

Johnson followed the 1964 law with the Voting Rights Act in 1965, sweeping legislation that codified federal intervention in race relations and sparked partisan realignment in the South.

The change in the voting patterns of the South was also caused by economic growth and the in-migration of middle-class northerners. These patterns are particularly evident in the growing suburban areas of cities such as Dallas, Houston, and Atlanta. Until recent decades, a substantial part of the southern electorate was poor and living in rural areas. But the in-migration and economic growth in the South has changed the socio-economic composition of the region, making it more like the rest of the country in many ways:

> The rise of a middle and upper-middle class has produced millions of voters with substantial incomes subject to substantial federal and state taxation. Many of these upwardly mobile individuals, wanting to keep the lion's share of their earnings, view the Republicans as far more sympathetic than the Democrats to their economic interests and aspirations.[39]

These demographic patterns reinforced the changing partisanship of southerners since the 1960s.

While the shift in southern presidential voting was swift, the southern realignment was of a more secular nature (see Figure 7.12). In fact, most southerners continued to affiliate with the Democratic Party for decades following the 1964 election, and they continued to vote for conservative southern Democratic candidates for congressional, state, and local offices. However, conclusive evidence of the realignment of southern white voters was revealed in the 1994 midterm elections, in which the GOP won a majority of the House seats from southern and border states. The Republicans also held a majority of the Senate seats from the states of the old Confederacy after the 1994 elections. By 2000, white southerners' identification with the Democratic Party had reached its lowest level in the history of the party.

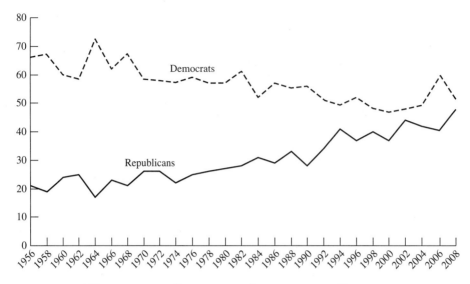

FIGURE 7.12 | PERCENTAGE OF SOUTHERNERS AFFILIATED WITH DEMOCRATIC AND REPUBLICAN PARTIES (INCLUDING INDEPENDENTS LEANING TOWARD EITHER PARTY), 1956–2008

Source: National Election Studies.

The Plains states and the Mountain states have also shown a distinctive partisan orientation. These regions have tended to be the core areas of Republicanism, particularly in recent presidential elections. Throughout most of their history, they have been predominantly rural and characterized by relatively high economic and cultural homogeneity. William Schneider has characterized Nebraska and Kansas as archetypal farm belt states:

> [They are] overwhelmingly agricultural and white Anglo-Saxon Protestant, and not marked by major class or cultural stratification. For example, the largest foreign-stock group in Nebraska, Kansas, and the Dakotas is German, but the Germans in these states are mostly Protestants, whose culture is close to that of their Protestant neighbors.[40]

Schneider has also observed that the farm belt and Mountain states never experienced the same level of internal class conflict as the northeast, southern, and progressive states during the late nineteenth and early twentieth centuries. These areas have not been immune to protest movements (e.g., populism), but a leftward-leaning class constituency never developed because protest movements were confined to a native-stock agrarian milieu. However, there is a sense of sectional protest in the farm belt and Mountain states that tends to be directed against the federal government (e.g., claims by western ranchers and timber and mining interests that the Clinton administration through its land use and natural resources policies was waging a "war on the West"). Republicans have successfully appealed to the powerful anti-Washington sentiment in western states.

| BOX 7.4 | DID RACE MATTER IN 2008? |

With Obama's historic candidacy as the first major party African American candidate for president, many commentators and scholars wondered whether race would play a role in the extent to which Americans supported or opposed his candidacy. Political science research conducted prior to the 2008 campaign indicated that an African American candidate would face greater challenges winning over white voters than a white candidate; yet, some initial analyses of Obama's victory suggest that his race did not significantly depress white support for his candidacy. As Ansolabehere and Stewart noted, "Obama won because of race—because of his particular appeal among black voters, because of the changing political allegiances of Hispanics, and because he did not provoke a backlash among white voters." In fact, many election post-mortems argued that part of the reason that Obama did not provoke a backlash among whites was because "economic issues trumped race." Nevertheless, there are some indications that race did play a role in depressing support for Obama. First, while Obama improved on Kerry's share of the vote in almost every part of the country, he actually performed worse than Kerry in a belt of counties in the Appalachia region of the South. Second, a study conducted by Brian Schaffner found that whites were substantially less likely to support Obama when (1) they held conservative views on racial issues; and (2) they placed more importance on race than others. Schaffner's analysis suggests that Obama's share of the national vote would have been approximately 5 percentage points larger if race had not been salient for any whites in 2008. Thus, Obama's race did not cost him the election, but it may have cost him so votes.

Source: Brian F. Schaffner, "Racial Salience and the Obama Vote." Paper presented at the annual meeting of the Southern Political Science Association, 2010.

RACIAL DIFFERENCES

The first major step toward enfranchising black citizens was ratification of the Civil War amendments—the Fourteenth Amendment, which guaranteed all persons the equal protection of the laws, and the Fifteenth Amendment, which banned denials of voting rights on the basis of "race, color or previous condition of servitude." However, the Democratic Party in the southern states, where the black population was concentrated, circumvented these amendments through such devices as the poll tax, literacy tests, and white primaries. Requiring payment of a poll tax prior to Election Day and administering literacy tests in a discriminatory manner meant that it was very difficult for blacks to have their names entered on the official voting rolls. The white primary further disenfranchised black citizens by excluding them from participation in Democratic primary elections, the real elections in most of the South until well into the 1960s. Physical force and intimidation were also all too frequent techniques used to prevent southern blacks from voting. For these reasons, before the 1930s, black Americans were overwhelmingly Republican. They supported the party of Lincoln. However, during the Depression and New Deal era, they began shifting toward the Democrats. Their support for Republican candidates remained substantial, however, as Eisenhower received 39 percent of the black vote in 1956 and Nixon gained 25 percent four years later.

Through judicial decisions (e.g., the Supreme Court banned the white primary in 1944) and the federal Civil Rights Acts of 1957, 1960, 1964, and 1965, racial barriers to voting were largely removed. Particularly important was the Voting Rights Act of 1965, which was passed on the strength of northern Democrats and signed by Democratic President Lyndon Johnson. In the 1964 presidential election between Barry Goldwater and President Lyndon Johnson, the images of the parties became sharply differentiated on civil rights issues, with the Democrats clearly perceived as the more liberal of the parties. In that election, blacks voted overwhelmingly for the Democratic candidate and have continued to do so in succeeding elections. Even though Ronald Reagan scored a landslide victory in the country as a whole in 1984, he won only 9 percent of the black vote. A growing black population, higher levels of voter turnout, and massive support for Democratic candidates have meant that blacks constitute an expanding and increasingly important share of the Democratic vote. Strong black support is now essential for Democratic electoral victories in national, state, and many local contests.

Voters of Latin American heritage also show a strong but less pronounced tendency to support Democratic candidates. Whereas Bush lost the black vote to Kerry 11–88 percent in 2004, his losing margin among Hispanic Americans was 44–53 percent. Likewise, Obama won 95 percent of the black vote in 2008, compared to two-thirds of Hispanics. There are significant differences among Hispanics in their political preferences. Mexican Americans tend to be Democrats, but Cuban Americans, who have done relatively well economically in this country, tend to be Republicans for economic as well as foreign policy reasons.

Hispanic voters are likely to become an important demographic group in the next few decades for several reasons.

- Hispanics comprise the fastest growing racial or ethnic group in the United States, accounting for more than half of the nation's population growth since 2000. Because of this growth, their political impact on elections, especially in the Southwest, is likely to be profound and result in both parties investing resources to win their allegiance.
- Hispanics participate in elections at a much lower rate than other racial or ethnic groups. In 2008, only 50 percent of eligible Hispanics voted (compared to 64 percent of eligible whites and 65 percent of blacks). Thus, a substantial portion of the potential Hispanic electorate has not been tapped. The parties may benefit from spending considerable resources attempting to mobilize Hispanics as a result.
- Hispanic voters appear to be unsettled in their partisan loyalties. In 2000, 34 percent of Hispanics voted for Bush; this increased to at least 40 percent in 2004. However, in 2008, Obama won two-thirds of the Hispanic vote. The Democratic Party tends to appeal to Hispanic voters because of its concern for social welfare issues, its traditional attention to civil rights issues, and its more liberal stance on immigration. On the other hand, Republicans often appeal to Hispanic evangelicals on social issues. Protestant evangelicals accounted for one-third of the Hispanic electorate in 2004, and they voted 56–44 in favor of Bush. Republicans can have some success in appealing to Hispanic voters on cultural issues, whereas Democrats will be more successful on social welfare issues.

BOX 7.5	LOSING LATINOS? IMMIGRATION REFORM AND THE REPUBLICAN PARTY'S PROSPECTS WITH HISPANIC VOTERS

As governor of Texas, George W. Bush worked hard to win a substantial share of the Hispanic vote. He continued to court Hispanics in his 2000 and 2004 campaigns for the White House, seemingly establishing inroads to the community for the Republican Party. But in 2006, the debate over immigration reform made national headlines and threatened to disrupt Bush's effort to bring Latinos into the Republican Party. Bush proposed a guest worker program that would allow illegal immigrants to stay in the country legally for a limited period of time. The proposal stopped short of eventually allowing the illegal population a path to citizenship, but it was a step toward a more liberal immigration policy. As it turned out, even this step was too much for Republicans in the House of Representatives, who strongly opposed efforts to give legal status to undocumented workers. House Republicans stepped up the rhetoric by lambasting any proposal that would give illegal aliens "amnesty," while Hispanic Americans took to the streets of America's cities in large protests that attracted substantial attention. House Republicans eventually defeated Bush's proposal as well as Democratic proposals that would have provided a path to citizenship for illegal immigrants.

Will the immigration debate eventually cost the Republican Party the support of the fastest-growing demographic in the nation? In a 2005 survey, 56 percent of Hispanic Americans favored a guest worker program like the one Bush proposed, while 84 percent supported more liberal proposals to allow unauthorized immigrants to eventually gain citizenship. In 2006, a similar survey found that Latinos overwhelmingly favored the Democratic Party over the GOP on the immigration issue. While the issue is not always a priority for Hispanic voters, there may still be electoral consequences for the Republican Party. Indeed, in 2008, Obama won two-thirds of the Latino vote. And given the rate of growth among the Latino community, such consequences could have a substantial effect on the electoral landscape.

Source: Thomas B. Edsall and Zachary A. Goldfarb, "Bush Is Losing Hispanics' Support, Polls Show," *Washington Post,* May 21, 2006, p. A06; and Pew Report.

Thus, because of its growing population, potential for mobilization, and unsettled partisan loyalties, the Hispanic population will be a target for appeals from both parties in the coming decades and the success or failure in winning this constituency may have an important effect on the partisan landscape.

PARTISANSHIP AND POLARIZATION AT THE TURN OF THE CENTURY

Many journalists, pundits, and academics see twenty-first-century America as being highly polarized along partisan lines. But how polarized are American citizens? Political scientist Morris Fiorina argues that the partisan polarization of the twenty-first century is a phenomenon among political elites that does not translate to the masses. He explains,

> Americans are closely divided, but we are not deeply divided, and we are closely divided because many of us are ambivalent and uncertain, and consequently reluctant

| BOX 7.6 | "DIVIDED THEY BLOG?" POLARIZATION ON THE WEB |

Bloggers became a much-discussed part of the 2004 campaign as one of every ten Internet users reported that they regularly or sometimes read a political blog. Usually, these blogs approached the political discussion from a particular point of view, such as the conservative blog, instapundit.com or the leading liberal blog, dailykos.com. But do blogs provide a venue for debating alternative viewpoints, or are they mostly a polarizing forum for like-minded partisans to discuss politics with each other? To answer this question, two researchers examined the top 20 liberal and conservative blogs during the campaign. Among other findings, this is what they discovered:

- Liberal blogs primarily linked to discussions on other liberal blogs and conservative blogs linked mostly to other conservative blogs. In general, bloggers ignored discussions on blogs run by the opposing side.
- Liberal and conservative blogs also tended to discuss different topics and personalities.
- Liberal blogs were more likely to cite and link to articles produced by more liberal news outlets such as the *New York Times* and Salon.com, whereas conservative bloggers linked more often to conservative news outlets such as Fox News and the National Review.

Overall, the authors concluded that bloggers act much as other citizens, preferring to exchange information with fellow partisans and shying away from the conflicting points of view generated by opposing blogs and news outlets.

Source: Lada Adamic and Natalie Glance, "The Political Blogosphere and the 2004 U.S. Election: Divided They Blog," http://www.blogpulse.com/papers/2005/AdamicGlanceBlogWWW.pdf, 2005.

to make firm commitments to parties, politicians, or policies. We divide evenly in elections or sit them out entirely because we instinctively seek the center while the parties and candidates hang out on the extremes.[41]

Fiorina argues that American citizens are mostly moderates, caught somewhere in between the polarized parties. As a result, much of the American electorate is uncomfortable with and turned off by such polarizing partisan politics, leading them to avoid politics altogether.

Are Americans polarized or inherently moderate? It depends on how one defines the electorate. Alan Abramowitz and Kyle Saunders find that while a majority of citizens hold positions on issues near the center of the ideological spectrum, the most politically engaged and active citizens take very polarizing positions. In essence, party identifiers have become more polarized in recent decades, while independents remain ideological moderates. As Abramowitz and Saunders state:

There are sharp divisions between supporters of the two major parties that extend far beyond a narrow sliver of elected officials and activists. Red state voters and blue state voters differ fairly dramatically in their social characteristics and political beliefs. Perhaps most importantly, there is a growing political divide in the United States between religious and secular voters. These divisions are not the result of artificial boundaries constructed by political elites in search of electoral security. They reflect fundamental changes in American society and politics that have been developing for decades and are likely to continue for the foreseeable future.[42]

In addition, the authors argue that polarization is not harmful to political participation; rather, it encourages it. This assertion certainly appears to be valid on its face, as the highly polarized presidential election in 2004 witnessed the highest turnout in decades. When citizens see larger differences between candidates and parties, they care more about who wins and loses and are more likely to become engaged in the campaign as a result.

Thus, even though many citizens choose to think of themselves as independents, partisanship among the electorate continues to be an important force. Most independents lean towards one party or another, and even these "leaners" report important differences between the parties and act quite partisan. A polarized political atmosphere has only increased the importance of partisanship to voters and possibly led to an increase in political participation in recent campaigns. This reflects the important role that parties play in mobilizing and engaging the electorate in the political process, a point we expand on in Chapter 8.

Web Sites on the Party-in-the-Electorate

The National Election Studies available from the University of Michigan's Institute for Social Research constitute the most extensive collection of data on voting in the United States.
http://electionstudies.org

The Pew Research Center for People and the Press provides up-to-date data on public opinion and the electorate.
http://www.people-press.org

The Annenberg Public Policy Center of the University of Pennsylvania has been conducting continuous surveys of American voters during the last two presidential elections. Reports from these data are included on this Web site.
http://www.annenbergpublicpolicycenter.org/naes/index.htm

This blog is operated by Mike Blumenthal, a longtime political pollster. On this blog, he discusses the science and pitfalls of polling, including commentary on current political polls.
http://www.pollster.com

A statistician by the name of Nate Silver operates this blog, which focuses on the analysis and prediction of election outcomes in the United States.
http://www.fivethirtyeight.com/

Notes

1. Steven Rosenstone and John Mark Hansen, *Mobilization, Participation, and Democracy in America* (New York: Macmillan, 1993), pp. 177–188.
2. Robert Jackson, "The Mobilization of U.S. State Electorates," *Journal of Politics* 59 (1997): 520–537; and Samuel Patterson and Gregory Caldeira, "Getting Out the Vote: Participation in Gubernatorial Elections," *American Political Science Review* 77 (Sept. 1983): 675–689.

3. Jae-On Kim, John R. Petrocik, and Stephen Enokson, "Voter Turnout among the American States: Systematic and Individual Components," *American Political Science Review* 69 (March 1975): 107–123; M. Margaret Conway, *Political Participation in the United States* (Washington, D.C.: CQ Press, 2000), ch. 2.

4. Raymond E. Wolfinger and Steven J. Rosenstone, *Who Votes?* (New Haven, Conn.: Yale University Press, 1980), p. 41. For a cross-national analysis of factors influencing turnout, see G. Bingham Powell, "American Turnout in Comparative Perspective," *American Political Science Review* 80 (March 1986): 17–43.

5. Michael D. Martinez and David Hill, "Did Motor Voter Work?" *American Political Quarterly* 27 (July 1999): 296–315.

6. Jeffrey A. Karp and Susan A. Banducci, "Absentee Voting: Mobilization and Participation," *American Political Research* 29 (March 2001): 183–195.

7. William H. Flanigan and Nancy H. Zingale, *Political Behavior of the American Electorate*, 9th ed. (Washington, D.C.: CQ Press, 1998), p. 41.

8. Paul R. Abramson, John H. Aldrich, and David W. Rohde, *Change and Continuity in the 1992 Elections* (Washington, D.C.: CQ Press, 1994), pp. 123–128.

9. Paul R. Abramson, John H. Aldrich, and David W. Rohde, *Change and Continuity in the 2000 Elections* (Washington, D.C.: CQ Press, 2002), pp. 92–93.

10. Pew Research Center for the People and the Press, "Obama Leads McCain 52% to 46% in Campaign's Final Days," November 2, 2008; Cooperative Congressional Election Study; Author's analysis of data from the 2008 Cooperative Congressional Election Study.

11. Gregory A. Caldeira and Samuel C. Patterson, "Contextual Influences on Participation in U.S. State Legislative Elections," *Legislative Studies Quarterly* 7 (Aug. 1982): 359–381; Patterson and Caldeira, "Getting Out the Vote"; see also Gregory A. Caldeira, Samuel C. Patterson, and Gregory A. Markko, "The Mobilization of Voters in Congressional Elections," *Journal of Politics* 47 (May 1985): 490–509.

12. Ivor Crewe, "As the World Turns Out," *Public Opinion* 4 (Feb./March 1981): 52.

13. See John R. Petrocik, "Voter Turnout and Electoral Preference," in Kay Schlozman, ed., *Elections in America* (Boston: Unwin Hyman, 1987), pp. 261–292; Abramson et al., *Change and Continuity in the 1992 Elections,* ch. 4.

14. Benjamin Highton and Raymond E. Wolfinger, "What If They Gave an Election and Everyone Came?" *Public Affairs Report* (Institute of Governmental Affairs, University of California, Berkeley), July 1999, pp. 11–13.

15. Kim Quaile Hill and Jan E. Leighley, "Lower-Class Mobilization and Policy Linkage in the U.S. States," *American Journal of Political Science* 39 (1997): 75–86.

16. A classic statement of the concept of party identification is contained in Angus Campbell, Phillip E. Converse, Warren E. Miller, and Donald E. Stokes, *The American Voter* (New York: Wiley, 1960); see especially pp. 121–128.

17. Fred I. Greenstein, *Children and Politics* (New Haven, Conn.: Yale University Press, 1965), p. 71.

18. Herbert B. Asher, *Presidential Elections and American Politics*, 5th ed. (Pacific Grove, Calif.: Brooks/Cole, 1992), p. 69.

19. Morris P. Fiorina, *Retrospective Voting in American National Elections* (New Haven, Conn.: Yale University Press, 1981); Richard G. Niemi and M. Kent Jennings, "Issues and Inheritance in the Formation of Party Identification," *American Journal of Political Science* 35 (Nov. 1991): 970–988.

20. "Party Affiliation: What It Is and What It Isn't," The Pew Research Center for the People and the Press, September 23, 2004.

21. Robert Huckfeldt, Jeanette Mendez, and Tracy Osborn, "Disagreement, Ambivalence, and Engagement: The Political Consequences of Heterogeneous Networks," *Political Psychology* 25 (2004): 65–95.

22. The Pew Research Center for the People and the Press, "News Audiences Increasingly Politicized," June 8, 2004.

23. National Annenberg Election Survey Press Release, "Daily Show Viewers Knowledgeable about Presidential Campaign, National Annenberg Election Survey Shows," September 21, 2004.

24. Los Angeles Times Poll, February 1, 1998.

25. Seymour Martin Lipset, "The Elections, the Economy and Public Opinion," *P.S.* (Winter 1985): 35.

26. Morris P. Fiorina, "An Outline for a Model of Party Choice," *American Journal of Political Science* 78 (Aug. 1977): 601–624.

27. Paul Allen Beck, "The Changing American Party Coalitions: 1952–2000," paper prepared for the State of the Parties: 2000 and Beyond conference, Bliss Institute, University of Akron, Akron, Ohio, Oct. 17–19, 2001.

28. Pew Research Center for the People and the Press, "Growing Doubts about McCain's Judgment, Age and Campaign Conduct," October 21, 2008.

29. For a summary of the impact of candidate image on voting in recent elections, see Flanigan and Zingale, *Political Behavior of the American Electorate*, pp. 166–170.

30. Norman Nie, Sidney Verba, and John R. Petrocik, *The Changing American Voter* (Cambridge, Mass.: Harvard University Press, 1976), ch. 10; Flanigan and Zingale, *Political Behavior of the American Electorate*, pp. 173–178.

31. Abramson et al., *Continuity and Change in the 1996 Elections*, Washington, D.C.: Congressional Quarterly, pp. 129–130.

32. Arther H. Miller and Martin P. Wattenberg, "Throwing the Rascals Out: Policy Performance Evaluations of Presidential Candidates," *American Political Science Review* 79 (June 1985): 359–373. See also Morris Fiorina, *Retrospective Voting in American National Elections* (New Haven, Conn.: Yale University Press, 1981).

33. Abramson et al., *Continuity and Change in the 1996 Elections*, pp. 143–163.

34. John R. Petrocik, "Issue Ownership in Presidential Elections, with a 1980 Case Study," *American Journal of Political Science* 40 (1996): 825–850.

35. Ibid., pp. 97–99; Flanigan and Zingale, *Political Behavior of the American Electorate*, pp. 101–103.

36. Brian F. Schaffner, "Priming Gender: Campaigning on Women's Issues in U.S. Senate Elections," *American Journal of Political Science* 49 (4) (2005): 803–817.

37. Jody Neuman, "The Gender Story: Women as Voters and Candidates in the 1996 Elections," in Regina Dougherty et al., *America at the Polls 1996* (Storrs, Conn.: Roper Center for Public Opinion Research, 1997), pp. 102–106.

38. Earl Black and Merle Black, *The Rise of Southern Republicans* (Cambridge: Harvard University Press), p. 77.

39. Ibid., p. 5.

40. William Schneider, "Democrats and Republicans, Liberals and Conservatives," in Seymour Martin Lipset, ed., *Party Coalitions in the 1980s* (New Brunswick, N.J.: Transaction, 1981), pp. 203–204.

41. Morris P. Fiorina, Samuel J. Abrams, and Jeremy C. Pope, *Culture War? The Myth of a Polarized America* (New York: Longman), p. ix.

42. Alan I. Abramowitz and Kyle Saunders, "Why Can't We All Just Get Along? The Reality of a Polarized America," *The Forum* 3 (2) (2005): 19.

THE GENERAL ELECTION: CAMPAIGN FINANCE AND CAMPAIGN STRATEGY

Once the field of candidates has been narrowed through the nomination process, the scene of the party battle shifts to the general election. Nominations are intraparty struggles, whereas the general election is an interparty struggle that operates in a different type of political environment. In the general election competition, there is normally a higher level of citizen interest, an expanded electorate, larger campaign expenditures, and greater media exposure. The nomination is an interim stage in the process of selection of government officials. In the general election, all decisions are final.

FINANCING ELECTIONS

Without substantial funds, it is rarely possible to run a credible campaign. Money is not the only critical campaign resource—name identification, charisma, incumbency, volunteers, party organizational support, interest group backing, and a favorable balance within the constituency of party voters are also important. But without money, the basics of a campaign are impossible to obtain. Money purchases a headquarters, consultants and staff, polls, media advertising, and travel. As the technology of campaigning has become more advanced and the electronic media has become an indispensable part of major campaigns, campaign costs have escalated dramatically. Retaining professional campaign consultants to advise on the use of the modern campaign technology has become a standard feature of most campaigns for major office.[1] These experts frequently demand large fees for their services, including a commission fee on media booking and production costs and substantial monthly retainers.[2]

The escalating cost of campaigns for the House and Senate is demonstrated in Figure 8.1, which shows the average expenditures between 1992 and 2008 for incumbents, challengers, and open seat candidates. The figure reveals that House campaigns costing $1 million or more are now commonplace. Even $3 million House campaigns (37 in 2008) are no longer unusual. Twelve Senate candidates spent more than $10 million in 2008, and thirty campaigns spent over $5 million. Campaigns for state office have also become costly. For example, in the 2002 Illinois gubernatorial race, Democrat Rod Blagojevich spent over $14 million to win the general election. Even state legislative races can be extremely expensive, with some candidates spending approximately half a million dollars in states where a switch in party control of a few seats could result in the change of party control of a legislative chamber.

The level of campaign spending is related to the candidates' chances of winning and the closeness of the contest. For example, in House elections, incumbents and open seat (where no incumbent is running) candidates have the best chance of victory and normally spend at higher-than-average levels. The parties are also more likely to provide open seat candidates with funds and other valuable resources. Closely fought races also cause high spending by both incumbents and challengers. The nineteen challengers who defeated House incumbents in 2008 spent an average of nearly $2 million, while the incumbents they defeated spent, on average, over $2.3 million.

Analyses of campaign spending and election outcomes have shown that the level of expenditure by a candidate can affect the result, but the individual who spends the most does not necessarily win. Sufficient funds to run an adequate

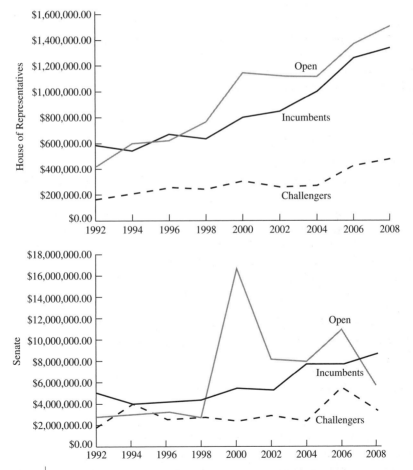

FIGURE 8.1 | AVERAGE EXPENDITURES OF HOUSE AND SENATE CANDIDATES, 1992–2008

campaign are absolutely essential, and large disparities in financial resources can be hurtful to the disadvantaged candidate. Research on House elections demonstrates that campaign spending is particularly important for candidates challenging incumbents. The more challengers spend, the better known they become to the voters and the better able voters are to make an evaluation of them (as well as more critical evaluations of the incumbents). Large-scale spending by a challenger can cut the incumbent's advantage in voter recall and recognition in half. Spending by incumbents, however, has less impact. As campaign finance expert Gary Jacobson has observed, for incumbents "the campaign adds little to the prominence and affection they have gained prior to the campaign by cultivating the district and using the many perquisites of office."[3]

Because of the escalating cost of campaigns, the inevitable differences among candidates in their financial resources, and the recurring charges of improprieties, there have been periodic demands for regulation of campaign finance. The resulting statutes at the national and state levels have used the following methods to regulate campaign finance: (1) public disclosure of contributions and expenditures; (2) contribution and expenditure limits; and (3) public funding of campaigns.

BOX 8.1 | Campaign Finance Terminology

The difficult subject of campaign finance regulations is compounded by the jargon used to describe these rules. Here are some of the terms that are useful to keep in mind:

BCRA: Acronym for the Bipartisan Campaign Reform Act of 2002, also known as McCain-Feingold, after Senators John McCain (R-Ariz.) and Russ Feingold (D-Wisc.).

Express Advocacy: Communication that expressly advocates for the defeat or election of a particular candidate. According to the FEC, this type of communication uses the words like "elect," "defeat," "vote for," and "vote against." These words are often referred to as "magic words" and are identified as such by the Supreme Court in the 1976 landmark decision, *Buckley v. Valeo*, 424 U.S. 1.

Election Cycle: A federal election cycle is a two-year period beginning on January 1st of an odd year (e.g., 2005) and ending December 31st of the following even year (e.g., 2006).

FEC: The Federal Election Commission, created by Congress in 1975, is the executive agency charged with administering and enforcing campaign finance regulations.

FECA: The Federal Election Campaign Act, passed in 1971 and amended in 1974, 1976, and 1979.

Hard Money: Any money raised or spent that is subject to federal limits.

Issue Advocacy: Any communication that does not expressly advocate for the defeat or election of a particular candidate.

Soft Money: Any money raised or spent that is not subject to federal limits.

Public Disclosure

The Federal Election Campaign Act (FECA) requires that all contributions of $200 or more must be identified and all expenditures of $200 or more must be reported. Candidate committees and parties must also file periodic preelection reports and a final postelection report with the Federal Election Commission (FEC). Using these reports, the FEC maintains an online searchable database of candidates, parties, PACs, and donors (http://www.fec.gov/finance/disclosure/disclosure_data_search .shtml). Visitors to the site can search for contributions made by particular individuals or by all individuals in any zip code. The site also allows users to browse a particular candidate's record of contributors in order to increase the transparency of the sources of candidates' financial support.

Contribution and Expenditure Limits

Candidates for federal office may raise money from individuals, political action committees (PACs), and party committees.

- *Individuals.* Individual contribution limits to federal candidates were doubled after the BCRA from $1,000 to $2,000 and are indexed for inflation (see Table 8.1). Thus, they increase with each election cycle. In 2010, individuals could contribute no more than $2,400 to any one candidate per campaign, up to a total of $45,600 for all candidates. Primary elections and general elections are considered separate contests, so an individual could give a candidate $2,400 for the primary campaign and an additional $2,400 for the general election campaign. Candidates running unopposed in the primary can still raise money for the primary contest and use that money for their general election campaigns.
- *PACs.* Nonparty political action committees may give no more than $5,000 to any one candidate per campaign (primary and general elections considered separate). This remained unchanged after the BCRA, and this limit is not adjusted for inflation.

Table **8.1** | Change in Individual Contribution Limits Under the BCRA

Type of Contribution	Pre-BCRA Limit	Post-BCRA Limit
Federal candidates	$1,000	$2,000 (indexed for inflation)
National party committee	$20,000	$25,000 (indexed for inflation)
State or local party committee	$5,000	$10,000
Political action committee	$5,000	$5,000
Aggregate limit	$25,000 per year	$95,000 total per election cycle
		$37,500 to candidates
		$57,500 to party committees and PACs (all indexed for inflation)

- *Parties.* In House elections, party committees are restricted to direct contributions of $5,000 per candidate per election. This means that party committees can contribute up to a total of $10,000 to House candidates ($5,000 for the nomination campaign and $5,000 for the general election). Both the national committees and the congressional campaign committees are permitted to make contributions at this level. As a result, national-level party committee contributions to House candidates may total $20,000. State party organizations may also contribute directly to congressional candidates. Direct party contributions to senatorial candidates are restricted to $37,300 per campaign, but this limit is shared by the national party committees and congressional campaign committees. This amount is also indexed for inflation and increases in each election cycle.

In addition to direct contributions, *party* committees are also authorized to make *coordinated expenditures* on behalf of the party and its candidates. Coordinated expenditures involve spending by the parties to support candidates (e.g., for polls, media production, campaign consultants), which benefits specific candidates but does not entail direct financial contributions to a candidate's campaign committee. The amount of coordinated expenditures a party may make depends on the type of election:

- *House Campaigns.* In 2010, the amount of coordinated expenditures authorized by law to assist a particular House candidate was $43,500. This amount increases in each election cycle based on cost-of-living adjustments to the original $10,000 limit set in 1974. In the seven states with only one congressional district, national party committees were permitted $87,000 in coordinated expenditures in 2010.
- *Senate Campaigns.* National party committees are permitted to spend more extensively in Senate races. Party-coordinated expenditures are based upon a formula of two cents per eligible voter in the state (adjusted for inflation since 1974). The "two cents per voter" formula, when applied to large states like California or Texas, means that party committees are in a position to be of major assistance to their party's nominee for the Senate ($2.4 million for California and $1.6 million for Texas in 2010). State party committees are also permitted to spend two cents per voter in coordinated expenditures to support senatorial candidates. However, most state parties are not in a financial position to take full advantage of this provision in the law. To compensate for the inability of most state parties to spend to the legal limit in support of senatorial candidates, the Republicans pioneered the development of the "agency agreement" technique. Under this procedure, state parties assign their quota of coordinated expenditures to the national party to act as their agent. As a result of this procedure, the Republican and Democratic senatorial campaign committees have been able to double the level of their coordinated expenditures in key races.

Traditionally, Republican Party committees played a more significant role in funding their candidates than did Democratic Party organizations (see Figure 8.2). Since 2004, however, Democratic Party committees have achieved parity with Republicans.

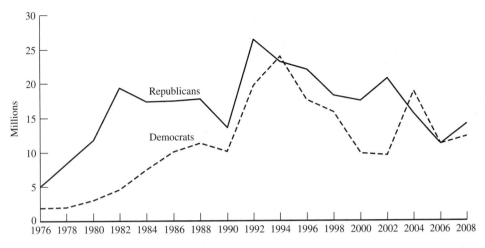

FIGURE 8.2   Political Party Contributions and Coordinated Expenditures for Congress, 1976–2008

Source: Federal Election Commission.

Although political parties are restricted in terms of how much they may spend to support congressional and senatorial candidates, there are no overall limits on the amount the candidates' organizations may spend. The outer range of expenditures in races for positions on Capitol Hill, therefore, can be extremely high. For example, in 2008, Al Franken (D-Minn.) spent over $20 million to defeat incumbent Senator Norm Coleman (R-Minn.) who also spent over $20 million. And in the most expensive House race of the cycle, incumbent Representative Kirsten Gillibrand (D-NY) spent $4.5 million to defend her seat from a Republican challenger who spent over $7 million.

Nor are there limits on how much of their own money candidates may spend in pursuit of public office. The Supreme Court has ruled that the limit on candidate contributions to their own campaigns contained in the FECA of 1974 was unconstitutional. As a result, some wealthy candidates have lavishly funded their own campaigns. Democrat Jon Corzine holds the record for candidate funding of a campaign. In 2000, he spent over $60 million of his own money to run for—and win—a New Jersey Senate seat. The least successful self-funded candidate was Blair Hull (D-Ill.) who spent over $28 million to lose the 2004 Democratic primary for the Senate to Barack Obama (D-Ill.).

Because of concern about the growing number of successful self-financed candidates, the BCRA included a provision typically referred to as the millionaire's amendment. In an attempt to level the playing field, the clause increased the contribution limits if a candidate's opponent spent a certain amount of his or her own money on the campaign. It also removed the limits on party coordinated expenditures. However, this portion of the law was ruled unconstitutional by the Supreme Court in June, 2008. The majority opinion in the case noted that it was unconstitutional to penalize candidates who exercised their rights to spend freely on their own campaign.

| BOX 8.2 | IS MONEY SPEECH? THE SUPREME COURT ON CAMPAIGN FINANCE REGULATIONS |

After Congress passed the FECA in 1971, a host of politicians, including New York Senator James L. Buckley, challenged the constitutionality of the new regulations in a case that eventually reached the Supreme Court. In 1976, the Supreme Court's decision in Buckley v. Valeo upheld the constitutionality of contribution limits but struck down limits on how much candidates could spend. The Court explained that while contribution limits served a government interest in "safeguarding the integrity of the electoral process," the limits on candidate expenditures amounted to "substantial restraints on the quantity of political speech." This decision meant that the government could not mandate limits on candidate expenditures; such limits could be opted into only by a candidate receiving public funding (as in presidential campaigns).

After the BCRA passed Congress in 2002, many suspected that, under the same logic as in Buckley v. Valeo, the Court would strike down the new limits on soft money and issue-advocacy advertisements as curtailment of free speech. However, in a 5–4 decision in McConnell v. FEC (2003), the Court upheld these limits as prudent given the dangerous effects of soft money and issue-advocacy ads on the electoral system. In 2006, the Court ruled again on campaign finance restrictions in the case of Randall v. Sorrell. This case involved a challenge to a Vermont law enacted in 1997 that would have set extremely restrictive limits on contributions and spending by candidates for state office. Candidates for statewide office would be limited to spending $300,000 for the entire campaign, and the limit for state legislative campaigns would have been just $4,000. However, the Supreme Court ruled the law unconstitutional, arguing that such low spending and contribution limits would be too restrictive of political speech. In 2008, the court again cited free speech concerns when it ruled the millionaire's amendment of the BCRA unconstitutional in Davis v. Federal Election Commission. And the Supreme Court's landmark decision in Citizens United v. FEC again referenced free speech concerns when ruling that the federal government could not limit the ability of corporations to spend on behalf of candidates during a campaign. These recent cases demonstrate that the Court is willing to allow restrictions on contributions and some regulation on particular types of spending, but campaign finance regulations that are viewed as too limiting will be struck down for impinging on the First Amendment guarantee of free speech.

INDEPENDENT EXPENDITURES, ISSUE ADVOCACY, AND SOFT MONEY

The Supreme Court struck down as a violation of the First Amendment rights to freedom of speech and association a provision in the FECA that restricted to $1,000 the amount that groups could spend to support candidates. This FECA provision limited so-called independent expenditures by PACs and individuals in support of candidates. These were expenditures made by organized groups or individuals without consultation or coordination with the candidate's organization. Independent expenditures are a campaign activity that is mainly the domain of large, well-funded groups such as the National Rifle Association, the American Medical

Association, the AFL-CIO, the Sierra Club, the National Association of Realtors, and the U.S. Chamber of Commerce.

In 1996, 1998, and 2000, voters were bombarded with television advertising costing uncounted millions and paid for by political parties and interest groups engaged in *issue advocacy*—defined by the FEC as "public advertisement, not sponsored by a federal office candidate or political committee, encouraging readers or listeners to take action to advance whatever public cause is being promoted." This type of advertising, which cannot contain "express advocacy" of the election or defeat of a candidate for federal office, was not regulated by FEC, and hence there were no limits on how much parties and groups could spend on issue ads or when they could air these ads. Although these ads did not expressly advocate the election or defeat of specific candidates, they were carefully crafted in such a way that the average viewer finds them almost indistinguishable from conventional ads for candidates. For example, during the 2004 campaign, MoveOn.org aired extensive issue-advocacy ads criticizing President Bush and the Republican Congress for the Iraq War but did not expressly advocate for their defeat in the coming election. An Annenberg Public Policy Center study found that 87 percent of the issue ads run in 1996 named individual candidates and that these ads were significantly more negative in tone than regular political commercials run by the candidates.[4] Subsequent research by the Wisconsin Advertising Project on the 2000 and 2004 elections has confirmed that issue ads tend to be more negative in tone.[5]

Beginning in 1996, the use of issue-advocacy advertising by political parties exploded. Issue advocacy was particularly attractive to party organizations because it provided a means of getting around contribution and spending limits in the FECA (issue ads could be funded to a significant extent using soft money outside the restrictions of the FECA). As a result, the parties raised ever larger amounts of soft money and became increasingly dependent upon it. Taking advantage of FECA rules that made it advantageous to have state parties actually pay for the television ads and mailings, the national-level committees of the Democratic and Republican parties made massive transfers of soft money to state affiliates. In 2000, $106.5 million was transferred by national-level Democratic committees and $98.6 million by GOP national party units to their respective state parties. This explosion in issue-advocacy advertising funded largely through soft money created several problems in the campaign finance system:

- *The Soft Money Loophole.* The FECA contained major "soft money" loopholes that enabled individuals, unions, and corporations to evade federal contribution limits or prohibitions and permitted parties to exceed their spending limits in support of federal candidates. "Soft money" involved contributions, sometimes in denominations in excess of a million dollars, that went to national and state parties or auxiliary committees set up by the national Republican and Democratic parties. It was used for "party building"—activities such as voter registration drives, get-out-the-vote (GOTV) campaigns, generic advertising that urged voter support for a party's full slate of candidates rather than for specific candidates—and it was used extensively by both parties for "issue advocacy" ads that were in fact thinly disguised commercials, mainly for top-of-the-ticket candidates rather than those at the bottom. Thus, a major consequence of the growth of issue-advocacy advertising by parties and interest groups through the use of soft money was to render the contribution limits of the FECA virtually meaningless.

- *Interest Group Influence.* Not only did the growth of issue-advocacy advertising create massive loopholes in the federal campaign finance laws, it also worked to take control of campaign strategy out of the hands of the candidates because outside groups could enter campaigns and engage in saturation advertising without advance warning to the candidates.

- *Accountability.* One of the problems with the extensive use of issue advocacy by the parties and a wide range of interest groups was that no one is really accountable for the content or tone of campaigns. Candidates at times even disavow interest group and even party ads run on their behalf. Yet voters often assume that it is the candidates who are responsible for the ads they see and hear in the media, when in reality the candidates' own ads are only a portion of what is being done in support of their candidacies.

THE BCRA: BANNING SOFT MONEY AND REGULATING ISSUE ADVOCACY

In 2002, Congress passed the most significant campaign finance legislation since the FECA in 1974. In addition to the adjustment of contribution limits noted earlier, the BCRA also aimed to tackle the problems created by the rise of soft money and issue advocacy in recent elections.

- *Ban on Soft Money.* The BCRA mandated that the national party committees could only raise and spend money subject to contribution limits. This effectively eliminated the use of soft money by the parties. Individual contributions were limited to $25,000 in 2004 (an increase of $5,000 from the FECA limit) and are now indexed for inflation (the limit is $26,700 in 2006). Previously, individuals could give an unlimited amount of soft money for the parties that could be used for issue advocacy.

- *Limits on Issue-Advocacy Spending.* Under the BCRA, labor unions or corporations could not contribute to a committee that paid for advertising identifying a candidate for federal office within thirty days of a primary or sixty days of a general election. The purpose of this clause was to reduce the prevalence of issue-advocacy advertisements; the standard of not even mentioning a candidate is significantly more stringent than the previously established prohibition on express advocacy. Before the BCRA, advertisements paid for with unregulated funds could mention federal candidates as long as they did not expressly advocate for their election or defeat.

- *"Stand by Your Ad" Disclaimer.* To attempt to create more accountability in political advertising, the BCRA required all candidates, interest groups, and parties to include a statement of responsibility for their broadcast advertisements. These statements became very familiar in 2004 as candidates typically appeared at the end of their advertisements repeating into the screen, "I approve this message."

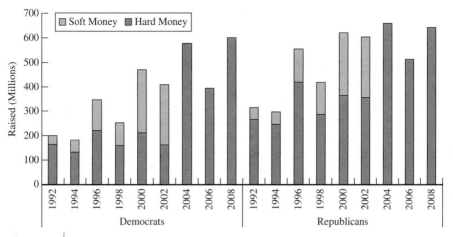

FIGURE **8.3** | PARTY FUNDRAISING OF HARD AND SOFT MONEY, 1992–2008

Source: Federal Election Commission.

Arguably the most important part of the BCRA was the ban on soft money. Until it was banned for national parties by the BCRA, soft money was by far the fastest growing source of campaign money (see Figure 8.3). The $263.5 million in soft money raised by the two parties in the 1995–1996 election cycle was triple the amount raised four years earlier; and the $487.4 million collected in 1999–2000 was 1.8 times more than was raised in the prior presidential year election cycle. After lagging behind the Republicans in the competition to collect soft money, the Democrats achieved parity with their opposition in the 1999–2000 election cycle, and the Democratic congressional and senatorial committees actually outpaced their Republican counterparts in raising soft money. The reason soft money was so popular with the parties is that it allowed the parties to collect funds in large amounts from big donors who did not have to abide by the contribution limits that federal law imposed on other types of contributions, such as direct contributions to federal candidates. For corporations, labor unions, and other groups, soft money contributions were attractive because the money could be taken directly out of their treasuries—something they could not legally do in making direct contributions to federal candidates.

Issue-advocacy ads also had become a prevalent feature of American campaigns in the decade before the BCRA took effect. The BCRA sought to reduce interest group influence via issue-advocacy advertisements by limiting the time period during which such ads could be aired.

POLITICAL PARTIES AFTER THE **BCRA**

By giving money to candidates, not parties, the FECA reinforced the decentralized qualities of the American party system and confirmed the conception of the party as a candidate-dominated structure. Candidates are given discretion to accept or reject federal campaign subsidies, and candidate organizations control the federal funds. Each candidate is required to set up a single central campaign committee that accepts all contributions or federal subsidies and makes expenditures.

The FECA, however, did contain provisions that were beneficial for parties. As noted previously, national party committees were permitted to make coordinated expenditures to support House and Senate candidates. State parties benefited from the FECA party-building provisions that encouraged the national parties to transfer funds or channel soft money contributions their way. This routing of resources to state parties enabled these organizations to play a more significant role in campaigns. The national party organizations were major beneficiaries of the soft money loophole in the FECA, which enabled them to collect millions of dollars that were used to defray operating expenses, engage in issue and generic advertising, and fund registration and GOTV drives in key states.

Given the parties' recent dependence on soft money contributions and issue-advocacy advertisements, changes made by the BCRA threatened to undermine the health of national party organizations. But in 2004, the first post-BCRA election, the parties did not appear to have lost a step. In a book evaluating the effects of the BCRA on the 2004 elections, Michael Malbin argues that rather than being undermined by the new campaign finance regulations, "the parties were remarkably resilient—raising more money and playing a more significant role in the 2004 elections than even BCRA's supporters had predicted."[6]

The DNC and RNC responded to the BCRA by increasing their emphasis on soliciting contributions subject to limits. For example, both parties increased their efforts to attract small donations from citizens by modernizing their direct mail and Internet donation programs, which led to significant increases in the amounts raised in contributions of $200 or less (see Figure 8.4). Both parties also focused on raising large donations under the increased individual limits. These efforts were very successful, as the national party committees raised more hard money in 2004 and 2008 than they had accumulated in hard and soft money combined in previous campaigns (see Figure 8.3). The BCRA also provided the parties with the ability to spend unlimited amounts of this money on behalf of their candidates. While coordinated expenditures were limited to $16.2 million for each party in 2004, the party committees were allowed to make unlimited independent expenditures—money spent on behalf of candidates but without coordination with those candidates. The DNC took advantage of the independent expenditures route, spending more than $120 million independently of the Kerry campaign. The RNC took a different tack by co-funding advertisements with the Bush campaign. These advertisements did not count as coordinate expenditures, since they made general appeals for voters to support Republicans rather than in support of any specific candidate.[7]

While the national committees more than made up for the loss of soft money in the first post-BCRA campaign, other party organizations did not fare as well. While all four Hill committees increased the amount of hard money that they raised during the 2004 election cycle, the increase was not sufficient to overcome the loss of soft money. Furthermore, the 2008 presidential election, the second following the BCRA, provided new insight into how the BCRA might diminish the influence of the national party committees. During that campaign, Barack Obama chose to rely almost exclusively on funds raised by his own campaign rather than support from the DNC. Thus, the DNC spent just $1.1 million in independent expenditures on behalf of Obama's candidacy, compared to over $53 million that the RNC spent independently on behalf of McCain.

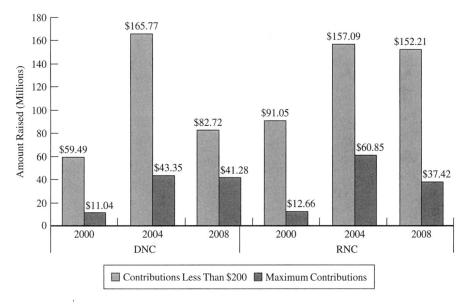

FIGURE 8.4 | PARTY FUNDRAISING FROM SMALL AND LARGE DONORS, 2000–2008

Source: Federal Election Commission.

The largest effect of the BCRA on state parties was to eliminate the large amounts of soft money that national parties previously transferred to them. Previously, the national parties would raise soft money and then transfer those funds to state parties, which would spend them on television and radio advertisements aimed at influencing elections for Congress and president. With national parties no longer able to raise soft money, the transfers declined markedly in 2004 and the amount of advertising purchased by the state parties virtually disappeared. However, when accounting for the loss of soft money transfers, the state parties did raise roughly the same amounts as they had in 2000. This money was largely spent on grassroots mobilization, administration, and direct mail efforts. Thus, the state parties did lose the large soft money transfers from the states, but these funds had usually been funneled directly into advertising anyway. Other activities that the state parties engage in appear not to have been affected by the BCRA.

PACs AND 527s

Political action committees and the newer 527 committees compete with and complement the parties in the campaign process. As previously noted, the FECA of 1971 and amendments of 1974 significantly expanded the role of PACs, especially corporate PACs. PACs are a type of "political committee" to which the statutes grant the right to solicit and accumulate funds for distribution to candidates. The law provides an exemption for corporate PACs from the general rule against federal campaign contributions by corporations and federally insured institutions. These institutions may now use corporate funds to offset the costs of setting up a PAC

BOX 8.3	POLITICAL SPAM? THE FEC PASSES ON REGULATING INTERNET COMMUNICATION

In 2006, the FEC decided unanimously that the only type of Internet communication that was subject to campaign finance regulations were paid political advertisements appearing on Web sites. Thus, political appeals made via Web sites, blogs, and e-mail are not subject to any campaign finance restrictions. One political consultant explained the practical consequences of this decision:

> A wealthy individual could purchase all of the e-mail addresses for registered voters in a congressional district ... produce an Internet video ad, and e-mail it along with a link to the campaign contribution page.... Not only would this activity not count against any contribution limits or independent expenditure requirements; it would never even need to be reported.

In 2004, over 1 billion unsolicited e-mails were received by American voters, and many experts believe that this number could increase substantially over the coming years. Since paid issue-advocacy advertisements mentioning federal candidates cannot be aired within sixty days of the general election, groups and individuals may turn to unregulated e-mail campaigns during the final stages of the campaign. But many political consultants believe that e-mail campaigns will not be effective in mobilizing or persuading voters during a campaign. As one consultant noted, "It is spam after all, and there are few things that annoy us more than spam."

Source: Jeffrey H. Birnbaum, "Loophole a Spigot for E-Mail; Critics Fear Voters Will Be Deluged as Fall Elections Near," *Washington Post*, June 11, 2006, p. A06.

and soliciting contributions to them from stockholders, administrative personnel, and their families. Labor union and trade association PACs are also given legal recognition by the law and given the right to solicit funds from their members. There are also independent PACs, organized by like-minded persons interested in promoting a particular ideology or policy position. All PACs must meet minimum statutory standards concerning the number of contributors (at least 51) and candidate recipients (at least 5) of PAC contributions.

Prior to the 1960s, PACs were largely a labor union phenomenon, patterned after the example of the AFL-CIO's Committee on Political Education (COPE), though the National Association of Manufacturers and the American Medical Association also maintained PACs. The statutory changes of the 1970s, however, spurred an explosion in the number of PACs (see Figure 8.5). Not only has the number of PACs proliferated, but so has their role in campaigns. One of the most striking characteristics of PAC contribution patterns to House and Senate campaigns is their preference for incumbents (see Figure 8.6). In fact, the propensity to donate to incumbents has become increasingly strong; in the 2007–2008 election cycle, nearly 80 percent of all PAC contributions went to incumbents, while 12 percent went to challengers and 8 percent to open seat candidates. Because the Democrats until 1995 had by far the largest share of incumbents in the House, they received the largest share of PAC contributions to House candidates. After the Republicans won control of the chamber in the 1994 elections, their share of PAC money majorities jumped dramatically from

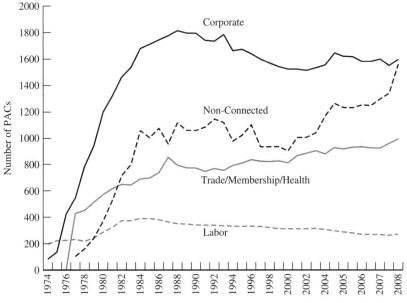

FIGURE 8.5 | THE GROWTH OF POLITICAL ACTION COMMITTEES, 1974–2008

Source: Federal Election Commission.

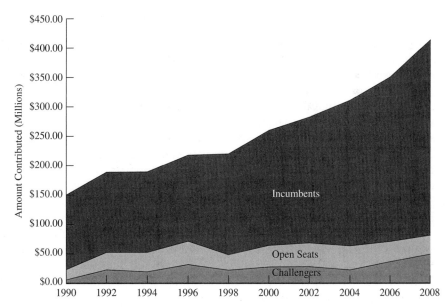

FIGURE 8.6 | AMOUNT OF PAC CONTRIBUTIONS TO INCUMBENTS, CHALLENGERS, AND OPEN SEAT CANDIDATES IN HOUSE AND SENATE ELECTIONS, 1990–2008

Source: Federal Election Commission.

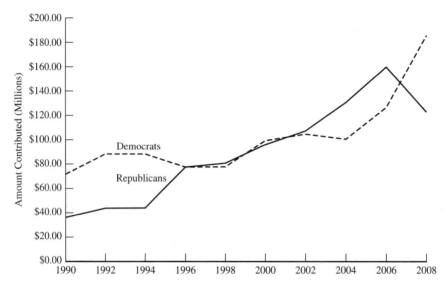

FIGURE 8.7 | PAC CONTRIBUTIONS GOING TO REPUBLICAN AND DEMOCRATIC CANDIDATES FOR THE HOUSE AND SENATE, 1990–2008

Source: Federal Election Commission.

33 percent in 1994 to an average of 50 percent in the 1996, 1998, and 2000 elections. With the Republicans holding only a narrow House majority after 1994, most PACs have hedged their bets and contributed almost equal amounts to both parties' candidates. Only in 2004 did Republicans gain a clear advantage in contributions from PACs. But that advantage quickly evaporated when the Democrats regained control of Congress after the 2006 election. The ebb and flow of PAC money to the parties' House and Senate candidates in recent elections is shown in Figure 8.7.

The conventional wisdom is that PAC growth has weakened the parties. However, there is evidence that both the Democratic and Republican parties have adapted to the PAC phenomenon. The parties solicit funds from PACs and encourage them to contribute directly to needy candidates. In an effort to channel PAC money into targeted races, the parties' national-level committees have revealed the results of party-commissioned polls to PAC directors, held special candidate receptions for PAC personnel, and set up candidate interviews with PAC representatives. Some PACs form close alliances with parties and become a dependable source of support for party candidates; organized labor's relationship with the Democratic Party is one example.

The BCRA largely ignored the role of PACs. It maintained previous limits on contributions to and from PACs (PACs can receive $5,000 from individuals and can give $15,000 to national party committees and $5,000 to a candidate or another PAC). These limits are not adjusted for inflation; thus, as individual contribution limits continue to increase over time, their value relative to the static PAC limits will also rise, which may reduce the influence of PACs in future election.

The rise of 527 committees during the 2004 campaign also overshadowed PACs. 527s were not new in 2004, but their influence was significant. Groups existing under section 527 of the tax code are tax-exempt and may engage in political activities, but they cannot expressly advocate for or against candidates for federal office. These committees can raise unlimited amounts of money from individuals and organizations and can spend unlimited amounts on activities such as voter mobilization and issue advocacy. Like the issue-advocacy advertisements of the pre-BCRA era, these ads typically leave no doubt who the 527 committee favors. For example, the Swift Boat Veterans for Truth aired advertisements attacking John Kerry's service in Vietnam and his later protests against that war, but these ads never expressly urged citizens to vote against Kerry or for Bush.

Before the 2004 campaign, most 527 organizations were tied to interest groups that also maintained PACs. Interest groups used PACs to donate to candidates and often used their 527 organization to air issue-advocacy ads and make other independent expenditures. However, in 2004, new 527 committees that were not necessarily tied to existing interest groups appeared. According to Steve Weissman and Ruth Hassan at the Campaign Finance Institute, "The two major parties, including their leading paid consultants and active notables, were involved, in varying degrees, in the creation, operation or funding of several prominent 527 groups."[8] The parties encouraged the formation of these new 527 organizations as a new venue for the raising and spending of soft money. For instance, The Media Fund was formed by Harold Ickes, former deputy chief of staff for Bill Clinton and previously a member of the DNC's executive committee. He left this position at the DNC specifically to manage the new 527 organization without violating campaign finance rules about coordination.

The new 527 committees received significant funding in the form of large contributions from wealthy individuals. In fact, just twenty-four donors accounted for roughly half of all individual contributions to 527s in 2004 by each contributing at least $2 million. This list was headed by George Soros and Peter Lewis, who each gave more than $20 million to Democratic-affiliated 527s. An analysis of the most lucrative 527 donors found that many had previously been contributors of soft money to the national party committees. In fact, many of these donors also contributed far more to 527s in 2004 than they had to the parties in previous campaigns, though most of the former soft money contributors did not become 527 donors in 2004. It is also important to note that 527s were not nearly as prevalent or influential in 2008 as they had been in 2004.

PUBLIC FINANCING OF ELECTIONS

The Federal Elections Campaign Act authorizes public funding of general election campaigns for those presidential candidates who qualify and wish to accept the federal subsidy. Major party candidates (defined by the law as the nominees of parties receiving at least 25 percent of the popular vote in the last election) automatically qualify for public funding of their campaigns. Although public funding is not mandatory, a candidate who accepts it must agree to restrict expenditures to the amount of the federal grant and forego all private fund-raising. The amount of public funding stipulated by the FECA of 1974 is $20 million, adjusted for inflation ($84.1 million in 2008). Minor parties' presidential candidates are also eligible for a proportionate share of public funding, provided their party received at least 5 percent of the popular vote for president in the previous election. Until the

2008 campaign, every major-party candidate has chosen to accept public funding of his or her campaign since the program was initiated in 1976. Acceptance of the federal funds removes from candidates the burden of private fund-raising. Another reason why candidates traditionally elected to accept public funds is that they were fearful that failure to do so would alienate some voters and make them vulnerable to the charge of being beholden to special interests. Because presidential candidates receive saturation coverage by the news media, the spending limits that the public funding provisions of the FECA impose on candidates are not thought to create any major advantages for either party or for incumbents or challengers. Clearly, however, the use of public funding in presidential elections has tended to equalize the resources available to the Republican and Democratic parties.

Much as with public funding of presidential nomination campaigns, the public funding of general election campaigns is now in jeopardy. In 2004, John Kerry seriously considered refusing the general election funds so that his campaign could raise and spend an unlimited amount of money. Buoyed by his unprecedented fund-raising success during the 2008 nomination campaign, Barack Obama became the first presidential candidate to decline public funding for the general election campaign. To deflect criticism that the move would make him beholden to special interests, Obama frequently cited the fact that he did not accept money from lobbyists or PACs and that much of his funds were raised from small donors. However, there were several strategic reasons for Obama to eschew public funds for the general election:

- *More money*. It sounds simple, but a necessary pre-condition for declining the $84.1 million check that the federal government would have handed him was the confidence that his campaign could raise substantially more than that amount. Since he had raised hundreds of millions for the Democratic nomination campaign, it seemed to be a safe bet that he could raise hundreds of millions more for the general election campaign. And by raising large sums of money, Obama felt confident that he would be able to outspend McCain and the RNC during the general election campaign.
- *More control*. The general election grant from the federal government comes with the stipulation that the candidate's campaign will not raise or spend any additional monies after the party's convention. This has traditionally meant that candidates had to rely on the national party committee and outside groups (such as 527s) to supplement the candidate's own expenditures. However, there are limits on the extent to which this supplemental spending can be coordinated with the candidate's campaign. Thus, by raising similar sums through his own campaign organization, Obama could exercise much more control on how the money was spent.
- *Reduced cost of raising money*. In the past, the amount of time and effort that it would have taken a presidential candidate to raise hundreds of millions of dollars would likely not have been worth the benefits of doing so. However, much of the money that Obama raised did not come from time-consuming fund-raising events, but rather from contributions made to the candidate online. Thus, the cost of raising money was relatively low compared to the benefit of being able to outspend his opponent and have more control over the campaign.

BOX 8.4	Small Donors or Small Donations?

During the 2008 campaign, Barack Obama revolutionized campaign fund-raising. He raised and spent, by far, more money than any candidate in the history of American elections. Even more notable was the fact that so many of his contributions came in small amounts. Nearly half of the amount Obama raised during the campaign came in the form of contributions of $200 or less. This led many news reports to focus on the notion that Obama's campaign was fueled mostly by small donors, a point that Obama himself often repeated as justification for forgoing public financing.

In reality, however, Obama's contributors may not have been that unique compared to previous campaigns. Political scientist Michael Malbin noted, "The myth is that money from small donors dominated Barack Obama's finances. The reality of Obama's fund-raising was impressive, but the reality does not match the myth." While nearly half of Obama's funds came in small contributions, many of those contributors donated money to his campaign several times, meaning that their total contributions to his campaign exceeded $200. In fact, the percentage of money he raised from contributors who gave $200 or less was roughly the same as what George W. Bush raised from small contributors in 2004 (about 25 percent).

Nevertheless, Obama did far out-pace Bush's total fund-raising, meaning that he still attracted a much larger number of small donors than candidates in previous campaigns. In fact, the Obama campaign estimated that approximately 2.5 million small donors gave an average $62 each to the campaign. The 2.5 million small donors that Obama attracted in 2008 was likely greater than the small contributors attracted by all candidates who ran in 2004 combined. Thus, while the notion that Obama's war chest was fueled largely by small donors may have been a myth, his success in attracting financial support from millions of small donors is still an impressive accomplishment.

Source: Michael Malbin, "Reality Check: Obama Received About the Same Percentage from Small Donors in 2008 as Bush in 2004." Campaign Finance Institute.

By all accounts, Obama's decision to become the first candidate to decline public funding was a smart one. Obama spent more than $300 million during the fall campaign, which easily eclipsed the $84.1 million in public funding that the McCain campaign spent combined with the $53.5 million that the RNC spent independently on behalf of its candidate. This spending turned in to a significant advantage in contacting voters. For example, the Wisconsin Advertising Project found that during the last two months of the campaign, Obama ran substantially more television advertisements than McCain on all but a handful of days. Citizens were also more likely to report that they had been contacted by Democrats than by Republicans during the campaign. Obama even spent more than $3 million to produce a thirty-minute infomercial program that aired during primetime on NBC, CBS, Fox, Univision, MSNBC, and BET.

Unless the federal public funding system is reformed to make it more attractive to candidates, John McCain may have been the last person to use the system in 2008. Similar to what happened with the matching fund system for presidential nomination campaigns, now that a candidate has demonstrated the value of working outside of the system, other candidates are likely to follow a similar blue-print in the future.

In addition to public funding of presidential campaigns, approximately half of the states have public-funding statutes for state elections. These statutes vary from state to state in terms of how the money for public financing of elections is raised, whether the funds are controlled by the candidates or the parties, and which races are eligible to be subsidized. Most plans involve taxpayer check-offs of one or two dollars per income tax form, although six states use an add-on procedure in which taxpayers indicate on their tax forms a willingness to add a small contribution to the campaign fund. Check-off plans tend to produce higher response rates from tax-payers than do add-on procedures. In most states, the contribution goes into a general campaign fund. However, in several states (including Arizona, Idaho, Iowa, Ohio, Virginia, and Utah) the citizens designate on the tax form which party is to receive their contribution.[9]

Public funding of campaigns may also be accomplished indirectly by channeling funds through the state and county party organizations (e.g., in Arizona, Idaho, Iowa, New Mexico, Ohio, Utah, and Virginia). However, the more common practice among the states is for the funds to go directly to candidates. In four states (Kentucky, Minnesota, North Carolina, and Rhode Island), a combination of these allocation procedures is used. When the money goes through the party organization, the major consequence of public funding is to permit the party to engage more actively in a broad range of electoral activities. Ruth Jones found that when the public subsidy goes to the candidates, the public funding was more important to legislative candidates than to statewide candidates, to candidates for the state house of representatives than to candidates for state senate, to Democratic candidates than to Republicans, and to challengers than to incumbents.[10] However, as campaign costs have escalated, public funding tends to be inadequate to finance campaigns at a level commensurate with candidates' needs. The evidence from a recent nation-wide study provides no compelling evidence that state public-funding programs have increased electoral competition, as was hoped by the reformers who pressed for adoption of public-funding legislation. Public funding has not removed the advantages of incumbency; and it has not encouraged challengers to take on state legislative incumbents.[11]

THE ELECTORAL COLLEGE

When voters within a state go to the polls and mark their ballots for the presidential candidate of their choice, they are in fact voting for a slate of presidential electors who will cast that state's electoral votes for president. The election of an American president is not a direct popular vote, but rather an indirect election process in which the voters select electors who in turn make the actual choice of a president. In designing this system, the Founders envisioned the presidential electors as a council of wise men from each state who would render an independent judgment on the best person to hold the nation's highest office. They also expected that the Electoral College would, in effect, "nominate" presidential candidates in those instances when no candidate received an Electoral College majority, because the House of Representatives would then choose a president from among the top three

Electoral College vote getters. The Founders also envisioned a nonpartisan selection process. Only the first two elections of George Washington came close to fulfilling the Constitution writers' expectations. Washington was indeed chosen by the Electoral College on a nonpartisan basis. But in the ensuing elections, the contests for president became highly partisan. Competing parties ran slates of candidates for the position of presidential elector within the states, and these elector candidates were pledged to support their party's nominee for president and vice president.

ALLOCATION OF ELECTORAL VOTES AMONG THE STATES

Each state's allocation of electoral votes is determined by its representation in the Congress. An electoral vote is assigned to each state based upon its number of senators and representatives (e.g., California, with two senators and fifty-three representatives, has fifty-five electoral votes; Vermont, with two senators and one representative, has three electoral votes). The District of Columbia, in accordance with the Twenty-Third Amendment, is entitled to three electoral votes.

ALLOCATING A STATE'S ELECTORAL VOTES: WINNER-TAKE-ALL

In every state but Maine and Nebraska, the allocation of a state's electoral votes among the presidential candidates is on the basis of a winner-take-all system. The candidate who receives a *plurality* of the state popular vote for president receives *all* of that state's electoral votes, no matter how narrow the candidate's margin of victory. In Maine and Nebraska, the state's electoral votes are allocated on the basis of two electoral votes for the candidate gaining a plurality in the statewide vote, and one electoral vote for the winner in each congressional district. Although an exception to the winner-take-all rule, Maine has consistently cast all its electoral votes for one presidential candidate, as has Nebraska since it initiated the district system for the 1992 presidential election.

MAJORITY IN THE ELECTORAL COLLEGE REQUIRED FOR ELECTION

To be elected president, a candidate must receive an absolute majority of the votes in the Electoral College (i.e., 270 of the total 538 electoral votes). If no candidate for president receives an Electoral College majority, the election is thrown into the newly elected House of Representatives, which chooses from the three candidates who received the largest number of electoral votes. In making its selection, the House votes by state delegation, with each state having one vote and with a majority of the states required for election. When no vice presidential candidate has a majority of the electoral votes, the Senate chooses the vice president from between the two candidates with the largest number of electoral votes.

The House of Representatives has been required to choose the president only twice. The first time was after the election of 1800, when Thomas Jefferson and his vice presidential running mate, Aaron Burr, both received the same number of electoral votes. This tie vote occurred because electors could not differentiate in casting their two votes between which candidate they preferred for president and vice president under the Constitution as originally written. Rather, the candidate with the largest number of votes was elected president and the candidate in second place became vice president. This system of balloting, which was not well adapted to the emerging party system, in which candidates for president and vice president ran as a ticket, resulted in the tie vote between Jefferson and Burr. The House ultimately resolved the tie in Jefferson's favor. In consequence of this bitter controversy, the Twelfth Amendment was added to the Constitution. It provided for electors to vote separately for the offices of president and vice president. The other instance of the House having to decide the election occurred in the election of 1824, when four persons received electoral votes: Andrew Jackson (99 votes), John Quincy Adams (84), William Crawford (41), and Henry Clay (37). With the support of Henry Clay, Adams was selected as president by a majority of one vote.

ELECTORAL COLLEGE TENDENCY TO EXAGGERATE THE POPULAR-VOTE MARGIN OF THE WINNING CANDIDATE

In four instances, the presidential candidate who was the winner of the popular vote failed to gain a majority in the Electoral College. In 1824, Andrew Jackson received a plurality of the popular vote in the eighteen states that chose their electors by popular vote (there were twenty-four states in the Union at that time, and in six the state legislatures chose the electors). The other cases of the popular-vote winner not gaining an electoral vote majority took place in the 1876 contest between Samuel J. Tilden (Democrat) and Rutherford B. Hayes (Republican), when Hayes was awarded disputed electoral votes of Oregon plus four southern states; in 1888 when Grover Cleveland (Democrat), with a 95,096 popular-vote plurality, lost in the Electoral College to Benjamin Harrison (Republican) by a 168 to 233 margin; and most recently in the 2000 election between George W. Bush and Al Gore. Gore won 48.4 percent of the popular vote and a plurality of 537,179 votes nationwide. He carried twenty states plus the District of Columbia, but his electoral vote of 266 fell four short of a majority. Bush won a narrow majority in the Electoral College (271 electoral votes while carrying thirty states) even though he trailed Gore by 0.5 percent of the popular vote. His electoral vote majority was sealed after the U.S. Supreme Court ruled in the dispute over Florida's twenty-five electoral votes in a way that resulted in his gaining the state's twenty-five electoral votes.

Most public discussion of the Electoral College, especially since the 2000 election, has focused upon the possibility that the popular-vote winner is not assured of an Electoral College majority and election to the presidency. However, because this circumstance has occurred rarely, Electoral College reform has not been high on the public's list of concerns. Indeed, the Electoral College normally has operated in such a way as to exaggerate the popular-vote winner's margin in the Electoral College. For example, Richard Nixon's 43.4 percent of the popular vote was less than 1 percent greater than Hubert Humphrey's 42.7 percent. In the Electoral College, however, Nixon's margin was a more comfortable 55.9 percent. A more striking example of the extent to which the winner of the popular vote can have his margin of victory exaggerated by the operation of the Electoral College occurred in 1980, when Ronald Reagan received 50.7 percent of the popular vote and 90.9 percent of the electoral

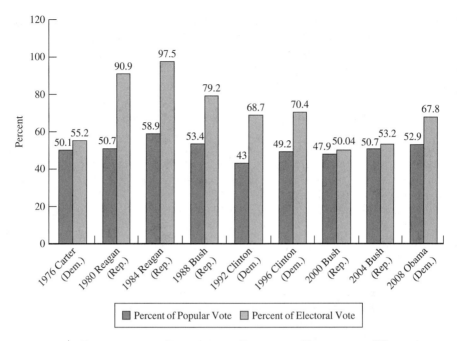

FIGURE **8.8** | PERCENTAGE OF POPULAR AND ELECTORAL VOTE OF THE WINNING CANDIDATE, 1976–2008

Source: http://www.uselectionatlas.org.

vote. This pattern of the winning candidate's proportion of the electoral vote normally being greater than his popular-vote percentage is shown in Figure 8.8. Because the popular-vote winner and the electoral-vote winner were the same from 1888 through 1996, there was little interest within the Congress—especially before the 2000 election—in changing the Electoral College system. Bush's election without a plurality of the popular vote in 2000 did spark some interest in plans to reform the Electoral College, but most Americans accepted the legitimacy of his election with an Electoral College majority. The usual tendency of the Electoral College to exaggerate the winning presidential candidate's margin of victory, it has been argued, gives the president an opportunity to claim an electoral mandate to govern and implement the policies that were advocated in the campaign.

ENCOURAGING TWO-PARTY POLITICS

The Electoral College system works to the advantage of the two major parties and to the detriment of minor parties. The combination of a winner-take-all system to determine the allocation of the states' electoral votes and the requirement of a majority in the Electoral College to be elected makes it almost impossible for third parties to win a presidential election. To win any electoral votes and have any impact on the electoral vote, a third-party candidate must have voter support that is geographically concentrated the way George Wallace's was in the southern states in 1968 or Strom Thurmond's was in 1948. When a third-party candidate's support is more evenly spread across the country, as in the case of Ross Perot in 1992 and 1996, the candidate has virtually no hope of winning any electoral votes.

If the Electoral College tends to be stacked against third parties winning elections, this does not mean that third parties are without influence. By garnering votes that might otherwise have gone to one of the major-party candidates, third parties can affect the outcome of the vote. Theodore Roosevelt's Progressive Party in 1912 split the normally Republican majority in the country and enabled the minority Democratic candidate, Woodrow Wilson, to be elected. The presence of significant third-party candidates in the 2000 election also illustrates the potential these parties have to affect presidential elections. Most analysts believe that if Ralph Nader had not been running as the Green Party nominee, Florida's twenty-five electoral votes would have gone to Gore, resulting in his election.

Although third-party candidates played a role in determining the outcome of the 2000 presidential election, their more common impact is to affect the distribution of electoral votes within particular states but not decide who is elected president. For example, in 1992 a *Washington Post* analysis of exit poll data showed that had Perot not been in the race, Ohio would have been in the Bush column, but Clinton still would have won 349 electoral votes to Bush's 189.[12] Running on the Reform Party ticket in 1996, Perot again had no effect on the presidential election result, although he did deprive President Clinton of a majority of the popular vote.[13]

BIG STATE VERSUS SMALL STATE ADVANTAGES

Small states are mathematically overrepresented in the Electoral College. This is because their overrepresentation in the House (every state is provided one representative irrespective of population) and the Senate (each state has two senators irrespective of population) guarantees them overrepresentation in the Electoral College. Following the 2000 reapportionment, Wyoming had an electoral vote for every 169,000 people in the state while the five most populated states (Illinois, New York, Florida, California, and Texas) had more than 600,000 people for every electoral vote. Because of the winner-take-all system, however, it is the large, populous states that mainly benefit from the Electoral College. California, with fifty-five electoral votes, has more electoral votes than the thirteen smallest states combined (six states with three electoral votes and seven states with four electoral votes). This means that narrow victories in large states yield a much higher return in terms of electoral votes than do large pluralities in small states. A vote in California holds the potential of influencing fifty-five electoral votes, whereas a vote in South Dakota can influence only three.

The critical nature of the big states to a presidential nominee is illustrated by the data contained in Table 8.2. The ten largest states have a combined total of 255 electoral votes (47 percent of the total), just 15 short of the 270 needed for election. Without carrying at least some of these large states it is almost impossible for a candidate to be elected president. It is, therefore, small wonder that presidential candidates tend to concentrate their campaign efforts in those large states where they believe they have a chance of victory. Because large states are normally quite competitive between the two major parties, they are major battlegrounds in presidential elections. Since the Electoral College makes large competitive states so

TABLE 8.2 | THE IMPACT OF STATE SIZE ON THE ELECTORAL COLLEGE[a]

State	Electoral Votes	Percent of Total Electoral College	State	Electoral Votes	Percent of Total Electoral College
Smallest States (13)			Largest States (10)		
Vermont	3	0.56	California	55	10.22
Delaware	3	0.56	Texas	34	6.32
Montana	3	0.56	New York	31	5.76
South Dakota	3	0.56	Florida	27	5.02
North Dakota	3	0.56	Pennsylvania	21	3.90
Wyoming	3	0.56	Illinois	21	3.90
Alaska	3	0.56	Ohio	20	3.72
Maine	4	0.74	Michigan	17	3.16
New Hampshire	4	0.74	New Jersey	15	2.79
Rhode Island	4	0.74	North Carolina	14	2.60
Nevada	4	0.74	Total	255	47.4
Idaho	4	0.74			
Hawaii	4	0.74			
Total	45	8.36			

[a]Based on 2000 census figures.

important in presidential elections, it also benefits those groups that are geographically concentrated in these states (e.g., racial and ethnic minorities).

TIGHT ELECTORAL COLLEGE COMPETITION IN 2000 AND 2004

With the Republicans winning 271 electoral votes and the Democrats 266 in 2000, the nation witnessed the closest Electoral College contest in over a century. The 2004 result was also relatively close, with George W. Bush's capturing a 286–251 victory and Ohio proving to be the pivotal state swinging the election to Republicans. Recent elections demonstrated that the Republican Electoral College base is the Mountain, Plains, and southern states, while the Democratic base is in the Northeast, West Coast, and industrial states of the Midwest. These partisan bases of support provide the potential for highly competitive contests for Electoral College majorities. However, recent elections have also witnessed regional polarization that has left fewer states up for grabs, meaning that campaigns have become increasingly focused on a narrowing battlefield.

In 2000 and 2004, Democratic hopes were largely tied to winning Florida or Ohio to complete a narrow majority in the Electoral College. In both cases, this strategy fell short. In 2008, Barack Obama expanded the field of contested states by competing in southern and southwestern states that had increasingly more urban and affluent electorates (Virginia, North Carolina, Colorado, New Mexico, and Nevada). Obama also extended his campaign efforts in the Midwest by running an active campaign in Iowa and even Indiana, a state where Kerry received less than 40 percent of the vote just four years earlier. Ultimately, Obama prevailed in eight states that Kerry lost in 2004—Colorado, Florida, Indiana, Iowa, Nevada, New Mexico, North Carolina, and Ohio.

THE GENERAL ELECTION CAMPAIGN

Each campaign is unique. Campaigns differ depending upon who the contending candidates are, the nature of the office being sought (executive, legislative, or judicial), the level of government (national, state, or local), the applicable campaign finance and election regulatory statutes, the campaign resources of the candidates, type of nominating campaigns that were conducted, the nature of the constituency, and the tenor of the times (e.g., which issues are salient to the voters). For the incumbent, the campaign is usually a matter of protecting one's inherent advantages of name familiarity and a favorable image while maintaining a favorable balance of campaign resources. For the challenger, who is often underfinanced, the campaign is frequently a time of frantic scrambling to accumulate adequate campaign resources and seeking to find the point of vulnerability in the incumbent's record. In every election cycle, elections are won and lost because of campaign decisions. For example, during the 1992 presidential race, the Clinton campaign was successful in keeping its message zeroed in on blaming the Bush administration for the economy's performance and the need for a new economic plan. The focused nature of its advertising, plus the use of a quick response technique to any charge made by the Republicans, enabled the Clinton organization to keep the campaign agenda on its chosen issue—the state of the economy. By contrast, Bush's message lacked focus; he wavered between claiming that the economy was better than his opponents asserted, blaming the Democratic Congress for the state of the economy, and attacking Clinton's character.

In 1996, the Clinton campaign again was successful in setting the campaign agenda through advertising, campaign events, and speeches. It succeeded in framing the electorate's choice as a referendum on the Republican Revolution that followed the party's takeover of Congress after the 1994 elections. Clinton's message was that the Republicans were uncaring and insensitive and should not be trusted with America's future. By contrast, Republican Bob Dole did not find an issue that made an impact until the last weeks of the campaign, when he began to stress the issue of Clinton's character amid news media reports of Democratic campaign finance irregularities.[14]

In the 2000 presidential campaign, Vice President Al Gore's campaign themes failed to take advantage of running on the administration's record, a favorable economy, and criticism of the Republican Congress. Instead, he allowed the race to become a contest between two individuals and their programs for the future. This strategy failed to capitalize on the Democrats' slight advantage among voters in terms of party identification. It also gave a small edge to George W. Bush, whose personal qualities were generally perceived to be more attractive to voters than Gore's.

In 2008, Obama's blueprint was much the same as Clinton's had been sixteen years earlier. With a struggling economy following two terms of a Republican presidency, Obama relentlessly focused on economic themes. When the difficult economic conditions became the focal point of America's attention, the Republican nominee was bound to fare poorly. McCain did himself few favors when the financial crisis began to surface during the fall campaign. He initially claimed that the "fundamentals of the economy are strong," a quote the Obama campaign quickly seized on as evidence that McCain was out of touch and did not understand how hard the economy was hitting the American public. Perhaps realizing his misstep, McCain changed course nine days later and announced abruptly that he was suspending his campaign to return to Washington to help assist in the passage of an economic bailout package. But Democrats were again to criticize McCain's "erratic" behavior and his campaign was never able to regain momentum.

WHEN THE VOTER DECIDES

Most voters (normally around 60 percent) in presidential elections make up their minds about the candidate for whom they will vote before or during the nominating conventions. A substantial portion of the electorate, however, does not make its decision until after the conventions and during the general election campaign (see Figure 8.9). Therefore, the impact of the campaign can be significant. Analysis of Gallup Poll and National Election Studies data by James Campbell shows that in presidential elections between 1948 and 2000, the campaigns after the conventions were probably determinative in Truman's win in 1948 and Kennedy's narrow victory in 1960. Campbell also concludes that it is quite possible that the campaigns were decisive in 1976 (Carter), 1980 (Reagan), and 2000 (Bush). For example, in 1976 more voters identifying with the Democratic Party decided during the campaign than before it (53 to 47 percent), and Carter garnered three-fourths of their votes. The one common condition that works against making campaigns decisive is the presence of a popular incumbent president—Eisenhower (1956), Johnson (1964), Reagan (1984), and Clinton (1996). In these cases, it appears that voters were familiar with and quite satisfied with the performance of the incumbent, and hence they might assume that there was little need to learn more about either the incumbent or his opponent. By contrast, when incumbents have been in trouble, the campaigns seem to have been important. Thus, Truman's Democratic Party was badly divided in 1948; Ford in 1976 carried the burdens of being an unelected president, Watergate, and his pardon of Richard Nixon; and Carter faced the voters in 1980 during one of the worst economic downturns since the Great Depression.[15]

In 2004, the presence of a polarizing president also appeared to have diminished the importance of the campaign to some extent. A much smaller percentage of the public than usual said that they had made their decision after the party conventions. Most Americans had a strong view on President Bush's record on the economy, terrorism, and the Iraq War, and their view on Bush's record largely determined their vote choice before the campaign had even begun. Even in 2008, without an incumbent running, the fall campaign appeared to make little difference. Obama held a consistent lead in the polls for almost the entire year and exit polls indicated that he did just as well among voters who made up their minds before September as he did among those who made up their minds closer to the day of the election.

INCUMBENCY

Incumbency normally carries with it advantages. The resources and privileges of public office enable incumbents to publicize themselves and build support through the positions they take and the decisions they make. Incumbents are better known than challengers, and they have built-in ways of reaching the voters. Incumbent members of Congress stay in contact with their constituents through newsletters, surveys of constituent opinion, special targeted mailings, news releases, radio and television interviews, and meetings with constituent groups. Skilled incumbents use the rights and duties of public office in a way that projects the image of caring and conscientious legislators fulfilling their obligations to constituents. Voters, however, often see these tactics, such as newsletters, office hours in the district, casework to help constituents having problems with the federal bureaucracy, and advocacy of programs to benefit the constituency, as instances of members of Congress merely performing their official duties. By contrast, voters see challengers as "politicians" or "campaigners" interested primarily in winning votes on Election Day. The self-advertisement efforts of all incumbent members of the House have meant that they are not only well known to their constituents, but they are normally

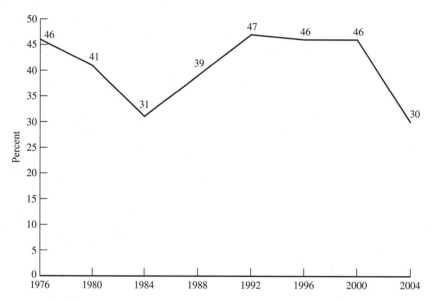

FIGURE 8.9 | PERCENT OF VOTERS WHO SAID THEY DECIDED ON THE PRESIDENTIAL CANDIDATE THEY VOTED FOR AFTER THE CONVENTIONS, 1976–2004

Source: National Election Studies.

thought of in positive terms. By contrast, most House challengers are not well known to the voters, who have difficulty making an evaluation of their qualifications.[16]

Incumbent executives, especially the president and governors, are also in a position to claim credit for all the positive things that have occurred during their tenure. Presidents Eisenhower, Reagan, and Clinton were thus able to run on themes of peace and prosperity during their reelection campaigns of 1956, 1984, and 1996. Incumbency is, however, a two-edged sword. Presidents can also be held accountable for the negative things that have happened while they have been in office. Presidents Ford (1976), Carter (1980), and Bush (1992) found that the voters were unforgiving about a faltering economy and foreign policy setbacks. It makes little difference that presidents cannot control all aspects of our domestic and international condition. They are still likely to be held accountable.

Incumbent senators and representatives have fewer problems than presidents with being held accountable for adverse conditions in the nation and world. Members of the Congress tend to be judged by their constituents not on the basis of the record of the institution of which they are members but rather upon their own individual records. Therefore, they are somewhat insulated from voter resentment about the state of the union, provided they have used their incumbency to build voter trust.

A further advantage of incumbency, especially in the case of legislative campaigns, is the ease incumbents have in raising money. Incumbents consistently have more money to spend on their campaigns than do challengers in House or Senate races. This pattern is illustrated in Table 8.3, which presents the mean funds raised in 2008 House races for incumbents and challengers of both parties. Incumbents raised over $1 million more than challengers, on average. Such financial advantages for incumbents affect the way they campaign. Incumbents are much more likely to have campaign staffs composed of paid professionals than are their opponents, who must rely more heavily on volunteer assistance. Thus, in 2008, just one House incumbent was defeated by a challenger spending less than $1 million.

Normally, over 90 percent of the House incumbents gain reelection (94 percent in 2008; see Figure 8.10). Even in 1994, when the Republicans won control of the

Table 8.3 Mean Expenditures of House Candidates, 2007–2008	
Type of Candidate	**Mean Fund-Raising**
Incumbents	$1,423,875
Republican Incumbents	$1,435,004
Democratic Incumbents	$1,415,647
Challengers	$179,333
Republican Challengers	$225,848
Democratic Challengers	$265,408
All Candidates	$469,359

Source: Federal Elections Commission.

House—ousting thirty-five incumbent Democrats—incumbents enjoyed an overall reelection rate of 92 percent. House incumbents benefit from the relatively homogeneous nature of their districts when compared to the larger and more socially diverse statewide constituencies of senators. The distinctive socioeconomic character of individual House districts frequently gives a clear advantage to the candidate of one party or the other (e.g., predominantly black inner-city districts are safely Democratic, as are most big city districts with concentrations of blue-collar workers of eastern and southern European heritage; middle- and upper-middle-class suburban/small town districts are normally strongly Republican).

Incumbents are in a position to engage in extensive self-advertisement (e.g., mass mailings, constituent surveys, press releases, radio and television interviews, constituent service, town hall meetings) designed to project a favorable image. Of particular benefit to incumbents is the fact that major campaign efforts are not normally made on behalf of their challengers. Through skillful use of the advantages of public office, incumbents in most House districts are able to make their constituencies relatively safe for themselves for extended periods of time. Major struggles for control of the House, therefore, are fought out in the small proportion of districts in which incumbents are considered electorally vulnerable and in open seats, where no incumbent is seeking reelection. Thus, the average margin of victory for House incumbents in 2008 was 40 percentage points.

The incumbent reelection rate for senators, however, is substantially below that of members of the House of Representatives (see Figure 8.10). This was particularly true during the 1976–1980 period, when less than 65 percent of incumbents were successful in retaining their seats. The relatively high levels of incumbent senator defeat reflect several factors:

- The generally higher levels of interparty competition that exist in statewide constituencies as compared to the smaller and more demographically homogeneous House districts
- The higher levels of campaign resources plowed into challenger races for the Senate
- The higher visibility of Senate contests

A substantial proportion of Senate incumbents, however, are normally elected by wide margins. In 2008, slightly more than half of the incumbents (eighteen of thirty-three) gained at least 60 percent of the popular vote in their states.

There is one particular set of candidates for whom incumbency has traditionally created severe difficulties. These are incumbent vice presidents seeking to succeed a president of their own party. Vice presidents running for president in their own right find themselves in a particularly restricted position in terms of campaign strategy. One of their claims to being qualified for the presidency is their service as vice president. Most claim that they were involved in the major decisions of the administration in which they served. The problem with such claims is that every administration after it has been in office for a time makes decisions that offend sizable numbers of voters. This presents the vice president with a dilemma. If the vice president gives unqualified support to the administration's policies, he or she risks losing the support of key voter groups. But if the vice president suggests disagreement with some aspects of administration policy, this could be interpreted as lack of influence in the administration in which he or she claims to have been a key policy maker. And if the vice president

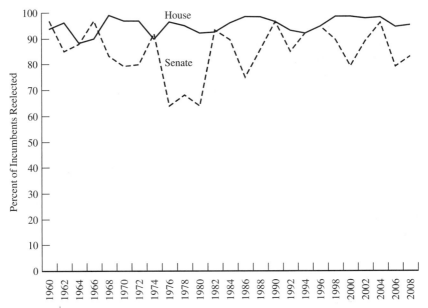

Figure **8.10** Percent of House and Senate Incumbents Reelected, 1960–2008

Source: Table 1-19 Incumbent Reelection Rates: Representatives, Senators, and Governors, General Elections, 1960–2008. CQ Press Electronic Library, Vital Statistics on American Politics Online Edition, vsap09_tab1-19. Originally published in *Vital Statistics on American Politics 2009–2010*, edited by Harold W. Stanley and Richard G. Niemi (Washington: CQ Press, 2009).

seeks to put distance between him- or herself and the president, there is a real risk of losing the support of the president's supporters. The liabilities inherent in the vice presidency were major problems for Richard Nixon in 1960, Hubert Humphrey in 1968, and Al Gore in 2000. Walter Mondale found in 1984, four years after leaving office, that service in the vice presidency during the Carter administration was a serious drawback for his campaign. Even George H. W. Bush, who in 1988 became the first incumbent vice president to be elected to the presidency since Martin Van Buren in 1836, had to endure and overcome charges that he was a "wimp" because of his reluctance to distance himself from Reagan administration policies.

Majority versus Minority Party Status

Candidates have customarily placed differing emphasis on partisan themes depending on whether they were the nominees of the majority or minority party. Majority party candidates have normally stressed party-type appeals and sought to rally the faithful to turn out and vote because if the faithful respond to the call, then the party's candidate is assured of victory. As the dominant party in terms of the electorate's party identification since the Great Depression of the 1930s, nationally the Democratic Party has more frequently emphasized partisan Democratic appeals to the electorate than have the Republicans. Past accomplishments of the party and its heroes have been stressed along with negative characterizations of the Republicans (e.g., "the party of the rich"). Because pro-Democratic voters groups have tended to have lower rates of turnout than Republican-leaning voters, special efforts have been made to mobilize Democrats to get to the polls on Election Day.

As partisan appeals have become less effective in presidential elections, the significance of majority/minority status in determining campaign strategy has been reduced. In addition, surveys conducted in the 1980s through 2004 have revealed that the two major parties are approaching parity in terms of the party identification of the voters. If this division between the parties continues within the electorate, it will further reduce the impact of majority/minority party status on campaign strategy. In keeping with this, a study conducted by the Brennan Center for Justice found that only 15 percent of issue-advocacy ads used in the 1998 midterm elections even mentioned a political party by name. However, in a reflection of the candidate-centered nature of campaigning, 99 percent of the ads gave a candidate's name.[17]

DEBATES

Debates have now become a standard part of presidential campaigns, and debates or forums are common in contests for other offices. Because the media tends to hype the presidential debates and give them prime time coverage, the candidates tend to see them as make-or-break events.[18] With a massive television audience (over 60 million tuned in for the second presidential debate in 2008), debates have the potential to damage or help presidential nominees. As a general rule, the candidate who is perceived to have "won" the debate tends to make a modest gain in the polls.[19] For example, in 1996, Clinton was generally perceived to have won the debates. By presenting a positive image of his record and policies while avoiding angry reactions to Dole's attacks, he was able to maintain his double-digit lead in the polls after the debates. In 2004, John Kerry made up some ground on Bush in the polls after he was widely perceived as having won the first two debates. But in 2008, the presidential debates appeared to produce little, if any, movement in the daily tracking polls.

Political scientist Nelson W. Polsby has observed that "it's nearly impossible to win a debate but it is possible to lose one....Therefore, whoever is perceived going in as having the higher level of expectations is the one that's most at risk."[20] As a result, the candidates' organizations try to raise the expectations for their opponents' performance before the first debate and lower expectations for that of their own candidates. In the last two weeks of September 2000, for example, the Bush camp went so far as to describe Gore as a "world class debater" who had bested debate opponents a dozen times. Consistent with Polsby's thesis, the expectations for Gore were greater than those for Bush, and it was Bush who in the end benefited most from the debates.[21] Bush, whose performance in the debates was more consistent than that of Gore, entered the debates trailing by approximately 5 percentage points and emerged from the debates in the lead.

The "winner" of the debates may receive a modest upward "bump" in the polls, but it is unlikely that the bump will be of a sufficient magnitude to alter the course of the race unless the contest is extremely close going into the debate. The impact of the debates is further limited by the fact that, for many viewers, the debates tend to reinforce their preexisting candidate preferences. That is, most viewers think their preferred candidate won the debate, and those who are dissatisfied with their candidate's performance are likely to say that the debate was a tie.[22]

The history of televised debates also demonstrates that it is not so much the substance of what is said that matters as it is the image of the candidates that is conveyed. The press tends to judge the debates in terms of winners and losers and press judgments affect the public's assessment. Voters in general do not follow the content of the debates carefully and do not normally have great confidence in their ability to make judgments concerning the substance of the debate. But voters often do make personal judgments about the candidates based on how they present themselves in this uncontrolled environment. In 2004, Bush lost the first debate more because of personal tics picked up by the cameras than for any substantive problems with the answers he gave to questions he was asked. Prior to the debate, the candidates had agreed that the cameras would not show one candidate while the other was speaking, but the networks were not bound by this agreement and they made extensive use of split screens to show both candidates at the same time. This decision was problematic for Bush, who was captured looking frustrated and annoyed while Kerry was speaking. These visuals led most of the public view the debate as a clear win for Kerry, which helped reinvigorate his campaign.

Voters also tend to rely rather heavily on media commentaries on the debates. As a result, immediately after the event, there is frequently a rather even split between the candidates in the viewers' minds about who won the debate. However, after several days of press commentary, there is usually a shift by the public in the direction of the verdict rendered by the press. In 2000, polls conducted immediately after the first Bush-Gore debates showed a slight advantage for Gore. However, after media commentary, including ridicule of Gore on *Saturday Night Live*, Gore's debate "victory" was reinterpreted as a defeat.[23]

ISSUES

Throughout the years from the Great Depression in the 1930s until the 1980 election, Democratic candidates generally had a clear advantage over the Republicans when dealing with domestic issues. Through their sponsorship and expansion of a vast array of government programs, which Republicans frequently opposed, the Democrats were in a position to seek support from virtually every major group in American society. The party has also had a favorable image on economic issues. When asked which party they believed was best for the economy, employment, and jobs, voters from the 1930s to 1980 consistently favored the Democrats. As a result, in elections when pocketbook issues were salient (e.g., 1960, 1976), the Democrats were at a distinct advantage. Indeed, during much of this period, Republican candidates sought to downplay domestic issues and emphasize foreign policy concerns. The public's perceptions of the parties changed significantly during the Carter administration and the 1980 campaign. For the first time since the 1930s, voters began to view the GOP candidate as best for the economy, no doubt reflecting the double-digit inflation, rising unemployment, and high interest rates of the later years of the Carter administration.[24] The Republicans lost their economic policy advantage during the serious 1981–1982 recession that occurred during the first Reagan administration. However, an improved economy during 1984 and 1988 enabled the Republicans to achieve a favorable rating from the electorate in terms of their ability to handle the economy. Until the late 1990s, Democrats trailed behind Republicans in being viewed as better able to handle the economy, but they took the advantage on this issue during George W. Bush's second term (see Figure 8.11).

With partisan advantage on the economy and domestic issues having shifted frequently between the two parties in recent elections, it is clear that American politics has emerged from the New Deal era and that neither party has a continuing lock on these issues. Rather, the electorate appears quite capable of venting its frustrations on either party, depending upon which one it holds responsible for the state of the nation. Thus, an electorate that in 1992 banished the Bush administration from the White House for its seeming lack of sensitivity to the public's economic concerns turned right around two years later and gave the Republicans a resounding victory that included control of the Congress for the first time in over forty years. Then, amid the prosperity of 1996, the voters rewarded Bill Clinton with a second term and continued GOP control of Congress. The 2000 elections were a virtual tie that resulted in a Democratic administration being replaced by one led by Republican George W. Bush, while the GOP in Congress sustained losses in both chambers. Republicans entered the 2006 elections suffering from widespread public disapproval and this dissatisfaction was evident in the public's propensity to trust the Democratic Party more on a wide array of issues (see Figure 8.11).

The Republicans' traditional disadvantage on domestic issues was partially off-set by an advantage they carried regarding foreign policy. For example, in 1992,

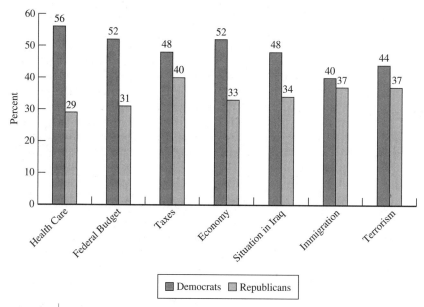

Figure 8.11 | Which Party the Public Trusts to Handle Issues, February, 2008

Source: The Washington Post/ABC News Poll, February 4, 2008.

voters preferred Bush to Clinton when it came to handling foreign affairs. The voters' preference for Bush over Clinton was small consolation to the GOP, however, because few voters considered foreign policy a basis for making their decisions on Election Day. Following 9/11, security issues became very important to citizens, who tended to trust the Republican Party to better handle terrorism and the Iraq War. Thus, while voters who were concerned about the economy in 2004 favored John Kerry by a large margin, a nearly equal proportion of the electorate who placed more emphasis on terrorism was far more likely to vote for Bush. Nevertheless, the lingering difficulties for the military in Iraq began working against Republicans by the midterm elections in 2006, threatening the Republicans' dominance on foreign policy issues (see Figure 8.11).

A third cluster of issues involves social issues such as crime, traditional morality, law and order, abortion, race relations, and school prayer. These are issues that often stir deep emotions, and they tend to affect the parties in different ways. Previously, the GOP was a coalition of free-market libertarians and social conservatives, and could usually stay united as long as it concentrated on economic issues, where both factions are in essential agreement on government's limited

---

BOX 8.5 | **Do Young Adults Get Real Knowledge from a Fake News Show?**

During the 2004 presidential campaign, the popularity of Comedy Central's The Daily Show, hosted by Jon Stewart, soared with an average of more than 1 million viewers nightly. The show is particularly popular with young adults (ages 18–29), over one-fifth of whom said they watched The Daily Show regularly. Stewart's show became such an important political player during the campaign that John Edwards chose it as the venue to announce his run for president and John Kerry appeared on the program after securing the Democratic nomination. The popularity of this show among young Americans drew some criticism from pundits such as conservative talk show host Bill O'Reilly, who claimed that Daily Show viewers were nothing but "dopey kids." However, a study conducted by the Annenberg Public Policy Study found that this was hardly the case. The survey asked citizens to answer six factual questions about where the candidates stood on the issues, and viewers of The Daily Show not only performed better than citizens who do not watch late night comedy, they outperformed those who are regular viewers of network television news or regular readers of the newspaper. In fact, another study found that Daily Show viewers were just as informed about current events as those who watch Bill O'Reilly's show on Fox News.

The increased knowledge of Daily Show viewers may be attributable both to the fact that the show attracts a more politically engaged audience because of its content and because in satirizing politics, the show does present content that can be informative. As one Annenberg researcher noted, "The Daily Show segments are less likely than a Leno or Letterman joke to use a quick punch-line to make fun of a candidate. Instead, Stewart's lengthier segments employ irony to explore policy issues, news events, and even the media's coverage of the campaign."

Source: Annenberg National Election Study, "Daily Show Viewers Knowledgeable About Presidential Campaign, National Annenberg Election Survey Shows," September 21, 2004; Pew Research Center for the People and Press, "News Audiences Increasingly Polarized," June 8, 2004.

role. However, in recent years, social issues have done more to unify the party, such as in 2004 when the Bush campaign used the issue of gay marriage to rally Republican voters to the polls.

Social issues do hold the capacity to split the Democratic coalition. Traditional Democrats—often white, middle-class southern voters—do not share the enthusiasm that the party's liberal, egalitarian elements have for such policies as implementing affirmative action, cutting defense, protecting a woman's right to an abortion, or supporting gay rights. Figure 8.12 demonstrates the large gap between liberal and conservative Democrats on values issues. This divide has caused problems for recent presidential nominees like John Kerry as well as other Democratic candidates who have been forced to make choices on divisive issues such as school prayer, gay marriage, and "partial birth abortion." Nevertheless, these issues generally affect voters only when other concerns are not tantamount. Thus, since most voters were preoccupied with concerns about the economy in 2008, the candidates' positions on social issues became less important.

CANDIDATE IMAGE

There are no hard and fast rules to guide candidates in terms of how to conduct their campaigns to achieve a favorable personal image, though homilies abound—appear decisive, don't appear trigger happy, the best defense is a strong offense,

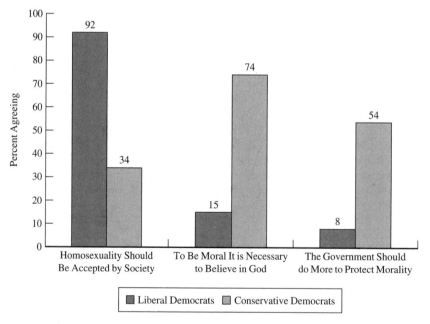

FIGURE 8.12   DIFFERENCES BETWEEN LIBERAL AND CONSERVATIVE DEMOCRATS ON SOCIAL ISSUES, 2005

Source: The Pew Research Center, "Beyond Red vs. Blue: Republicans Divided about Role of Government–Democrats by Social and Personal Values," May 10, 2005.

carry the attack to your opponent. Personal characteristics that voters believe are important tend to vary depending upon the condition in which the country finds itself. In 2000, both Gore and Bush had image problems. For Gore it was the image of pandering to voters, whereas Bush faced the question of whether he was prepared to be president. Because he had been part of the Clinton administration, which had had its share of both accomplishments and scandals, Gore faced a difficult dilemma on the image front: how to claim credit for the accomplishments of the Clinton administration while distancing himself from the unpopular image of Clinton as a person. This proved to be extremely difficult. Exit polls on Election Day revealed that no single issue dominated voters' choices, but one personal quality did—honesty and trustworthiness. Of the 25 percent who said that this quality was most important to their vote, 80 percent voted for Bush.[25] In 2004, Bush's image was one of a strong leader who was willing to take unpopular stands on the issues while Kerry suffered from being perceived as a "flip-flopper." Kerry worked hard to project his own strong image at the Democratic Convention and during the debates, but his efforts were not entirely successful. Exit polls revealed that those who placed a priority on the winner being a strong leader voted overwhelmingly for Bush. With a faltering economy and two stagnant wars, voters in 2008 were looking for the candidate who best represented "change," and Obama had the clear advantage over McCain on that quality (see Figure 8.13).

There is frequent commentary about how candidates manipulate their images through skillful use of the mass media. In fact, however, candidate images are not easily created and altered. For example, candidates cannot control the topics that will

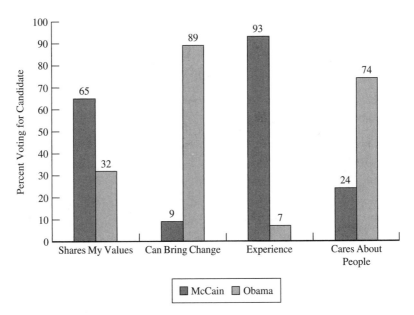

FIGURE 8.13 | VOTE CHOICE OF EXIT POLL RESPONDENTS BASED ON MOST IMPORTANT PERSONAL QUALITY, 2008

Source: National Election Poll Exit Survey.

be raised by their opponents or journalists, nor can they erase their past records. Candidates for major office that are not well known to the public have the greatest opportunity to create a favorable image during the early stages of their campaigns. Although candidate image can be influential in affecting voter choice for high-visibility races, such as those for president or governor, the impact of candidate image normally declines as one goes lower down the ballot, because these candidates are less well known and less visible.[26]

To a significant degree, elections are about performance—voters render a verdict on an incumbent and the incumbent's party's record in office. That is, elections involve retrospective voting on the part of the citizenry. This was certainly the case in 2008, when Obama benefited from the fact that many voters were voting against how Republicans had handled the economy and the military conflicts in Iraq and Afghanistan during the previous several years.

THE ROLE OF PARTIES IN MODERN CAMPAIGNS

In the modern campaign, the candidate tends to be the focus, not the party. Most candidates build a personal organization devoted almost exclusively to their own election rather than the election of the party ticket. These organizations recruit volunteers and raise funds independently of the party. Indeed, any campaign for a major office run by a party organization is now a rarity in American politics. The candidate organizations tend to use professionals for the various phases of the campaign. These campaign technicians—pollsters, media consultants, direct-mail specialists, Internet experts, targeting experts, and management specialists—operate as private entrepreneurs outside the regular party organization. Campaign consultants tend to work, however, for the candidates of only one party. There has grown up, therefore, two sets of consultants—one group works almost exclusively for Democratic candidates and another for Republicans. Candidates and consultants have found that it is extremely difficult to develop a relationship of trust and confidence unless it is understood from the beginning that both are on the same side politically. The partisan orientation of consulting firms is reinforced by the fact that the national party organizations, such as the national committees and the congressional campaign committees of both parties, each maintain approved lists of consultants whom they recommend to their parties' candidates.

Although the party organizations are seldom involved in the day-to-day management of campaigns, they can provide essential and timely financial support and in-kind contributions of services such as polls, computer analyses of voting patterns, and phone banks for contacting contact voters. Indeed, the role of national party organizations in campaigns for the House and Senate has been growing rather than declining. Parties often aid candidates by conducting public opinion polls on their behalf. During the 2004 election cycle, state parties spent over $13 million on polling. Survey research is now combined with demographic targeting techniques to sharpen the impact of campaign activities. For example, if polls reveal that a particular set of voters, such as blue-collar workers of eastern and southern European heritage, are undecided about their vote, it is important to be able to find these voters within the constituency. Computer analyses of census and marketing data can aid in the identification of where these voters reside. With these targeting data in hand, the party

BOX 8.6	HOW DO CITIZENS PERCEIVE THE CANDIDATES' STRATEGIES?

Candidates and political parties generally choose to target some demographic groups more than others during the campaign. These choices are an inevitable result of the fact that candidates have limited resources and their appeals are likely to work better with some groups than others. But does the public take note of the decisions?

A 2008 survey asked respondents which groups they thought Barack Obama and John McCain were paying most attention to during the campaign. The figure below presents the findings from this survey. If a group appears above the upper left-hand quadrant, it means that many people thought that Obama was focusing attention but few thought McCain was doing so; when a group fell in the bottom right-hand quadrant, the opposite was true. Groups who are located in the top right-hand quadrant were thought to be attracting attention from both candidates, and those in the bottom left-hand quadrant were thought by the public to have been targeted by neither Obama nor McCain.

According to these results, the public thought that young adults, lower income Americans, African Americans, liberals, and union members were among the groups Obama was focusing most on while few thought McCain was targeting those groups. Instead, the public thought that McCain was focusing most of his attention on whites, upper income Americans, conservatives, and men; groups that the public did not see Obama trying to win votes from. According to the public, some groups drew significant attention from both sides. In particular, middle income Americans and women were singled out for being the subject of both sides' campaign efforts.

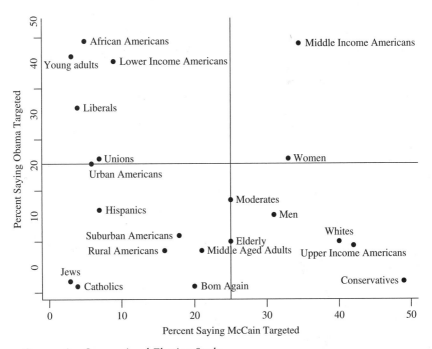

Source: Cooperative Congressional Election Study.

organizations can help develop an appropriate plan for directing the campaign's direct mail, phone banks, door-to-door canvassing, and media purchases.

A large share of candidates' and parties' budgets in national and statewide races is devoted to television advertisements. Indeed, in big states like California, campaigns have become largely television advertising campaigns, as the opposing candidates "debate" each other and seek to influence voters via thirty-second television spots designed by media consultants. In 2008, over 2 million television advertisements were aired for elections to positions at all levels of government.[27] Over $500 million was spent on advertising for the presidential campaign alone.

Often these media campaigns emphasize attack ads, featuring harsh criticism of an opponent's record and character. Criticism of an opponent, particularly one's record in public office, has always been a standard and legitimate part of American electoral politics. However, in recent elections television attack ads have, in the view of many close observers, crossed over the line between legitimate criticism of an individual's record and outright distortion. In presidential and congressional campaigns, candidates often seek to avoid the backlash that might come with airing negative ads. Rather, they defer to parties and interest groups to run the most negative attacks against their opponents, while their own campaigns take responsibility for the less controversial and more positive.

Parties are often instrumental in funding targeted appeals during campaigns as well. Direct mail allows candidates and parties to target their appeals to selected voter groups with a message that is apt to strike a responsive chord with the group being courted. Candidates, parties, and interest groups are all involved in producing direct-mail appeals during campaigns. This strategy is often reserved for more targeted and emotional appeals aimed at attracting supporters in critical areas. In 2004, the national party committees produced and distributed eighty-two different mailers for Ohio, while the state parties were responsible for another seventy-seven unique pieces of direct mail.[28]

Direct mail can also be used as part of larger mobilization efforts conducted by candidates, parties, and interest groups. Parties often focus particular attention on these GOTV efforts because getting supporters to the polls tends to aid all of the party's candidates. For instance, in the presidential campaign, the DNC and RNC spent more than twice as much on their grassroots efforts as the candidates (see Figure 8.14). The state parties reported spending over $70 million on GOTV efforts in 2004, including more than $15 million in Florida.

In attempting to mobilize voters, the parties used a two-step process: finding those who needed to be mobilized and then contacting those potential supporters to encourage them to vote. To identify potential supporters, the parties relied on a combination of voter files and marketing data. The voter files were used to keep track of how often a citizen voted, allowing parties to distinguish between who was registered to vote and, among registered citizens, who was an occasional voter and who was a regular voter. The marketing data provided parties and groups with clues as to the partisan leanings of the citizen. As two *Washington Post* reporters explained:

> Republican firms ... delved into commercial databases that pinpointed consumer buying patterns and television-watching habits to unearth such information as Coors beer and

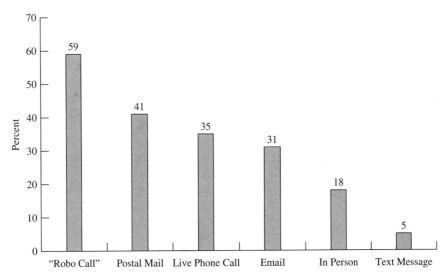

FIGURE **8.14** | HOW VOTERS WERE CONTACTED DURING THE 2008 PRESIDENTIAL CAMPAIGN

Source: Cooperative Congressional Election Study.

bourbon drinkers skewing Republican, brandy and cognac drinkers tilting Democratic; college football TV viewers were more Republican than those who watch professional football; viewers of Fox News were overwhelmingly committed to vote for Bush; homes with telephone caller ID tended to be Republican; people interested in gambling, fashion and theater tended to be Democratic.[29]

To complement the information taken from marketing and voter files, parties and groups also attempt to use information they collect themselves when canvassing neighborhoods door-to-door.

In 2008, Democrats were able to surpass the Republican Party's recent dominance in GOTV efforts. The massive resources of the Obama campaign were combined with the warehouse of data collected by Catalist (see Box 7.2) to generate the largest and most efficient mobilization effort to date. In previous years, Democrats focused their efforts on mobilizing people who lived in particular *precincts* that appeared to hold a lot of potential supporters who might not otherwise turn out to vote. However, in 2008, Democratic data and technology had developed sufficiently so that Democrats were targeting *individuals*. In particular, they focused on mobilizing individuals who either (1) habitual voters who were likely to be persuadable; or (2) citizens who were likely to be supportive of Democrats, but were less likely to turn out without encouragement.

Once parties have identified the targets for their GOTV efforts, they turn to contacting these citizens in a variety of ways, including by phone, e-mail, mail, and in person. The grassroots efforts of candidates, parties, interest groups, and party-affiliated 527 organizations during the 2008 campaign were unprecedented in their scope and sophistication. At the end of the campaign, two-thirds of

TABLE 8.4 | EFFECT OF MOBILIZATION TECHNIQUES ON TURNOUT

Method	Effectiveness	Cost per New Voter
Door-to-door	1 new voter for every 14 people contacted	$19
Phone call	1 new voter for every 35 people contacted	$39
Direct mail	1 new voter for every 177 people contacted	$59
E-mail	No evidence of mobilization effects	3

Source: Alan Gerber and Donald Green, *Get Out the Vote.*

Americans reported being contacted by either a candidate, party, or some other campaign organization. These contacts came in a variety of forms. Three in five Americans received a pre-recorded phone call while one-third of the population was called by a live campaigner. Approximately 40 percent reported receiving direct mail from at least one of the campaigns while over 30 percent received an email. And 18 percent of Americans reported being contacted in person by one of the campaigns (see Figure 8.15). These grassroots efforts are somewhat successful in generating new voters. Research by Donald Green and Alan Gerber demonstrates that contacting potential voters in person has the most significant effect on turnout, followed by phone calls and direct mail. According to their research, e-mail contact has no effect on turnout (see Table 8.4).[30]

While the "air war"—campaign advertising on television and radio—is typically the most visible aspect of the campaign, the importance of the "ground war"—the grassroots efforts to mobilize voters—has become an increasingly important aspect of the parties' strategies for winning elections. As technological advancements have made targeting voters more cost effective, candidates, parties, and interest groups have devoted more resources to these GOTV strategies. This has become a particularly important venue for political parties, who have contacted more voters in recent campaigns than at any time during the previous decades (see Figure 8.15).

ELECTION OUTCOMES

Elections are the culmination of candidates' campaigns and voters' decisions, and they are played out as contests for specific offices, in different constituencies, at various times. Office, constituency, and timing factors, therefore, combine to produce diverse patterns of election outcomes.

PRESIDENTIAL ELECTIONS

Despite the fact that Democrats have enjoyed a substantial advantage in party identification for most of the period from 1956 to 2008, the Republicans have been at least as successful in capturing the presidency. In fourteen presidential elections held during this period, the Republicans have won eight times and the Democrats six. Obviously, short-term factors of candidate image, issues, and

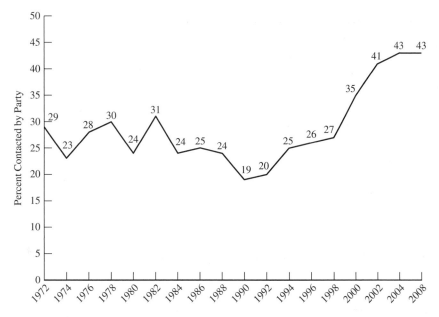

FIGURE 8.15 | PERCENT OF CITIZENS REPORTING THAT THEY WERE CONTACTED BY THE PARTIES, 1972–2008

Source: National Election Studies.

party image have overridden the normal Democratic advantage in party identifiers to produce this pattern of outcome in presidential elections. Among the most dramatic aspects of this pattern is the changing allegiance of the South in presidential elections.

In each of their presidential victories between 1956 and 2004, the Republicans were beneficiaries of major internal splits within the dominant Democratic Party. Democrats are divided on such matters as affirmative action, crime, gun control, gay marriage, and national defense issues that have become more important than they were in the 1940s through the early 1960s. At the same time, the old New Deal agenda of national government responsibility for the social welfare of individuals and the regulation of the economy has either lost some of its salience or the perceived "superiority" of the Democrats on these issues for the party's traditional voters has become less obvious.[31] These changes have given the GOP the opportunity to compete effectively in presidential elections.

CONGRESSIONAL ELECTIONS

Whatever advantages the Republicans may have had in presidential contests had been substantially offset by Democratic domination of the Congress. Until the 1994 midterm elections, which gave Republicans control of both the House and Senate, the voters had denied the party control over both chambers for forty years. Democratic dominance had been so pervasive and persistent that there had even been talk of the GOP being a "permanent minority" in the House.[32] During their forty years in the congressional wilderness, the Republicans did achieve temporary majority status in the Senate during the Reagan era (from 1981 through 1986), but they never controlled the House of Representatives.

REGIONAL PATTERNS   The same regional patterns that are discernable in presidential elections are also present in congressional elections. The most significant regional change during the second half of the twentieth century was southern realignment. The long-standing Democratic control of Congress was anchored by the party's dominance of southern politics, which enabled it to control nearly every Senate and House seat in the region. In fact, southerners constituted the largest regional bloc within the congressional Democratic Party in 1960—making up 33.8 percent of the party membership in the Senate and 40 percent in the House. Of the 2,565 congressional elections held in the South during the first half of the twentieth century, Republicans won just 80 times. Because Democrats could count on dominating southern Congressional elections, they had a substantial head start in controlling Congress; winning just one-third of the seats outside of the South was usually sufficient to guarantee control.

The realignment of the southern electorate began in the mid-1960s as a response to the Republican and Democratic parties taking clear sides on racial issues. Yet this realignment was not immediately evident in the outcomes of congressional elections in the South (see Figure 8.16). Even as recently as 1990, Democrats won two-thirds of southern House contests. Much of this continued Democratic success in the South was due to the ability of southern Democratic office holders to vote conservatively

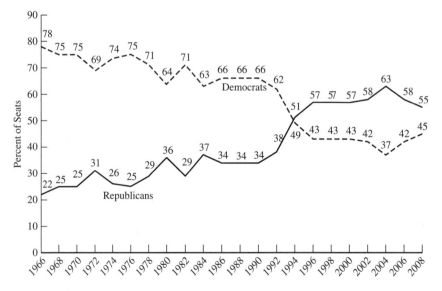

FIGURE 8.16 | DEMOCRATIC AND REPUBLICAN PARTY SHARE OF SOUTHERN CONGRESSIONAL DELEGATION, 1966–2008

Source: Results of House elections, by party, 1928–2008. (2001). In *Guide to U.S. Elections 2010* (Vol. 2). Washington: CQ Press, 2010.

on social and race issues while voting more with the mainstream Democratic Party on other issues. In addition, it took several decades to build a viable GOP party organization in the South capable of seriously competing with Democrats.[33]

The culmination of the partisan realignment in the South was the 1994 midterm elections, when Republicans won a majority of southern House seats for the first time since Reconstruction. This Republican advance in the South was instrumental in handing Republicans control of Congress for the first time in forty years. It also represented a substantial shift in the regional composition of both parties' congressional delegations. After the 1994 elections, the Democratic Party became substantially less southern and western in membership. Southern states constituted less than one-quarter of the party's membership in Congress, and Mountain state senators were less than 15 percent. As southern influence in the congressional Democratic Party has declined, it has grown significantly among the Republicans. Southern Republicans moved from being an insignificant segment of the party in 1960 to the largest regional contingent after the 1994 elections. This shift was symbolized in 1995 by the selection of Newt Gingrich of Georgia to be Speaker of the House and Richard Armey of Texas to be the Majority Leader and in 1996 with the selection of Trent Lott of Mississippi as Senate Majority Leader.

REDISTRICTING   After the decennial census, state governments are obligated to redraw congressional district lines to assure that districts maintain approximately equal populations. The redistricting process varies from state to state, but in most cases the state legislature is responsible for drawing new maps while the rest use a commission process. In most cases, redistricting plans address the goals of protecting incumbents and gaining a partisan advantage.[34] When a state's government is divided and neither party has complete control over the process, the parties tend to compromise and draw lines that make incumbents from both parties more secure. Incumbents' high reelection rates are at least partially attributable to the tendency of redistricting plans to draw districts favorable for sitting incumbents.

By most accounts, the redistricting performed by the states after the 2000 census went especially far in creating large numbers of seats that were safe for either Republicans or Democrats. Only eight incumbents lost reelection campaigns in 2002, and four of those losses were to other incumbents in states that had lost a congressional district. And these incumbents not only won but won easily; their average margin of victory was 40 percent. The reason for this security appeared to be favorable redistricting. In fact, Sam Hirsch's analysis of redistricting noted that of 108 incumbents whose districts were relatively competitive before redistricting, only four districts became more competitive while forty-five were made safer.[35]

In addition to safer incumbents, Hirsch also notes that redistricting after the 2000 census had an overall partisan bias that favored Republicans. Indeed, when a single party controls a redistricting process, that party often acts to draw district lines to help elect more of their own party members. Democrats in Georgia controlled the legislature and governorship in 2001–2002 and used this power to draw district lines intended to benefit Democratic congressional candidates. Unified Republican governments in Pennsylvania, Florida, and Michigan acted at the same time to benefit Republican candidates in those states. According to Hirsch's analysis, Republicans were able to partisan gerrymander more congressional districts

BOX 8.7	DO SINGLE-MEMBER DISTRICTS CREATE BIAS IN THE HOUSE?

The single-member district-plurality system of election has meant that a party's percentage of the House membership will not necessarily be proportionate to its national popular vote for Congress. If one party's voters tend to be concentrated in districts that it wins overwhelmingly, and if the opposition party tends to win most of the marginal districts by narrow margins, then the composition of the legislative chamber is not apt to reflect accurately the share of the total vote received by either party. A disparity between popular votes and a party's share of the legislative seats is an inevitable consequence of the uneven manner in which adherents of the two parties are scattered across the country and the way boundary lines are drawn. Of course, overt gerrymandering of congressional district lines designed to enhance the advantage of one party or the other can magnify the disparity between seats won and a party's share of the national two-party vote.

From 1960 through 1992, the Democrats were advantaged by the single-member district-plurality system of election. However, in 1994 through 2004, it has been the GOP that gained the advantage from the single-member district system. For example, even though Al Gore won the popular vote in 2000, he would have carried only 198 of the 435 (45.5 percent) congressional districts created for the 2002 midterm elections. Part of this bias against Democrats results from the fact that Democratic populations tend to be more compressed in urban areas, where they comprise overwhelmingly Democratic districts, whereas Republican voters are distributed more efficiently.

Source: Sam, Hirsch. "The United States of Unrepresentatives: What Went Wrong in the Latest Round of Redistricting." *Election Law Journal* [2 (2003): 179–216.]

after the 2000 census than Democrats, creating a twenty-five-seat redistricting bias in favor of the Republican Party. In other words, Republicans would not have had a majority in the House of Representatives after the 2002 and 2004 elections without the gains they achieved from redistricting.

Despite the partisan redistricting in several states before the 2002 elections, the clearest effects of partisan gerrymandering were actually evident in Texas in 2004. Prior to the 2002 election, Texas' legislature was under divided party control and was not able to reach a compromise on how to draw new congressional districts. Because of the stalemate, a state judge chose the districts used in the 2002 election. However, Republicans gained full control of the Texas legislature following the 2002 elections, which motivated U.S. House Majority Leader Tom DeLay to urge Texas Republicans to pass a new map that would favor Republicans. Democratic state legislators attracted national media attention when, in an effort to keep Republicans from drawing new districts, they fled the state for Oklahoma and later New Mexico so that there would not be enough legislators for a quorum. After these standoffs, Democrats eventually returned to the legislature and the new map was passed and implemented for the 2004 elections. The Republican gerrymander was successful; the Democrats lost six seats to the Republicans in Texas, including four held by Democratic incumbents with a combined sixty years of congressional seniority.

Largely due to the national media attention garnered by the Texas redistricting controversy and the overall decline in competitive House districts, many scholars and politicians are considering ways to reform the redistricting process to make it less partisan. One example that many reformers point to is Iowa, which uses a non-partisan commission for its redistricting. In 2001, the commission used a computer program to draw congressional districts without accounting for partisanship or incumbency, and neither party benefited from the new lines (nor did most of Iowa's incumbents).[36] In 2005, Governor Arnold Schwarzenegger (R-Calif.) campaigned for a ballot proposition that would have implemented a similar system in California, but the proposition was rejected by California voters. Nevertheless, if the process is to be reformed, the initiative will have to come from the states themselves; the Supreme Court has consistently upheld redistricting plans that are based on protecting the interests of parties or incumbents. With the next round of redistricting on the horizon following the 2010 elections, both parties will be looking to carve out districts to their advantage.

GUBERNATORIAL AND STATE LEGISLATIVE ELECTIONS

Despite setbacks in presidential politics, the Democratic Party dominated gubernatorial and state legislative elections during most of the post–World War II era (see Figure 8.17). Between 1956 and 1994, the GOP controlled a majority of the nation's governorships only twice—following the 1968 and 1994 elections—and the party never controlled both state legislative chambers in a majority of the states. The post–World War II pattern of Republicans winning the largest share of presidential elections and Democrats tending to dominate governorships and state legislatures (as well as House elections) created a two-tiered political system. Analysts considered this two-tiered system to be a reflection of voters' differing expectations

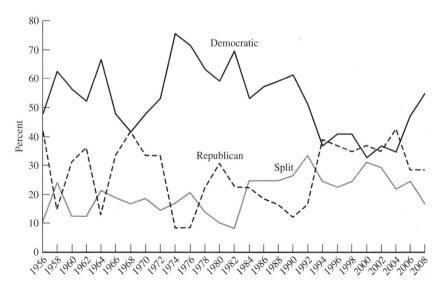

FIGURE 8.17 | PERCENTAGE OF STATE LEGISLATURES UNDER DEMOCRATIC, REPUBLICAN, AND SPLIT CONTROL, 1956–2008

Source: National Conference of State Legislatures.

for governmental institutions and their perceptions of which party was best able to operate those institutions. Thus, voters seemed to expect the House of Representatives and state officials to protect specific government programs from which they derived benefits. In protecting those benefits, they saw the Democrats as doing a better job than the GOP. At the same time, voters viewed the presidency as the office responsible for protecting broad national interests, and for this responsibility they favored the Republicans in most postwar presidential elections.[37] However, the 1992 and 1994 elections, which brought a Democrat to the White House and Republicans into control of Congress and a majority of governorships, have turned this theory on its head. Recent research into split election outcomes has cast further doubt on the theory that voters engage in ticket balancing. Contrary to the theory that voters intentionally engage in split-ticket voting to produce divided government and moderate policies, most cases of split outcomes are a byproduct of lopsided congressional campaigns characterized by well-funded, high-quality candidates versus unknown competitors plus cross-pressured voters holding candidate evaluations at odds with their partisan leanings.[38]

With the exception of Democrats in the South from 1960 until 1994, there has been no consistent pattern of regional party dominance of governorships. Rather, party fortunes within regions have shown substantial variation over relatively short periods of time. For example, Republican control of the five midwestern governorships ranged from zero to five between 1960 and 1980 and stood at four after the 1994 and 1998 elections. Even before the 1994 GOP sweep, the South had not escaped the rising tide of interparty competition. Every southern state had elected at least one Republican governor between 1966 and 2004.

One of the most interesting patterns of regional voting during the Reagan–Bush era was the ability of the Democrats to win governorships in the Mountain states, one of the GOP's areas of greatest strength in presidential elections. Between 1980 and 1990, the Democrats never held less than five of the eight governorships in this region, and after the 1982 elections they held all eight. Clearly, these Democratic governors were able to differentiate themselves from their national party and effectively appeal to voters. Even before the 2006 elections (which favored Democratic candidates), Democrats held the governorships in four of the eight Mountain states.

PROFESSIONALIZED LEGISLATURES As a part of the 1970s movement to reform state legislatures, salaries were increased and additional staff and other resources were provided to legislators. This process of legislative professionalization made legislative service virtually a full-time job in many states. With legislatures professionalizing, campaigning for legislative seats has become almost a full-time vocation. In addition, legislative campaigns have become more expensive and professional, employing consultants and sophisticated techniques.

Research by Morris Fiorina has shown that the trend toward full-time legislators tended to advantage the Democrats by making legislative service more attractive to the party's pool of potential candidates. By contrast, the pool of persons from whom the GOP recruited its candidates tended to find that full-time legislative service was incompatible with another career, thereby hurting the party's candidate recruitment efforts and contributing to the Republicans' minority status in most state legislatures since the 1970s. Fiorina also found that there is a relationship between professionalized legislatures and divided party control of state governments because entrenched professional legislators can often withstand adverse political tides much as members of the U.S. House have done.[39]

The increased professionalization of legislatures also appears to have increased the incumbency advantage in state legislatures.[40] Full-time legislators have extensive opportunities to engage in self-advertisement through use of their perquisites of office and normally have a much easier time raising campaign funds. In addition, they often enjoy the support of party caucus staffs and aggressive legislative campaign committees. As a result, defeating incumbent legislators has become more difficult. The Council of State Governments reported that in 2008 34 percent of all state legislative seats up for election went uncontested and just 39 percent of state legislative races attracted candidates from both major parties.

CAMPAIGNS, ELECTIONS, AND GOVERNANCE

Although candidates can vary their campaign strategies and can hire experts to devise the seemingly most effective strategy, all are restricted by conditions over which they have little or limited control—election laws, the state of the economy, international conditions, campaign resources, public images of the parties, and the partisan division of the electorate between Republicans and Democrats. Candidates, therefore, must tailor their campaigns to fit conditions or run the risk of defeat or a serious decline in electoral support. The eventual electoral outcomes reflect the decisions of voters influenced by long-term affiliations with either the GOP or Democratic Party and more short-term considerations relating to candidates and issues. The voters' electoral choices produce a wide array of different patterns of partisan control over governmental offices. These patterns of party control mirror the effects of regional diversity, incumbency, economic conditions, campaign effort, and the timing of elections.

Those who assume governmental office as a result of elections constitute the party-in-government. It is these partisan leaders who carry major responsibility for the enunciation of party policy and for shaping the public's image of the party. They are also responsible for the content of governmental policies that affect the nation and the world. The role of the party-in-government and its impact on policy making are the concerns of Chapter 9.

WEB SITES ON CAMPAIGNS AND ELECTIONS

Campaign Finance
The Federal Election Commission's Web site includes information on candidates and donors as well as reports on overall trends in campaign finance.
http://www.fec.gov/

The Center for Responsive Politics also maintains campaign finance databases and presents easy to use information on overall trends. One feature even allows you to search for all donations made in your zip code.
http://www.opensecrets.org/

The National Institute on Money in State Politics serves a similar function as the Center for Responsive Politics, but for state elections.
http://www.followthemoney.org/

The Campaign Finance Institute is affiliated with George Washington University and provides analysis of campaign finance regulations as well as suggestions for reforms. http://www.cfinst.org/

Candidates
Project Vote Smart is an organization that provides voters with information about candidates' issues positions. Their Web site includes candidates' responses to issue questionnaires as well as information about vote ratings of elected officials. http://www.vote-smart.org

Campaign News
CNN's home for election news includes a wealth of information, including surveys, issue positions, news, and results. http://www.cnn.com/ELECTION/

The Note is ABC News' daily political update, which keeps close track of campaign news. http://abcnews.go.com/sections/politics/TheNote/TheNote.html

National Journal's Hotline On Call is a blog used by the Hotline staff to post political news of interest, including news about congressional and presidential races. http://hotlineblog.nationaljournal.com/

The Columbia Journalism Review's site monitors and criticizes campaign coverage. http://www.cjrdaily.org/

Election Results
Extensive Web site of presidential, gubernatorial, and senatorial results, with information on turnout, statewide and county-level results, and colorful maps. http://www.uselectionatlas.org/

NOTES

1. For a detailed consideration of the role and impact of campaign consultants, see James A. Thurber and Candice J. Nelson, eds., *Campaign Warriors: Political Consultants in Elections* (Washington, D.C.: Brookings, 2000).

2. Michael Weisskopf, "The Professional Touch," *Washington Post*, Nov. 8, 1994, p. A3 Dennis W. Johnson, "The Business of Political Consulting," in James A. Thurber and Candice J. Nelson, eds., *Campaign Warriors: Political Consultants in Elections* (Washington, D.C.: Brookings, 2000), pp. 37–52.

3. Gary C. Jacobson, *The Politics of Congressional Elections*, 5th ed. (New York: Longman, 2001), p. 122. On the impact of campaign spending, see also Paul Herrnson, *Congressional*

Elections, 3rd ed. (Washington, D.C.: CQ Press, 2000), ch. 9.

4. David S. Broder and Ruth Marcus, "Wielding Third Force in Politics," *Washington Post*, Sept. 27, 1997, pp. A1, A6; David E. Rosenbaum, "Groups Spending $260 Million on Ads to Promote Agendas," *New York Times* (national edition), Oct. 15, 1998, p. A21.

5. Michael M. Franz, Joel Rivlin, and Kenneth Goldstein, "Much More of the Same: Television Advertising Pre- and Post-BCRA," in Michael J. Malbin, ed., *The Election After Reform: Money, Politics and the Bipartisan Campaign Reform Act* (Lanham, Md.: Rowman & Littlefield, 2006).

6. Michael J. Malbin, *The Election After Reform: Money, Politics and the*

Bipartisan Campaign Reform Act (Lanham, Md.: Rowman & Littlefield, 2006).

7. Anthony Corrado, "Party Finance in the Wake of BCRA: An Overview," in Michael J. Malbin, ed., *The Election After Reform: Money, Politics and the Bipartisan Campaign Reform Act* (Lanham, Md.: Rowman & Littlefield, 2006).

8. Steve Weissman and Ruth Hassan, "527 Groups and BCRA," in Michael J. Malbin, ed., *The Election After Reform: Money, Politics and the Bipartisan Campaign Reform Act* (Lanham, Md.: Rowman & Littlefield, 2006).

9. Michael. J. Malbin and Thomas L. Gais, *The Day After Reform: Sobering Campaign Finance Lessons from the American States* (Albany, N.Y.: Rockefeller Institute Press, 1998), pp. 52–54, 66–70.

10. Ruth S. Jones, "Financing State Elections," in Michael J. Malbin, ed., *Money and Politics in the United States: Financing Elections in the 1980s* (Chatham, N.J.: Chatham House, 1984), p. 203.

11. Malbin and Gais, *The Day After Reform*, pp. 136–138; see also Kenneth R. Mayer and John M. Wood, "The Impact of Public Financing on Electoral Competitiveness: Evidence from Wisconsin 1964–1990," *Legislative Studies Quarterly* 15 (Feb. 1995): 69–88.

12. E. J. Dionne, "Perot Seen Not Affecting the Vote Outcome," *Washington Post*, Nov. 8, 1992, p. A36.

13. Paul R. Abramson, John H. Aldrich, and David W. Rohde, *Change and Continuity in the 1996 Elections* (Washington, D.C.: CQ Press, 1998), p. 248.

14. Darrell M. West, *Air Wars: Television Advertising in Election Campaigns, 1952–1996*, 2nd ed. (Washington, D.C.: CQ Press, 1997), pp. 141–142.

15. James E. Campbell, "When Have Presidential Campaigns Decided Election Outcomes?" *American Politics Research* 29 (Sept. 2001): 437–460.

16. Jacobson, *The Politics of Congressional Elections*, pp. 30–32 and ch. 5.

17. Study reported by David S. Broder, "Ads Sham," *Washington Post*, May 28, 2000, p. B7.

18. For a thorough analysis of the impact of presidential debates and of the scholarly literature on debates, see Thomas M. Holbrook, *Do Elections Matter?* (Thousand Oaks, Calif.: Sage, 1996), ch. 5.

19. Holbrook, *Do Elections Matter?* p. 114.

20. Quoted in Richard L. Berke, "Debate Stakes Seen as Critical by Candidate," *New York Times*, on the Web, Oct. 1, 2000, p. A1.

21. Majorie Randon Hershey, "The Campaign in the Media," in Gerald M. Pomper, ed., *The Election of 2000* (New York: Chatham House, 2001), pp. 60–63.

22. Holbrook, *Do Elections Matter?* p. 123.

23. Hershey, "The Campaign in the Media," p. 62.

24. William Schneider, "The November 4 Vote for President: What Did It Mean?" in Austin Ranney, ed., *The American Elections of 1980* (Washington, D.C.: American Enterprise Institute, 1981), p. 231; Gallup Poll Index, Report No. 181, Sept. 1980, p. 19.

25. Kathleen A. Frankovic and Monika L. McDermott, "Public Opinion and the 2000 Election: The Ambivalent Electorate," in Gerald M. Pomper, ed., *The Election of 2000* (New York: Chatham House, 2001), pp. 87–88.

26. William H. Flanigan and Nancy H. Zingale, *Political Behavior of the American Electorate*, 9th ed. (Washington, D.C.: CQ Press, 1998), pp. 166–170.

27. Based on figures calculated by the Wisconsin Advertising Project.

28. David B. Magleby and Kelly D. Patterson, "Stepping Out of the Shadows: Ground War Activities in 2004," in Michael J. Malbin, ed., *The Election After Reform: Money, Politics and the Bipartisan Campaign Reform Act* (Lanham, Md.: Rowman & Littlefield, 2006).

29. Thomas B. Edsall and James V. Grimaldi, "On Nov. 2, GOP Got More Bang for Its Billion, Analysis Shows," *The Washington Post*, December 30, 2004, p. A1.

30. Donald P. Green and Alan S. Gerber, *Get Out the Vote! How to Increase Voter Turnout* (Washington, D.C.: Brookings Institution Press, 2004).

31. John R. Petrocik and Frederick T. Steeper, "Realignment and 1984: New Coalitions and New Majorities?" *Election Politics* 2 (Winter 1984–85): 8.

32. William F. Connelly, Jr., and John J. Pitney, Jr., *Congress' Permanent Minority? Republicans in the U.S. House* (Lanham, Md.: Littlefield Adams, 1994).

33. Earl Black and Merle Black, *The Rise of Southern Republicans* (Cambridge: Harvard University Press, 2003).

34. Andrew Gelman and Gary King, "Enhancing Democracy through Legislative Redistricting," *American Political Science Review* 88 (1994): 541–59.

35. Sam Hirsch, "The United States House of Unrepresentatives: What Went Wrong in the Latest Round of Congressional Redistricting," *Election Law Journal* 2 (2) (2003).

36. See Adam Clymer, "Why Iowa Has So Many Hot Seats," *New York Times*, October 27, 2002.

37. Gary C. Jacobson, *The Electoral Origins of Divided Government, 1946–1988* (Boulder, Colo.: Westview, 1990), ch. 6; see also Byron E. Shafer, ed., *The End of Realignment* (Madison: University of Wisconsin Press, 1991), ch. 3.

38. Barry C. Burden and David C. Kimball, "A New Approach to the Study of Ticket Splitting" *American Political Science Review* 92 (Sept. 1998): 533–544; and Franco Mattei and John S. Howes, "Competing Explanations of Split-Ticket Voting in American National Elections," *American Politics Quarterly* 28 (July 2000): 379–407.

39. Morris P. Fiorina, "Divided Government in the American States: A Byproduct of Legislative Professionalism?" *American Political Science Review* 88 (June 1994): 304–316; see also Peverill Squire, "Another Look at Legislative Professionalization and Divided Government in the States," *Legislative Studies Quarterly* 22 (Aug. 1997): 417.

40. Malcolm E. Jewell and David Breaux, "The Effect of Incumbency on State Legislative Elections," *Legislative Studies Quarterly* 13 (Nov. 1988): 477–494; Malcolm E. Jewell, "State Legislative Elections: What We Know and Don't Know," *American Politics Quarterly* 22 (1994): 483–509.

PARTIES IN THE GOVERNMENT

CHAPTER CONTENTS

In national and state government, Republicans and Democrats "make the major decision about who pays and who receives."[1] Only leaders of these two major parties have occupied the Oval Office in the White House since the Civil War; only an occasional independent ever gains election to the House or Senate, and those who do quickly associate themselves with one of the major parties for organizational purposes and committee assignments. Since 1942 only five people have been elected to governorships as third-party candidates or independents (most recently Angus King of Maine in 1994 and 1998, and Jesse Ventura of Minnesota in 1998); and following the 2008 elections, less than twenty state legislators out of 7,382 were independents or belonged to a minor party (not including the nonpartisan unicameral legislature of Nebraska). American government is organized on a partisan basis. Presidents and governors customarily appoint fellow members of their party to key posts within their administrations and to judicial vacancies. In Congress and most state legislatures, key leadership posts go to members of the majority party and committees are aligned to give the dominant party numerical control. Partisans and partisanship pervade American government. Even so, American parties face major obstacles in guiding the policy-making machinery.

The party-in-government must operate within a constitutional order that was designed to make coordinated and cooperative action difficult. Federalism and separation of powers were conceived as checks and balances on organized factions, not as facilitators of cooperation. American parties are divided geographically by federalism, which creates thousands of separate constituencies in which elected officials can operate with relative autonomy. Separation of powers divides the parties functionally and reduces the need for cooperation among party leaders in the executive and legislative branches. In a parliamentary system, legislators who fail to support their party's prime minister run the risk of forcing the cabinet to resign and the calling of new parliamentary elections. American legislators, however, are not required to support the policies of a president or governor of their party in order to maintain partisan control of the executive branch or to preserve their own positions in the legislature. Separation of powers assures executives of fixed terms of office irrespective of which party controls the legislature, and it imposes no special obligations of loyalty to the executive's policies upon the party's legislators.

Within America's separation-of-powers system, there exists a *separation of party organizations*[2] as well. When President George W. Bush was called the leader of the Republican Party, or President Obama is said to be head of the Democratic Party, there is an implication that these men head a single organizational entity. But American parties are not of this type. There is a "presidential party" composed of presidential appointees to the executive branch, national convention delegates, the national committee, and the president's personal campaign organization. There is also a "congressional party" with fully organized structures in both chambers that operates quite autonomously from the presidential party. In addition, there are gubernatorial and legislative parties in the states.

The separateness of these organizations is particularly noticeable in terms of nominations. Presidents play no significant role in the selection of party nominees for the House and Senate. Rather, they are chosen by their districts and states in primary elections. Presidents may encourage particular individuals to seek party nominations, but they cannot prevent others from running or guarantee the nomination to their favorite candidates.

In a similar manner, representatives and senators have only the most limited influence upon presidential nominations. The largest proportion of national convention delegates are selected by presidential primaries in which congressional endorsements are of scant value. Nor are congressional leaders in a strong position to win presidential nominations for themselves. Winning a presidential nomination requires virtually full-time campaigning for two to four years—time that is not available to a senator or representative with major congressional leadership responsibilities. As Austin Ranney has observed, members of Congress have about "as little power over whom their party nominates for the presidency as the president has over whom his party nominates for the House and Senate."[3] Presidents have even less influence over the selection of congressional leaders than they do over nominations. Representatives and senators strongly resent presidential intrusion into their leadership-selection processes. As a result, even expressions of support by presidents are rare, and there are no verified instances of presidents seeking to oust a speaker, floor leader, or whip.[4] Just as presidents do not influence selection of congressional party leaders, representatives and senators do not exert significant influence upon the organization of the White House staff, which normally consists of principal advisors to the president.

The separateness of the presidential and congressional parties at the national level is replicated in most of the states, where distinct gubernatorial and legislative party structures normally exist. Just as the national constitutional provisions for separation of powers make a unified party difficult to achieve, similar provisions in state constitutions cause party fragmentation.

For all their diffuseness, American parties do have a center of gravity. They tend to be executive-centered coalitions.[5] The president is the only party leader with a truly national constituency, and it is his or her nomination and general election campaigns that are the chief activities of the national party. Visibility makes the president and his or her policies the symbols of the party to the mass electorate. The leverage derived from his or her visibility and mass support enhances the ability of the president to lead the government and persuade others in public office to support his or her policies. Even with all the difficulties that confront any president seeking to exert party leadership, his or her position is infinitely stronger than that of any competing party leader. In state government, governors tend to enjoy a similar level of prominence to that of presidents in national politics. The existence of a separate and distinct "presidential party" alongside a "congressional party" has, in the words of Theodore J. Lowi, provided the basis for a *real separation of powers*" within the government. That is, the separation of organizations within the parties reinforces and makes meaningful the separation of powers created by the writers of the Constitution.[6]

THE PRESIDENT AS PARTY LEADER

Presidential leadership involves exerting influence over the national party organization, the Congress, the executive branch, and even the judiciary. In his or her relations with each of these institutions, the resources of the president are substantial, but the president operates under severe constraints imposed by the Constitution and the party system.

THE PRESIDENT AND THE NATIONAL PARTY

A president needs to assert dominance over the party's organizational structure lest it become an independent power center during his or her administration or be used by rivals working against his or her policies and renomination. Of particular importance is controlling the national committee. It is the most inclusive party organization in the country because its membership includes representatives of all the state parties and key party constituencies. It operates a year-round headquarters, staffed by professionals in contact with political leaders around the country, and it has resources that can be used to underwrite White House political activities—polls, fund-raising expenses, and presidential travel. The national committee also exerts substantial influence over presidential nominations through its role in developing national party rules, administering those rules, and handling the arrangements for national conventions. These activities require that presidential interests be protected within the national committee.

Although the president has no formal role in the national committee, his or her informal influence over the selection of the national chair is nearly total. The president's "recommendations" are customarily accepted without dissent. For example, even with the Watergate scandals washing over the Nixon administration and threatening to sink it, the president was able to designate George H. W. Bush as Republican National Committee chairman. The presidential prerogative to select a national committee chair was most recently reaffirmed when Barack Obama selected Virginia Governor Tim Kaine to become chair of the Democratic National Committee before his inauguration in January, 2009. For the party controlling the presidency, national committee subordination to the White House is almost complete, as presidential interests are given priority.

The leadership of the national committees customarily finds it necessary to work under the supervision of White House aides charged with responsibility for protecting the president's political interests. This partnership between the White House and the national committee is generally strengthened by the fact that many of the President's former campaign staffers inevitably end up serving in staff positions for the party. For example, Jennifer O'Malley-Dillon, who directed field operations for the Obama campaign in 2008, took on the role of DNC executive director of the DNC in 2009. Countless other staffers also ended up in DNC positions.

White House personnel and political operatives have also assumed responsibility for handling administration patronage appointments. This reflects unwillingness on the part of presidents and their supporters to place their executive appointments at the disposal of the party organization for purposes of party building. There is instead an emphasis on building a personal organization supportive of the president. The creation of personnel and political offices in the White House, operating with substantial autonomy from the national committees, is a departure from past practice, when the national committees were the chief patronage-dispensing agents. Until 1953, when Dwight Eisenhower stopped the practice, the national party chair had in a few instances even served simultaneously as postmaster general and handled the vast patronage available to the party within the postal system.[7] The reform of the postal service in the 1970s removed the agency from the patronage system and precluded national committee involvement in its hiring practices.

National committees have also seen their presidential campaign roles restricted since the 1960s. National party chairs formerly served as the campaign managers of presidential reelection campaigns, and the campaigns were run out of the national committee headquarters. The last national chair charged with responsibility for a presidential reelection campaign was Leonard Hall, who as RNC chairman managed the 1956 Eisenhower campaign. Since then, incumbent presidents have set up their own personal campaign organizations and relegated the national committee to a supportive role. The Federal Election Campaign Act (FECA) encourages this separation of the national committee from the presidential campaign committee responsible for the receipt and expenditure of funds, while also permitting separate national committee spending on presidential campaigns that are receiving public financing.

The assumption of traditional party functions by the White House staff and the subordination of the national committee to the White House have made being national chair of the president's party a frequently frustrating experience. Based on his experiences as RNC chairman under President Richard Nixon in 1972, Senator Bob Dole (R-Kans.) commented, "When your party's in power, the chairman doesn't have any decision-making role."[8]

As was noted in Chapter 4, governors frequently exert influence over their state party committees that is at least as pervasive as that of the president over the national committee. Like presidents, governors work to prevent their state committees from becoming competing or hostile centers of power within the party. Unlike the national committee–presidential relationship, however, there have periodically been instances of alienation and conflict between governors and state party committees. The most common pattern, however, has been for governors to play a substantial role in the selection of state chairs, to be consulted on state party issues, and to assist the party in such activities as fund-raising and candidate recruitment.

Presidential Nominations and the Building of Governing Coalitions

The pattern of national committee subordination to the president and his or her staff and the tendency of presidents to set up their own personal political operations within the White House is a reflection of the changed process of coalition building involved in gaining presidential nominations. As noted in Chapter 6, winning a presidential nomination involves intense personal campaigning and an organization equipped to contest presidential primaries and party caucuses, which are open to almost any interested citizen. It is no longer a process of forging a coalition among state and local party leaders, governors, senators, congresspersons, mayors, and interest groups aligned with the party. Prior to the 1970s, candidates for presidential nominations were required to build electoral coalitions around party leaders and elected officials. In the process of their negotiations with these leaders, presidential candidates became well acquainted with many of the people who would be important to them once they entered the Oval Office. In effect, presidents began to forge a governing coalition while they sought their party's nomination. The changes in the nominating process, which have substantially diminished the power of party and elected officials, have had the effect, according to Austin Ranney, of separating "the process of building the coalition needed for the nomination from the process of building the coalition needed for governing."[9] Presidential leadership of the government, already made difficult by the constitutional restrictions of federalism and separation of powers, is made even more difficult by the nature of the nomination process. *Washington Post* columnist David Broder noted the consequences of the changed nominating process for governance while comparing the experiences of John F. Kennedy and Jimmy Carter:

> Kennedy ran in four contested primaries in 1960. Contrast four with the thirty-four that await anyone who wants the nomination in 1980. After Kennedy won West Virginia, he still had to persuade the leaders of his party—the governors, the mayors, the leaders of allied interest groups—particularly organized labor—that they could stake their reputations on his qualities as the best man to be the standard bearer for the party. Contrast that with Jimmy Carter, who never had to meet, and in fact, in many cases, did not meet, those similar officials until after he had achieved the Democratic nomination.
>
> The significance of the difference for the presidency is that in one case, a man, if he is elected, comes with the alliances that make it possible for him to organize the coalitions and support necessary to lead a government.
>
> In the present nominating system, he comes as a fellow whose only coalition is whatever he got out of the living rooms of Iowa (precinct caucuses). If there is one thing that Jimmy Carter's frustration in office ought to teach us, it is that the affiliation and commitment that is made on Iowa caucus night and New Hampshire primary day is not by itself sufficient to sustain a man for four years in the White House.[10]

The difficult leadership position in which an American president finds himself or herself upon entering the White House is quite different from that of most chief executives in other Western-style democracies. In the United Kingdom, for example, the leader of the opposition party is in an officially recognized governmental position. The Opposition leader stands ready to assume the prime ministership in the event the cabinet is forced to resign or his or her party wins a national election. The Opposition leader's governing coalition is already in place, and he or she is, therefore, in a stronger position than an American president to exert leadership over the government. American presidents, by contrast, only assume leadership of their party upon winning a presidential nomination, and they continue to hold the leadership only if they can win the general election.[11]

THE PARTY, THE PRESIDENT, AND CONGRESS

The president's policy-making powers are shared with the Congress even in areas such as international relations and national security. Much of what a president can accomplish in terms of policy making requires the cooperation of the Congress. In gaining policy influence with the Congress, presidents are constantly required to use the kinship that they share with their party colleagues in the legislature. These partisan ties, however, are not of a truly binding character, and tensions always exist between the president and Congress.

SOURCES OF PRESIDENTIAL-CONGRESSIONAL DIFFERENCES

ELECTORAL BASES The circumstances of elections to Congress and the presidency carry the seeds for conflict between the president and his or her fellow partisans on the Hill. As noted previously, presidents are nominated and elected without the development of mutual obligations between the president and the congressional party. The president owes them nothing for his or her victory. But by the same token, members of the Congress also perceive that they have achieved their office largely through their own efforts. Since the president has no real control over the party's congressional nominations, presidential leverage with legislators is fractured early in the electoral process.

Nor does the president derive substantial influence over members of Congress from the general election process. Presidential coattails have become rather threadbare in recent decades.[12] In 2008, Obama ran ahead of a winning Democratic House candidate in just 37 districts. The declining influence of coattails has weakened the position of the president vis-à-vis the Congress because it has diminished the perception among members that they owe their election at least in part to the president's popularity and that they should, therefore, support his or her policies.

The differing constituencies of members of Congress as compared to presidents and the timing of elections also create differing perspectives. Legislators are ultimately responsible to the constituents in their states or districts. No matter how pressing national problems may be, reelection requires attention to local or state interests. Representatives and senators have few electoral incentives to view issues from a national perspective. By contrast, the president has a national constituency and is forced to take a more comprehensive view of issues than is required of legislators. Further tension is introduced into presidential-congressional relations by the staggered timing of elections. Because senators are elected for six-year overlapping terms, only one-third of the senators are ever elected simultaneously with the president. Those who are elected with the president know their next reelection campaign will be fought during a midterm election, when the president is not on the ballot. House members, of course, are also on a different election schedule than presidents. Their two-year terms require them to run without the president on the ballot during midterm elections. The staggered timing of elections means that the president, senators, and representatives must confront the voters at different times and under divergent circumstances. They are, therefore, apt to view their electoral mandates quite differently.

INSTITUTIONAL BASES Complementing the electoral basis for differences between the president and Congress are institutional sources of tension. The executive branch is organized on a relatively hierarchical basis, with the president in charge and held accountable for its actions. With their sweeping responsibility for policy development and implementation, presidents are forced to consider the trade-offs that must be made among various policies and to take a comprehensive national view of policy. The hierarchical character of the executive enhances the president's ability to propose policies that are comprehensive and consistent in character.

By contrast, the Congress is structured in a more decentralized manner. Major decision-making responsibilities are delegated to committees and subcommittees, which often have memberships that are not particularly representative of their parent chambers. Senators and representatives tend to gravitate toward committees that have special significance for their constituencies (e.g., westerners to the Natural Resources committees, farm-state legislators to the Agriculture committees, and urban legislators to the Banking Committee or committees with jurisdiction over labor and education issues). Committees, therefore, often become centers of narrower interest concerns than are found among leaders of the executive branch. Differences between the branches are further encouraged because Congress considers issues serially—one at a time—rather than comprehensively. That is, Congress often considers issues with little reference to other related policies. The decentralized power structure of Congress and its reliance on the committee/subcommittee system for a detailed review of policy proposals make it almost impossible for the institution to consider policies in a manner as integrated and comprehensive as the executive branch.[13] The relatively hierarchical structure of the executive branch and the more decentralized character of Congress also cause the president and legislators to have a different sense of accountability to the voters.[14] Because presidents are so visible and are responsible for the development and implementation of a full range of policies, they are held accountable for the performance of the government as a whole. The representatives and senators are substantially less visible, and the decentralization of power within Congress makes it virtually impossible to hold any of its members accountable for the actions of the Congress, let alone the national government. Legislators, therefore, are evaluated on the basis of their own records, not the performance of the government as a whole. This frees them to engage in activities that will enhance their standing with constituents, irrespective of the national implications of those actions. Many even campaign by running against the Congress and its record, knowing full well that individually they will not be judged by Congress' institutional record.[15] Presidents also operate on a different time perspective than do legislators. Whereas the president's term in office is fixed and he or she has a limited time to accomplish his or her objectives and establish his or her a place in history, representatives and senators normally think in terms of lifetime careers in the Congress. Presidents are concerned about problems of the moment—passing high-priority proposals. Members of Congress, instead, worry about how to advance their long-term influence in the chamber, promote the policies to which they attach importance, and maintain electability within their constituencies.[16] Presidential leadership of Congress is also made more difficult because of the separation-of-powers system, which makes possible divided partisan control of the presidency and Congress. Indeed, since the mid-1950s, divided government has been more common than single-party control (see Table 9.1). Except during Eisenhower's first two years in office and George W. Bush's four years of presidency, Republican presidents have consistently had to face a Congress in which at least one chamber was controlled by the Democrats. Democratic presidents have been more fortunate. Until the Republican sweep in the 1994 midterm elections left President Bill Clinton facing a Republican-controlled Congress every Democratic president starting with Harry Truman in 1948 had the benefit of a Democratic Congress. President Obama also had the good fortune of taking office alongside a Democratic majority in Congress.

Separation of powers has had similar consequences for state government. Since 1952 every state has experienced divided government at least once. In

TABLE 9.1	SINGLE-PARTY VERSUS DIVIDED CONTROL OF THE NATION GOVERNMENT, 1955–2008

Years	Condition	Party of President	Party Controlli...
1955–1956	*Divided*	Republican	Democrats
1957–1958	*Divided*	Republican	Democrats
1959–1960	*Divided*	Republican	Democrats
1961–1962	Unified	Democrat	Democrats
1963–1964	Unified	Democrat	Democrats
1965–1966	Unified	Democrat	Democrats
1967–1968	Unified	Democrat	Democrats
1969–1970	*Divided*	Republican	Democrats
1971–1972	*Divided*	Republican	Democrats
1973–1974	*Divided*	Republican	Democrats
1975–1976	*Divided*	Republican	Democrats
1977–1978	Unified	Democrat	Democrats
1979–1980	Unified	Democrat	Democrats
1981–1982	*Divided*	Republican	Split
1983–1984	*Divided*	Republican	Split
1985–1986	*Divided*	Republican	Split
1987–1988	*Divided*	Republican	Democrats
1989–1990	*Divided*	Republican	Democrats
1991–1992	*Divided*	Republican	Democrats
1993–1994	Unified	Democrat	Democrats
1995–1996	*Divided*	Democrat	Republicans
1997–1998	*Divided*	Democrat	Republicans
1999–2000	*Divided*	Democrat	Republicans
2001–2002	*Divided*	Republican	Split[a]
2003–2004	Unified	Republican	Republicans
2004–2005	Unified	Republican	Republicans
2006–2008	*Divided*	Republican	Democrats
2009–2010	Unified	Democrat	Democrats

[a]Republicans briefly controlled the Senate in 2001, until Senator James Jeffords switched from Republican to independent on June 5, 2001.

some states, it has been a common occurrence (e.g., Illinois, Michigan, New York, Ohio). Following the 2008 elections, twenty-four states had divided partisan control between the governor and at least one house of the state legislature.

PARTY LOYALTY AS A BASIS FOR PRESIDENTIAL-CONGRESSIONAL COOPERATION

While the tensions between the president and Congress are substantial, the extent of conflict can be overstated. Partisanship does provide a basis for cooperation and for keeping inevitable conflicts within reasonable bounds. The claims of party loyalty are important within the Congress. Studies of roll call voting have consistently found that the best single predictor of the way members of Congress will vote is their party affiliation. With major portions of the congressional agenda determined by presidential policy initiatives, the party membership that the president shares with congressional colleagues is of substantial importance in promoting cooperation between the executive and legislature. Table 9.2 presents evidence of the extent of support received by presidents from their congressional party members and the opposition. In the forty-six years between 1954 and 2008, presidents have been able to count upon their party members in Congress to support them approximately two-thirds of the time. During the first year of the Obama administration, support came from Senate Democrats 72 percent of the time and from House Democrats the figure was 79 percent (see Table 9.2).

In seeking to influence the Congress, presidents tend to work closely with the elected party leadership of their party in the House and Senate. Party leaders on the Hill are normally quite supportive of presidential policy initiatives because they have a stake in the president's legislative successes. If the president fails in

TABLE 9.2	AVERAGE LEVEL OF CONGRESSIONAL SUPPORT FOR THE PRESIDENT'S POSITION, 1954–2008 (PERCENT)

Year	President	Members of the President's Party			Members of the Opposition Party		
		Party	House	Senate	Party	House	Senate
1954–1960	Eisenhower	Rep.	64	70	Dem.	46	44
1961–1963	Kennedy	Dem.	72	64	Rep.	37	40
1964–1968	Johnson	Dem.	68	58	Rep.	43	48
1969–1974	Nixon	Rep.	64	62	Dem.	44	41
1974–1976	Ford	Rep.	60	62	Dem.	38	47
1977–1980	Carter	Dem.	63	66	Rep.	37	46
1981–1988	Reagan	Rep.	64	74	Dem.	31	42
1989–1992	Bush	Rep.	69	77	Dem.	30	43
1993–2000	Clinton	Dem.	74	84	Rep.	31	38
2001–2008	Bush	Rep.	78	87	Dem.	21	50
2009–2010	Obama	Dem.	72	79	Rep.	26	50

Source: Norman J. Ornstein, Thomas E. Mann, and Michael J. Malbin, *Vital Statistics on Congress, 1999–2000* (Washington, D.C.: AEI Press, 2000), pp. 198–199; *Congressional Quarterly Weekly*, January 6, 2001, p. 61; *Congressional Quarterly Weekly*, January 11, 2010, p. 112. Used by permission.

gaining adoption of his or her legislative program, they also fail. Through acting as presidential spokespersons on Capitol Hill and as conduits for communication between the White House and the Capitol, party leaders gain influence and leverage with their congressional colleagues. They, therefore, zealously guard their prerogatives as the principal presidential contact persons within the Congress. Presidents also benefit from working through the party leadership in Congress. As David Truman has pointed out:

> The clock provides no hours for the cultivation of rank-and-file legislators which direct leadership of the Congress would require.... If the agenda ... [the President] ... sets is to emerge in a product he favors, he must have the information and means for day-to-day assessment, if not actual guidance of Congressional activity. The elective leaders wield no monopoly here, but standing as strategic communications points, they are, for the President as much as for their legislative associates, an important source of intelligence, entirely aside from their capabilities as facilitators or obstructers of his program.... Relations with the leaders of the Congressional party can be supplemented ... but no substitutes have appeared on which he can rely with equal confidence. To the degree that the mechanism of the Congressional party is relied upon, however, it must be taken as it is, with the leaders it has produced.[17]

Although the presidential–congressional leader relationship is, in Truman's words, "collaborative and mutually useful," it is not necessarily smooth. The most important constituency of congressional party leaders is not the president, but their legislative colleagues. To hold their leadership positions, they must protect the interests of their congressional colleagues. Thus, when President George W. Bush tried to pass his immigration plan through Congress in 2006, he was rebuffed by Republican leaders in the House who refused to bring the bill up for a vote since a majority of their caucus members opposed it. As a result, the measure was defeated and Bush was denied the possibility of signing a landmark piece of legislation during his second term.

In seeking to influence Congress, recent presidents have expanded the resources of the White House. Eisenhower created an Office of Congressional Relations in the White House to complement the formal party structures. Since then, this office has become one of the key units in the White House. It has a contingent of personal presidential lobbyists, who are dispatched daily to the Capitol to win votes for the administration's program. The Office of Congressional Relations also seeks to coordinate its activities with those of the congressional liaison personnel in each of the agencies of the executive branch. The White House also maintains an Office of Public Engagement, which was formerly called the Office of Public Liaison. Presidents have frequently used this office as an effective mobilizer of grassroots constituency and interest group pressures on Congress. President Obama appointed one of his closest and most trusted friends and advisers, Valerie Jarrett, to run the Office of Public Engagement, indicating the importance he places on that operation.

As the numbers in Table 9.2 demonstrate, presidents can rarely expect nearly unanimous support for their programs from party colleagues in Congress. Even if such support were forthcoming, it could be insufficient to pass legislation, because the president's party does not necessarily control the Congress. It is, therefore, often necessary for presidents to build bipartisan legislative coalitions. The recurring need for support on both sides of the aisle tends to dampen partisan conflict and forces bipartisan consultation on the formulation of legislation. It also permits members of both parties to claim credit for presidential policy initiatives that have support among legislators' constituencies. A dramatic example of a president having to rely on a bipartisan coalition to pass high-priority legislation occurred in 2001 when George W. Bush assiduously courted and cooperated with one of the Senate's most liberal Democrats, Ted Kennedy (Mass.), to win chamber passage of an education-reform bill.

Of course, the need for bipartisan support may create difficulties for the president within his or her own party. To the extent that he or she negotiates and makes deals with the opposition party in order to build legislative majorities, the president runs the risk of alienating his or her loyal supporters. Loyalists in the president's party often perceive that White House largesse seems to be flowing toward members of the opposition party, whom they view as less deserving than themselves. But if the president fails to accommodate some elements in the opposition, he or she is likely to leave the governance responsibilities unfulfilled. Balancing the need for both party loyalty and bipartisan support is a constant juggling act that presidents are compelled to perform.[18]

DOES UNITED OR DIVIDED PARTY CONTROL OF GOVERNMENT REALLY MAKE A DIFFERENCE IN LAWMAKING?

The discussion of party influence on presidential-congressional relations thus far has stressed that united party control of the government eases the president's burden in gaining congressional approval of his or her legislative agenda. Left as yet unanswered, however, is the question of whether or not united party control of the government is really critical to the passage of major, innovative legislation. Interestingly, exhaustive research by David R. Mayhew of major policy enactments from 1946 through 1994 reveals that there has been no great difference in the amount of major initiatives passed during periods of united versus divided party control of the government.[19] The basic reason for this unexpected finding is that lawmaking is affected by a variety of forces over and above party control of government and these forces tend to "even out" lawmaking across both conditions of united and divided party control.

It should be pointed out that Mayhew's conclusions, which stress the importance of factors other than whether or not there is united or divided government in evaluating legislative productivity, have been challenged recently by several political scientists who believe that divided government results in less important legislation being passed than is the case in united government.[20] The combination of intensified partisanship, intense battles for control of the House and Senate, and divided government in recent years has often led party leaders to shape legislative proposals and parliamentary maneuvers for their publicity value rather than their likelihood of enactment. In this kind of an environment, it takes uncommon leadership and skillful interbranch bargaining to overcome divergent political stakes and the resultant inertia. As congressional scholar Roger M. Davidson has observed,

> Frustration in achieving their policy goals psychologically wears down presidents, legislators, and their staffs. Policy decisions may be deferred or compromised so

severely that the solutions have little impact ... each blames the other for failing to resolve pressing national problems or enact coherent policies.[21]

Even issues that contain broad areas of agreement, such as adjustments in Social Security and health-care reform, invite partisan rhetoric and position taking. The debate over health-care reform in 2009 and 2010 provided just such an example of such heated partisan rhetoric. For example, when President Obama addressed a joint session of Congress to speak on behalf of the health-care reform legislation, he received a chilly response from Republicans. At one point, as Obama was making a claim about his health-care plan, Republican House member Joe Wilson shouted "you lie" from his seat in the chamber, a spectacular breech of etiquette that drew condemnation from members of both parties. And after the Senate cast its first health-care vote in December, 2009, Senator Jay Rockefeller (D-W. Va.) noted, "It has gotten so much more partisan. This was so wicked. This was venal."[22]

THE PARTY, THE PRESIDENT, AND THE EXECUTIVE BRANCH

For a president to influence the direction of national policy requires more than influence with Congress. The president must also exert influence *within* the executive branch because it is here that policy initiatives are developed and implemented. Government organization charts often depict the president at the pinnacle of the executive branch with direct control over the far-flung departments and agencies. Most presidents, however, have found organizational chart depictions of their power to be illusionary. A multitude of factors hamper presidents' ability to exercise effective control over the executive establishment.

Each agency and department has a separate congressionally enacted statutory mandate governing its organizational structure, policies, and budgets. Presidents and their appointees within the agencies must operate within the constraints imposed by these statutes. In addition, each agency has its own permanent civil service staff. These persons are committed to the mission of the agency and often have developed a policy orientation and style of operation—a bureaucratic culture—that even presidents find almost impossible to alter. Conservative presidents are normally highly suspicious of bureaucrats who administer what they perceive as liberal programs and who insist on maintaining these programs when the president sees less need for them. Liberal presidents often complain about the bureaucracy for different reasons. They see the bureaucracy as being unwilling to break out of its traditions and move in new directions. The federal bureaucracy is, however, essential for the successful administration of presidential policies. Presidents of either ideological stripe must, therefore, reconcile their style of operation with this relatively independent force within their administrations.[23] The programs administered by the various agencies develop a clientele of beneficiaries who have ties to the civil service and to the congressional committee members involved in passing agency authorizations and appropriations. These clientele groups are normally prepared to mobilize political influence to protect their interests within the agency. Therefore, cabinet secretaries charged with carrying out presidential policies are confronted frequently with having to cope with the combined influence of their department's bureaucracy, clientele groups, and attentive congresspersons and senators. Because any of these forces has the political resources to make the life of a cabinet officer difficult in the extreme, there is a tendency on the part of many department heads to come to an accommodation with these interests. However, to the extent that they become responsive to these so-called iron triangles, presidents lose influence over their cabinet officers. Presidents and White House staff are constantly concerned that cabinet secretaries will become more responsive to pressures arising within their departments than to presidential initiatives. The cross-pressures operating upon department heads were once captured in somewhat exaggerated form by President Coolidge's vice president, Charles Dawes, who quipped that "the members of the Cabinet are a President's natural enemies."[24] Presidential leadership of the executive branch has become more difficult in recent decades because of what Hugh Heclo calls "policy congestion." As the involvement of the government in society and the world has expanded, the policy concerns of the government have become more complex. "There are," Heclo concludes, "more issues to be coordinated affecting any given agency, and there are more agencies in need of coordination for any given issue." As a result, the president, "rather than simply deciding on the government agenda, is increasingly involved in sorting out relationships among agendas—for economic management, international affairs, social policy, intergovernmental relations, and so on."[25] The end product of this synthesis is apt to appear diffuse and unfocused. As a result, the executive branch has difficulty speaking with one voice, and presidents who seek to balance these conflicting values often appear ambiguous and indecisive.

The difficulties a president faces in trying to initiate and coordinate policies within the various federal departments and agencies were vividly on display in the aftermath of the September 11, 2001, terrorist attacks on the United States. To cope with the terrorism threat, President Bush designated a close friend and political ally, Pennsylvania governor Tom Ridge, to be director of the new White House Office on Homeland Security. Ridge was faced with the daunting task of overseeing forty-six federal agencies involved in counterterrorism. These agencies employed thousands of staff, while Ridge had only a small staff (twelve persons at the end of 2001). Congressional critics were quick to assert that Ridge lacked the authority to safeguard the country.[26] The massive expansion of governmental programs in the 1960s and 1970s has also spawned additional organized interests capable of political mobilization to protect their special policy interests. They range from grassroots neighborhood organizations, to state and local government officials who administer federal programs, to conservative public interest law firms, to high-priced Washington lawyers maneuvering to protect their clients' interests. There are now more interests to be reconciled by a president seeking to coordinate governmental policy.

By centralizing appointment decisions in the White House Personnel Office, presidential control and bureaucratic responsiveness to the White House have been increased. At the same time, there have been unintended and potentially less-than-desirable consequences. White House centralization of personnel decisions has permitted job seekers, interest groups, campaign contributors, and members of Congress to press their claims more directly upon the White House staff, moved more conflicts into the White House, and caused conflict between the appointments staff and administrative units.[27] Given the loose nature of American parties, appointment of fellow partisans does not assure a president that his or her appointees will be inclined to faithfully follow his or her policy initiatives. As previously noted, cabinet members often find it necessary to make an accommodation with their staffs, clientele groups, and congressional committees. In addition, prominent party leaders appointed to the cabinet have their own networks of supporters and are likely to be inclined toward periodic spells of independence.

White House staff operate in a quite different environment than do presidential appointees to the departments and agencies. In the White House, the president and his or her key aides reign supreme. Actions taken to facilitate presidential objectives bring rewards, not responsiveness to Congress, interest groups, or the civil service. Presidents have, therefore, tended to expand the size of the White House staff as a mechanism to monitor and supervise the rest of the executive branch. Of course, increasing the size of the White House staff in itself creates problems of control and increases the potential for elements of the staff to engage in activities that create embarrassments for the administration. For Republican presidents, the Office of Management and Budget (OMB) has been a key control and coordinating agency. Democratic presidents, who have had a greater interest in expanding governmental programs, have tended to rely more heavily on the domestic policy staff at the White House.[28] In both Republican and Democratic administrations, however, there is heavy reliance on the domestic and foreign policy staffs in the White House because of their responsiveness to presidential concerns. The creation of policy development and evaluation staffs within the White House, of course, creates tensions between the senior officials of the departments and their counterparts in the White House. The most notable recent example of such a conflict occurred when George W. Bush was determining whether to invade Iraq following 9/11. Secretary of State Colin Powell and Central Intelligence Director George Tenet had significant disagreements with White House foreign policy officials, as well as Vice President Dick Cheney, and Bush generally favored Cheney and the White House officials in these disputes.

Recent presidents have followed a variety of strategies designed to achieve control over the executive branch. Reagan's unusual success in controlling his administration can be attributed to four factors.[29] First, he and his key staff members dramatically limited their policy priorities and focused upon economic issues. The president was, therefore, perceived as rising above the policy congestion with a clear agenda for action. Second, the Reagan administration entered the White House with a program. It was, however, not so much a party program as it was a program developed by conservative policy activists. The Heritage Foundation, a conservative, Washington-based think tank, for example, produced a 1,080-page compilation of 1,270 policy recommendations for the administration. After the first year of the Reagan administration, the Foundation claimed that 61 percent of its recommendations had been acted upon.

A third factor in the administration's management strategy was finding a body of like-minded people to staff the executive branch. Loyalty to Reagan and to his conservative philosophy was an essential prerequisite for appointment. For example, John Kessel's comparative study of White House personnel has revealed that

Reagan appointees were not only highly conservative, but they showed a greater level of agreement with each other than did the staffs of Presidents Nixon and Carter.[30] Unlike Presidents Nixon and Carter, who allowed their department heads to have a free hand in filling subordinate positions, job applicants in the Reagan administration were checked out by the White House Personnel Office for their loyalty to the president's objectives. Indeed, the Reagan White House even went so far as to fill many of its subcabinet posts with conservative loyalists before cabinet officers were designated. As Bert Rockman, an expert on executive politics, has observed, Reagan "cabinet officers provided the administration's public face, but the subcabinet officials in particular were chosen for their commitment to the goals of the White House."[31] The final factor contributing to presidential control of the executive branch during the Reagan administration was a concerted effort to reinforce central rather than department loyalties among leaders of the executive branch. Initial policy proposals for the various departments were developed by transition teams of conservative activists from outside the government. The newly appointed heads, therefore, were given little time or opportunity to try and develop their own policy directives. In addition, much of the negotiation with the Congress on key issues was handled by White House staff personnel, not the various department heads. The administration also made extensive use of the cabinet councils—policy groups composed of cabinet members dealing with related policy matters and key White House staff members (e.g., the cabinet council on economic affairs).

Clinton, in staffing his administration, stressed gender and racial and ethnic diversity. This severely limited his ability to put people speedily in place and also made it difficult to build a team founded on clear and coherent directions.[32] The George W. Bush administration also faced problems caused by the increasingly intrusive checks into prospective appointees' finances, ethics, and personal backgrounds. These background checks by federal authorities inevitably created lengthy delays in the appointment process and prevented the president from actually having his own people staffing policy-making posts within federal agencies and departments even months after he had moved into the White House.

In all administrations, the party in the executive branch is used primarily for purposes of governing and not for the building up of the party organizations. The party in the executive, of course, is also a resource that can be used to help secure the president's renomination and reelection. It is not, however, an institution over which the party organization exerts substantial influence.

THE PARTY, THE PRESIDENT, AND THE JUDICIARY

The president and his or her White House staff can exert direct pressure upon the Congress and the executive branch. Party and presidential influences upon the judiciary, however, follow a much more indirect route—largely through the process of appointing federal judges. Presidents normally select approximately 90 percent of their judicial nominees from within the ranks of their own party. The impact of these appointments on judicial policy making can be profound. During his eight years in office, President Clinton appointed mainly liberal Democrats to 367 federal judgeships. His appointees (87.5 percent Democrats) constituted nearly half of the federal bench when he left office. During his two terms, President George W. Bush

| BOX 9.1 | NUCLEAR MELTDOWN IN THE U.S. SENATE? |

The filibuster in the Senate has been a key for empowering the minority party to bargain for compromises or to endlessly stall items the majority wishes to pass. It also becomes an important consideration in the confirmation of judicial nominees, effectively allowing a unified minority party the ability to veto nominees that are too far from the mainstream. In 2005, Republican leaders who were frustrated with Democratic filibusters of several of President Bush's nominees decided to attempt to ban the use of the filibuster on judicial nominations. While a two-thirds supermajority is necessary to change Senate rules, this "nuclear option" (so named because of the disastrous effect it would have had on civility and cooperation in the Senate) would have used parliamentary maneuvering to force a simple majority vote on ending filibustering on judicial nominees. Democrats quickly cried foul and threatened to delay all Senate business if the Republicans exercised the option. As the vote approached, fourteen Senators—seven Republicans and seven Democrats— broke from their parties to compromise. The Democratic members of the group agreed to allow votes on some of the nominees the Democrats had been filibustering, while the seven Republicans promised to vote against any attempt to change Senate rules during the 109th Congress. The compromise averted a potential partisan meltdown and proved that bipartisan compromise is still possible in the Senate.

appointed more than one-third of the federal appeals court judges who were on the bench at the end of his term in office. However, his influence on the courts was somewhat mitigated by the fact that only one-fourth of his appointees replaced a justice who had been appointed by Democratic president. During his first year in office, President Barack Obama appointed over twenty justices to the federal bench, 40 percent of whom were replacing a Republican appointee.

In making federal district and court of appeals appointments, presidents are forced to share power with their party's senators. The practice of senatorial courtesy enables senators of the president's party to block federal appointments within their own states if they disapprove of the nominee. To a significant degree, therefore, the initial screening of judicial candidates is done by senators of the president's party from the state in which the appointment is to be made. Because federal judicial appointments are among the most prized patronage plums at the disposal of a president and his party, there is often substantial jockeying for influence among home state senators of the president's party, the Justice Department, White House staff, concerned interest groups, bar associations, state party organizations, and presidential supporters from the state where the appointment will be made. The ultimate decision on a judicial nomination is a presidential prerogative. However, disputes between the Justice Department and senators of the president's party over judicial appointments within their home state can become rancorous if the president declines to nominate the individual preferred by a senator. In such cases, Senate colleagues are likely to rise in defense of senatorial courtesy by stalling all pending judicial nominations.

In those states in which there is no senator of the president's party, presidents normally give substantial weight to the recommendations of House members of the president's party, governors, and campaign officials. To a significant degree, any administration is dependent upon knowledgeable people within the states in making judicial appointments because the Justice Department and the White House staff do not have detailed knowledge of the legal fraternity in the various states.

In selecting nominees for the Supreme Court, the president has substantially more leeway than in making appointments to the federal district courts or the courts of appeals. The practice of senatorial courtesy does not operate in the confirmation process, though it is essential for presidents to nominate candidates capable of securing the necessary votes for confirmation by the full Senate. The direction of national judicial policy can be dramatically changed through Supreme Court appointments. The reliable liberal majorities that existed on the Warren Court have ceased to exist because Republican presidents were able to appoint a majority of the justices that currently sit on the Court, including two who were appointed by George W. Bush (Chief Justice John Roberts and Associate Justice Samuel Alito).

Because of the Supreme Court's potential to affect controversial public policy issues like abortion, affirmative action, and presidential war powers, it is not surprising that Court appointments can become an issue in presidential campaigns. In 2000, Democrats charged that Bush would appoint Supreme Court justices would deny women the right to have an abortion, while Bush stated that he would not impose a pro-life litmus test on judicial nominees. In 2008, Barack Obama made the Supreme Court an issue again, particularly by playing to fears that a McCain presidency would create an even more conservative Court. While only 7 percent of voters reported that future Supreme Court appointments were the most important factor in determining their vote, Obama won 57 percent of these voters. As judicial politics expert Sheldon Goldman has aptly observed, "when we elect a president, we're electing a judiciary."[33]

RECENT APPOINTMENTS TO THE SUPREME COURT

Prior to Bush's second term, there had not been a vacancy on the Supreme Court since 1994. In 2005, the Court suddenly had two vacancies to fill due to the retirement of Sandra Day O'Connor and the subsequent death of Chief Justice William Rehnquist. Prior to Rehnquist's death, Bush nominated John Roberts to fill O'Connor's seat on the Court. However, when Rehnquist passed away, Bush nominated Roberts for Chief Justice. The Roberts nomination proceeded relatively smoothly. While he drew some opposition from liberal interest groups concerned about his record on civil rights, Roberts' relatively short record as a judge and his much-praised performance during the Senate confirmation hearings led to an easy confirmation. The final vote was 78–22, with the entire Republican caucus unified in favor of his confirmation and the Democratic Party split 22–22 (James Jeffords, an independent, voted in favor of the confirmation).

While the Roberts confirmation went smoothly, Bush ran into a significantly more difficult time with his nomination for the second vacant seat on the Court. His first nominee for the position was Harriet Miers, a longtime friend who worked as White House counsel. Her nomination quickly drew criticism not just from liberal Democrats but also from the conservative Republican base, whose reaction to her quickly sank her nomination. In the 1980s, Miers donated to the presidential campaign of Al Gore and the Democratic National Committee. Conservatives were concerned not only with her prior support for Democrats but also her seeming lack of consistency on issues such as abortion. Many Republican senators openly criticized her nomination, an indication that her confirmation was very much in doubt. Within a few weeks of Bush naming her as his nominee, Miers withdrew from consideration for confirmation to the Court.

After the repudiation from the right on the Miers nomination, Bush sought to reach out to the Republican base by nominating Samuel Alito. Unlike Miers, Alito was a favorite of conservatives based on his fifteen-year record as a conservative federal judge. But in appealing to Republican conservatives, Bush drew criticism from much of the Democratic Party. While they had been relatively quiet during the Roberts confirmation hearing, liberal interest groups geared up to strongly oppose the Alito nomination. Alito's confirmation was less certain prior to his hearing in the Senate Judiciary Committee, and even after the hearing, Senator John Kerry (D-Mass.) led an attempt to filibuster to keep the Senate from confirming him. Ultimately, the filibuster failed by a vote of 72–25 and Alito was confirmed by a vote of 58–42. Alito's vote was not nearly as bipartisan as Roberts'—all but four Democrats voted against confirming him to the Court—but his confirmation to the Senate did succeed, much to the delight of the conservative Republican base.

Just a few months after taking office, President Barack Obama had his first opportunity to nominate a Supreme Court justice when David Souter announced his retirement from the court. Obama selected Sonia Sotomayor, who was originally a U.S. District Court justice appointed by George H.W. Bush and later was placed on the U.S. Court of Appeals by President Clinton. Sotomayor's nomination created some controversy, as has been common with recent nominations, but given the large Democratic majority in the Senate, the confirmation never seemed to be in much doubt. The Senate voted 68–31 to confirm Sotomayor, with every Democrat and nine Republicans voting in favor of confirmation, who became the first Hispanic to serve on the Court.

PARTIES IN CONGRESS

From the period after World War I until the 1980s, the congressional environment was not conducive to high levels of party unity or strong leadership by the parties, and even in the current era of almost record-high levels of party unity and intense partisan conflict between Republicans and Democrats, there are forces that limit the strength and unity of the parties. The party leadership of Congress has been forced to adapt to the fact that members of the House and Senate are individually responsible for their own renomination and reelection. Because the congressional party organizations can guarantee members neither safe seats nor extensive campaign resources in return for loyalty on roll call votes, members frequently assume a highly independent orientation when voting on the House and Senate floor. They must protect themselves with their constituents, irrespective of party policy positions.

As noted previously, the separation-of-powers system further reduces the incentives for party loyalty within the party of the president. Unlike parliamentary system participants, members of Congress who desert their president on key votes do not risk losing control of the executive branch or the calling of new

BOX 9.2 | WHAT DO MEMBERS OF CONGRESS ADVERTISE ON THEIR WEB SITES? EVERYTHING BUT THEIR PARTY

It has long been understood by congressional scholars that incumbent members of Congress tend to be committed first and foremost to their constituents, not their party, a factor that makes life more difficult for congressional party leaders. In fact, the desire of members to downplay their partisan affiliation affects how they present themselves in a wide array of forums, even the Internet. When Sharon E. Jarvis and Kristen Wilkerson analyzed the content of House members' Web pages in 2001, they found that all members presented information about things they were doing for their constituents. Most also provided a biography of the member, a discussion of state concerns, and legislation the member was promoting in Congress. However, members were not eager to mention their party affiliation on their homepages. In fact, only 17 percent of House members in 2001 made note of their party; not even Nancy Pelosi (Calif.), who was then Democratic Whip, identified herself as a Democrat on her Web site.

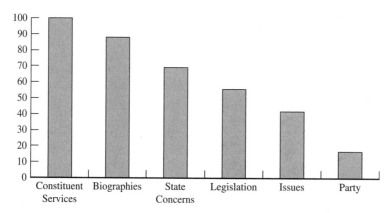

Source: Sharon E. Jarvis and Kristen Wilkerson, "Congress on the Internet: Messages on the Homepages of the U.S. House of Representatives, 1996 and 2001," Journal of Computer-Mediated Communication (Vol. 10, No. 2) January 2005.

congressional elections. The Constitution assures both the president and members of Congress fixed terms in office, even when presidential programs lack congressional support.

The parties of Congress also have to contend with the committee/subcommittee system, which has major responsibility for the development of policy proposals. Strong congressional committees and subcommittees result in power over various aspects of public policy being scattered among hundreds of House and Senate subcommittees and committees. With each committee and subcommittee zealously guarding its jurisdiction and prerogatives, policy development and coordination by congressional party leaders is extremely difficult.

Although electoral forces and institutional arrangements operate to frustrate party influence within Congress, evidence of partisanship abounds in the organizational structure, decision making, and social life of Congress. Although it is not an

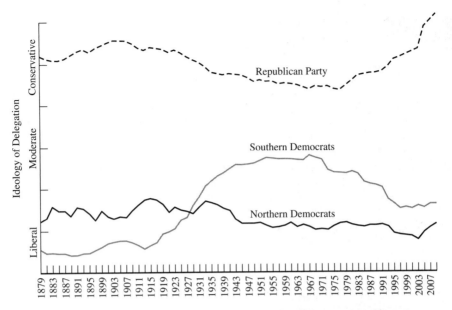

FIGURE 9.1 | MEAN IDEOLOGY OF ROLL VOTING BY REPUBLICANS AND NORTHERN AND SOUTHERN DEMOCRATS IN THE HOUSE OF REPRESENTATIVES, 1879–2009

Source: Keith T. Poole, University of California at San Diego, http://voteview.com

all-pervasive or disciplined type of partisanship, it is nevertheless an everpresent influence that has grown stronger since the mid-1980s.

This intensification of partisanship is mainly the result of changes in the composition of the parties' membership in Congress. As a consequence of the electoral realignment in the South, there has been a sharp decline in the proportion of conservative southerners among House and Senate Democrats, as well as a corresponding increase in conservative Republican members from the region. The southern Democrats that do remain are more ideologically liberal than their predecessors, meaning that the Democratic Party in Congress is now more cohesive and more liberal (see Figure 9.1). At the same time, northeastern moderate Republicans have gradually been replaced by liberal Democrats, producing a more cohesive and conservative Republican Party in Congress as well. The net result of these membership changes has been the creation of two polarized parties, each of which is united in terms of ideology and policy orientation. One is overwhelmingly conservative and the other is overwhelmingly liberal. Few members can now find like-minded colleagues on the other side of the aisle, as they did in the 1950s–1980s. This condition works against bipartisan cooperation and instead produces intense partisan conflict. The sharp policy disagreements between congressional Republicans and Democrats spring from and are reinforced by the sharp differences that exist over policy between the activists within each party and, to a lesser extent, the differences between the parties' rank-and-file voters.

Another factor contributing to heightened partisanship is the narrow margins by which the parties have controlled the House and Senate, especially since 1994.

This is in sharp contrast to the decades from the 1950s through the 1970s when the Democrats were assured of majority status. As long as party control of the House and Senate was safely in Democratic hands, the two congressional parties were only minimally affected by maneuvering designed to influence who would have majority status in the next election, and bipartisan cooperation was possible. All that changed when the GOP gained control of Congress by narrow margins after the 1994 election. With just a few seats now capable of determining which party would have majority status, partisan maneuvering for advantage in the next election has become a constant feature of congressional politics. If there was one thing that the members of both parties have learned and agreed upon since 1994, it is that it is much better to be a member of the majority rather than the minority party.

EVIDENCE OF PARTISANSHIP

Congress is organized on a highly partisan basis. Members of the majority party hold the key leadership posts—Speaker of the House, majority floor leader of the Senate, and all committee and subcommittee chairships in each chamber. By holding these positions, the majority party maintains procedural control of the Congress. This enables the majority-party leadership to determine which bills will be scheduled for action, as well as when they will be on the agenda and under what conditions. With majority status, there are other benefits as well—additional staff assistance to facilitate action on policies supported by the members of the party, and committee ratios of Democrats to Republicans that assure the majority party of at least a numerical advantage in each committee and subcommittee. In the House, for example, the majority party has set the ratio of majority to minority members of key committees, such as Rules, Ways and Means, and Appropriations, at a level that assures the majority party of control on most issues. These majority-party advantages often make life in the minority a frustrating experience. In the 1980s and until 1994, when they gained control of the House after forty years in the wilderness of minority status, Republicans grew increasingly frustrated. With the combative Newt Gingrich (Ga.) as their leader, a group of junior Republican members decided to forego attempts to win minor concessions from the majority Democrats through cooperation and compromise. Instead, they adopted a highly confrontational style on the House floor designed to raise issues that could be used in the next election. A leader of these aggressive and highly conservative Republicans explained their actions as follows:

> There is ... a sense of trying to force confrontation as a ... permanent way for the Republican minority to operate. More confrontation rather than cooperation.... Another way to put it from our perspective would be that we receive absolutely none of the benefits for helping you guys [Democrats] pass your bills. We're never going to be committee chairmen as long as we're in the minority. We're never going to move up, we're never going to be subcommittee chairmen, and as long as we don't have that option, we'll confront instead of cooperate.[34]

With the Congress under the control of Republicans after the 1994 elections, it was the Democrats' turn to feel the frustrations that go with minority status, especially in the House of Representatives. As the House Republicans exhibited a high

| BOX 9.3 | HOW PARTY LEADERS USE THE RULES TO THEIR ADVANTAGE |

While congressional party leaders do not always demonstrate great power in compelling their members to vote a particular way, their influence can be felt through the imaginative use of parliamentary rules. For example, occasionally party leaders can use their discretion in scheduling and managing floor votes to win when they might have otherwise lost. In 2003, Republican leaders held a vote on Medicare legislation in the middle of the night, a vote they were about to lose by a narrow margin. To prevent defeat, they held the vote open for three hours, much longer than the fifteen minutes normally allotted, until they were able to convince two Republican members to switch their votes. A frustrated Nancy Pelosi (D-Calif.) complained that the vote had been "stolen" and that Democrats should have "won it fair and square." However, when they held power, Democrats also used this trick from time to time.

Because Republicans maintained only a small majority after taking control of the House in 1994, they often used the rules to their advantage in other ways as well. For example, before they lost control of Congress after the 2006 elections, Republicans were becoming increasingly apt to limit the ability of members to offer amendments to legislation that might be unwanted by the leadership. Through the Rules Committee, party leaders can restrict what, if any, amendments members can propose to legislation being considered. While Republicans initially reduced the use of such restrictive rules when they came to power in 1995, they used them extensively after 2001, employing the restrictions on more than two of every three bills considered in 2003–2004. After regaining control of Congress in 2007, Democrats continued the trend toward using more restrictive rules. During the 110th Congress, just 12 percent of all bills in the House were considered under an open rule, while nearly nine of every ten pieces of legislation were debated under restricted rules.

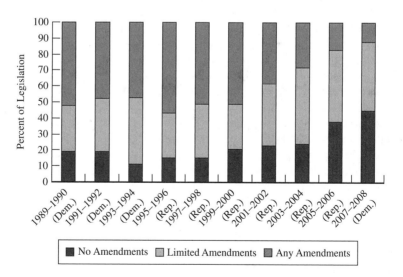

Source: Susan Milligan, "Back-Room Dealing a Capitol Trend," Boston Globe, October 3, 2004; Richard E. Cohen, Kirk Victor, and David Baumann, "The State of Congress," National Journal, January 9, 2004. Data for the 109th and 110th Congresses come from Sarah A. Binder, Thomas E. Mann, Norman J. Ornstein, and Molly Reynolds, "Assessing the 110th Congress, Anticipating the 111th," Mending the Broken Branch 3 (Washington, D.C.: Brookings Institute, 2009).

degree of party unity and now exercised the same sorts of powers that the Democrats had previously used to severely limit minority-party influence over legislation, Democrats complained about being shut out of a meaningful decision-making role. These minority party frustrations have continued in the first decade of the twenty-first century as party control changed hands again in 2007.

The parties tend to loom large in the minds of junior members because it is through the congressional party organizations that members receive their committee assignments. Assignment to preferred committees is often essential, especially in the House, if members are to achieve such congressional career goals as reelection, power in the chamber, or policy influence.[35] During the days immediately after their first election and before they have even taken the oath of office, members-elect must campaign among their senior party colleagues for support in gaining good committee assignments. Thus, at the beginning of their life in the Congress, they are confronted with the importance of partisanship. Often the leadership will impress upon members the importance of loyalty before granting assignment to a key committee.

The party leadership is also important as a source of needed information—the legislative schedule, the expected outcome of a roll call, the position of the president on a key amendment, the strategy of interest groups on an issue, and the electoral consequences of a yea or nay vote. The party leaders are obviously not the only source of information on such matters, but with their larger staffs and wide range of political contacts, they are an important source of political intelligence for rank-and-file members. The leadership can also be extremely useful in helping members acquire the financial resources for reelection campaigns.

The social contacts of members of Congress tend to be within their own party. The physical layout of the two chambers encourages this. The House and Senate floor arrangements feature a center aisle with the Democrats on one side, the Republicans on the other. One's seatmates, with whom one shares information, political gossip, and small talk, are fellow partisans. The same pattern holds true in the committee and subcommittee meeting rooms, where the seating arrangement divides the members of the two parties. Even the cloakrooms off the House and Senate floors are segregated along party lines.

Partisanship is also encouraged because of the ideological bonds that exist among party members in Congress. Most national legislators share strong ideological affinities. Through their political socialization processes, fellow partisans come to develop compatible ideological orientations. They are also likely to have a common interest in supporting similar voter groups and interest groups.

The extent of partisanship in the Congress may also be seen in member voting patterns on House and Senate roll calls. Figure 9.2 shows the percentage of time that a majority of voting Republicans have aligned themselves against a majority of voting Democrats on roll call votes in the House and Senate between 1879 and 2008. Since 1960, the percentage of party votes in the two chambers steadily increased to a high point in the 1994–1995 House, the first Congress after Republicans took control of both chambers. This indicates the increased partisanship in Congress during the past few decades. However, when viewed in historical perspective, the recent level of partisan division portrayed in Figure 9.2 constitutes a decline from the period around the turn of the previous century, when over

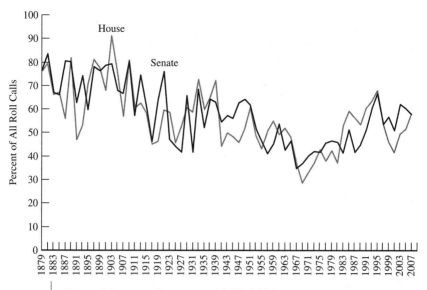

FIGURE **9.2** | PARTY VOTES IN CONGRESS, 1879–2008

Source: Keith T. Poole, University of California at San Diego, http://voteview.com

70 percent of House roll calls involved a majority from each party voting on opposite sides.[36] Similarly, the current levels of partisan voting in Congress appear low when compared to the more intense partisanship found in other Western democracies. However, considering that each chamber held between 800 and 1,000 roll calls during each Congress (a two-year period) and that many of the bills were of a minor or noncontroversial character, the data in Figure 9.2 give evidence of substantial partisan division within the House and Senate.

The extent of partisanship in Congress can be explored further by examining the degree of party unity on those roll calls that pit a majority of Democrats against a majority of Republicans. Figures 9.3 and 9.4 show the percentage of Republicans and Democrats voting in agreement with a majority of their party colleagues on issues that divided the two parties. The data from 1879 to 2008 reveal that average party unity scores for a session of the Congress have rarely dipped below 75 percent and have climbed to above 85 percent in recent years. The data show substantial evidence of partisanship and party loyalty that has been trending upward since the mid-1980s. Recent levels of party unity are comparable to those at the beginning of the twentieth century, when congressional partisanship was at an apex.

Yet, even in a highly partisan era, not all members support consistently support their party's position. Consider intraparty disunity in the House and Senate in the first year of the 111th Congress (2009). Twenty or more members of each party's caucus supported a majority of their party colleagues on fewer than 80 percent of the roll call votes. Two Democratic House members actually voted against their party a majority of their time on party-line votes. Not surprisingly, both of these legislators represented districts in Republican states; one represented constituents

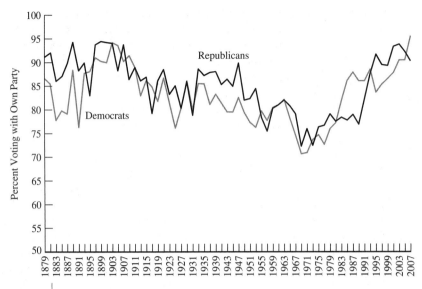

FIGURE **9.3** | PARTY UNITY IN THE HOUSE OF REPRESENTATIVES, 1879–2008

Source: Keith T. Poole, University of California at San Diego, http://voteview.com

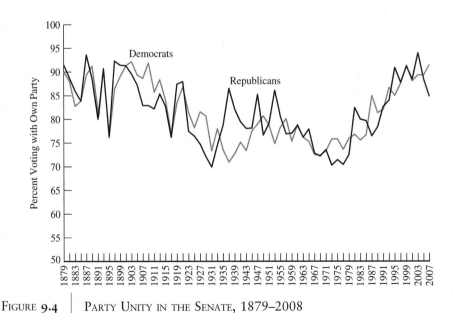

FIGURE **9.4** | PARTY UNITY IN THE SENATE, 1879–2008

Source: Keith T. Poole, University of California at San Diego, http://voteview.com

in Idaho while the other represented Alaska. Senators also displayed significant variation in their support for the party. Ben Nelson (D-Neb.) and Evan Bayh (D-Ind.), both representing traditionally Republican states, voted against their party more than one-third of the time. On the other side of the aisle, Susan Collins (R-Maine) and Olympia Snowe (R-Maine) dissented from their party on over half of all partisan roll call votes, a pattern that is undoubtedly related to the fact that President Obama won nearly 60 percent of the vote in their state in 2008.

While senators and representatives do not move in lock step to support the position of their leaders, it is clear that both parties on Capitol Hill have become substantially more unified in recent years. Even so, the internal cleavages that exist within the congressional parties and the resulting lack of party unity mean that legislative majorities must sometimes be forged with bipartisan coalitions. For example, when President Bush and congressional leaders were faced with the financial crisis in 2008, they found it necessary to push a highly unpopular bailout package through Congress. Facing significant opposition from members of both parties, the Republican president teamed with Democratic leaders in Congress to build a bipartisan coalition of legislators willing to support the bill. The legislation ultimately passed the House with 91 Republicans and 172 Democrats voting in favor.

PARTY ORGANIZATION IN THE HOUSE

Because of its large size (435 members), the House has rules that strictly regulate the processing of legislation and limit the effectiveness of dilatory tactics. These rules, which bring an element of order to the chamber and enable it to fulfill its legislative responsibilities, also have the effect of severely limiting the power of the minority party and individual members. In the House, the majority party, if it is reasonably united, is in a position to work its will on most issues, and minority-party and individual members have only the most restricted powers of delay and obstruction. These procedural rules strengthen the position of the party leaders, especially the Speaker and majority floor leader, who tend to dominate the setting of the House agenda (see Box 9.3—"How Party Leaders Use the Rules to Their Advantage"). Table 9.3 outlines the House and Senate party leadership positions for 2009–2010.

THE SPEAKER OF THE HOUSE   The most prominent and influential member of the House is its Speaker, who serves as both its presiding officer and the leader of the majority party. Early in this century, the speakership was brought to the zenith of its power by the legendary and autocratic Joseph G. Cannon ("Uncle Joe"), an Illinois Republican who served as Speaker from 1903 to 1911. He dominated his party and the House through his extensive formal powers, which he used aggressively to ensure that his faction of the Republican Party controlled the House. These powers included serving as presiding officer of the House, controlling member committee assignments, designating committee chairs, whom he both appointed and removed, and regulating the work schedule of the House through his chairship of the Committee on Rules. Cannon, however, lost his majority on procedural issues within the House during 1910 and 1911. In a revolt

Table 9.3 | Party Leadership in the 111th Congress, 2009–2010

House of Representatives

Speaker
(Nominated by the Republicans and elected by the full house)

Majority Party (Democrats)	Minority Party (Republicans)
Floor Leader	Floor Leader
Whip	Whip
Caucus Chairman	Conference Chairman
Policy Committee Chairman (Position held by minority floor leader. Committee helps develop party policy.)	Policy Committee Chairman (Committee helps develop party policy.)
Steering Committee Chairman (Position held by minority floor leader. Committee makes Democratic committee assignments.)	Steering Committee Chairman (Position held by the Speaker. Committee makes Republican committee assignments.)
Chief Deputy Whips	Chief Deputy Whips
Democratic Congressional Campaign Committee Chairman (Committee recruits and supports Democratic House candidates.)	National Republican Congressional Committee Chairman (Committee recruits and supports Republican House candidates.)

Senate

President Pro Tempore
(Most senior member in terms of service in the majority party)

Majority Party (Democrats)	Minority Party (Republicans)
Floor Leader	Floor Leader
Whip	Whip
Conference Chairman (Position held by minority floor leader.)	Conference Chairman
Policy Committee Chairman (Position held by minority floor leader. Committee consults on policy.)	Policy Committee Chairman (Committee consults on policy research.)
Policy Committee Co-Chairman	
Conference Secretary	Conference Secretary
Steering and Coordination Committee (Committee makes Democratic committee assignments.)	Committee on Committees Chairmen (Committee makes Republican committee assignments.)
Chief Deputy Whip	Chief Deputy Whip

continued

TABLE 9.3	PARTY LEADERSHIP IN THE 111TH CONGRESS, 2009–2010 *continued*

Senate	
Majority Party (Democrats)	Minority Party (Republicans)
Technology and Communications Committee Chairman (Develops methods of communicating party message.)	
Democratic Senatorial Campaign Committee Chairman (Committee recruits and supports Democratic senatorial candidates.)	National Republican Senatorial Committee Chairman (Committee recruits and supports Republican senatorial candidates.)

of Progressive Republicans and Democrats, the Speaker was stripped of his position as chair of the Rules Committee, his power to make committee assignments, and some of his powers to recognize members on the floor. The formal powers of modern Speakers are not as extensive as those that were available to Cannon; modern Speakers must lead their parties and the House by relying more heavily on informal means—persuasion, bargaining, and negotiation.

In the 1970s, the Democrats made a series of rule changes that revived some of the formal power of the Speaker. The Speaker was made chair of the Steering and Policy Committee, which made committee assignments for Democratic members. This gave the Speaker the ability to exert a significant impact on the careers of rank-and-file members and to influence the composition and therefore the policy orientation of committees. The Speaker was also given authority to name Democratic members of the Rules Committee and through the Rules Committee to control the flow of the legislation to the floor as well as the procedures under which bills were considered by the House. As the presiding officer of the House, the Speaker is also in a position to make strategically important parliamentary rulings. Backed by a relatively cohesive party membership, these formal powers in the hands of an aggressive speaker, such as Jim Wright (D-Tex., 1986–1989) or the previously mentioned Newt Gingrich (1995–1998), provide the bases for strong and policy-oriented party leadership.

Even though recent Democratic and Republican Speakers have been able to centralize power to a degree that was unknown in the House from the 1950s through the 1970s, there is one political reality with which all Speakers must cope. This is the fact that their power is only as great as their colleagues will permit. When significant numbers of their party colleagues become disenchanted and withdraw support out of concern for policy outcomes and/or electoral survival, then the power of the Speaker is threatened.[37]

NEWT GINGRICH AND THE REPUBLICAN REVOLUTION   In 1994, the Republicans won a stunning electoral victory and took control of both chambers of Congress for the first time in 40 years. Newt Gingrich's rise and fall are illustrative of the possibilities and perils faced by party leaders in Congress.[38] According to congressional scholar David Rhode, several characteristics were important in giving Gingrich unprecedented influence when Republicans took control of the House in 1995:[39]

- The congressional parties were more ideologically polarized and cohesive than they had been in decades. A more homogenous party is easier to lead because intraparty disagreements are less common and leaders do not have to worry as much about defections.
- Despite the stunning victory, Republicans only held a narrow majority in the House. This meant that any missteps by the House Republicans could possibly cost them their majority in the next election. In addition, such a narrow majority meant that every Republican vote in Congress was important for the success of the party's policies. Thus, Gingrich often appealed to members of the party by citing the importance of party unity given the narrow margin for error.
- Gingrich was credited by most House Republicans, particularly first- and second-term members, as being responsible for the party's return to power. As a result, these party members were willing to trust Gingrich as Speaker when the 104th Congress convened.
- Gingrich also displayed personal leadership skills that complemented the situation. As Rhode explains, "He wanted power, he was willing to exercise it, and exhibited significant skills in using it."[40] While Gingrich would eventually make some mistakes that would cost him and the party, he demonstrated considerable leadership skills as Republicans took power.

Shortly after the Republicans took over Congress in 1994, Gingrich took a number of steps to consolidate power among the party leaders. Many of these steps dealt with undermining the power of committees and their chairs since they represented a competing source of power in Congress. He took unprecedented control over committee assignments and control over which Republicans would serve on the powerful House Rules Committee. He used these powers to select committee chairs (who would support his legislative agenda), sometimes in violation of the seniority principle. And, like his Democratic predecessors, he used the Rules Committee to develop procedures for consideration of legislation that would severely limit the influence of the minority party. In the first one hundred days of the 104th Congress in 1995, the Gingrich-led Republicans succeeded in gaining House passage of an almost unprecedented amount of major legislation that was contained in their ten-point campaign manifesto: the Contract with America.

Gingrich's first year as Speaker appeared to represent the most powerful party leadership in the House since Joseph Cannon, but subsequent years illustrated just how limited his influence was. At the end of 1995, budget negotiations between President Clinton and the Republican leadership broke down and forced a shutdown of the federal government. Eventually, public opinion sided with Clinton, not the Republicans, and Gingrich was forced to compromise on key pieces of the Republican agenda to end the shutdown. This budget compromise and shifting public opinion led to the first erosion of trust among rank-and-file House Republicans. In 1997, Gingrich was threatened by a revolt led by the most conservative members of his party, who believed that he was failing to deliver on the conservative agenda

| BOX 9.4 | DECLINING CIVILITY IN THE FACE OF POLARIZATION |

When Republicans took control of Congress in 1995, it ended a long period of Democratic dominance. Democrats now had to deal with minority status for the first time in their careers, while Republicans were learning to cope with being the majority party. The increased polarization in Congress and the thin margins by which Republicans controlled the chamber further stressed interparty relations. During this period of increased partisanship, the partisan battles in Congress occasionally became physical and even involved Capitol Hill police:

- In 1995, while the House was debating U.S. involvement in Bosnia, Representatives Randy "Duke" Cunningham (R-Cal.) and Jim Moran (D-Va.) got in a shoving match on Capitol Hill that required the intervention of police officers.
- Also in 1995, an episode that became known as "the brawl in the hall" was captured on television cameras. Several members of a House committee engaged in a shouting match, and Representative Sam Gibbons (D-Fla.) yanked the necktie of Representative Bill Thomas (R-Cal.).
- In 1997, Tom DeLay was involved in a shoving match with Representative David Obey (D-Wisc.) on the floor of the House of Representatives.
- In 2003, Democrats on the House Ways and Means Committee used a parliamentary maneuver to gain time to strategize in a meeting room adjacent to where the committee hearing was taking place. Thomas, the committee chairman, was frustrated by the move and instructed Capitol Hill police to evict the Democrats from the room.

and was too accommodating to President Clinton and party moderates. Gingrich was able to quell this attempted coup, but he was left in a weakened position due to factionalism between moderates and conservatives within his own party's ranks, each of whom could exert leverage on the Speaker because his party's majority in the House was only eleven seats. When the GOP lost five seats in 1998, Gingrich's position was further weakened, and with only a six-seat majority in the Chamber, he chose to resign.

MADAM SPEAKER: NANCY PELOSI   When the Democratic Party won control of Congress following the 2006 midterm elections, Nancy Pelosi (D-Calif.) was in line to become the first female Speaker of the House. Pelosi has achieved power in the chamber that is comparable to what Newt Gingrich enjoyed in the 1990s. In 2009, Congressional Quarterly noted that Pelosi was "as hard-nosed as any high-level figure in Washington" and described the effectiveness of her top-down leadership style in bringing "unity to a group that had been known for infighting." During her first two years in office, Pelosi's primary challenge was to manage a narrow Democratic majority in the chamber during the last two years of the Bush presidency. Her biggest challenge came in the fall of 2008 when she marshaled the votes necessary to pass a wildly unpopular $700 billion bill to rescue the nation's financial institutions (though the legislation failed an initial vote). In many ways, Pelosi's job became much tougher after Democrats captured the White House and built up the largest House majority (257 Democrats) that either party had enjoyed since 1994. The expanded Democratic majority also meant more ideological heterogeneity, particularly since many of the new Democrats came from traditionally Republican districts. Nevertheless, Pelosi succeeded in achieving the majorities necessary to pass even the most controversial programs such as economic stimulus legislation and health-care reform.

She did this by creating a leadership structure in the House that was filled with members loyal to her and has used this team to cajole rank-and-file members of the party into supporting the party's agenda. But Pelosi often does her own cajoling as well. Indeed, Pelosi's hands-on leadership style was never more evident than when she had to muster the necessary votes to pass the health-care reform legislation in 2010. Many Democrats were on the fence and concerned about their reelection prospects if they voted for the bill. When the Democratic leadership identified sixty-eight members that they would need to lobby, she did not follow the usual routine of dividing the names among her whips; instead, she told them, "I'll take all 68." Pelosi successfully lobbied her members to support the legislation, which narrowly passed the House. As Republican Majority Leader John Boehner admitted, "She is a strong speaker, there isn't any question about that."[41] As proof of her strength as Speaker, Democrats won 473 of the 502 (94 percent) party-line votes in 2009.

| BOX 9.5 | WHAT EXPLAINS DEMOCRATIC DEFECTIONS ON HEALTH-CARE REFORM? |

Late on a Sunday evening in March, 2010, 431 members of the House of Representatives cast historical votes on a major reform of the nation's health care system. Public opinion polls showed that the public was deeply divided on the issue, mostly along partisan lines. All 178 Republican House members were unified in their opposition to the legislation. After a significant amount of lobbying, Speaker Nancy Pelosi and the Democratic leaders were able to convince 219 Democrats to vote in favor of the bill, despite the fact that many worried the vote might significantly damage their prospects of being reelected. In trying to explain why thirty-four Democrats who voted against the bill went against their party to do so, a single reason stands out: re-election. Consider the following statistics regarding these thirty-four Democratic "no" votes:

- Twenty-six of these thirty-four Democrats represented districts that McCain had won in 2008.
- Eight of the thirty-four Democratic "no" votes came from members serving their first terms in office. Generally speaking, a House member's most difficult re-election campaign is their first one.
- Six of the thirty-four had won their previous re-election campaign by less than 5 percent of the vote.
- At least seventeen of the thirty-four members were listed by news organizations as facing a difficult re-election campaign in 2010.

When members vote against their parties on important votes, it is often because doing otherwise would put their seats at risk. The 2010 health care vote was no exception.

THE FLOOR LEADERS   Within the majority party, the Speaker's principal associate is the floor leader, who normally acts as the key party spokesperson and strategist on the House floor. With the Speaker, the floor leader helps to plan the legislative schedule of the House. He or she carries major responsibilities for persuading his or her colleagues to support party leadership positions on House votes and must also spend time talking with colleagues to gauge members' sentiments on various issues. Following the exit of Gingrich from the speakership, the majority leader took on a greater role by complementing Speaker Dennis Hastert. John Boehner (R-Ohio), who became majority leader in 2006 after DeLay was forced to resign the position because of ethics charges, had wide latitude in handling the day-to-day operations in the House. As Boehner noted, "[Hastert's] style is to let the majority leader lead."[42] However, Pelosi's hands-on leadership style has reduced the role of the majority leader since the Democrats regained control of Congress in 2006.

The minority floor leader is the highest-ranking position within his or her party. He or she is responsible for serving as party spokesperson and defender on the floor, developing legislative strategy to advance the minority goals, building bridges to dissident members of the opposition, and keeping in touch with the sentiments of his or her party colleagues. When his or her party controls the presidency, the minority leader has the responsibility of acting as a spokesperson for the White House and for advancing its legislative program. During the Reagan and Bush administrations, Republican leader Robert Michel of Illinois often found that serving the needs of the White House and his colleagues was extremely difficult. On the one hand, it was frequently necessary to make concessions to the majority Democrats in order to fashion a majority on the House floor. But frequently such concessions were not well received by his own hard-core partisans, who were seeking confrontations with the opposition to develop issues for the next election. Former House leader Richard Gephardt (D-Mo.) faced similar problems and frequently asserted his own and his Democratic colleagues' opposition to policies of the Clinton White House, including such key issues as welfare reform and trade. When the minority leader shares the same party as the president, he or she is constantly torn between his or her party's obligations to govern (thereby downplaying partisanship) and the party's desire for majority status.

Without the constraints imposed by having to maneuver a president's legislative program through the House, the minority leader gains considerable leeway in developing policy positions for his or her party, provided the leader stays in close touch with the sentiments of the party membership in the chamber. In these circumstances, the minority leader not only becomes the advocate for colleagues in the House, but also becomes one of the party's most prominent national spokespersons in the media on policy issues.

THE WHIPS   Both parties have assistant leaders known as whips. The term derives from the English hunt, where the job of the whip was to keep the dogs together. Similarly, the duty of the party whips is to encourage party discipline. The whips do not have the formal authority to "whip" their colleagues into line. Rather, they are information brokers, responsible for collecting and disseminating information to and from the rank-and-file. To the party members, whips provide information about the House schedule and where the party stands on the issues coming up for a vote. They often even provide members with evidence supporting the party's position as well as information about what messages members should be promoting to constituents and the news media on various issues. To the party leaders, whips report the sentiments of members on pieces of legislation by making advance nose counts to determine the likelihood for success of a leadership position on the floor. At times, whips even attempt to persuade members to vote with the party.

Each party has an elaborate whip organization composed of a deputy whip and regional whips responsible for contacting and persuading their colleagues. Just before key party votes and during the roll calls, whips can be seen roaming the floor rounding up votes for their side and standing by the doors of the chamber signaling members how to vote as they enter the House chamber from their offices and committee rooms. One of the most powerful whips in recent decades was Tom DeLay, who earned the nickname "The Hammer" for the heavy-handed way that he often used to compel Republicans to vote with the party leadership. Part of DeLay's influence was his ability to direct large amounts of contributions to rank-and-file members, a skill that made him a powerful party leader but also may have led to his demise for his part in lobbying scandals that made news in 2005 and 2006.

THE POLICY COMMITTEES   Party policy committees function as agencies to gauge party sentiments and to identify the party position on issues before they come to the House floor for a vote. For example, if there is substantial disagreement within a policy committee concerning what the party's position on an issue should be, the leadership will probably not take a formal party position on that issue. On the other hand, policy committee endorsement of a position on a bill tends to strengthen the leadership's position in winning party members' support for their viewpoint. The policy committees play a role of providing policy guidance to members, but they do not have the power to bind members to support their positions. Nor do the policy committees customarily seek to involve themselves in the deliberations of the standing committees. The policy committees instead enter the process at the stage when legislation has emerged from committee and is being scheduled for floor action. Therefore, they are not agencies for the development of a party program. The Congress and its parties are too decentralized for them to play such a role.

THE STEERING COMMITTEES   Each party has a steering committee, which is responsible for making committee assignments for party members. For the majority party, the Steering Committee also nominates members to serve as committee chairs, while in the minority party, it nominates members to be ranking minority members of committees. These nominations must be confirmed by their full party membership. By serving as chairs of their party's Steering Committee, the Speaker and Minority Leader exert a profound influence over the committee assignments and chairships and in the process strengthen their leverage with party colleagues.

PARTY CAUCUSES AND CONFERENCES   Party caucuses or conferences include all the members of the party in a chamber. The most important work of the party caucuses is done at the beginning of a new Congress when they meet to organize their parties in the House. It is at these meetings that party leaders are elected and party rules are adopted. In addition, these organizational meetings customarily ratify decisions of the steering committees concerning committee assignments and chairships or ranking minority member positions on the committees. Major intraparty struggles periodically erupt over the selection of leaders, which can affect the future course of the party. For example, in a spirited intraparty contest, the Democratic Caucus in 2001 elected Nancy Pelosi (Calif.) to be the party's whip, making her the first woman to hold a whip position in the history of the House and putting her in line for higher-level leadership posts in the future. Over the years, House Democrats have been less inclined to have contested elections for leadership positions than the Republicans. Democratic leaders have tended to move through a series of subordinate positions before becoming Speaker. For example, though Pelosi faced a tough election to become the Democratic whip, her ascension to minority leader in 2005 and then the speakership in 2007 were relatively easy. By contrast, minority Republicans have had a series of revolts that have toppled the minority leaders—for example, following the midterm elections of 1998, when the party lost seats in the House, Majority Leader Dick Armey (Tex.) had to fight off a strong challenge from Jennifer Dunn (Wash.) to retain his post.

Party caucuses are held on an almost weekly basis throughout a congressional session to allow members to express their sentiments on issues facing the House and to rally partisan support for leadership positions on key votes. Like the policy committees, however, the caucuses do not make decisions that are binding on their members in terms of how they will vote on the floor. Only rarely have the caucuses in recent years sought to instruct committee members concerning action on legislation being considered by a committee. Every member of the caucus is also a member of at least one standing committee and, therefore, has a stake in maintaining the autonomy and power of the committees. Strong expressions of sentiment in the caucus can, however, affect the actions and strategy of the party leadership.

The Democratic caucus has played a major role in reshaping the procedures of the House of Representatives. Through changes in party and House rules initiated in the caucus during the 1970s, the seniority system for selection of committee chairs was modified, members were restricted to one subcommittee chairship, subcommittees gained substantial autonomy from full committee chairs, the Steering Committee gained the power to make committee assignments from the Democratic members of the Ways and Means Committee, and the Speaker not only acquired the power to nominate Democratic members to the Rules Committee, but had his or her power to refer bills to committee strengthened as well. As a consequence of the Democrats' caucus-mandated rules changes in the 1970s and similar rules adopted by the Republican Conference, the party leadership in both parties has been strengthened and power has been considerably centralized in the once highly decentralized House.

INFORMAL PARTY GROUPS In addition to the regular party organizational structure that has just been described, there also exists within the House a series of informal party groups that can work under some circumstances to reinforce party unity and at other times to cause fragmentation. An important set of groups within each party are the state party delegations, which vary in size and in the formality of their organizations. Some meet regularly to discuss their position on legislation and to share information. As communications networks, state delegations can be used by both the leadership and dissident factions to line up support for floor votes. State delegations are particularly active during the time early in a Congress when committee assignments are being made. The various delegations lobby to get their members on key committees and often engage in complicated multidelegation bargaining schemes in order to secure the best possible assignments for their members.

Within both parties there are class clubs, which are organized on the basis of the Congress or year in which a member was first elected. Freshmen class clubs are the most active, as they seek to promote junior members' interests with the leadership and assert some influence through coordinated actions. As members gain seniority and positions of influence in the committee system and party organizations, however, they normally find the class clubs of limited usefulness.

There are also a series of ideologically oriented groups within each party that seek to pressure their parties' leadership to adopt policies compatible with the groups' views. One of the largest and most liberal groups within the Democratic Party is the Progressive Caucus, which in the 111th Congress (2009–2010) had over eighty members. Much smaller and less structured groups of moderate and conservative Democrats also operate in the House. The New Democratic Coalition, with about forty members, has as its goal moving the Democratic caucus to a more centrist policy orientation. Leaning somewhat to the right of the New Democrats is a smaller group, the Blue Dog Democrats, who have tried to play a brokering role on budgetary issues. The relatively small size of these moderate groups and their rather ad hoc character have limited their influence within the party. Additional and increasingly important subgroups among the House Democrats are the Black Caucus and the Hispanic Caucus.

The Republicans also have policy-oriented subgroups. The Republican Study Committee, a group of conservative Republicans, patterned their operations after the DSG. With over 115 members in 2010, their aggressiveness made them an important force within the House GOP. Like the Democrats, the Republicans also have moderate groups, such as the Main Street Partnership, which seek to steer the GOP toward a centrist course of policy.

PARTY ORGANIZATION IN THE SENATE

Whereas the average member of the House is a relatively anonymous figure, except in his or her own constituency, senators are much more visible and are frequently national figures. They represent major commonwealths. Most importantly, there are only one hundred senators. The smaller size of the Senate means that it can function with rules that permit the individual senators much greater leeway and influence. As a result, the average senator has significantly more formal power than the average representative. For example, much of the work of the Senate is done under unanimous consent agreements developed and negotiated by the majority leader. By refusing to agree to a unanimous consent request, an individual senator can hold up the work of the Senate until concessions are made to him or her. Senators also have available to them the filibuster or its threatened use as means of gaining leverage with their colleagues. The Senate's closure rule requires the votes of sixty senators to cut off debate. This means that a determined band of senators can often block action on legislation to which they are strongly opposed, or at least gain concessions in return for dropping their filibuster. In comparison to the House, influence is more widely dispersed in the Senate, and each member is more equal in power. Formal leadership positions (e.g., majority or minority floor leader, committee chairships) are important, but they are less important in the modern individualistic Senate than in the more hierarchical House.[43]

Unlike the House leader, the Senate's presiding officer is not a key majority party leader. The vice president is constitutionally empowered to preside but rarely does so except when his or her vote may be needed to break a tie or when he or she may be called upon to make an important parliamentary ruling. Nor is the position of president pro tempore an influential position. By tradition, this post is awarded to the majority party's most senior member in terms of Senate service. Like the vice president, the president pro tempore rarely presides over the Senate. This task is instead delegated to freshman senators as an apprenticeship task. It is not an onerous duty, because the Senate rules are relatively simple—unlike the complex House rules, which give substantial advantage to the party controlling the presiding officer.

THE FLOOR LEADERS   The key leaders of the Senate are the party floor leaders. The majority floor leader is responsible for the Senate schedule, which he or she handles mainly through negotiated unanimous consent agreements. This procedural prerogative gives the leader some bargaining advantage with colleagues. The leader also acts as his or her party's chief spokesperson and legislative strategist. But much more than in the House, the leader has only limited formal powers. The leader's influence rests upon his or her ability to find a compromise position and then persuade a majority of the senators to support his or her position. The minority floor leader serves his or her party in a capacity similar to that of the majority leader, except he or she has no responsibility for developing the schedule of Senate business.

Senate floor leaders are also responsible for steering presidential programs through the Senate when their party controls the presidency. This normally involves juggling the interests of fellow party members in the Senate and the concerns of the White House, while keeping lines of communication open to opposition party senators whose votes may be needed to build a majority. With senators on a different reelection schedule and often holding different policy priorities than the president, the majority leader can easily become ensnarled in intraparty and institutional rivalries. In addition, he or she must negotiate with the House leadership, whose views are apt to depart from those of the Senate or president. Thus, Majority Leader Harry Reid faced significant challenges during the 111th Congress (2009–2010) when he had to balance the interests of a Democratic president, a more liberal Democratic House caucus, and the more moderate views of the Senate Democrats he needed to win voters in the Senate. This balancing act was particularly difficult given that Reid himself was facing plummeting approval ratings and a significant re-election challenge in his home state of Nevada at the same time.

THE WHIPS   Each party has a whip who serves as an assistant floor leader. In both parties, the whip appoints a series of deputy whips to work with him or her in counting votes prior to key roll calls, persuading members to support the party position, and communicating leadership positions to the membership.

THE POLICY COMMITTEES   Senate policy committees do not make policy for the parties. The Republican Policy Committee meets on a weekly basis for lunch to discuss matters of mutual interest, but not to take positions on issues. It also has a staff that does research for the leadership and individual members, but it is not involved in the development of party policy. The Democratic Policy Committee has been used as an advisory body to the floor leader and assists him or her in scheduling Senate business when the party is in the majority.

THE COMMITTEES ON COMMITTEES   Each party has a committee on committees (called the Steering Committee in the Democratic Party) to handle member committee assignments. In making these appointments, the Republicans have tended to rely heavily upon seniority as a criterion for selection, whereas the Democrats have had a more open process in which candidates for committee posts waged campaigns to secure coveted assignments. Compared to the House, a larger share of Senate issues are resolved on the floor than in committee. As a result, the committee assignment process is of somewhat less importance to the individual senators than it is to House members. Senate rules permit each senator substantial opportunities to have an impact on floor deliberations, whereas the restrictive House rules do not permit rank-and-file members equivalent chances to influence the decisions of the full House.

THE CONFERENCES   The party conferences in the Senate are used primarily to organize the parties at the beginning of each new Congress. At these meetings, the leadership is elected and party rules are adopted. Senate party conferences meet irregularly to discuss legislative issues. These meetings provide the leadership with a sense of where their membership stands on an issue, but the sessions are not used to arrive at a party position or to intervene in the work of standing committees.

CONGRESSIONAL PARTIES AND NATIONAL PARTY ORGANIZATIONS

The congressional parties operate with substantial autonomy from their national committees. The principal constituencies of the national committees are the state party organizations and, when a party holds the White House, the president. Congressional party leaders, especially when the party does not control the presidency, zealously guard their prerogatives as policy spokespersons for the party and show little deference to, or interest in, the work of the national committees. The national committee's separation from the congressional parties is revealed by the existence of autonomous House and Senate campaign committees in both parties. Conscious that their constituency is members of the House and Senate, the congressional and senatorial campaign committees go about their business of seeking to elect representatives and senators, leaving presidential election politics and aid to state candidates to the national committees.

Nor do the congressional and senatorial campaign committees seek to enforce party loyalty or ideological purity by bestowing their campaign support only on incumbents who have adhered to the party line on roll call votes, or to nonincumbents who have pledged to do so. Table 9.4 presents the five House incumbents receiving the most support from the congressional campaign committees in 2004 and their party unity scores. Note that two of the Democrats receiving the most support had

TABLE 9.4	PARTY UNITY SCORES FOR HOUSE INCUMBENTS RECEIVING MOST COORDINATED EXPENDITURES FROM CONGRESSIONAL CAMPAIGN COMMITTEES, 2008

	Democrats			Republicans	
Member	Party Unity Score	Amount	Member	Party Unity Score	Amount
William Foster (Ill.)	92.0%	$301,719	Eric Cantor (Va.)	98.3%	$137,342
Travis Childers (Miss.)	68.4%	$172,032	Dave Reichert (Wash.)	73.6%	$85,288
Donald Cazayoux (La.)	75.3%	$144,053	Marilyn Musgrave (Colo.)	97.0%	$84,200
David Scott (Ga.)	96.6%	$83,506	Jon Porter (Nev.)	75.5%	$84,200
Andre Carson (Ind.)	98.9%	$81,932	William Sali (Idaho)	96.3%	$84,000
House Democratic Average	95.6%		*House Republican Average*	90.3%	

Source: Federal Election Commission and Keith T. Poole, University of California at San Diego, http://voteview.com.

party unity scores far below the House average and a similar pattern is evident on the Republican side. Rather than contributing to the most loyal party members, the campaign committees have granted aid to candidates on strictly electoral criteria: Which candidates are the strongest? Which races does the party have the best chance of winning? Which incumbents are in tough reelection contests? Given the diversity of viewpoints represented in the congressional and senatorial parties, it would be almost impossible for the campaign committees to enforce party discipline without causing bitter and counterproductive intra-party disputes. The campaign committees, therefore, function principally as candidate recruiters, fund-raisers, and campaign professionals rather than as party policy makers or enforcers of party discipline.

PARTIES AND POLICY IN THE CONGRESS

Political parties are the most inclusive institutions within the Congress. As such, they constitute Congress's strongest integrating and centralizing influence. For members of the president's party, this integrating force is often bolstered by the influence of the White House and its legislative program. Allied interest groups also help to reinforce party loyalty among members of Congress. Beginning in the 1980s, electoral factors, as has been noted previously, have helped to create congressional parties that are more internally united and distinct in their policy orientations than was true in prior decades. This has resulted in heightened partisan conflict with Congress and at times in policy gridlock in an era when divided party control of government has become almost the norm. But even with the parties' very substantial influence, the policy-making process of Congress cannot be characterized as party government, where disciplined parties with agreed-upon programs confront each other.

In spite of the trend toward stronger party influence upon government, the congressional parties continue to operate in an environment in which powerful decentralizing forces exist that make party government difficult to operate. Strong standing committees and their relatively autonomous subcommittees create multiple centers of influence over specific aspects of public policy. The centralizing influence of the parties is further weakened by the fact that most representatives and senators are what might be termed independent political entrepreneurs. They are personally responsible for the well-being of their own political enterprises. The party organization and the congressional parties did not get them nominated and elected, though they may have helped. Members are, therefore, unwilling to submit to any kind of party discipline that might jeopardize their electoral positions and their careers. If the congressional parties are relatively weak, it is, as David Mayhew has noted, because that is the kind of parties that the members want. They want parties that will be of assistance to them in securing their policy goals, but that will not impose burdens of discipline to party policy line that could cost them the support of their constituents.[44] Congressional party leaders recognize their colleagues' need for substantial freedom in making policy decisions. They also appreciate the dispersion of power through the committee/subcommittee system. Party leaders, especially in the Senate, must supplement their formal powers with informal techniques to build legislative majorities one issue at a time. Occasionally, they can enlist the support of outside forces like the administration or interest groups to reinforce party unity (though these same outside forces can also contribute to party disunity). And frequently they must seek votes on the other side of the aisle to forge a majority. It is an endless process of bargaining, negotiation, and compromise.

A PARTY-INFLUENCED GOVERNMENT, BUT NOT A PARTY-DOMINATED GOVERNMENT

The political parties' role in government is a paradoxical one. Party influence is pervasive in the organizing of both the executive branch and the Congress, and partisan considerations are constantly in evidence in the selection of federal judges. In addition, shared partisanship between members of Congress and the president does much to facilitate cooperation and bridge the gap created by a constitutional separation of power. Party affiliation has also been shown to be the single best predictor of how representatives and senators will vote on congressional roll calls. Despite this evidence of party influence, there also exists evidence of the parties' limited capacity to control American governmental institutions. Presidents have consistently found it difficult to maintain effective control over the far-flung executive establishment, including the White House staff, even though key policy-making posts are occupied by persons from the president's party. In Congress, the absence of strict party discipline has been shown to be even more pronounced. American government and policy making, therefore, is party influenced, but it is not party dominated. The looseness of the American party system gives governmental officials substantial flexibility and independence in shaping public policy.

Party-in-Government Web Sites

The Presidency
This is the official Web site of the White House and executive branch and includes many features, including podcasts of the president's speeches.
http://www.whitehouse.gov

Internet Public Library on the Presidency is a comprehensive site on the presidency.
http://www.ipl.org/ref/POTUS

Congress
These are the official sites for the Republican and Democratic Party organizations in the Senate.
http://republican.senate.gov
http://democrat.senate.gov

This site provides links to all the House Democratic and Republican Party Web sites.
http://www.house.gov/house/orgs_pub_hse_ldr_www.shtml

News
Congressional Quarterly and the National Journal are both authoritative sources for comprehensive information about the Congress.
http://www.cq.com
http://nationaljournal.com

The two sites above are to online versions of *The Hill* and *Roll Call*, both newspapers of Capitol Hill, and provide extensive coverage of congressional politics.
http://www.hillnews.com
http://rollcall.com

The *Washington Post* is the leading paper of the nation's capital and contains a wealth of information and detailed coverage of national politics, including a newly launched Congressional Votes Database, several blogs covering the political scene, and even a daily podcast on politics.
http://www.washingtonpost.com

Blogs
This blog contains mostly posts from members of Congress, giving you the ability to exchange views with those members.
http://blog.thehill.com/

The Hotline's blog, mentioned in earlier chapters, also includes timely information about proceedings in Congress and the executive branch.
http://hotlineblog.nationaljournal.com/

NOTES

1. Sarah McCally Morehouse, *State Politics, Parties and Policy* (New York: Holt, Rinehart, and Winston, 1981), p. 29.

2. Austin Ranney, "President and His Party," in Anthony King, ed., *Both Ends of the Avenue: The Presidency, the Executive Branch, and Congress in the 1980s* (Washington, D.C.: American Enterprise Institute, 1983), p. 137.

3. Ibid., p. 138.

4. Ibid., p. 139.

5. Paul Allen Beck, *Party Politics in America*, 8th ed. (New York: Longman, 1997), p. 383; Leon D. Epstein, Political Parties in the American Mold (Madison, WI: University of Wisconsin Press), pp. 80–89.

6. Theodore J. Lowi, "Party, Policy, and the Constitution in America," in William Nisbet Chambers and Walter Dean Burnham, eds., *The American Party Systems: Stages of Development* (New York: Oxford University Press, 1975), p. 248; see also Leon D. Epstein, *Political Parties in the American Mold* (Madison: University of Wisconsin Press, 1986), pp. 80–89.

7. Cornelius P. Cotter, "Eisenhower as Party Leader," *Political Science Quarterly* 98 (Summer 1983): 261. The development and extent of White House control over executive branch appointments is analyzed by C. Calvin Mackenzie, "Partisan Presidential Leadership: The President's Appointees," in L. Sandy Maisel, ed., *The Parties Respond: Changes in the American Party System* (Boulder, Colo.: Westview, 1990), ch. 13.

8. David S. Broder, "At White House Order," *Washington Post*, Jan. 1, 1991, p. A17; *New York Times*, Oct. 5, 1982, p. A24.

9. Ranney, "President and His Party," p. 143.

10. *Choosing Presidential Candidates: How Good Is the New Way*, John Charles Daly, moderator, AEI Forums (Washington, D.C.: American Enterprise Institute, 1979), p. 7.

11. Ranney, "President and His Party," pp. 141–142.

12. See John A. Ferejohn and Randall L. Calvert, "Presidential Coattails in Historical Perspective," *American Journal of Political Science* 28 (Feb. 1984): 127–146; Randall L. Calvert and John A. Ferejohn, "Coattail Voting in Recent Presidential Elections," *American Political Science Review* 77 (June 1983): 407–419.

13. George C. Edwards, III, *Presidential Influence in Congress* (San Francisco: W. H. Freeman, 1980), pp. 42–45.

14. Ibid., p. 45.

15. Richard E. Fenno, Jr., "U.S. House Members in Their Constituencies: An Exploration," *American Political Science Review* 71 (Sept. 1977): 914.

16. Nelson W. Polsby, *Congress and the Presidency*, 4th ed. (Englewood Cliffs, N.J.: Prentice Hall, 1986), pp. 193–194.

17. David B. Truman, *The Congressional Party* (New York: Wiley, 1959), pp. 297–298.

18. Polsby, *Congress and the Presidency*, pp. 194–196.

19. Mayhew, "The Return to United Party Control under Clinton," in Bryan D. Jones, ed., *The New American Politics: Reflections on Political Change and the Clinton Administration* (Boulder, Colo.: Westview, 1995), pp. 111–121; and David R. Mayhew, *Divided We Govern: Party Control, Lawmaking, and the Investigations 1946–1990* (New Haven, Conn.: Yale University Press, 1991).

20. John J. Coleman, "United Government, Divided Government, and Party Responsiveness," *American Political Science Review* 93 (Dec. 1999): 821–834; George C. Edwards, III, Andrew Barrett, and Jeffrey Peake, "The Legislative Impact of Divided Government," *American Journal of Political Science* 41 (April 1997): 545–563.

21. Roger M. Davidson, "Congressional Parties, Leaders, and Committees, 1900, 2000, and Beyond," in Jeffrey Cohen, Richard Fleisher, and Paul Kantor, eds., *American Political Parties: Decline or Resurgence?* (Washington, D.C.: CQ Press, 2001), p. 206.

22. David M. Herszenhorn, "In Senate Health Care Vote, New Partisan Vitriol," *New York Times*, December 24, 2009, p. A1.

23. Francis E. Rourke, "The Presidency and the Bureaucracy: Strategic Alternatives," in Michael Nelson, ed., *The Presidency and the Political System* (Washington, D.C.: CQ Press, 1984), p. 340.

24. Quoted in Neustadt, *Presidential Power*, p. 39.

25. Ibid., pp. 33–34.

26. Adriel Bettleheim, "Does Ridge Have the Clout to Carry It Off?" *Congressional Quarterly Weekly*, Nov. 3, 2001, pp. 2586–2590.

27. Norman C. Thomas and Joseph A. Pika, *The Politics of the Presidency*, 4th ed. (Washington, D.C.: CQ Press, 1997), pp. 252–253; and Thomas J. Weko, *Politicizing the Presidency: The White House Personnel Office, 1948–1994* (Lawrence: University of Kansas Press, 1995), pp. 149–151, 157.

28. David E. Price, *Bringing Back the Parties* (Washington, D.C.: CQ Press, 1984), p. 176.

29. Heclo, "One Executive Branch or Many?" pp. 42–47.

30. John H. Kessel, "The Structures of the Reagan White House," *American Journal of Political Science* 28 (May 1984): 235.

31. Bert A. Rockman, "The Federal Executive: Equilibrium and Change" in ed. Bryan D. Jones, The New American Politics (Boulder, CO: Westview), pp. 144–164.

32. Ibid., p. 160.

33. Quoted in Howard Kurtz, "Reagan Transforms the Federal Judiciary," *Washington Post*, March 31, 1985, p. A4.

34. Quoted in John F. Bibby, *Congress Off the Record: The Candid Analyses of Seven Members* (Washington, D.C.: American Enterprise Institute, 1983), p. 29.

35. For the most thorough analysis of member goals and committee politics, see Richard F. Fenno, Jr., *Congressmen in Committees* (Boston: Little, Brown, 1983).

36. David Brady, Joseph Cooper, and Patricia Hurley, "The Decline of Party in the U.S. House of Representatives, 1887–1968," *Legislative Studies Quarterly* 4 (Aug. 1979): 383–386.

37. See Charles O. Jones, "Joseph G. Cannon and Howard W. Smith: An Essay on the Limits of Leadership in the House of Representatives," *Journal of Politics* 30 (Aug. 1968): 617–646.

38. On the centralization of power in the hands of the Republican House leadership after the 1994 election, see John H. Aldrich and David W. Rohde, "The Transition to Republican Rule in the House," *Political Science Quarterly* 112 (Winter 1997–1998): 541–568; see also Lawrence W. Dodd and Bruce I. Oppenheimer, eds., *Congress Reconsidered*, 6th ed. (Washington, D.C.: CQ Press, 1997), pp. 29–60.

39. David Rhode, "The Gingrich Speakership in Context: Majority Leadership in the House in the Late Twentieth Century," *Extensions: A Journal of the Carl Albert Congressional Research and Studies Center*, Fall 2000.

40. Ibid.

41. Sheryl Gay Stolberg, Jeff Zeleny, and Carl Hulse, "Health Vote Caps a Journey Back from the Brink," *New York Times*, March 20, 2010, p. A1.

42. Patrick O'Connor, "'When Tom stepped down, I had to step in,'" *The Hill*, May 25, 2006.

43. Barbara Sinclair, *The Transformation of the U.S. Senate* (Baltimore: Johns Hopkins University Press, 1989), chs. 5–7.

44. David R. Mayhew, *Congress: The Electoral Connection* (New Haven, Conn.: Yale University Press, 1974), pp. 97–105.

POLITICAL PARTIES: IMPORTANT AND RESURGENT

CHAPTER 10

CHAPTER CONTENTS

I began this book by outlining the contradictory feelings Americans express about the role political parties play in elections and in government. In fact, although they are often underappreciated or avoided by the public, as we have noted throughout this text, parties are fundamental to the operation of the American political system. In this chapter, I conclude by providing further evidence of the significance of parties. First, I examine how American democracy functions in the absence of parties. Second, I discuss how the recent resurgence in partisanship has affected American politics.

POLITICS WITHOUT PARTIES: WHAT ARE THE CONSEQUENCES?

How do we know what parties contribute if we have never experienced politics without them? While we have outlined many of the vital functions that parties play in our political system, it is difficult to know how important political parties are without knowing how the political system would operate without them.

While there is little basis for comparing what politics might be like without parties at the national level, there is substantial opportunity for examining this question at the state and local level. In fact, approximately three-fourths of all municipal elections are contested on nonpartisan ballots—those without party labels identifying the candidates.[1] Nonpartisan elections are also used to elect many statewide offices and the entire Nebraska state legislature. The nonpartisan ballot was a Progressive-era reform, meant to address what Progressives viewed as the undemocratic nature of local party machines. Progressives sought to diminish the power of these machines by removing parties from the electoral process, an act they believed would give power back to citizens who they believed could make decisions without the aid of parties.[2] The movement toward nonpartisan elections was successful in many American locales, particularly in the western states. Minnesota and Nebraska even adopted the nonpartisan format for elections to their state legislatures, though Minnesota reverted to partisan ballots in the early 1970s. The conduct of politics in areas that adopted nonpartisan ballots provides us with clues about some of the significant effects parties have on our political system.

ELECTIONS WITHOUT PARTIES

In Chapters 7 and 8, we discussed how parties provide information to voters through the party label and their campaign activities. This information is an important contribution given that citizens are asked to cast votes in an extraordinary number of elections in the United States. Parties help to encourage citizens to participate in politics by informing them and mobilizing them during campaigns. Accordingly, we may not be surprised at the patterns discovered in nonpartisan elections:

- *Participation Declines.* Removing party labels from the ballot tends to diminish turnout in elections. Consider the case of Nebraska, which holds nonpartisan elections for its state legislature. From 1984 to 1990, roll off in these elections was almost 40 percent. In other words, four out of every ten voters who had already taken the effort to go to their polling place to vote in partisan races decided, once there, not to cast a vote in the contests for which party labels were not provided. In comparable partisan state legislatures, on the other hand, less than 10 percent of voters failed to vote in the state legislative contest when party labels were present. Similar patterns of lower voter participation are evident in studies of municipal and statewide nonpartisan contests.[3] This evidence suggests the importance of partisan information for many voters, and without such information, many citizens do not feel they know enough to participate in elections.

- *Less Educated Voters Are Especially Affected.* Partisan information is relatively costless in a partisan political world since the party labels appear on the ballot and most citizens have at least some notion of what the parties stand for. Thus, even citizens who might otherwise have trouble making sense of the political world are still able to do so when politics is boiled down to Democrats versus Republicans. But when the partisan structure to political conflict is removed, the most adversely affected group are those who have the least information about politics—those with less education. Indeed, research suggests that citizens with less education are less likely to cast ballots in nonpartisan elections than they are when party labels appear on the ballot.[4]
- *Voters Rely on Other Clues.* In elections with party labels, voters have a sense of where a candidate stands on the issues simply by knowing his or her party affiliation. Such is not the case when partisan information is absent. In the absence of such information, voters search for any clues they can discern to help them decide who to vote for. Sometimes they rely on whether a candidate's name sounds ethnic or gender-specific.[5] Alternatively, voters may be drawn to names that sound familiar. Thus, research indicates that because they are more familiar to voters, incumbents fare significantly better in nonpartisan elections than they do in partisan contests for no other reason than that their names are more familiar to voters.[6]
- *Voters May Vote "Incorrectly."* It is always difficult to determine which candidate a respondent would have preferred if he or she had known the party affiliations of those candidates. However, if citizens are choosing candidates based on name recognition or some other nonsubstantive factors, then we might expect citizens to make mistakes. In other words, they may be more likely to vote for a candidate they might otherwise oppose if they knew the candidate's party affiliation. Indeed, there is evidence that the party that is usually in the minority in an area tends to fare better in nonpartisan elections than in partisan contests.[7]

Overall, elections without parties demonstrate several characteristics that students of politics often find undesirable. By examining how nonpartisan elections operate, we can demonstrate more confidently some of the virtues of political parties; namely, that they encourage participation and provide voters with useful information as they decide how to vote.

GOVERNING WITHOUT PARTIES

In Chapter 9, we discussed the importance of parties in the governing process. Parties organize the government and allow for a more orderly and coherent process of considering and enacting policies. But how would Congress function in the absence of parties? To answer this question, one can look a century and a half into the past at the Confederate Congress or at contemporary politics in the Cornhusker state.

During the Civil War, the South convened its own Congress, which was identical to the U.S. version in every respect but one—it did not have political parties. This difference appeared to be an important one. Members of the Confederate Congress were less consistent in their voting patterns than members of the U.S.

Congress. While voting behavior in the U.S. Congress could largely be predicted by which party a member belonged to (Republican or Democratic), the ability to predict roll call voting by party in the Confederate Congress was substantially reduced. Two consistent coalitions in the Confederate Congress resembled parties, but the members of that body were not particularly loyal to either coalition when casting roll call votes. They frequently strayed from their coalition in unpredictable ways.[8]

The experience of Nebraska's legislature reinforces the importance of parties to the governing process. Parties do not exist in this unicameral legislature, and their absence significantly affects how legislators behave in the chamber. When running for office, Nebraska legislative candidates tend to express clear partisan ideologies just as candidates do in other states. However, once in the chamber, their votes on legislation reveal no such clarity. Rather, different members vote together on different issues without regard for party or other factors. The reason for the lack of consistent voting coalitions in the legislature is that the electoral advantage to such consistent cooperation is removed by nonpartisan elections. As Gerald Wright and Brian Schaffner explain:

> [In partisan environments,] the parties, in vying for electoral advantage, adopt positions on new issues to bring in new voters and, thus, package these with their existing issue stands. This provides a political connection among issues, which works its way into our general ideological way of looking at politics. Without parties, there would be no need to bundle these diverse issues, and legislators, activists, and the media would be much less likely to see any obvious connections between them.[9]

The importance of parties in bundling issues cannot be overstated. By creating a clear packaging of issues so that there is a Democratic and Republican side to each issue, parties help to clarify politics for citizens and provide them with more control over their elected officials. The study of the Nebraska legislature reveals that

> [In Nebraska] legislators are not connecting their clear ideological preferences on the issues to the bills that they vote on in the legislature. Indeed, it is hard to imagine how voters could achieve even general policy direction when conflict patterns in the legislature are unstable and unstructured ... nonpartisan elections effectively break the policy linkage between citizens and their representatives.[10]

Thus, political parties are not only an important force within legislatures in organizing members into consistent and durable coalitions, but they are also important in making those legislators accountable to the public. Studies of Nebraska and other state legislatures demonstrate that citizens' views are best represented in the state legislatures where parties have the strongest influence.

THE RELEVANCE OF PARTIES FOR THE AMERICAN PUBLIC

If parties matter so much to the political system, the point was lost on much of the American public during the latter half of the twentieth century. During this time, Americans became increasingly disconnected from political parties. As noted throughout this book, dealignment in the electorate is the primary evidence of the phenomenon. But it is not the only evidence of party decline. Citizens openly expressed their disenchantment with parties in public opinion polls. By 1990, 48 percent of those surveyed said that there were not any important differences in what the Democratic and Republican parties stood for. Throughout the 1990s, more than half of the public said that neither party would be better able to handle the most important problems facing the country. In 1994, less than half of Americans surveyed agreed that political parties "make democracy work better in this country," and compared to citizens in other nations, Americans were far less likely to think that political parties were necessary for the political system (see Figure 10.1).

Evidence of dealignment coupled with such expressions of ambivalence for parties during the 1970s and 1980s led political scholars to question whether parties were dying. As early as 1971, David Broder published a book titled *The Party's Over*. With the rise of candidate-centered elections and the increasing use of party primaries, the relevance of political parties was thought to have been forever diminished for Americans. Among the consequences feared by scholars was a decline in participation by and effective representation for the public. However, more recently, some political scientists saw hope for party renewal. Following the 1996 election, political scientist Martin Wattenberg argued that "the widely differing agendas of Democrats and Republicans have at least the potential to convince people who have been paying scant attention to party politics in recent years that parties do indeed matter."[11] Indeed, the renewed polarization evident during the twenty-first century appears to have rekindled the relevance of parties for American citizens.

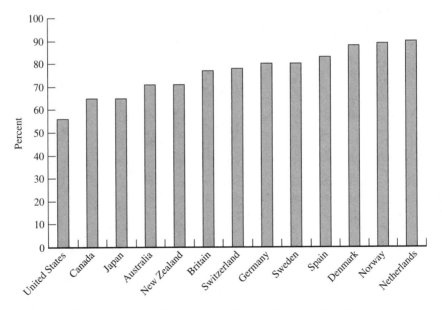

FIGURE 10.1 | PERCENTAGE OF RESPONDENTS SAYING PARTIES ARE NECESSARY FOR POLITICAL SYSTEM IN THIRTEEN NATIONS, 1996–2000

Source: Russell J. Dalton and Steven A. Weldon, "Public Images of Political Parties: A Necessary Evil?" *West European Politics* 28 (5) (2005) p. 934.

POLARIZATION AND THE RENEWED RELEVANCE OF PARTIES

As I have documented throughout the book, the parties have become increasingly polarized, offering clearer choices to the American people. The explanations for this polarization include the realignment of southern whites, the growing importance of social/moral issues, and even a growing cultural divide that reinforces party division. This partisan polarization has not been lost on the public. In 2006, 61 percent of Americans agreed that the parties were "more deeply divided" than in previous years.[12] And by 2009, two of every three people said that the country was more politically divided than in the past.[13]

Considering the fact that Americans see politics as more divided now, it is not surprising that they are also more likely to see important differences between the two major parties (Figure 10.2). In 2004 and 2008, three of every four Americans said they saw important differences between the two major parties—the highest level since at least 1960. Because citizens were more likely to see important differences between the parties during the past two presidential elections, they were also more likely to care which side won. In fact, citizens have become increasingly more interested in who wins the presidential election since the early 1990s, with only 20 percent saying that they did not care who won in 2008 (see Figure 10.3). Far from the critiques of previous decades that there was not a "dime's worth of difference" between the two parties, citizens now see a real distinction between Democrats and Republicans, making partisan politics more relevant to the contemporary American public.

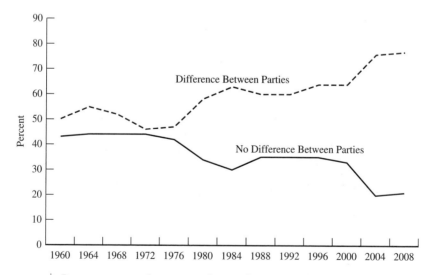

FIGURE 10.2   PERCENTAGE OF AMERICANS SEEING IMPORTANT DIFFERENCES BETWEEN THE PARTIES, 1960–2008

Source: National Election Studies, only presidential election years included.

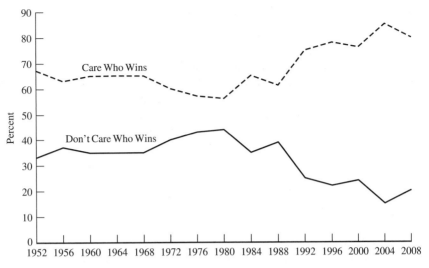

FIGURE 10.3 | PERCENTAGE OF AMERICANS THAT CARE WHO WINS THE PRESIDENTIAL ELECTION, 1952–2008

Source: National Election Studies, only presidential election years included.

THE EFFECTS OF PARTISAN POLARIZATION

The increased polarization in the American political system has been both praised and criticized by commentators, politicians, and scholars. This disagreement is born from the fact that polarization has had both beneficial and deleterious effects on politics.

THE GOOD: RENEWED INTEREST AND PARTICIPATION IN THE POLITICAL SYSTEM

When parties offer more distinct policies, citizens tend to view the choice between them as more important. When the salience of those electoral choices grows, so does interest and participation in the campaign. In 2008, 44 percent of the American public reported that they were very interested in the campaign, the highest value since the question was first asked in 1952 (though campaigns in 1992 and the 1960s came close). An additional 41 percent said they were somewhat interested in the 2008 campaign; only 16 percent said they were not interested.[14]

Driven by the partisan divide, public interest in the campaign spurred increased political participation. While scholars and commentators have been lamenting the decline in political participation for many years, polarization may, at least temporarily, be reversing this trend. As we discussed in Chapter 7, turnout in the 2008 election was higher than it had been in decades. But the act of voting is just one way that citizens can involve themselves in the political process. Figure 10.4 demonstrates that other forms of participation have also increased in recent years; in fact,

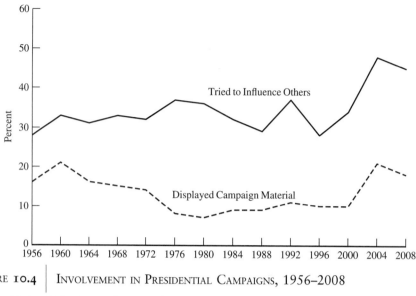

FIGURE 10.4 | INVOLVEMENT IN PRESIDENTIAL CAMPAIGNS, 1956–2008

Source: National Election Studies, presidential election years only.

nearly half of the American public reported trying to influence another person on how to vote in 2004 and 2008, a substantially higher proportion than at any other time since the survey question has been asked. Thus, partisan polarization not only led citizens to participate more in the political process, it also drove them to discuss politics with others, which reinforced the politically charged atmosphere in 2004 and 2008.

Political scientists have also observed over recent decades that citizens have come to feel less like they can have a say in how the government operates through their participation. For example, the percentage of the public saying that elections "make the government pay attention to what people think" has been declining since the 1960s (see Figure 10.5). Yet in 2004, 56 percent said that elections could have this effect, the highest percentage in a presidential election year since 1968. Not only have citizens been more involved in the last two campaigns than they had been in recent decades, they also felt as though their involvement could make a difference.

Because politics in recent years have become polarized, they have also become more important and compelling to citizens. The signs of higher turnout and increased engagement among the public are encouraging for those who believe that a political system represents the public interest best when the public is more involved in the process. By staking out clearly differentiated agendas and promoting those agendas through their efforts to inform and mobilize the electorate, the parties have contributed greatly to this trend.

THE BAD: INCIVILITY AND GRIDLOCK

While partisan polarization has likely been instrumental in sparking renewed interest and engagement among the public, it has not been embraced by all politicians

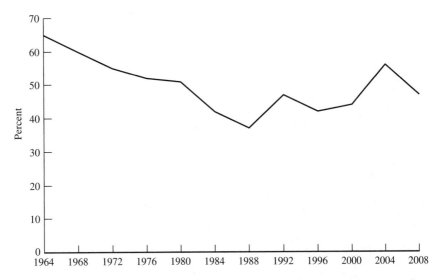

FIGURE 10.5 | PERCENTAGE OF AMERICANS WHO THINK ELECTIONS MAKE THE GOVERN-
MENT PAY A GOOD DEAL OF ATTENTION TO THE PUBLIC, 1964–2008

Source: National Election Studies, presidential election years only.

and political commentators. For example, former Senator William Brock (D-Tenn.) argued in a *Washington Post* column:

> We're increasingly moving to a political system that looks, and feels, like a political barbell: one where all the weight is at the ends of the spectrum, leaving those in the center with little voice or opportunity for impact. It's dangerous, it's counterproductive and I think it represents an assault upon the constitutional premise of balance which has so graced the first two centuries of this republic.[15]

Indeed, *Washington Post* columnist E. J. Dionne noted that in recent years "the political map of the United States takes on the coloration of the Civil War."[16] Why the alarm over polarization even while we recognize that it has sparked renewed interest in politics? One reason is that fierce partisan competition tends to breed strong feelings. For example, in 2008, half of those voting on election day said that they would be "scared" if the other candidate won. After the 2004 election, 74 percent of those who voted for Kerry were worried about the outcome, whereas 93 percent of Bush voters were relieved that he had won.[17]

As noted in Chapter 9, polarization has also created declining civility in Congress. The consequences of polarization may be more serious than just harsh words and some pushing in the House chamber, however. In fact, polarization may make it more difficult for office holders to pass legislation. Because there are few moderates left in Congress, it has become more difficult to broker bipartisan compromises to pass legislation. Some scholars argue that this has led to more legislative gridlock in Congress and frustration among elites in both parties. The public has also taken notice of the lack of compromise: A survey in 2009 found that 81 percent of the public believed that the year had been a "period of division where the parties held fast to their positions and showed little willingness to compromise."[18]

While many political theorists believe that passionate disagreement is central to democracy, the public tends to be turned off by political conflict. As John Hibbing and Elizabeth Theiss-Morse explain, "People despise pointless political conflict and they believe pointless political conflict is rampant in American politics today."[19] It is interesting to note that most Americans view most political conflict as pointless since they do not believe that political disagreements are difficult to resolve. Therefore, because polarization has caused an increase in political conflict among elites, the public has viewed these partisan battles with concern. In 2006, for example, 78 percent of Americans saw party conflict as either a very serious or somewhat serious problem.[20] Even many political scientists have warned that increasing polarization threatens to turn off many citizens, particularly partisan independents and ideological moderates. In the view of these scholars and commentators, political polarization harms rather than enhances democracy.

THE CONTRADICTORY NATURE OF POLITICAL PARTIES

Writing on the recent polarization in America, Geoffrey Layman, Thomas Carsey, and Juliana Menasce Horowitz note, "It remains somewhat ironic that political observers and political scientists have offered a primarily negative account of [partisan polarization] ... because they have long argued that the parties should be more programmatic, ideologically cohesive, and distinct from each other on policy issues."[21] As noted earlier in this chapter, scholars of the 1970s and 1980s worried about the declining relevance of the parties and what this meant for American democracy. Less than two decades later, many writing on the subject now worry that parties are *too relevant*. It is natural to be confused by the remarkable contradictions espoused by political scholars on a subject as fundamental as whether strong polarized parties are good for our political system. But part of the reason for this confusion is that many of the things we value in politics are themselves at odds:[22]

- We value political discussion, but we worry about passionate disagreement.
- We want people invested and involved in politics, but not so invested that they grow frustrated and angry when their side loses.
- We want our parties and elected officials to be principled and offer distinct policy proposals, but we also want them to compromise.
- We want the minority party to hold the majority party in check, but we do not want gridlock or stalemate.

Parties provide us with all of these things, good and bad, particularly when they are as strong and active as they have been in recent years. The parties took divergent positions during the 2004 campaign, and the public embraced those choices by becoming more involved and more interested in politics than it had been in decades. Yet political discussions sometimes turned into political arguments, both sides were fearful of the other side winning, and the outcome resulted in elation for committed Republicans and depression for loyal Democrats. Then, in the aftermath of the election, many Americans were disappointed to find that compromise eludes those parties took such divergent positions.

The seemingly incompatible views of polarization outlined above underscore the more fundamental contradictory nature of political parties discussed in Chapter 1. Parties represent the primary line of demarcation in the politics—they organize the public, candidates, and office holders into the teams that compete for control over government. They simplify political conflict for us, facilitating our involvement in and influence over politics. Yet because we associate parties with the political conflict that they help organize, we are never entirely comfortable with them. In short, Americans have never fully embraced their political parties, yet those parties have become a permanent and necessary part of the nation's political fabric.

Despite our unease with parties, they have proven a durable part of our system. Just in the past few decades, we have witnessed a general pattern of party decline that some believed foretold a partyless politics in the near future followed by dramatic partisan polarization that many see signs of substantial party revival.[23] Of course, it is dangerous to predict the future and to make too much of the recent polarization would be to repeat the mistake made by those predicting an end to parties a few decades ago. Indeed, based upon past history, it is probably safe to predict that American parties will maintain their record of proven durability and adaptability to changing and even hostile conditions.

The evidence of their durability and adaptability is striking. For almost 150 years the same two parties—the Republicans and Democrats—have dominated electoral politics. This is a record of durability unmatched in any other Western-style democracy. Remarkably, these two parties compete against each other across the nation, despite the obstacles of regional diversity and federalism. They have adapted to the Progressive Era reforms that stripped them of control over nominations and patronage, and they have adapted to the more recent reform environment of public funding of presidential elections and some state elections. The rise of political action committees (PACs) has not put parties out of business. Instead, the parties have sought to coordinate and channel PAC contributions. As campaigns became more professionalized, technical, and expensive, the parties increased their fund-raising potential through such techniques as direct mail and hired their own technical experts to provide in-kind services to candidates. At both the national and state levels, there is evidence of increased party organizational strength compared to that which existed in the 1960s.[24] Parties continue to play an important function in informing and mobilizing citizens. Parties also organize the Congress, state legislatures, the White House, and state administrations, exerting substantial influence on the decision-making processes at the national and state levels.

For all their acknowledged weaknesses, parties remain—and are likely to remain—the principal agents for recruiting leaders, making nominations, contesting elections, bridging the gulf created by separation of powers, and providing a link between the citizenry and their government.

NOTES

1. Victor S. DeSantis and Tari Renner, "Contemporary Patterns and Trends in Municipal Government Structure," in *The Municipal Yearbook* (Washington, D.C.: International City/County Management Association, 1992).

2. Richard Hofstader, *The Age of Reform: From Bryan to FDR* (New York: Knopf, 1955).

3. Brian F. Schaffner, Matthew Streb, and Gerald Wright, "Teams without Uniforms: The Nonpartisan Ballot in State and Local Elections," *Political Research Quarterly* 54 (1) (2001): 7–30.

4. Brian F. Schaffner and Matthew J. Streb, "The Partisan Heuristic in Low Information Elections," *Public Opinion Quarterly* 66 (4) (2002).

5. Peverill Squire and Eric R.A.N. Smith, "The Effect of Partisan Information on Voters in Nonpartisan Elections," *Journal of Politics* 50 (1988): 169–179.

6. Schaffner, "The Partisan Heuristic in Low Information Elections."

7. Brian F. Schaffner, Matthew J. Streb, and Gerald C. Wright, "A New Look at the Republican Bias in Nonpartisan Elections," Unpublished manuscript.

8. Jeffrey A. Jenkins, "The Bonding Effects of Party: A Comparative Analysis of Roll-Call Voting in the US and Confederate Congress Houses," *American Journal of Political Science* 43 (1999): 1144–1165.

9. Gerald C. Wright and Brian F. Schaffner, "The Influence of Party: Evidence from the State Legislatures," *American Political Science Review* 96 (2) (2002): 377.

10. Ibid.

11. Martin P. Wattenberg, *The Decline of American Political Parties, 1952–1996* (Cambridge: Harvard University Press, 1998), p. 240.

12. "Political Values in a 51%–48% Nation," The Pew Research Center for the People and the Press, January 24, 2005.

13. National Election Studies.

14. Ibid.

15. William E. Brock, "A Recipe for Incivility," *The Washington Post,* June 27, 2004, p. B7.

16. E. J. Dionne, Jr. "One Nation Deeply Divided," *The Washington Post,* November 7, 2003, p. 169–A31.

17. Data on those saying they would be "scared" if the other candidate won comes from the 2008 National Election Pool Exit Polls. The data on those who were "worried" and "relieved" about the 2004 outcome comes from a USA Today/CNN/Gallup survey conducted October 22–24, 2004. This percentage is much higher than when asked in 1996. USA Today/CNN/Gallup survey conducted October 22–24, 2004. This percentage is much higher than when asked in 1996.

18. NBC News/Wall Street Journal Poll, Dec, 2009. Retrieved Mar. 20, 2010 from the iPOLL Databank, The Roper Center for Public Opinion Research, University of Connecticut. http://www.ropercenter.uconn.edu.silk.library.umass.edu:2048/data_access/ipoll/ipoll.html

19. John R. Hibbing and Elizabeth Theiss-Morse, *Stealth Democracy: Americans' Beliefs about How Government Should Work* (New York: Cambridge University Press), p. 33.

20. DIAGEO/Hotline Poll, May 25, 2006.

21. Geoffrey C. Layman, Thomas M. Carsey, and Juliana Menasce Horowitz, "Party Polarization in American Politics: Characteristics, Causes, and Consequences," *Annual Review of Politics* 9 (2006): 102.

22. Bernard R. Berelson, Paul F. Lazarsfeld, and William N. McPhee, *Voting: A Study of Opinion Formation in a Presidential Campaign* (Chicago: University of Chicago Press, 1954).

23. Walter Dean Burnham, *Critical Elections and the Mainsprings of American Politics* (New York: Norton, 1970). See also David S. Broder, *The Party's Over* (New York: Harper and Row, 1972); and William Crotty, *Parties in Decline* (Boston: Little, Brown, 1984).

24. Cornelius P. Cotter and John F. Bibby, "Institutional Development of Parties and the Thesis of Party Decline," *Political Science Quarterly* 95 (Spring 1980): 1–28; Xandra Kayden and Eddie Mahe, Jr, The party goes on: the persistence of the two-party system in the United States (New York: Basic Books, 1985) and Cornelius P. Cotter, James L. Gibson, John F. Bibby, and Robert J. Huckshorn, *Party Organizations in American Politics* (New York: Praeger, 1984).

INDEX TO REFERENCES

Index